Hearing Brazil

Hearing Brazil

Brazil

*Music and Histories
in Minas Gerais*

Jonathon Grasse

University Press of Mississippi / Jackson

The University Press of Mississippi is the scholarly publishing agency of
the Mississippi Institutions of Higher Learning: Alcorn State University,
Delta State University, Jackson State University, Mississippi State University,
Mississippi University for Women, Mississippi Valley State University,
University of Mississippi, and University of Southern Mississippi.

www.upress.state.ms.us
The University Press of Mississippi is a member
of the Association of University Presses.

On the cover: Ouro Preto, Minas Gerais. After descending the steep hill from Ouro Preto's Church of Santa Efigênia in Alto da Cruz, after ceremoniously cleansing the entrance to that eighteenth-century Catholic church, members of the local Congado de Nossa Senhora do Rosário e Santa Efigênia prepare to enter the Padre Faria Chapel, constructed in 1704. Here, they will participate in a Mass delivered by the parish priest and will later raise flagpoles to mark the beginning of the early January festival known as the Faith that Sings and Dances. (Photo by Jonathon Grasse, 2018.)

First printing 2022
∞

Library of Congress Cataloging-in-Publication Data
Names: Grasse, Jonathon, 1961– author.
Title: Hearing Brazil : music and histories in Minas Gerais / Jonathon
Grasse.
Description: Jackson : University Press of Mississippi, 2022. | Includes
bibliographical references and index.
Identifiers: LCCN 2021059097 (print) | LCCN 2021059098 (ebook) | ISBN
978-1-4968-3827-8 (hardback) | ISBN 978-1-4968-3828-5 (trade paperback) | ISBN
978-1-4968-3829-2 (epub) | ISBN 978-1-4968-3830-8 (epub) | ISBN 978-1-4968-3831-5
(pdf) | ISBN 978-1-4968-3832-2 (pdf)
Subjects: LCSH: Popular music—Brazil—Minas Gerais—History and criticism.
| Folk music—Brazil—Minas Gerais—History and criticism. |
Music—Brazil—Minas Gerais—History and criticism. | Music—Social
aspects—Brazil—Minas Gerais—History. | Minas Gerais
(Brazil)—History.
Classification: LCC ML3487.B77 M554 2022 (print) | LCC ML3487.B77 (ebook)
| DDC 781.640981/51—dc23
LC record available at https://lccn.loc.gov/2021059097
LC ebook record available at https://lccn.loc.gov/2021059098

British Library Cataloging-in-Publication Data available

Contents

Preface and Acknowledgments

The idea for this book about music and regional identity in Minas Gerais, Brazil, grew from a course reader I wrote and developed for an undergraduate survey course on Brazilian music at the University of California, Los Angeles, beginning in the early 2000s. That material, designed for ethnomusicology majors and general students alike, had emerged from my extensive notes and personal writings dating to the late 1980s. The course reader wove diverse topics including samba and bossa nova, carnival, the music and life of Heitor Villa-Lobos, Afro-Brazilian religious music, and Música Popular Brasileira (MPB), among other subjects. These particular seeds of interest had been planted in the late 1980s, when I began regularly visiting Brazil and performing in a Berkeley, California, samba group. A new research focus on Minas Gerais emerged in 2006, exploring the social and historical strata of the region through music as disparate as the folk, popular, religious, and classical genres I pursued in my reader. The fresh challenge was not to objectively represent Minas musically but to examine a select set of cultural expressions to which I had been subjectively drawn, as a means of understanding the region as a cultural territory. Fieldwork came in the form of interviews, road trips from Belo Horizonte, readings of Brazilian publications, video and photo documentation of performances and festivals, and explorations of music traditionally adorned with exceptional regional meaning and local significance. Subsequently, I presented versions of my research of Minas music through Society for Ethnomusicology conferences, published journal articles, a book chapter, and a study on the seminal 1972 LP recording *Clube da Esquina* (Corner Club) by Milton Nascimento and Lô Borges.

Many have assisted in my search for these aspects of the musical soul of Minas Gerais. My wife Nanci, who was born and raised in Belo Horizonte, has been a profound inspiration and tireless supporter, sharing her love for the songs of the Corner Club music collective that emerged from that city in the 1960s. Additionally, the following people listed alphabetically are due my appreciation, none of whom are responsible for the book's representations: Corner Club members Márcio and Lô Borges, the late chair of the California State University, Dominguez Hills, music department, Rod Butler, University Press of Mississippi editor Craig Gill, UCLA ethnomusicologist Steve Loza, Belo Horizonte–based ethnomusicologist Glaura Lucas, University Press of Mississippi editor Lisa McMurtray and her staff, Corner Club member Tavinho Moura, Belo Horizonte–based scholar and choral director Arnon Sávio Reis de Oliveira, Corner Club member Nivaldo Ornelas, Belo Horizonte bookseller Simone Pessoa, Marcello Pianetti, ethnomusicologist Brenda Romero, Danilo Geraldo dos Santos, Shawn Usha, and Norman Ware for his skilled editorial corrections and inciteful suggestions. I am grateful for assistance and support from CSUDH College of Arts and Humanities Deans Munashe Furusa and Mitch Avila and their staff, officers of the CSUDH Graduate Studies and Research program (an RSCA grant), and the staff of UCLA's Charles E. Young Research Library. My deepest thanks go to members of my *família mineira*, who were of great assistance for many years: Dona Jane and Doctor Márcio, Teresa and Bruce, and Márcio Luis. Muito obrigado. This book is dedicated to the memory of my father, Marvin R. Grasse (1920–2005), who shared with me his love for words and whose humor and empathy greatly buoyed my upbringing and coming of age.

This work contains many specialized terms and place-names. While some effort has been made to standardize spellings where appropriate, in many cases, previous scholarship and conventional usage prevent such efforts, and spelling variations have been retained depending on context.

Hearing Brazil

Chapter 1

Introduction

Minas Gerais (General Mines) is a highland, interior state in Brazil's southeast (Sudeste), where inhabitants are known as Mineiros/as and where a rich tapestry of popular, traditional, and liturgical music contributes to forms of regional identity. This book's purpose is to interpret relationships between Mineiro society, history, and diverse music with strong regional associations, and to present Minas as a unique cultural territory through its music. The title's "Hearing," always in upper case, refers to the deep interpretation of music beyond casual listening and analysis of structure and style, in which music engages regional identity among three types of musical space: the physical places of a cultural territory's geography; the historical-temporal spaces of past events and development informing communities; and the figurative spatiality of individual consciousness.[1] Historian Robert Tombs stated that "most nations and their shared identities are modern creations, the products of literacy, urbanization, and state-led cultural and political unification."[2] However, in terms of a regional identity, I am suspicious of what is "shared" and cautious of both the nature and method of "unification." In this book, views on musical performance, genres, instruments, and histories of music often form a basis for interpreting heterogeneous communities and identities that resist assimilation and the reduction of social differences into a false sense of wholeness, seen with impartial familiarity and sameness. Fictive ideals of a transparent, civic public with claims to a common good and shared history veer dangerously close to the denial of difference and of the struggles within unequal power relations that form social and political worlds.[3] Music symbolizes, and enables, collective memories and cultural affiliations that communities and groups retain and celebrate, partly in order to participate socially.

Each of the following chapters approaches the challenge of regional meaningfulness in a different manner, their topics sharing insight into the processes and nature of Minas as a cultural territory. At times, the notion of place assumes fluid roles, less as bounded, bordered, and named and more as landscapes that engage the imagination, memories, and dreams. Places emerge, too, as correlates to stories and histories, to climates and biospheres, to moods and emotions. I observe historical cause and effect, and plain chronology, yet sometimes push discussion toward multiple narratives without a beginning, middle, and end. Regionalism is treated in this book as a challenge to understand ideas, places, peoples, and history, with music as the tool to create facets in the gem. This work is not about one particular place, a few musicians, or a single genre. The notion of music's iconicity of geographic place confronts the freedom with which music actually travels, imaginatively within ourselves and socially between us, occupying multiple places as emergent, potentially transcultural global forms. No geographic region is hermetically sealed from the world, and the technologies of printed music, radio, film, television, and the internet have brought rich varieties of international music streaming into Brazilian lives. Yet, as the French botanist Auguste de Saint-Hilaire wrote of his early nineteenth-century travels through the region, "If there is a region that could do without the rest of the world it is certainly the Province of Minas."[4]

Questions of the Mineiro connection to the world can perhaps best be approached by the story of "Oh, Minas Gerais," a song considered to be the region's unofficial anthem. At the dawn of Brazil's republic at the end of the nineteenth century, the waltz "Viene sul Mar" journeyed across the Atlantic with a touring Italian stage show. The musical troupe was soon competing in Rio de Janeiro theaters with popular French revues and other variety acts known as *companhias líricas* then flourishing in the tropical, capital port. The song became a hit, gaining exposure beyond the stage and entering popular repertoire. The remarkable Brazilian singer Eduardo das Neves penned a contrafactum, refitting "Viene sul Mar" with new, heroic lyrics dedicated to a Brazilian navy warship recently engaged in the suppression of the 1910–1911 Chibata naval mutiny, a revolt of black and mixed-race sailors protesting flogging with the lash (*chibata*) as a form of punishment.[5] The ship, named *Estado de Minas Gerais*, had emerged from the incident as a gleaming icon for proud nationalists, and its dreadnought vessel type became popularly known as the Minas Gerais class of navy ships. In a recording of Neves's 1917 hit song "Minas Gerais," we hear, "The strength of the Minas Gerais is enough for the defense of our Brazil," sung by legendary Rio de Janeiro musical fixture Cadete, registered as K.D.T. in Casa Edison's first catalog of Brazilian phonograph recordings.[6] Years later, in 1942, a radio singer from Minas Gerais, José Duduca de Moraes (1912–2002, b. Santa Maria de Itabira, MG), partnered with Manuel Pereira de Araújo in adapting Neves's "Minas Gerais," fitting yet another set of new lyrics that transformed the waltz theme into an homage to his home state, "Oh! Minas Gerais": "Your soaring lands, your pure indigo sky, it is all beautiful ... the hope of our Brazil."[7]

Fluid, global appropriation and adaptive processes define the song's creation and emergence as the region's hymn. Remarking on an early 2000s internet poll determining the state's most iconic song, Corner Club lyricist Márcio Borges noted that his 1970 collaboration with brother Lô Borges and Milton Nascimento, "Para Lennon e McCartney" (For Lennon and McCartney), earned second place in the poll to "Oh, Minas Gerais," which, he added, "is not even from Minas."[8] The classic, rock-infused tune that borrowed so heavily from foreign popular music sources shouts out an homage to the Beatles while proclaiming, "I am from South America ... I am of gold, I am you, I am of the world, I am Minas Gerais."[9] The social narratives of these two songs—their programmatic texts rather than their musical style—reveal their status as the region's most widely acknowledged symbolic anthems. Song lyrics convey the message, just as historical contexts cast light on how the music attains regional meaningfulness. "Para Lennon e McCartney" was written in the Santa Tereza neighborhood of Belo Horizonte, where, in the coming generations, young musicians would adopt a wealth of foreign styles, not unlike other places across Brazil. By the 1980s, members of the nationally renowned reggae- and ska-influenced band Skank had perfected their act beyond Santa Tereza and the city, as the neighborhood's death metal band Sepultura also forged an international stature. A few blocks from the seminal street corner of the Corner Club's origins in the late 1960s, Sepultura's band photos and gold record facsimiles hang on the walls of the Bolão Restaurant.[10]

Today, alt-rock styles, funk, hip-hop, and rap are popular genres that deserve attention in studies of Mineiro contemporary popular culture and identity. Imported popular music develops new modes of self-understanding for countless Mineiros, and Brazilians have a long track record of making foreign music their own. Oswald de Andrade's seminal 1928 analysis of Brazilian modernity, "Manifesto antropófago" (Cannibalist manifesto), characterizes the Brazilianization of imported ideas as a process of metaphoric digestion that the writer likens to cultural cannibalism. As foreign music entertains, it also potentially addresses Brazilian identities and social problems through appropriation, refitting, and new interpretations in collective quests for personal and social change, democratic voices, freedom of speech, status, and political resonance. While imported culture helps form valid Brazilian expression and identity, it takes a back seat here. Rather, this book focuses on music that arguably retains some degree of regional tradition, from which flows historical identities of place and contexts for understanding Minas. In partly signifying the Mineiro past, representations of historical musical cultures render into narrative form the practices generating heterogeneous cultural territories. Renato Ortiz was not alone among Brazilian writers when, during the 1980s, he debunked simplistic myths of a homogeneous national identity and culture: specifically, if in the 1970s one could "imagine the worlds of candomblé, of carnival, of soccer, and samba as metaphors for Brazilianness (*brasilidade*)," such simplistic essentialism no longer applied.[11] He argues that such stereotypes always fail to address Brazilian identity. In interpreting Ortiz's ideas on national identity and music, Michel Nicolau Netto stresses the importance of Brazil's diverse cultural territories, a simple, effective idea that informs part of this book's intentions.[12] Minas Gerais is its own slice of Brazil. As Brazilianist Stanley Blake comments in his study of the country's distinct northeastern culture, "regionalism and nationalism are not antithetical concepts,"[13] and indeed, case studies of the local, regional, and national may at times telescope or collapse into one another.

Indigenous Peoples

At the time of the region's first documented gold discovery in 1693, near what is now the city of Mariana, what became Minas Gerais had been called home by indigenous peoples for at least twelve thousand years. Within ten kilometers of Belo Horizonte's Tancredo Neves/Confins International Airport is the Lapinha cave network, the burial site of ten-thousand-year-old Lagoa Santa Man; and the Red Cave, where a twelve-thousand-year-old human female cranium was discovered in the 1970s. The trajectories of these hunter-gatherers carried through the highland and humid subtropical zones of mountains, limestone karst landscapes, savannas and *cerrado* scrub brush, desolate *sertões*, and formerly lush rainforests of the Atlantic rainforest (Mata Atlântica). The Gê language complex once common to western Minas joins Brazil's three other main indigenous language groups: Carib and Arawak of the Amazon basin, and the coastal Tupi-Guarani. The rainforests formerly separating central Minas from the coast were once dominated by nomadic tribes—the Puri, Pataxó, and those who became known derogatorily as the Botocudo. Most of the indigenous-language place-names in Minas are not in what would have been a local native tongue but rather in Tupi, the language of the coastal Indians who guided the first white settler-explorers known as *bandeirantes* (flagbearers). To illustrate this dynamic during these early years of Portuguese colonial settlement, the Tapuia ethnic group of southeastern Minas Gerais was renamed by the Tupi as Cataguases, meaning "people of the thick forest." The northern border with Bahia, a gradual topographic transition zone to the rough, arid *sertão* (drought-prone drybrush) east of the São Francisco River, with the Jequitinhonha River valley further west, was home to the Maxakali and Camaça people. The once nomadic Kayapo group, now found in the central Brazilian regions of Mato Grosso and Tocantins, roamed the western Triângulo of Minas Gerais into the nineteenth century, when they fled restless settlers relocating from the economically ruined mining district of central Minas. Other Native ethnic groups that faced violent colonial Portuguese expansion in Minas Gerais include the Xakriabá, Krenak, Kaxixó, Xukuru-Karriri, Mukurim, Hãhãhãe, and Pankararu.

There are contemporary recordings of traditional musical practices by descendants of some of these indigenous groups. For example, the first Festival of Indigenous Dance and Culture of the Serra do Cipó, held in 1998 and coordinated by Native Brazilian activist and environmentalist Airton Krenak, provided a stage for performances by Krenak, Maxakali, and Pataxó singers, which were recorded. Some of those recordings were released the following year on the CD *Krenak, Maxakali, Pataxó: O canto das montanhas* (Sonhos and Sons). The published proceedings of a conference held at Belo Horizonte's Federal University of Minas Gerais (UFMG), organized in part by ethnomusicologist Rosângela Pereira de Tugny, included two CDs featuring several tracks of indigenous music of Minas Gerais by Maxakali, Kamayurá, Pankararu, and Krenak performers.[14] By 2010, Minas was home to fewer than 14,500 Native persons belonging to ten ethnic groups. Those now living in roughly fifty communities spread throughout the northeastern part of the state make up less than 4 percent of Brazil's total indigenous population, including the roughly one thousand members of the Maxakali living along the Umburanas River, a tributary of the Mucuri River basin in the state's northeast. In addition to these communities forming a pillar of Mineiro society are generations of the mixed-race descendants of people with indigenous and European heritage, known as *caboclo* and *mameluco*.

Minas's eastern half, as well as its southern borders with Rio de Janeiro and São Paulo (specifically the Mantiqueira Mountains, Tupi for "crying mountains" due to their abundant lakes, streams, and waterfalls), were home to massive primordial rainforests as late as the nineteenth century. In an environmental ruination echoing the genocide of indigenous peoples, the southeast's Atlantic rainforest has been 95 percent destroyed, heavily deforested over two and a half centuries for subsistence agriculture, extensive coffee plantations, the harvesting of wood as a charcoal fuel source for iron foundry furnaces, and land and materials for the construction of settlements.[15] The remains of the original forest sit semiprotected among 113 very small federal reserves throughout the southeast. One of the largest federal reserves in Minas Gerais is smaller than four square miles, the Reserva Feliciano Miguel Abdala, near the town of Caratinga in the Rio Doce valley. In 2015, major environmental ruination continued within the iron mining sector as the catastrophic Bento Rodrigues mining dam break near Mariana, known as the Samarco disaster after the company that owned the mine (itself owned by Vale, a Brazilian multinational), killed twenty people and sent countless tons of toxic iron mine tail waste seven hundred kilometers down the Rio Doce into the Atlantic Ocean. In 2019, a similar tailing dam break at another Vale company site killed 259 near the small Paraopeba River town of Brumadinho, just southwest of Belo Horizonte. Minas Gerais has suffered painfully for its name.

Gold, Diamonds, and Gems

The baroque-era gold rush (1690s–1760s) remains the region's defining historical chapter, and propelled Minas as Brazil's most populous state into

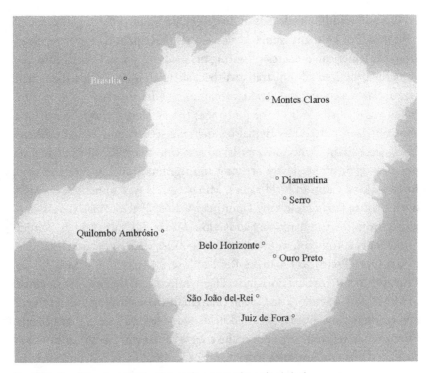

Figure 1.1. Map of Minas Gerais, Brazil, with some place-names referenced in the book.

Figure 1.2. The state of Minas Gerais highlighted in a map of Brazil.

the 1920s.[16] Within one decade of discovery, the value of Portugal's colonial "Eldorado" of gold and gems surpassed "all that Spain had ever received from her American possessions during the whole of the sixteenth century."[17] A highly protected administrative district also rich in diamonds, the region was declared a colonial *capitania* (captaincy, an administrative unit) in 1720, following the brief War of the Emboabas (hairy-legged ones). This armed confrontation pitted the original *bandeirante* settlers and their Brazilian-born descendants, who often enslaved and intermarried with indigenous peoples, against the newly arriving immigrants pouring into the gold fields staking claim to local riches. Minas Gerais was something to fight over, leading Portuguese king Dom João V to split the Minas Gerais captaincy from the Capitania de São Paulo e Minas do Ouro. Rough frontier settlements sprouted into towns, and into cities such as Sabará, Vila Rica (today Ouro Preto), São João del-Rei, São José del-Rei (Tiradentes), Vila do Príncipe (Serro), Arraial do Tijuco (Diamantina), and the first city founded in Minas, Nossa Senhora do Carmo (Mariana). These bustling urban centers and markets grew around key gold fields, some luxuriously. Minas became the crown jewel from where over the course of the eighteenth century it is estimated that 1 million kilos of gold and 2.4 million carats of diamonds were officially accounted for by Portuguese colonial officials. It is possible that similar amounts of each escaped royal taxes in illegal contraband.[18] In these gold-rich cities, a flourishing of artistic output dressed in techniques of the European baroque produced music, architecture, wood and stone sculpture, and painting celebrating religious, nativist, and regional expression. This period became known as the *barroco mineiro* (Minas baroque).

The original leg of the colonial-era Royal Highway network (Estrada Real) connected Vila Rica to the port of Paraty on the São Paulo coast and became known as the Old Road (*caminho velho*). A faster route to Vila Rica, the New Road (*caminho novo*), started out from Miner's Beaches (Praias Mineiras) on Rio de Janeiro's Guanabara Bay. It sliced northeast along what was a ten-thousand-year-old Native trail stretching into the mountains, across the imposing coastal range and river valleys of the once thick rainforest and the wild, meandering region still known as Campo das Vertentes (Rolling Fields). Traveling more than four hundred kilometers to the rugged, mountainous mining district (*zona metalúrgica*) required navigating an arduous two- to four-week journey by foot or horseback or with a mule train driver (*tropeiro*) on roads that flowed with mud during the rainy summer months, November through March. Further isolating the mountainous, urban mining centers from the coast stretched the unsettled "prohibited lands," restricted by crown surveillance and eagerly protected and defended by indigenous groups. Following the discovery of diamonds around Arraial do Tijuco, the Estrada Real network was extended there from Vila Rica along what became known as the Diamond Road.

The mines and agricultural fields of Minas produced one of the New World's most populous slave communities, an inland frontier of the Black Atlantic, perhaps the most concentrated African slave operation of its day, and one that also resulted in a large population of free people of color (*gente de cor*). Healing and religious rituals of the African-derived *calundú*, and the unique mining song genre of *vissungo*, flourished here (see chapters 2 and 3). Even by the earliest years of the 1700s, within a decade of the first gold discovery, free people of color had established livelihoods as artisans, musicians, independent miners, and agricultural and cattle-industry workers. *Forros* were those blacks and mixed-race Brazilians born free, and *libertos* were formerly enslaved Africans and Brazilians who purchased their freedom (by manumission). *Forros*, *libertos*, slaves, and the rest of colonial society fueled memberships of racially segregated lay Catholic brotherhoods (*irmandades*), corporate lay organizations whose members participated in public communal worship on saints' days and other special occasions, and in charitable acts organized by these mutual aid societies including care for the dying and burial of the dead. Colonial Mineiro society welcomed the popular Catholicism of the Afro-Mineiro Congado processions sponsored by black brotherhoods (see chapter 6). By the second half of the eighteenth century, Minas was home to one of the New World's largest populations of free black and mixed-race peoples.[19] Though neither Portuguese nor Brazilian colonial law guaranteed the enslaved access to manumission, as was suggested by Spanish law, it has been controversially claimed that rates of manumission in Minas Gerais were greater than in any other Brazilian region. Rafael de Bivar Marquese argues:

> It is no accident that a substantial number of the studies on this issue [of manumission] look to Minas Gerais during this period. . . . Two points set the mining experience apart within the context of Portuguese America: first, the fact that more slaves received their liberty during the height of the gold mining activities than during the decline; second, the most frequent presence of the practice of *coartação*, that is, the slave's purchase of his or her own freedom via installments.[20]

Mixed-race musicians were by this time filling official roles as professional instrumentalists, composers, and musical directors in some of the cities grown wealthy with gold and diamonds, producing the Minas School of liturgical composers (chapter 4). Coastal Brazilians joined a steady stream of Portuguese immigrants flowing into the region primarily from northern Portugal and the Azores. They brought musical instruments such as the ten-string guitar known as the viola (chapter 7). In attracting an estimated four hundred thousand Portuguese during the eighteenth century, an inchoate Minas later came to be regarded as the soul of Portuguese America, arguably its most Catholic region, a complex quilt of ethnicities and social groups soon producing a *mestiçagem* (racial mixture) among white settlers, enslaved Africans and their descendants, and Native Americans. Caio César Boschi notes:

> [O]nly 39 of the 174 families that the genealogist Cônego Raimundo Trindade considers "old trunk Mineiros" originate from São Paulo, which is to say the population of white colonial Minas was constituted by a vast majority of those [Portuguese regions of] Minho, Porto, Trás-os-Montes, Beira, and the Azores—almost all being countrymen of Portugal—including many "new-Christians," and children of other captaincies.[21]

Portuguese king Dom João V attempted to curb racial mixture in Minas Gerais, decreeing in 1726 that town council positions could be held only by white men or the widowers of white women, further writing that white men in Minas Gerais "are not in the habit of marrying because of the freedom and license of life there. It is not easy to force them to renounce their black and mixed-race concubines and for this reason every family is becoming tainted by the mixture of bloods."[22] Miscegenation flourished, with white men often taking harsh advantage of women of African and indigenous descent. Mineiro cities and towns swelled with populations of Brazilian-born, mixed-race *pardo* (later *mulato*), Euro-Indian *caboclo*, and the *cafuzo* offspring of blacks and Indians. Despite Dom João's proclamation, mixed-race Mineiros were being appointed to municipal and judicial offices in the eighteenth century.[23] Also defying rigid social norms, the Afro-Brazilian *batuque* circle dance (chapter 5) blossomed among non-blacks as the performative center of a society soon suffused with greater Brazil's sine qua non rainbow of skin color.

Minas is the size of France and features six distinct topographic sub-regions. The chaotic and disorderly mining towns were first subject to authoritative spatial administration by the Catholic Church's parish divisions undertaken in 1703. Toll houses (*barreiras*) and tax stations (*recebedorias*) were soon established on major roads and rivers, charging fees and collecting taxes on the movement of people, beasts of burden, dry goods, and the gold, gems, and diamonds from local mines. Well into the nineteenth century, non-Portuguese foreigners were generally barred from entering the safeguarded mining territory of the mountainous interior that lay far south of Salvador, Bahia, and well north of São Paulo. A substantial series of nineteenth-century travel and research books published by a string of European scientists allowed to travel through imperial-era Minas (1808–1889) still provide insight into a society in which printing presses were banned and no system of education established. The state is seen by many today as a historically rich gateway to an illustrious Brazilian past crisscrossed with old, pastoral roads and picturesque colonial-era towns bejeweled with baroque churches. The Mineiro network of colonial-era towns is recognized in the national psyche as a layer of "authentic" Brazil, removed from the busy cosmopolitanism of coastal cities. The poetics of Mineiro cultural identity emerging from this vastness and isolation include reflective introspection, themes of journey and escape, contact with a distant outside world, and a quiet distrust of outsiders. In tandem arose solipsistic themes of intimacy, a closeness to one's own self and to the natural world, and a self-reliance centered within an extended family.

Isolation from the coast did not create a cultural vacuum: the Mineiro past is populated by residents of small towns and cities, and by those who moved along paths, roads, and rivers, via ox carts, mule trains, and horses, between far-flung rural settlements. Now distant history, the ways of life of the traveling mule train drivers known as *tropeiros* were a foundation of the *toadas* and *modas de viola* (folk melodies and viola music) that also graced those trails and paths. Like the iconic *bandeirantes* before them, *tropeiros* became symbolic of Mineiro individuality and independence. The music of the *rebeca* (folk fiddle) and viola entered the back country (*caipira*) of weigh stations and lodgings known as ranchos, fazendas (large farms), and *roçinhas*—the small plots of subsistence crops cultivated by marginalized rural laborers.[24] Landless, impoverished people known as *agregados* lived on others' property, greatly contrasting with the relative comfort of the small towns and larger urban centers that grew around significant gold finds. The relationship between town and country is echoed today by the still under-developed interior and the gleaming modernity of Belo Horizonte, the state capital constructed only in the 1890s with a metropolitan area now home to nearly six million (chapter 8). Its rise coincided with that of the Old Republic (1889–1930), Brazil's first phase of postimperial nationhood.

A Conspiracy of Revolution: The Inconfidência Mineira

"In Minas, each one is his own architect," wrote French naturalist Alcide d'Orbigny following his visit to the region in 1832, a remark referencing the self-sufficiency and independence characterizing the Mineiro legacy.[25] In 1775, the Portuguese governor of Minas Gerais, Antonio de Noronha, observed that the establishment of many illegal manufacturing enterprises in the region represented a clear threat to Crown monopolies, and worse, a source for political independence. By the 1780s, Mineiros' disobedience toward the Crown, and their hushed, nativist talk of independence from Portugal, clandestinely echoed revolutionary movements in the United States and France. The Brazilian viceroy of the time, the Marquis of Lavradio, noted of Minas Gerais that "because of the vastness of the region and the spirit of the population, such independence was a matter of great moment and might one day produce consequences."[26] Portuguese diplomat Martinho de Melo e Castro wrote in a January 28, 1788, letter to Salvaterra de Magos, the Viscount of Barbacena (the *capitão-geral* of the Captaincy of Minas Gerais), that, "among all the peoples that make up the different captaincies of Brazil, none perhaps cost more to subjugate and subdue to the just obedience and submis-siveness of vassals to their sovereign, as have those of Minas Gerais."[27] The Portuguese Crown's subsequent hike in the gold tax proved the final straw in the tense buildup to revolution. In Ouro Preto, a small, secretive circle of civic leaders, intellectuals, heavily indebted local oligarchs, and spirited fol-lowers planned a 1789 political rebellion known as the Inconfidência Mineira (Minas Conspiracy). They sought not an independent nation of Brazil but rather a Mineiro republic with strong ties to the Rio de Janeiro captaincy and its port. The short-lived plot, which failed tragically, etched Minas Gerais into the national psyche as a remote, independent region of individualists with minds for liberty. The rebellion's hero was a young lieutenant named Joaquim

José da Silva Xavier, or Tiradentes ("Tooth Puller," 1746–1792), a soldier and occasional dentist who was arrested, tried, and drawn and quartered for treason against the king of Portugal.

Mining profits began sputtering in the late 1760s, and wealth gradually gave way to a regional economic decline (the *decadência*) that lasted for well over a century. Minas, once a wealthy, closely guarded captaincy of the colony, faced growing poverty and self-reliance. It remained Brazil's most populous province during the imperial era of independence (1822–1889) led by Emperors Dom Pedro I and his son, Dom Pedro II, a period later witnessing significant growth of coffee latifundia that bolstered the rural oligarchy's power in the province's southern subregions of Sul de Minas (Southern Minas) and the Zona da Mata (Forest Zone). The Mineiro interior was reached by dirt roads until the 1890s, when rail lines extended to Sabará to deliver construction materials for Belo Horizonte. The industrial modernity of the railroad's transport of people, goods, and ideas became a symbol of Mineiro development well into the twentieth century and further represented freedom and journey, social connection, and escape. Trains are celebrated by the Corner Club (chapter 9) in both song and image: the cover for Milton Nascimento's 1976 LP *Geraes* debuted his simple line drawing of mountains, the sun, and a train running right to left, with the steam from the *maria fumaça* (steam locomotive) languidly trailing behind. Today, an animated version of this logo welcomes visitors to Nascimento's website. Throughout the twentieth century, locomotives shared their iconic power only with Mineiro politicians: the Old Republic witnessed the quick emergence of *café com leite*, the "coffee with milk" metaphor for the near-domination of national politics by the states of São Paulo and Minas Gerais.

Mineiridade: Minas-ness and Regional Identity

Regionalist expressions weave permeable blankets of local identity and argot that distinguish ways of life, forming place-oriented norms, social relations, and both casual and formal resistance to modes of nationalism and globalism that can constitute collective solidarities and commemorations of suffering, struggle, and survival. Mineiro historian Zanoni Neves, in a discussion of work groups along the São Francisco River, sees in the totality of regionalism, constituted as it is in the case of Minas Gerais through diversity and

plurality, an emphasis not on geography and physical place but rather on
social relations and resistance to nationalist homogeneity.[28] Mineiridade
(Minas-ness) as a regional antidote to the outside world is best illustrated
by the many ways Mineiros tell their homespun stories (*casos*), and by the
many ways to "be Mineiro" (*ser mineiro*). The most Mineiro of all sensibilities, *mineiríssimo*, though resisting easy definition, is the very essence of that
notion and state of mind. Home, and the wide net of extended family kinship
(*parentesco*), define with gravity a great deal of the interiorized backdrop to
that experience.

Familial piety, pride in place and friendships, and an expressed content-
ment with local surroundings characterize the literary works associated
with this conservative, male-dominated tradition. Historian John D. Wirth
coined the abbreviation TMF for the overarching, patriarchic structure of the
"Traditional Mineira Family," as it stamped generations of a fundamentally
conservative and hierarchical society. The governing position of the patriarchic family unit was well established, and "the quality of town life reflected
the stable, conservative values of an agrarian society. . . . The small urban
concentrations of [the nineteenth century] faced toward the countryside
they serviced."[29] It is, though, the larger networks of the "spatially mobile
family system" that grew to define, along with racial markers of light and
dark skin, the closely guarded means of social control characterizing Mineiro
life. Wirth continues:

> Pride of family and of origin gave the Mineiro elite a strong sense of place. Their
> belief in a satisfying local world was more than a politician's delight, a journal-
> ist's feel for hyperbole. The extent to which this theme appears in their memoirs
> and creative literature shows it was a hallmark of Mineiro regionalism.[30]

Pioneering authors who promulgated Mineiro identity were led by historian Diogo de Vasconcelos (1834–1927), who came of age during the empire.
An "unshakable monarchist,"[31] he supported the return to power of Emperor
Dom Pedro II and was a fervent conservative who, for instance, favored only
the slowest rate of gradual slave emancipation.[32] As the dean of Mineiro historians, Vasconcelos conjured foundational myths of regional identity with
monolithic individuals of European descent, the *bandeirantes*. Positing them
as the most significant characters of their day, Vasconcelos further lamented
the struggles these white founding fathers faced with enslaved Africans,

Indians, and outsiders, dismissing both the brutal nature of slavery and the genocidal campaigns against Native Indians, uncritically normalizing these developments as evolutionary frameworks of regional history. In his view, the colonial power structure gave rise to a natural order and to the specific features of Mineiros, shaping their character, culture, and values. He characterized blacks as merely domesticated captives, deserving of charity as simply the poorest of the poor in postabolition Brazil. Vasconcelos's narratives of ethnic homogeneity characterized this notion of true *mineiridade*. He argued against the 1890s construction of Belo Horizonte, and the relocation of the state capital to the new city from his beloved Ouro Preto, where he had owned a newspaper and had served as mayor.

Vasconcelos was not alone among regionalist historians in romantically extolling the natural wonders of Minas as elemental to its social stratification. The Mineiro environment as a cradle of regional identity was a defining theme in the work of João Camilo de Oliveira Torres (1915–1973, b. Santa Maria de Itabira, MG), particularly his influential 1943 study *O homem e a montanha* (Man and the mountain), which carries the subtitle "Introduction to the study of geographic influences on the formation of the Mineiro spirit." Oliveira Torres also promoted certain brands of twentieth-century racist doctrine suggesting that the cultural practices of Africans and their descendants in Minas Gerais only benefited from slavery, stating outright that "blacks were an amorphous mass, without organization or defense. The brotherhoods [Catholic lay sodalities] contributed unequivocally to the integration of the African and his descendants into the Christian civilization, a task that was brilliantly completed by . . . the same group spirit of the old regime."[33] Ignoring the scope of Afro-Mineiro history in its own right, Oliveira Torres argued that it was the Catholic brotherhoods that singularly enabled "innumerable musical and choreographic creations of African origin that today enrich our folklore."[34] Regarding the region's vital Congado traditions, he famously suggested that the black community's celebrations linked to the church calendar's festival of Our Lady of the Rosary were "scandalously Afro-Brazilian."[35] The racially marginalized, often remaining nameless in this literature when not being lampooned, toiled outside of the narratives painted by elite Mineiro historians and writers, an exclusion that still haunts some portrayals of Minas and regional identity.

Mineiro scholars in the social sciences and humanities have added discursive layers of *mineiridade* from the fields of sociology, history, and economics, some turning away from *mineiridade*'s roots in colonialism, monarchic rule, and racist doctrine.[36] By the 1930s, a small, informal group of more progressive Mineiro writers and intellectuals found common ground in the haunts of Belo Horizonte and in their respective searches for new meaning in the local, the regional, and their broader Brazilian experiences. This twentieth-century oeuvre arose in the form of published letters, memoirs, journals, chronicles, poetry, short stories, and novels, including those of nationally recognized Mineiro authors. Quotidian, nostalgic, and sentimental observations augment the work of literary giants such João Guimarães Rosa (novelist, doctor, and diplomat, 1908–1967), Carlos Drummond de Andrade (poet, journalist, writer, 1902–1987), Pedro Nava (memoirist, medical doctor, historian, 1903–1984), writer and journalist Paulo Mendes Campos (1922–1991), memoirist Cyro dos Anjos (1906–1994), and João Dornas dos Santos Filho (1902–1962). Among other mostly white men born within a decade of Belo Horizonte's founding, they are lauded for having forged fresh connections with new European movements, creating a twentieth-century *mineiridade*. These near-conflict-free accounts, full of easy social interaction and hospitality, still conflict with the symptoms of the underclasses and the region's epochal transition from the aching legs of the *decadência* to the long road toward industrialism, urban self-awareness, and grinding social changes arising at the end of the nineteenth century and throughout the twentieth.

These writers strove for a renewed sense of regional identity fusing modernist tastes with some of the nationalist discourse surrounding the controversial work of Gilberto Freyre, and with the old spirits of Mineiro revolt, independence, and the more egalitarian potential of Minas's colonial-era urban heritage. Their "Minas-ness" arguably reflected aspects of the *brasilidade* arising in certain national circles of the 1930s and onward. On the national stage, this modernist turn came most notably from writer, composer, pianist, and musicologist Mário de Andrade (1893–1945), whose remarkable group of artists, writers, and dreamers were based in São Paulo. Two years earlier, this Paulista group had championed the highly influential Modern Art Week (Semana da Arte Moderna) in São Paulo, promoting, among other artists and new ideas, Heitor Villa-Lobos and his inimitable fusions of Brazilian contemporary fine art music. With his friends, writer Oswald de Andrade, French poet Blaise Cendrars, and painter Tarsila do Amaral, Andrade ventured north from São Paulo to Minas Gerais seeking out the meaningfulness of colonial Mineiro towns during Holy Week in 1924, like a modern *bandeirante* group waving flags of new artistic aesthetics and notions of national identity. Like the Mineiros, the Paulista modernists were looking for new ideas in Old Brazil, and a fateful meeting occurred at Belo Horizonte's Grande Hotel, spawning lifelong friendships, particularly between Carlos Drummond de Andrade and Mário de Andrade. Drawn together through their reevaluations of colonialism, the baroque civilization of gold, and the vital importance of Afro-Brazilian culture, these local modernists arguably threw a spotlight on what they perceived as outdated, nineteenth-century, European-derived thought and ideas, and the backwardness of the nation. In Minas Gerais, regarded as the most conservative, Catholic, and Portuguese of all the Brazilian states, these twentieth-century celebrations of folk culture, Afro-Brazilian traditions, and democracy were an antidote to what Michael Mitchell has called the conservative modernism of Brazil: strains of racist, proto-authoritarianism portraying blacks and the poor "as drags on modernization . . . [who were] made, consequently, the targets of social and political exclusion."[37]

Music and Regional Identity: Traditionality, Embodiment, and Musical Space

The term "Hearing," as used in the title of this book, remains capitalized and is a philosophically charged concept of interpreting the broader implications of music's social meaning. Music is understood here in relation to identities of place, and to the historical and contemporary institutions shaping Minas and Brazil such as slavery, colonialism, urbanization, ideas about race and racial politics, socioeconomic inequalities, and religiosity. However, because this is not a book about theory or philosophy, Hearing is not routinely elaborated upon, nor is it the only theoretical aspect of the book. Hearing regional identity requires ideas about *traditionality*, *embodiment*, and musical spaces. Traditionality is a variable condition of music, enabling participants in contemporary experience to recognize and reconstitute meaningfulness established in the past by historical others. I suggest a flexible universalism whereby general theoretical concepts apply in adaptive, positive ways to concepts discussed in this book. This determination is only indirectly a result of fieldwork and is not intended as a stand-in for any particular subject's ideas about their own self-understanding. Music's traditionality, existing before us as a condition emerging from the past, is met in the contemporary world as an "opportunity" for human consciousness, actions, and behavior that mindfully bring the past into the present. We sharpen the dullness of the past by bringing it to life, on our own social and individual terms, through music. And we do that with others, as musicians, listeners, dancers, readers, and mindful observers.

Music's condition of traditionality demands participation. Through music cognition, participants step into (embody, enact, emplace, emplot) the identity-producing social spaces of music. This concept of experience has no use for notions of an externalized, objectified "music," one that supposedly acts upon us from outside our consciousness, or is believed to retain an essentialist presence or a reified symbolism. We foster and mediate music's traditionality in a dual embodiment: first, by allowing ourselves to be transformed by music through our own, cognitive enactment of traditionality; and second, by imagining our own narratives that constitute transformations in which we ourselves invoke, reenact, or somehow participate in communal memories, welcoming and joining others as part of an affected community. Andrea Schiavio, whose enaction theory of music cognition draws from principles of neurophenomenology, suggests a music cognition arising from the whole body (including mind and consciousness) and emerging from interactions with the social and physical environment in which we are embedded.[38] Here, "sense-making" through music is a practical skill constituted by embedded and embodied forms of interactions with the environment, and with the past. Through a dynamic interplay with music, performers, audience members, and other participants enact their own identities of place by imaginatively situating themselves, a deep regionalism located in processual spaces of consciousness.

Participants bring places to life. Alex Lawrey reminds us that there is a "psyche of place, a 'living' identity to any given spatial situation that music may participate in."[39] In the context of regional identity, traditionality and embodiment engage the three notions of musical space mentioned at the start of this introduction: the geography of a cultural territory's physical places; the heterogeneous temporal spaces of social memory within and between historical communities; and the processual spaces of consciousness hosting identities of place as cognitive experiences enabling what some have termed *enactment*. Of these three, I devote the least amount of discussion to the space of consciousness in this book, yet it remains an important factor:

music is neither expressive nor symbolic unless participants consciously enact the meaningfulness of those symbols. I suggest a threefold concept of embodiment to include one's emplacement and emplotment within social spaces offered by music's traditionality, generating personal narratives that can form both social and individual identities. In terms of regional identities and music, a pragmatic theory of music's social meaning and understanding deals not with truth-conditions but rather with the bearing of our reconstruction of stability among change and conflict whereby tradition conveys an orderliness of continuance and survival.

Notions of Embodiment in Ethnomusicological Literature

Participatory enaction of traditionality, and processes of embodiment through music cognition, enable and heighten identities of place. In twenty-first-century ethnomusicological literature, place and embodiment have acquired various, sometimes interrelated meanings that I feel resonate with this book's concerns with regional identity. As Alessandra Ciucci suggests in her study of regional Moroccan sung poetry, the odes of the ʿaita genre express "a history that is critical to the communal memory, identity, and consciousness of the populations of the Atlantic Plains." She stressed how participants are given the opportunity to "invoke and reenact a vision of history and of the past on each occasion of performance."[40] Such an enactment of history characterizes the Congado processions described in this book. Nancy Guy examines Taiwanese popular music's referencing of an "embodied sense of being in a particular place," in the larger context of *ecomusicological* relationships linking us to natural phenomena and physical settings.[41] She further considers the sense of *being* in relation to specific places, physical settings, and phenomena of nature, stemming from textual representation and programmatic content, musical style, and other expressive and symbolic devices such as instrumentation and timbre. This book's chapter on the viola (chapter 7) stresses the symbolic cultural timbre of that instrument and its connection to the rural past of Minas Gerais.

In his discussion of Chayantaka music in highland Bolivia, Thomas Solomon echoes similar ecomusicological concerns in invoking collective memory as conjoining emplacement and embodiment "[To] encounter a culturally defined place is to encounter the experiences and feelings of those who came before and made that place, and interpolate those experiences and feelings with one's own. Emplacement becomes inseparable from embodiment; the senses make places and places literally make sense—they are cultural ways of organizing felt experiences of the environment."[42]

Many culturally defined places are examined in this book, many of which conjure the past while welcoming encounters with the living. Senses of place engendered by embodiment are expanded via *emplotment*, the narrative-like mimetic role play of participants facilitating regional identity in musical encounters. To borrow from David Kaplan, emplotment brings participants toward a type of culmination providing contexts of fulfillment or unification in which meanings are recognized.[43] In her study of Hindu nationalism and music, Anna Schultz considers associations among performers, audiences, and music's strong narratives of belonging.[44] Transformations occur within the participant's identity consciousness and outward collective behavior, often in relation to spiritually and ritually invoked, yet physically *unreal*, nonpresent entities and figurative participants in personal narratives of emplotment. Here, embodiment involves identity-generating collective memories and stories tied to place, not unlike the power of the Congado with its plot-driven basis and public devotion to patron saints. According to Schultz, certain formal attributes of music, such as call-and-response vocal styles and cyclic structure, facilitate entrance into such processes and encourage participation in deeper musical experiences.[45] Musical contexts help create a chance not just to display competence but, equally important, to manifest identities with an empathetic potential, leading to what Schultz describes as "a blurring of distinctions between real and invoked participants."[46] From music's "theater of embodiment," empathy arises from togetherness and self-reflective role playing in which the individual is imaginatively accompanied by others in mental configurations. Social music encounters within communities and groups suggest types of *intersubjective communication* in the sense of collective identity and memory. In our social groups, we expect/suspect that fellow group members understand meaningfulness in some manner similar to our own, particularly in ritualized, formal behavior.

Concepts of traditionality, embodiment, and identities of place are not mechanical explanations of mysterious, metaphysical phenomena and are to be considered in fluid ways as they are applied to this investigation of Minas Gerais as a cultural territory. Music is a catalyst for regional identities of place throughout physical spaces, communities of historical narratives, and the consciousness of participants. Similar notions easily figure into what Fiona Magowan and Louise Wrazen write of in the introduction to their edited volume *Performing Gender, Place, and Emotion in Music*, that "performance is to a large extent contingent on performers' imagined and emotional relationships with place."[47] Lillie Gordon interprets these authors as seeking to understand "how music mediates embodied connections to place by engaging issues of landscape, geography, environment, home, country, and indigeneity."[48] Chris Gibson and Peter Dunbar-Hall note Aboriginal popular music's "closeness to, love of, and responsibility for land."[49] Here, I think of the discussion of Clube da Esquina songs in chapter 9. Embodiment is thus recognized in ethnomusicological literature partly as the individual's presence with, and participation in, the temporal musical spaces of a cultural territory. The social body becomes part of music's "place-making" in its meaningful relationship to physical environment and local social history among the heritage of culturally defined spaces. I argue for the notion that the participants discussed in this book in their own ways, individually and collectively, have embodied their ideals of their own identities of place in making Minas Gerais their home.[50]

This book is about communities. "One does not remember alone," says Paul Ricoeur in his survey of Maurice Halbwachs's notions of collective memory.[51] In communal performance spaces, and in dislocated spatialities such as the internet that figuratively spawn contemporary connections, we intuit and sense the collective experience and memory of others arising from the *shared* sound worlds of musical performance, their social narratives, and their meaningfulness. We understand ourselves through music due greatly to social others. Music can be interpreted as a performance of social memory within and across social groups where spaces function as a stabilizing force, whether private or public, formal or informal, sacred or profane. Music, meanwhile, is *from somewhere*, a condition of our surroundings, influencing our individual and collective feelings of belonging, subjective orientations of place, and sensibilities of *being somewhere*. These spatial ontologies of music create conditions for action, consciousness, and integration of experiences with physical place as part of a cultural territory's musically enhanced sociogeographic dimension. Timothy Rice comments on the sociogeography of music as "multiple social settings in which people produce, experience, and understand music."[52] There are also the borderless, (re)imagined landscapes of our individual memories, upon which our remembrances of images and soundscapes of the past reside and grow. Our personal, interiorized representations of the past, of the world, may appear as images both visual and auditory living on in spaces conjured by memory and imagination, interpretations of the lay of the land, the landscapes of our experiences. As an outsider in Minas Gerais, I hold many personal biases toward the strength of this sensibility of place in the music discussed below. In a wide sense, music is behavior (performing, listening, dancing, discussing, and writing), a partner in memory and remembrance, and a vehicle for consciousness-defining experiences. Music is people and community.

Minas Gerais as a Socially Constituted, Heterogeneous Cultural Territory

The poetics of the Mineiro state of mind are revealed in flashes, then recede into the natural forms that flow here, and stubbornly intermingle with elements of a semihidden past. In the imagination's subtropical melody, the wide intervals of mountain air move in time with ornamented, colonial-era embellishments of noble architecture graced with birdsong and glinting river light. Humid landscapes generate their own cosmos, linked as they are in visions of vast skies of blue and the blackest, star-filled nights. Brazil's human rainbow lives here, a vibrant sonority modulating among foreground, middle-ground, and background relief to a sun-drenched world and to environments they have sculpted into the earth. Hard-core cadences of noisy change stop and start their rush among urban iron and steel, rain-stained cement walls, and asphalt either baked under a humming sun, cooled by overcast, or lavished with cloudbursts. In following some of these city streets one might transition stage by stage, down bustling, dense avenues to nondescript suburbanscapes that gradually merge into scattershot hovels along gravel roads, and then beyond city limits onto narrow red dirt paths slicing into the greenest of green hills and fields. Shaded only by trees, what are now ancient trails eventually disappear into moonlit streams and hillsides.

History, Paul Ricoeur reminds us, "will contain the inventory of social practices governing the bonds of belonging to places, territories, fragments of the social space of communities of affiliation."[53] It is common for iconic performers; music instruments, genres, and styles; and pieces of music to be associated with specific geographic origins such as a region or city. Although the singular aspect of territoriality is not an obvious characteristic of music's abstract sound worlds, multifaceted territorial dimensions nonetheless develop as bonds of belonging, forming experiences leading to local, regional, and national identity. In Neil Brenner and Stuart Elden's analysis of Henri Lefebvre's seminal theories of territory, the term *territoriality* applies to the social spaces of physical place; *territory* applies to the historically and geographically specific cultural organization and thought of a regional population.[54] Territory is created by social groups, growing from large-scale, long-term organization and confrontation. The geographical fixedness of territories emerges as a spatial analogue to historical time, where and when individual lives, communities, and social groups have existed pluralistically and in temporal relationship to each other. Within a heterogeneous region, Mineiros create, experience, and interpret music within multiple socially constituted settings forming along complex interstices of political histories and ethnic diversity. It is not all about only music, as political corruption, high rates of street violence, and social injustices also characterize contemporary Brazilian life. It is better that this reality is understood rather than ignored: music plays an inspirational role in Brazilian lives partly because of these social ills. Music in Minas has mediated these challenging struggles for three centuries. Some music can be best interpreted as growing from, or being a part of, suffering.

Lines of political demarcation such as state borders act as discursively symbolic institutions reflecting and generating spatialized identities. Yet borders suggest both the state-sponsored enclosure of cultural territories and the invitation for crossings of people, material, media, and ideas. As much as bordering speaks to inclusion, separation, and territoriality, a telling osmosis easily highlights the transnational and transregional fluidity of musical experiences. How musical borders bring people together while also underlining social divisions reflects the binaries of bordering's tendency to circumscribe/connect, isolate/encompass, separate/meet, confine/approach, and limit/touch.[55] Music's potential iconicity of geographic place confronts the very freedom with which music actually travels, imaginatively within ourselves and socially between us, occupying multiple places as emergent, potentially transcultural global forms defying specific place.

Ideas about Race

This book does not approach race as being a uniform marker for collective attitudes or beliefs of self-identity, musical taste or practice, cultural expression, or religious belief. I do not advocate an essentialist attribution of musical behavior and aesthetics based on skin color, race, ethnicity, or parental background. Neither is this book based upon ethnographic studies or beliefs aimed at determining how Brazilians racially self-identify. Race is a socially determined concept, and the vast literature on Brazilian race relations reveals richly fluid concepts of race, skin color, and their social meanings in ways markedly different from, for instance, the situation in the United States. However, the label "African-derived," notions of blackness (negritude), and categorical racial terms such as white, black, mixed-race, *mestiço* (mixed-race), and *pardo* (brown, mixed-race) are routinely referenced in the following chapters. For instance, the popular Catholic practice of Congado has been termed by a few scholars as "Black Catholic," a designation I share, not to arbitrarily racialize the practice but rather to celebrate and valorize practices developed over centuries within Afro-Brazilian communities. Certainly, not all black Brazilians who are Catholic practice popular forms of the religion, or "Black Catholicism," while some non-blacks do.

The term "Afro-Mineiro" is used throughout to designate black musical traditions of Minas Gerais—"Afro-" rather than "African Mineiro" or "Africano-Mineiro" simply because the former, despite its throwback status in the United States, remains standard in Portuguese and is used widely in Brazil. The black cultural history of Minas Gerais is rarely mentioned in twentieth-century English-language scholarship by Brazilianists, who have tended to focus their discussions of Afro-Brazilian expression within the coastal cultural poles of black Bahia and black Rio and who often betray a near-bias toward West African–derived Afro-Brazilian cultural heritage. The historical legacy of African-derived culture in Minas Gerais, and more broadly in the southeastern interior, is dominated by a Central African lineage often referred to by scholars as Bantu, or pan-Bantu. Throughout Mineiro history, mentalities and attitudes among Afro-Mineiros toward cultural Africanisms have ranged from acceptance and emulation to rejection on the basis of their own, self-determined Brazilianness and general westernization. Degrees of "Africanness" cannot be assigned in blanket terms to all qualities of past "Afro-Mineiro-ness." Chapters 2, 3, 5, and 6 do their part in arguing these details in the analysis of calundú, vissungo, batuque, and Congado, respectively.

The racial and phenotypic categorization terms *non-white* and *non-black* are also used in this book, not always as hard-and-fast historical cases of inclusion and exclusion but most often as a general support and guide for discussion. The designation *gente de cor* (people of color) is common in some dialogue on race in Brazil, a term that, like others, is problematic and open for contestation. White and mixed-race Brazilians readily participate in "black" music, and countless Afro-Brazilians practice and enjoy European-derived "white" music, though few Brazilians would apply these gross delineations. Left unspecified and unsubstantiated, overgeneralized categorizations of the relationships between skin color and musical practice are misguided, damaging, and confusing. I have never met a Brazilian who would define these relationships in "black and white," and I reference these generalities only as an indication of the far deeper complexities enveloping issues of music, culture, race, and skin color in Brazil. In some sense, certain "black" music arguably became nationalized culturally, as in the case of samba, and in what became the middle-class, multiracial urban forms of African-derived Umbanda religious practice at the dawn of the twentieth century.

Regardless, serious racially based social disparities are readily seen throughout the world, including Brazil. If race is a socially determined concept, then so, too, is racism. Slave society and its violently white supremacist ideology grew from, and was reinforced by, rigid racialization and segregation through laws and social norms. The brutality of enslavement, and the often rough nature of sexual violence and miscegenation among white males and women of Native and African descent, historically transitioned to pseudo-rational scientific racism and the eugenics-based policies of "whitening" (*branqueamento*) in postabolition, nineteenth-century Brazil. Later, in valorizing the considerable rates of miscegenation, Gilberto Freyre attempted in the twentieth century to liberate Brazil's mixed-race profile from the spotlight of Eurocentric, white supremacist ideology and scientific racism that marked nineteenth- and early twentieth-century thought. One in a series of influential books, his *Casa-grande e senzala* (Master's house and slave quarters, 1933) lifted up the racial mixture of *mestiçagem* and the *pardo* population as proud aspects of a new nationalist ideology. Yet in celebrating the country's mixed-race, *mestiço* heritage, often in a condescending, patriarchic manner legitimizing white privilege, Freyre and his followers presented apologist defenses concerning the inequality faced by twentieth-century Brazilian blacks (*pretos*). One Freyrian argument is that slavery's institutionalized racism generated a historical inertia that overwhelmed the twentieth-century ruling class's ability to address, for example, the poverty and lack of access to education experienced by darker-skinned Brazilians of African descent. This apologist belief easily masked theories of white supremacy and tended to ignore racial injustices embedded in contemporary customs and laws, instead placing the blame for racial inequality on disparity engendered in the past. According to this argument, the notable and often obviously color-based inequities in education, health care, income, and living standards were naturalized and attributed primarily to slavery. In authoritarian circles, Freyrian theory was used by nationalists to refute claims of racism and became a basis for the criminalization of black political movements that called for progressive change in racial politics and government policy, labeling them subversive and anti-Brazilian.

Another aspect of what many have referred to as the myth of a Brazilian "racial democracy" includes what has been termed the *deracializing* of social differences. This analysis forms the basis of Elisa Nascimento's "Sorcery of Color" thesis, which suggests that substituting race with skin color "allowed the nation to cultivate pretentiously antiracist ideology that obscured the existence of an extremely efficient system of racial domination."[56] As Edwin E. Telles argues, Freyrian views on race in Brazil were "horizontal" in their focus on lateral sociability and interracial social relations, whereas the subsequent generation of researchers disavowed notions of a so-called racial democracy in favor of "vertical" views of inequality, discrimination, and real social distance between blacks and whites.[57] In this sense, I use the term *marginal* in this book to reference inequalities in living conditions, general socioeconomic disparity, and lack of opportunities in education and social advancement, and to stress what I see as a near anonymity, or a type of nonappearance, of black narratives in official Brazilian histories. Often, I use the terms marginal and *marginalized* to convey what are, in reality, more complex notions of social, political, and historical exclusions from arenas of power based on race, gender, and socioeconomic status.

Furthermore, racial issues are not limited to arguments of African-descendant black versus European-descendant white. Brazilians' incredibly diverse range in self-perception of race, skin color, and their meanings defy simplistic categories. Importantly, Native American ancestry, and Near

Eastern immigrant communities beginning in the early 1900s, for instance, are essential to understanding contemporary Brazilian attitudes about race. Waves of Near Eastern Christians, including Syrians, Lebanese, and Turks fleeing the collapse of the Ottoman Empire and the ruin of World War I, settled in São Paulo, with some making it to Belo Horizonte and Sul de Minas. Many Japanese immigrants settled in Brazil's southeast. Juiz de Fora retained a quasi-cosmopolitan, global demographic due to its easy access to Rio de Janeiro, an open port since 1808.

Book Chapters

Each of the following chapters attempts to locate a musical realm of the Mineiro soul. Chapter 2, "*Calundú:* 'Winds of Divination,'" investigates a lost healing and religious practice of Central African origin, and in introducing calundú's musical attributes presents a window into a cross section of colonial society and key social characteristics of eighteenth-century Minas. The chapter seeks out voices from the first generations of Afro-Mineiros within the burgeoning frontier slave society that embraced calundú's music, dance, chant, and incantations before its violent demise at the hands of colonial administrators, regional church authorities, and the Portuguese Inquisition. The chapter concludes with a discussion of calundú's cultural inertia and speculates on possible connections between its drumming and trance possession legacies and those of subsequent musical practices. Chapter 3, "*Vissungo*'s 'Songs of the Earth': A Vanishing Tradition of the Serro Frio," looks at an extinct tradition once specific to Minas Gerais and elaborates upon aspects of the Afro-Mineiro heritage introduced in chapter 2. It establishes a picture of the gold- and diamond-mining industry, and the free labor that drove Mineiro civilization. Broader consideration of vissungo allows discussion of the social spaces of the work song, and of a further connection provided by Brazilian scholars to runaway slave settlements known as *quilombos* and their important role in Mineiro society. The chapter brings readers through the colonial and imperial eras into the 1940s, when vissungo was documented through the efforts of Brazilian musicologists working with the US Library of Congress, becoming an inspiration to popular musicians of Rio's black consciousness movement of the 1960s and 1970s. Chapter 4, "Sacred and Fine Art Music of the Colonial and Imperial Periods," considers the unique legacy of the liturgical music

of the Minas School of eighteenth- and nineteenth-century composers of
sacred church music. The chapter includes brief biographical reflections on
the musicians and their times, spotlighting the repertoire's rediscovery and
contemporary social place as a valued regional heritage of sacred musical
art. The chapter concludes with a discussion of *choromeleiros*, bandas, and
the imperial-era modinha as elements of fine art music emerging from town
plazas, salons, and concert halls. This volume's appendix 1 augments this look
into colonial-era music with information about important musicological
publications drawn from essential regional archives.

The subject of chapter 5 is batuque, an African-derived circle dance
that represents a coming together of diverse Brazilians across varied social
strata despite state and church opposition. Tracing the dance's key narratives from Africa to contemporary Minas Gerais reveals vital changes in the
Mineiro social landscape. A secondary theme of the chapter is the remarkable power of dance and joyous drumming to create a common ground
among Brazilians across racial and class lines. "Congado in Minas Gerais:
The Feast Day of Our Lady of the Rosary and the Election of a Black King"
is the title of chapter 6, completing the cycle of four chapters dedicated to
Afro-Mineiro musical history. Although found throughout much of Brazil,
this genre of popular Catholicism is special to Afro-Mineiro history and is
often termed "Congado Mineiro." Appendix 2 of this volume is a brief yet
detailed auxiliary to chapter 6, outlining the five-hundred-year history of
this processional genre dedicated to the Virgin Mary and black saints, which
celebrates the crowning of a black king.

Chapter 7 examines the guitar-like viola, presenting the instrument as both
symbolic of the rural past and central to contemporary masters who have
assigned it a new role in defining regional musical identity. Musicians have
played the viola for several hundred years, and twenty-first-century players
(*violeiros*), luthiers, and collectors continue navigating the instrument's history. "The Viola in Minas Gerais: Rural Dreams and Urban Realities" attempts
to define the instrument's meaningfulness for a cultural territory across time,
and enters the "interior" world of rural Mineiro history. That hinterland
perspective on regional identity is contrasted by chapter 8, "Belo Horizonte
Nocturne: Subtropical Modernism, 1894–1960," which presents a musical
profile of a brand-new city, examining music's multiple social spaces and
crucial role in twentieth-century Minas Gerais. The city's classical music
scene has formed a link to the fine art past of liturgical music, bandas, and

modinhas discussed in chapter 3. The chapter identifies the city's key musicians, conductors, performance organizations, and conservatories that have
defined this slice of regional musical identity. In addition to continuing chapter 3's focus on regional fine art music history by presenting many individual
musicians, chapter 8 sketches a brief picture of dance clubs, carnival, and
popular music that formed the backdrop to the growing capital's nightlife and
musical trends. Belo Horizonte was the primary locus for Milton Nascimento
and his friends, the collective known as the Corner Club. The final chapter,
"Regionalist Themes in the Songs of the Corner Club," examines how images
and concepts of Minas Gerais figure prominently in some of the collective's
most important, well-loved songs. The region's rurality and historical character as portrayed in some of these songs played a foil to themes of political resistance to the authoritarianism of the country's military dictatorship
(1964–1985), which mapped to the time line of the rise of the Corner Club
collective and subsequent stages of its success.

The particular styles and types of music I present in this book have greatly
informed my understanding of Minas Gerais since my first visit there in
1987. The book's scope precludes deeper immersion into any one particular topic and excludes more than it includes: my subjective choices come
nowhere near a complete profile, a project both undesirable and impossible.
Although I greatly value music notation as a composer and guitarist, any
musical examples that may have been relevant for this book illustrating, for
example, various tunings of the viola, drumming patterns found in Congado,
or stylistic considerations of the Minas School composers, would only get in
the way of what I wanted to write about. For this project, I consider music
for its narrative role in descriptively exploring a multicultural, heterogeneous
society. Neither analysis nor technical explanation of musical structures and
styles were of primary concern during the writing of this book. These pages
do not examine music in relation only to itself.

Select audio examples illustrating some of the genres discussed in this book
are available on the *Hearing Brazil* YouTube channel.

Chapter 2

Calundú

"Winds of Divination"

The incantations and percussion-laden music of *calundú* religious and heal-ing practices involving human possession animated cities, mining towns, and farms in eighteenth- and nineteenth-century Minas Gerais. Although calundú had appeared in Brazil by the mid-seventeenth century, particularly in Bahia and the northeast, its presence in Minas Gerais was even stronger a century later, during and after one of the world's first gold rushes. And in another context of its prevalence in this interior, mountainous region of Brazil, Portuguese Inquisition documents speak of these rituals as being common, daily ceremonies in the lives of Mineiros during the eighteenth century.[1] This chapter seeks to more clearly understand this African-derived belief system, its cultural sources and relationships to music, and its meaningfulness as a long-lost yet once vital sacred healing tradition in an understudied region of the African diaspora. Examining eighteenth- and nineteenth-century music and black religiosity, and calundú's fate, offers insight into Minas Gerais as a cultural territory. As Daniela Buono Calainho maintains, "[A]lthough com-mon in Bahia, it was in the region of Minas where references [to calundú] more consistently appeared in documentation, generalized during the eigh-teenth century as a social function of the region's large contingent of slaves, the process of urbanization, and of the local production of gold."[2] Colonial-era oppression spearheaded by the Portuguese Inquisition led to calundú's fragmentation and transformation, with the likely absorption of its musical inertia into other drum-based Afro-Mineiro genres, including syncretic religions Macumba and Umbanda, the Black Catholic Congado, the quasi-sacred circle dance batuque, and the popular, secular couple's dance *lundu*.

Calundú's functional religious music has prompted some scholars of Atlantic creole religion to argue for a so-called African-derived parallelism with Christianity. For instance, historian James Sweet suggests that some early eighteenth-century African religions in Brazil were often less syncretic or creolized than they were "independent systems of thought" paralleling Catholicism; Sweet characterizes calundú as "Central African religion in action."[3] In addition to its very religiosity running counter to Christian beliefs, calundú's African-derived liturgical music, and language, helped to distinguish it from later processes of creolization, syncretism, and hybridization in other Afro-Brazilian cultural developments.[4] Drumming, both figuratively doctrinal as sacred communication and imagistic in its sensual timbre and attractive musical patterns that induce dance and trance possession, is a primary conduit for ancestor worship and spirit communication. A key to this parallelism, drumming here remains in a sense what anthropologist José Jorge de Carvalho qualified as "uncompromisingly African."[5] Further speaking to parallelism was calundú's uncompromising chant, calling forth spirits and ancestors in African languages including a "dialect of the mines" (*falar Africano,* or *Calunga*) specific to Minas Gerais and southeastern Brazil, which, like calundú itself, became shrouded in secrecy, decreased in prevalence, and ultimately shrank into isolation.[6]

From Africa to Brazil

Calundú's alternative, dynamic social spaces define a chapter of Minas Gerais's history, when a cross section of colonial Mineiro society, dominated by a Catholic Portuguese minority, sought the services of clandestine black healers, both male and female (*calundeiros/as*), who performed trance possession rituals within an increasingly hidden subculture. This music, dance, and chant contrasted with the very public soundscapes of other Afro-Mineiro music such as batuque, capoeira, and the Congado religious processions of popular Catholicism. Calundú sessions attracted paying clients seeking remedies for illness and pain, spiritual protection, and good fortune in matters of love and finance. Directors of calundú ritual relied upon the efficacy of music, chant, and dance for trance possession, inviting ancestral spirits (sometimes known as *zumbi*) to prescribe treatments and advice. Enslaved Africans and their descendants formed an ethnically diverse population of Afro-Mineiros contributing to the transformed traditions of an increasingly pan-Bantu culture dominated by Congolese and Angolan influences; *nganga* priests and priestesses from Angola, now forced laborers, likely contributed to calundú's presence. This, too, may have been the case of the slavery-shattered remnants of secretive Congolese *kimpasi* religious societies, and the music-filled *xinguila* possession cults common to regions of Angola during the seventeenth century.[7] The Bakongo people, for instance, placed *nganga* practice alongside the work of spiritual advisers (*itomi*), who encouraged fertility and resolved family disputes, and fortune-tellers (*ndoki*) practiced in divination. As the Portuguese and missionaries had first spread Catholicism in Africa two centuries before the start of the Mineiro gold rush in the mid-1690s, Europeans interpreted Native, paganistic rituals as creolized concepts of fetish (*feitiço*) and sorcery (*feitiçaria*), with practitioners becoming known as fetishists (*feitiçeiros*). Early eighteenth-century Portuguese Inquisition testimony given by Matheos, a Jesuit College estate slave in Bengo, Angola, described *quilundu* (calundú) as the ritualized spirit possession of a living person.[8]

> They also had a pot placed over a fire. In the pot [were] blood, wild honey, red feathers, and bones of animals. Three men danced around the fire, accompanied by musicians playing *maconzas* [a scraper idiophone known in Brazil as *reco-reco* and *canzala*]. The purpose of the ceremony was to cure a sick black woman. Paulo, the master of the ceremony, invoked a spirit named Angola, clearly a reference to the title *ngola*.[9]

In subsequent descriptions, rituals were accompanied by combinations of percussion instruments such as the frame drum (*adufe*, later *pandeiro*), friction drum (*cuíca* or *puíta*), wooden or bamboo-notched scrapers (*reco-reco* or *canzala*), shakers (*chocalho*), bead or shell net-covered gourds (*chekere*), basket rattles (*caxixi*), struck metallophonic bells (*agogó*), and/or shaken bells with clappers (*adjá*). We can surmise that these sacred timbres combined with syncopated, polyrhythmic patterns similar to those heard in other African and Afro-Brazilian percussion music. Arguing for timbre and rhythmic style as primary contexts for religiosity allows us to assume through conjecture calundú's historical continuity of musical traits with other Afro-Brazilian religious practices, and to ascribe to calundú its proper musical import. As Sweet reminds his readers:

> [E]very *calundú* ceremony included a small entourage of helpers who aided the *calundeiro* in his or her invocations—dancers, musicians, and so on. By including other slaves in the proceedings, the *calundeiro* ingratiated himself or herself to others in the community, reinforcing not only the religious importance of *calundú*, but also the social "freedoms"—music, dance, and food—that came along with it.[10]

To varying degrees, enslaved people of Central and West African origin in Minas Gerais shared music's role in articulating aspects of healing and divination rituals. Commonalities likely revolved around religious beliefs concerning everyday social roles, relationships, fluidity between the worlds of the living and the dead, and belief in the eternal force of human souls. Music's relationships with spirit pantheons and ancestors remained a cornerstone belief that joined communal vocabularies of performative gestures engaging the explanation, prediction, and control of life experience through spirit forces. In the transformed social spaces of urban and rural Minas Gerais, *calundeiros* possessed by the "winds of divination" mediated cosmological forces with drumming, chant, dance, and sacred objects designed to bring about the embodiment of healing spirits, from whom arose fortune and misfortune, health and harmonic balance, or illness and bad luck caused by spiritual imbalances.

Though of great historical value, sources such as the observations published by nineteenth-century European travelers in Minas Gerais, Christians who were often ignorant of the sacred music functions they witnessed, were prone to racist and religiously bigoted views conflating calundú with satanic pacts.[11] Misidentification of cultural functions likely went both ways: secular entertainment interpreted and conveyed as sorcery; sacred rituals described as simple dance music. "Feast" and "dance" labeled what could have been calundú. In Minas Gerais, some white and mixed-race Brazilians participated in calundú, as some African descendants did not, creating a heterogeneous admixture of the practice's demographic. Ladinos, acculturated Africans who often turned away from their ancestral traditions such as calundú, more readily looked toward the Catholic beliefs and practices accepted by lay brotherhoods. Catholic missionaries had made inroads into sixteenth-century Africa, long before slave shipments to Minas began: some enslaved Africans had already been converted to, or deeply influenced by, Catholicism, some practicing both Catholicism and parallel African beliefs. It was the potential in calundú's healing powers and economic gain that attracted whites both poor and wealthy, a characteristic of broad social engagement documented in Inquisition testimony and other ecclesiastical hearings. In subscribing to divination and healing ritual beliefs, certain white Brazilians in authority tacitly allowed calundú to flourish, a social fact conflicting with the intent of authorities.

Calundú was driven into secrecy and fragmentation by secular and church law, the latter enforced via the repressive apparatus of the Portuguese Inquisition. Papal agreements granting the Portuguese royal court patronage over the church made the Inquisition equally an agency of the Portuguese state, and its Tribunal of the Holy Office of Inquisition operated between 1536 and 1821.[12] As Goa, India, was the tribunal's only outpost in the Portuguese colonies, Brazil answered directly to the Lisbon tribunal. Proceedings in Salvador, Bahia, began in 1646, seeking to punish Jews and Muslims for heretical worship to a singular deity standing contrary to Christian belief. Calundú, however, constituted in these hearings the lesser religious crimes of enchantment, magic, and giving aid to sorcery. Practitioners of "magic" were persecuted less harshly than heretics, the latter defined as followers of organized religions who engaged in idolatry. Despite calundú's religious import, the Inquisition declared that it amounted to deception and trickery, a repertoire of lesser evils and nonheretical strategies for solving everyday problems and for healing.[13] Testimony was further shaped to portray African religious practice, including its music and dance, as demonic. In denouncing its performative components and criminalizing its medical practices, the Inquisition associated all of African religion with satanic worship. Not surprisingly, testifying witnesses frequently played up descriptions of alleged satanic witchcraft in calundú's courtroom profile. Popular literature of the time also made erroneous connections between calundú and the Christian concept of the devil. Brazil's celebrated baroque-era poet Gregório de Matos e Guerra (1636–1696) depicted calundú as satanic witchcraft in verse he completed during his stay in Bahia (1679–1694), prior to the Minas Gerais gold discovery. Here, *quilombo* refers not to a runaway slave settlement but rather to a forest clearing: "I know of *quilombos* with superlative masters / In which they teach at night calundú and witchcraft ... What I know is that in such dances Satan is engaged / There is no scorned lady or disfavored gallant / Who misses going to the *quilombo* to dance his little bit."[14]

Inquisition activities in Brazil were most frequent and broadest in scope in Minas Gerais, occurring there between the 1720s and the early 1800s. Holy Office familiars closely observed colonial populations, documenting calundú and batuque dance circles as offenses prosecutable by the Lisbon tribunal.[15] A large majority of familiars active in Minas Gerais were single white men who owned slaves, who conducted business in the slave trade, mining, livestock, and agriculture, and who were predominantly from northern Portugal, a region with the lowest number of blacks and enslaved Africans in the entire kingdom. Inquisition familiars in Minas, whose numbers peaked between 1740 and 1770, exceeding 430 throughout that century, were concentrated in the four *comarcas* dominating the mining regions: Vila Rica, Rio das Mortes, Rio das Velhas, and Serro.[16] A very small Mineiro network of Inquisition notaries was composed of Portuguese-born clergy entrusted with transcribing tribunal proceedings, keeping records, and performing other duties overseen by a handful of commissars. Separate from the Inquisition, ecclesiastical inquiries (the *Devassas eclesiásticas*) were investigative church hearings examining the lives of suspect Mineiro citizenry, at which individuals testified about religious behavior, suspicious activities, and sexual conduct. *Devassas* were first held in Minas in 1721, by a Mariana ecclesiastical unit that became that city's office of the archbishop in 1745. As with the Holy See's Inquisition records, the *Devassas* offer valuable descriptions of calundú manifest through music, dance, chant, and language. However, these testimonies were the products of complex, authoritarian methods frequently tainted by racist bigotry and potentially spurious witnesses reporting malicious hearsay. Some of those testifying against *calundeiros* may have libeled their fellow citizens or misled investigators in an attempt to conceal their own involvement in calundú. For instance, slave owners were known to have received percentages of receipts from their slaves' professional rituals. They and other whites risked exposure in having profited from, participated in, or formed a willing audience to calundú.

In Minas, *calundeiros* and *curandeiros* (healers, used also in contexts unrelated to calundú) engaged even the lives of Catholic clerics. During his 1819 expedition from Rio de Janeiro to southwestern Minas, French naturalist Auguste de Saint-Hilaire noted that in the city of São João del-Rei, the local parish priest recommended a black slave *curandeiro* who had treated his father.[17] In a not atypical case from the early eighteenth century, military officer Silvestre Marques da Cunha paid higher than market value for four enslaved Africans sold by Mineiro merchant Pedro Nunes de Miranda: each was a highly skilled *curandeiro* specializing in remedies and treatments for illnesses. Sixteen kilometers east of Queluz (today Conselheiro Lafaiete), farmer (*fazendeiro*) Antonio Gomes da Cruz rented out his healer and diviner slave Matheus Monjolo throughout the region.[18] Criminalized yet commodified, calundú settled into the social fabric of this mountainous Brazilian interior among diverse agents, forming an uneasy regional identity that "can be seen as a way in which the slave protected and redefined his culture in the face of hierarchical cultural values imposed by Luso-Brazilian authorities, while at the same time served to create links of friendship and fraternity with elements of the dominant society. This popular culture uniting currents arising from Africa and of popular Portuguese culture impeded the full imposition of Portuguese hierarchical culture."[19]

The spiritual and medicinal efficacy of sacred objects was often necessary to calundú ritual. Joining the Catholic crucifix, puppets and dolls, and other empowered, syncretic materials were protective amulets known as the Mandinga pouch (*bolsa de Mandinga*) designed to "close the body" (*fechar o corpo*) against misfortune. From their earliest contact with Muslim Mandinka *marabous* in the fifteenth century, the Portuguese noted the prominence of these sacred pouches, into which were sewn quotations from the Koran and other items. In Brazil, as Roger Sansi-Roca writes, they contained seemingly unrelated objects such as "altar stones, pieces of paper with Christian orations, rocks, sticks, roots, bones, hair, animal skins, feathers, powders and consecrated particles."[20] Mandinga pouches were also known to be imbued with Catholic meanings, a trend reflected in Atlantic creole Christian beliefs and practices. People throughout the Iberian Catholic world carried protective amulets as well as gold and silver chains, diamonds, gems, trinkets, charms, and stones such as the local *itatiaia* common to Minas. The use of these pouches spread throughout Brazil, including Minas, where they were prepared and sold by specialists (*mandingeiros*) whose clients included "both slaves and masters, black and white, African and Portuguese." Sansi-Roca continues: "[B]olsas were used by people of all social origins and social classes.... Feitiçaria was a part of everyone's everyday life.... The discourse of the Mandinga pouch and of *feitiçaria* in general, is in many ways a discourse about everyday power and the violence of all against everything that pre-ceded and succeeded the Atlantic slave trade."[21] Possession, manufacture, and distribution of Mandinga pouches were crimes regularly prosecuted by the Inquisition in Minas Gerais. In 1752, Vicente José de Tavora denounced three slaves belonging to Vila Rica resident José de Barros Araujo: each was accused of being a "grand master" of the Mandinga.[22] Medical practices in colonial Minas Gerais incorporated the use of statues of saints made more powerful as prayerful healing icons through decoration with valuable objects: gold itself was employed in the healing of the sick.[23] In Vila Rica in 1791, the Angola-born *liberto* Pai Caetano da Costa employed lizard-skin *bolsas de Mandinga* containing brass relics in "doing his dances called *calundus*," and in creating magic spells against informers.[24] In Mariana sometime during 1790, Joaquina Maria de Conceição visited several doctors seeking a cure for an undisclosed illness. After exhausting contacts in that city's established medi-cal community, the white woman twice attended "calundu dances" directed by two Central African slaves, the "Benguelas" Maria and Thereza. Witnessing a possession ritual, Joaquina provided damning testimony that "the blacks pretended that they died and started to speak in delicate voices, saying that it was the Devil speaking." Also participating were other slaves, the *fazendeiro*'s daughter, Joaquina's sister Anna, and two other white women.

Four *Calundeiras* in Colonial Minas Gerais: Women and Their Healing Practices

The historical record affords valuable glimpses into Inquisitional cases against several alleged *calundeiras* in eighteenth-century Minas Gerais, including the practices of Rosa Gomes, Gracia, Rita, Luzia Pinta, and Rosa Courana. These brief descriptions go far in considering this once widely practiced ritual. Black freedwoman Rosa Gomes was a store owner and highly regarded official in her Catholic brotherhood in Conceição do Mato Dentro, a town in the Serra do Cipó region forty kilometers from the Afro-Mineiro communi-ties of Açude and Mato do Tição, two locations renowned in the twenty-first century for maintaining the Afro-Mineiro music tradition of *candombe* (see chapter 6). Rosa represented a significant Mineiro demographic: the free person of color who either owned or operated a bar or general store (*venda*). Her weekly ceremonies constituted to authorities a creolized Catholic worship that masked African-derived religious practices, and in 1764, she was denounced by the Portuguese Inquisition for hosting "celebrations that were clearly African in origin," including batuque dances for feast days and Sundays.[25] The case language conflates an unspecified religious practice that was likely calundú with the drumming, dancing, and song of the otherwise secular batuque drum circle. Although the simultaneity of Catholicism and "parallel" ritual is apparent, the details of Rosa's celebrations remain a mystery. Four generations of Africans and African descendants had been making Minas their home by the time of her trial. Rosa was either a *calundeira*, or one whose community leadership position empowered her to simply host ceremonies on her property.

An enslaved Central African named Gracia hosted racially mixed Saturday-evening gatherings in the small Mineiro town of Rodeiro, near Ubá, in the Zona da Mata region. Lisbon Tribunal testimony from 1721 details three "African" dancers performing a ritual aimed at locating runaway slaves and curing blindness, among other goals. A witnessing Catholic priest testified that during spirit possession, Gracia channeled a venerated ancestor identified as Dom Felipe, likely referencing the King of Ndongo (1626–1664), who was known by that name.[26] Gracia's clients knelt before her, offering great reverence and addressing her as Dom Felipe.

Also telling is the case of Rita, an enslaved African from the Mina coast living near Mariana, home to eleven thousand slaves by 1718 and an important Roman Catholic diocese by 1745.

> Her cures were made "in the presence of various blacks who had found the sound of drumming from their land. . . . [A]s she danced, the more they wanted the sound of the drum to be played according to the custom of their land." During her ceremonies, she spoke "at the same time using her Mina language," . . . accompanied by African instruments, and she "prayed and made those watching pray on their knees in front of a small altar with lovely images of Christ, the Virgin Mary, and other saints." The cures made by Rita used divination, natural products such as herbs and powdered roots, African music, and elements of the Catholic religion, [and] are a window into a popular culture in formation. . . . [T]he participants played music "of their land." The preferred instruments were drums also "of their land," [and] speaking in languages "of their land."[27]

In the 1740s, a fifty-year-old Angolan-born healer in Sabará who had purchased her own freedom directed drumming, dance, and chant to bring about calundú's "winds of divination." Stressing the presence of calundú within Mineiro popular culture, Inquisition testimony describes Luzia Pinta's many visits to the gold-mining town of Caeté.[28] She traveled with her practice and was widely known. As described by her accusers, drums called forth her transformative, cosmological healing power of the spirit world, and according to the official letter sent with her to the Lisbon Tribunal, this "feitiçeira" was known for invoking the devil by means of dances called calundús. One of her accusers was a prominent Portuguese-born white landowner and head of the local militia (*capitão-mor*) who testified in 1739 concerning Luzia's calundús in which he had participated. Diogo Sousa de Carvalho stated to the Inquisition tribunal:

> [S]inging were two negresses, also Angolans, and an African male playing a *tabaque*, which is a small tambourine; and they say that the negresses and the black male are [Luzia's] slaves; and playing and singing for a space of one to two hours she became as if out of her mind speaking things that no one understood; and the people who were to be cured lay down on the floor, [and] she passed over them various times; on these occasions, it was said that she had the winds of divination.[29]

Such testimonies relate that the practice of calundú was sought out by elites as well as commoners. The most prestigious of Luzia's clients was Dr. Bathesar de Morais Sarmento, a graduate of Portugal's esteemed University of Coimbra and a prominent judge (*ouvidor*) of the captaincy of Minas Gerais, who visited her for pain relief.[30] Luzia was shipped to Lisbon and coerced into confessing that her spiritual practice was an illness, tortured for allegedly forming satanic pacts, and in her exile ordered never to return to Sabará.

The Vila Sabará of Luzia Pinta's day was one of the most important Mineiro cities. Her calundús flourished in a bustling, wealthy urban center that was demographically dominated by Africans and their descendants; less than 15 percent of Sabará's population was white, a number almost doubled by the category of free women of color.[31] The area's gold mines attracted outsiders well into the late eighteenth century, and by 1776, more than five thousand free blacks lived in the city. Due to the low ratio of white women available for white men, colonial Minas witnessed widespread concubinage among rich, poor, slave, and free. While fining citizens for violations of religious doctrine, the church could not stop widespread interracial sexual encounters, nor white men living unmarried, public lives with black and mixed-race women. Years later, the 1808 Sabará *comarca* census revealed among the 76,215 total population, 64,927 people of color, including 21,980 black slaves, 8,884 free blacks, 32,465 free mixed-race persons, and 786 mixed-race slaves. Children of mixed racial parentage, many the result of sexual abuse, would sometimes be granted manumission if the mother was a slave. The free mixed-race population swelled throughout Minas by the middle of the eighteenth century. Those of mixed parentage likely strayed more readily from strongly parallel religious practice like calundú toward syncretic belief and Catholicism. Religious hybridism occurred, with some calundú practitioners baptized as Christians and molding Catholic beliefs into their daily lives. An Africanization of Catholic practice, and a Christianization of African practice, had begun three centuries earlier in the Congo, with belief in the embodiment of a ritual object by the divine being one shared tenet. In 1790, Joaquina Maria de Conceicão attended "calundú dances" in Mariana directed by the "Benguelas" Maria and Thereza, labeled after the Angolan slave port of Benguela. Also in attendance were some local slaves, the *fazendeiro*'s daughter, and three other white women. Included in Joaquina's testimony was malicious hearsay claiming that "the blacks pretended that they died and started to speak in delicate voices, saying that it was the Devil speaking."[32] Rural Mineiros, including fazenda owners, also relied on African-derived medicinal practice. In his study of coffee fazenda culture in the county of Vassouras in Rio de Janeiro's Paraíba Valley, Stanley Stein comments on what could most likely have been said about nineteenth-century coffee fazendas in Sul de Minas:

> Where fazendeiros knew little home medicine, their wives and their slaves exchanged views or finally called in the *curandeiro*, a figure of long standing in African cultures. Known among Vassouras slaves as *curandeiros, quimbandeiros,* and *cangiristas,* and to Portuguese as *feitiçeiros,* curandeiros employed a variety of remedies including herbs and other substances prescribed in accordance with set rituals.[33]

The case of Rosa Courana (ca. 1719–ca. 1761), later known as Rosa Maria Egipcíaca da Vera Cruz, offers profound insight into the calundú-influenced society of eighteenth-century Minas Gerais.[34] Of the West African Courá people, Rosa was sold into slavery at age six in Whydah (today in Nigeria), and thus was likely too young to have received substantial religious training while still living in Africa. Sold again in 1725 at Rio de Janeiro's infamous Valongo slave market, she was later raped at age fourteen by her owner. She was sold a third time, to Ana Garces de Morais of Inficionado, Minas Gerais, a small town of five hundred residents a few kilometers from Mariana: the settlement's name means "infested," and it was changed to Santa Rita Durão in 1895. There, Rosa lived as an enslaved prostitute until the age of thirty-one. A so-called public woman, one of many "women of the fandango in Minas Gerais" during the height of the gold rush, Rosa befriended a young woman named Leandra, a *crioula* (creole) from Pernambuco believed to have been an initiate (*ekédi*) of the Xangô religion centered in the city of Recife. Another acquaintance was Padre Francisco Gonçalves Lopes, a traveling exorcist who diagnosed Rosa's epilepsy as satanic possession and whose friendship led to her gradual conversion to Catholicism and acquisition of literacy.

Rosa's painful journey, including her eventual transformation into a popular saint, is characterized by forms of cultural and religious syncretism manifested in Minas Gerais and reflects the viciousness with which authorities punished an innocent victim whose behavior was linked to calundú's possession-based trance. She crossed paths with church authorities in 1749 when she suffered a severe epileptic seizure in Nossa Senhora do Pilar Church in São João del-Rei. Following her immediate arrest and subsequent jailing, she was mercilessly whipped for the heretical crime of satanic possession at the pillory in Mariana's main square on orders issued by the recently installed bishop of Mariana, Dom Frei Manuel da Cruz. Carrying scars for the remainder of her life and partially paralyzed by her public torture, Rosa was adopted and freed from slavery by her exorcist priest. She left Minas Gerais in 1751. In Rio de Janeiro, her written accounts of visions, of having a direct relationship with Jesus Christ, and of hearing divine orders directly from God won admirers and sparked a movement to have her canonized. Rosa Maria produced the earliest known autobiographical work of any black woman in history, *Sagrada teologia do amor divino das almas peregrinas* (Sacred theology of divine love of the pilgrim's souls). Historian Luiz Mott describes her as

[a] Saint who prayed in Latin, who knew how to touchingly sing liturgical hymns, but who, as a good African from the Mina coast, never dispensed

with her inseparable *cachimbo* drum; who in her mystical rapture could be convincingly compared to the prophets canonized by Rome, but who could not occasionally resist the temptation to worship Jesus Christ by dancing frenetically to the rhythm of batuque.[35]

Calundú Drumming: Brazilian Transformation of the *Ngoma*

While the celebratory rhythms of Afro-Mineiro drumming brought certain freedoms from, and generated resistance to, slavery's brutality and injustice, the functional sonic worlds and rhythmic patterns of calundú coaxed the presence of ancestors and healing spirits, forming sacred alliances with incantations, dance, ritualized objects, and medicinal treatments. Trance possession signaled the stage in which the healer appeased the spiritual entity, channeling its diagnosis and treatment of illness while revealing remedies and instructions for their application. Revisiting the drum's role in the argument that African-derived beliefs in Afro-Mineiro practice ran parallel to Catholicism, we note that in Central Africa, drumming engendered successful ancestral healing overseen by specialized communities:

> In some circles these communities are called "drums of affliction," reflecting the significance of their use of drumming and rhythmic song-dancing, and the colloquial designation in many societies of the region of the whole gamut of expressive dimensions by the term *ngoma* (drum). The drumming is considered to be the voice or influence of the ancestral shades or other spirits that visit the sufferer and offer the treatment.[36]

In Brazil, the word *ngoma* is still used in reference to drums and musical functions as well as extramusical contexts, and transformed into *ingoma*, *angona*, and similar corruptions. In certain Mineiro communities, its meanings have broadened to indicate the people, events, and social spaces associated with festive drumming. Ethnomusicologist Glaura Lucas finds local, contemporary uses of the term *ingoma*, noting designations for a group of Congado dancers (a genre discussed below) and an adjectival expression for a "very good" performance.[37] Her ethnography of the Os Arturos community documents Congado and other Afro-Mineiro musical practices in Contagem, a city in the Belo Horizonte metropolitan region. In another study of Os Arturos, Núbia Pereira de Magalhães Gomes and Edimilson de Almeida Pereira write of that community's spiritual connection with ancestors of the Afro-Mineiro past, specifically the community's nineteenth-century founder and "father of the drum" (*dono de ingoma*), Arthur Camilo Silverio. They state that "the *ingoma* is the group of people, the instruments, the ceremony, the party, and the sacred cultural space."[38]

Some accounts of calundú refer to *tabaques* (atabaque drums), its root term dating to the ancient Akkadian *tabalu* and shared by the Indian tabla, later entering Iberia through the Arabic *tabl*. *Tambor* (*tambu* is a common Afro-Brazilian corruption) and *caixa* (box) are common Portuguese terms for drums throughout Minas, the latter resonating with *cachá* (drum), the Congolese root for the drum known in Brazil as *caxambú*. On the Brazilian coast, African-derived ritual found its fullest voice in the trio of cylindrical, single-head drums common to Candomblé, Xangô (primarily in Recife), and Tambor de Mina (São Luís) religious practices, relying on drum patterns that call forth the pantheon of spirits known as *orixás*, or *voduns* in the case of Tambor de Mina. Here, trance-possession rituals hinge on the drum's call for the desired spirit to descend into the initiated.

Lodging overnight in a fazenda during his 1720s journey through Minas Gerais, the Portuguese priest and writer Nuno Marquez Pereira was kept awake by drumming and slave festivities. The *fazendeiro* explained the following day that the calundú they had heard was brought from Africa, and he described the varied divinational functions of calundú dance and music: "They were used for discovering various things, such as the cause of illnesses and the location of lost things, and also for having good luck in hunting and agriculture."[39] In Inquisition testimony, calundú practitioners wearing ritualistic costumes danced "to the sound of drums or cymbals" performed by an encircling group. Shakers, rattles, bells, or scraper instruments added meaningful color to calundú's sacred sound world. These idiophonic timbres, from bright metallophonic tones to various wooden-instrument punctuations, find significant roles in other Afro-Brazilian religious and secular traditions, past and present, offering discrete roles in repetitive, interlocking patterns in ritual music otherwise dominated by drumming and chant.

The Sound of Medicine

Music, dance, and chant also worked in tandem with the spiritual and medicinal efficacy of sacred objects, a characteristic stronger in the profile of West African "Mina" ritual than in that of the Central African, whose greater reliance on trance possession and spiritual leaders likely made more use of music, chant, and dance. Mina healers and diviners in Brazil employed a large basket that might contain "powders, shells, bones, hair, teeth, feathers, and other powerful substances from the natural world, all of which might be endowed with spiritual power," contents enabling the *curandeiro* to ritualistically diagnose illness.[40] The use by some *calundeiros* of figurines and drawings of Saint Anthony, the symbolic healer and finder of lost things, offers transformative links between Christian and African cosmologies. Embodiment of the ritual object by the divine is a shared tenet across beliefs of Atlantic creole Christianity. Wooden sculptures of men, women, and anthropomorphized figures imbued with spiritual power were known in Bantu-speaking Africa as *nkisi*. The protective amulets known as the *bolsa de Mandinga* are discussed above.

A widely respected leader in the Mineiro War of the Emboabas (1706–1709), Manoel Nunes traveled throughout Minas offering for sale the magical healing and fortune-telling calundú powers wrought by his slave, a "black *mandingeiro*" of the African tradition.[41] That a prominent citizen of the colony overtly supported, and profited from, the distribution of African "fetish" practice speaks to the needs of the population as much as to the popular defiance of social norms and authority: the sick and dying had few other hopes for cures. The Saint John's Day practices of Pedro Teixera, a colonial-era resident of São Sebastião, near Mariana, relied on a ritually imbued three-legged doll. His annual ceremony included this spirit-channeling doll and "divination, healing, and fortune telling," followed by "a specially prepared dish . . . sordid evening dances, and abominations called calundús," realized by "black men and women of his spiritual community." According to Teixera's wife, who had been forced to provide Inquisition testimony against her husband, the sacred dish included cut-up images of Jesus Christ and saints mixed with herbs in a mortar.[42]

Devassa eclesiástica witnesses testified to music rounding out ritualized applications of herbs and foliage, ceremonial uses of chicken feathers and eggs, the presence of dolls, and applications of colorful skin paint derived from clay and soil pigments. In Vila Rica, property owner Miguel Rosário claims to have been visiting a household to collect a debt payment when he witnessed a calundú ritual. In 1791, as one of ten eyewitnesses against an Angolan-born *calundeiro* named Pai Caetano da Costa, mentioned above, Rosário helped convict the man to a sentence of public flogging and three years of forced labor: "We know that we saw a puppet they called Dona Crentina.... When doing their calundú dances, there entered a *biola* [*viola*, a ten-string Brazilian guitar]. And the sound of such playing made the puppet dance, and also in such calundús there were images of St. Anthony, crucifixes, and candles."[43] Luiz Mott interprets further Inquisition testimony regarding a *calundeiro*'s use of sacred objects and substances in Minas:

> Also, the black Antonio Barbosa, resident of Queluz [now Conselheiro Lafaiete], was reported in 1799 for "doing their dances they called calundú" in his home full of blacks, creoles, and mixed-race persons, and using smoke and rubbing unguents on their hands and feet, calling on them to kiss a crucifix to remove spells, and passing a crucifix and the image Saint Antonio through the legs of those who were to see their fortune.[44]

The dearth of effective Western medicine encouraged even social elites to seek black healers regarded by authorities as criminals engaging in cabalistic pacts. The colonial-era ban in Minas Gerais of the Sacred House of Mercy brotherhood (Santa Casa de Misericórdia), a social institution responsible for public hospitals and burial services, fueled demand for calundú. Only in 1734 did the first professional, European-trained doctor officially register in Vila Rica, then a city of twenty thousand. Exotic medicinal treatments drawing from the spice trade formed the basis of the then innovative European practices, reflecting Portuguese maritime access to South Asian Indian pepper, myrrh, dates, cinnamon, musk, sandalwood, ginger, and nutmeg. Pharmacy inventories in Mineiro cities featured medical panaceas of Islamic origin, African products, and ancient Eastern remedies such as red coral dissolved into a warm liquid and ingested to decrease the blood's acidity. Eighteenth-century barber-surgeons, many of whom were Afro-Mineiros joining untrained Portuguese immigrants in the trade, were neither doctors nor apothecaries yet were seriously engaged in premodern European medicine, prescribing and manufacturing drugs.[45] Later in the eighteenth century, Mineiros Luís Gomes Ferreira, José Antonio

Mendes, and João Cardoso de Miranda self-published local handbooks on medicine, incorporating their ideas about new herbs, medicines, and bloodletting and purging treatments for illnesses encountered among free and slave populations alike.

Black Communities in Early Minas Gerais

Who were the Afro-Mineiros behind calundú? Prior to the mid-1690s gold discoveries in Minas, the Portuguese had already been enslaving black Africans for 250 years. Military confrontations between European colonial powers and shifting commercial relations among Brazilian ports, European markets, and Atlantic slave traders were factors in defining which African ethnicities were brought to Minas as slaves. During the early period of the gold rush, Portugal's West African slave trade east of São Jorge da Mina (Saint George of the Mine fort, in what is now Elmina, Ghana) centered on four Bight of Benin ports along what became known as the Mina coast, namely Grand Popo, Whydah (Ajuda), Jaquin, and Apa. Victims of slavery from those sources spoke mostly the languages of the Niger-Congo family including Yoruba, Fon, Ewe, Igbo, Edo,[46] and also Akan, the language of modern-day Ghana. Enslaved Africans received ethnic labels and generalized descriptors (*grupo de procedência*) making up the system of "nations," often a hodgepodge of inaccurate, culturally arbitrary labels assigned by slavers based on ports of embarkation that often ignored genuine African ethnicity. The first "nations" sent to Minas Gerais include Jeje for the Fon (also associated with the Kingdom of Dahomey), and Nago for Yoruba peoples who were further distinguished as Ijexa, Ketu, and Egba, among others. Mina-Jeje is thus a designation for Fon people coming from the slave factories of the Mina coast. The so-called Mina slaves, and the broader, Old World term Guinean, consisted of dozens of ethnicities, including the Fanti and Ashanti, and accounted for a vast majority of slaves shipped to Minas Gerais for the first few decades of the eighteenth century.[47] Those "Mina" slaves, renowned for their mining skills perfected in West African gold mines, became legendary in Luso-Brazilian history for their role in the Minas Gerais gold boom. Entering the Mineiro interior through Salvador, Bahia, they were marched overland to the gold and diamond mines of the Serra do Espinhaço and its subregions of Serro Frio and Serra do Cipó, and the mining center cities of

Ouro Preto, Diamantina, Mariana, and São João del-Rei. Others went to the cotton fields and cattle fazendas of northern Minas.

The number of imported West Africans waned in the mid-eighteenth century, and they remained a majority of Africans in Minas only until roughly 1750. Bahia's powerful merchants faced Salvador's loss of colonial and financial status after the colony's capital moved to Rio de Janeiro in 1763, partly owing to the latter's proximity to the gold mines. Central Africans entering Rio de Janeiro and bound for Minas were shipped from ports in Loango, Cabinda, Benguela, and Quelimane and quickly began to outnumber West Africans in the Mineiro interior during the second half of the eighteenth century. The rise of a regional pan-Bantu cultural influence began around this period. To this complex cultural array entered enslaved laborers from Angola and the Congo. The Bakongo, and their Congo basin neighbors the Punu, Teke, Suku, and Yaka, became "Congo" slaves, as did many other ethnicities from surrounding lands falling victim to Portuguese slavers.[48] "Angolans" shipped to eighteenth-century Minas included Ovimbundu, Casanje, Umbengala, Quimbundo, and Bakongo peoples, among others. Enslaved "Moçambiques" were Makua, Yao, and Tumbuka peoples forced onto ships in various East Africa ports as far north as Mombasa, in present-day Kenya. These diverse Central and East African groups were often narrowed down in name to Benguela, Congo, and Angola people.[49] In terms of their reception by authorities in colonial Minas, their rich African lineages of ethnic particularity fell into a fog of disinterest, abandoned in favor of their new roles as chattel slaves.

The southeast's coffee boom beginning in the 1830s would be accompanied by a truly massive reintroduction of slaves into the region. Minas Gerais of the colonial and imperial eras, a socially and racially complex mosaic of urban and rural elements, became a prominent region for Afro-Brazilian religious practices. Laura de Mello e Souza states:

> Placing Minas ahead of Bahia in this context, where the slave population was even greater, is attributable to the fact that [Minas] constituted a more complex slave system and was being more intensively urbanized. In Minas, conflicts erupted at any moment, disrupting the mining towns. Probably appearing there also was the greatest concentration of *quilombos* during the colonial period. It was also in Minas that the African cultural complex was better preserved.[50]

In the hinterland of the Black Atlantic in Portuguese America, Minas Gerais became a cultural outpost of African cosmology. Although calundú had by the start of the eighteenth century became familiar throughout the colony, it flourished in the Mineiro interior. African-derived cosmological concerns with social spaces, and the actions required to maintain the goodwill of territorial spirits, spoke to a regionally specific power of place to Afro-Mineiro culture and its localities. The formation and bordering of Afro-Mineiro communities helped define their spiritual links to a past articulated by ritualized behavior aimed toward ancestors, memory, and ancient, lost territory. Calundú space became sacred space: slave quarters (*senzalas*), forest clearings, private homes, and runaway slave *quilombos*. In his study of Central African religion in eighteenth-century Minas, Kalle Kananoja invokes notions of borders and territory when he states: "[M]any slaves from varied origins in Central Africa would have held shared beliefs in the strong association of territorial spirits and water, and the need to propitiate those spirits for the well-being of the community."[51] Vestiges of calundú also remained in the isolated *quilombos*, which contrasted sharply with the zones of wealth, stability, and political power of colonial-era cities before their post–gold rush decay. Free to a great extent from the terrors of the Inquisition and Crown authorities, runaway slaves likely practiced increasingly fragmented forms of calundú in the many *quilombos* found throughout Minas, though few details of such cultural practices are known. Brazilianist Roger Bastide noted in these rural Mineiro locations a pan-Bantu religious ceremony known as *canjeré*, a dance and sacred gathering (from the Kimbundu *kanzare*, to spin, shake, or whirl):

> Although the term *calundú* is as common in Minas as elsewhere in Brazil, African religious ceremonies were commonly known in that province as *canjeré*. Little remains of them today. Aires da Mata Machado Filho [a Mineiro author discussed in chapter 3 below] discovered what may be the last moribund survivals of these old Bantu religions in the area of Minas, where the *quilombos* were most numerous, and the vocabulary he recorded does indeed show that there were priests known as *ngangas* or *ugangas* as well as witch doctors called *caquis*.[52]

It was, however, in the burgeoning colonial-era urban areas enriched with mining wealth where accomplished *calundeiros/as* were able to find paying clients for healing and divination rituals. As Mello e Souza comments:

They flourished in Minas more than anywhere else in the colony during the eighteenth century; at least available references to Minas calundús are more numerous—even more so than references to calundús in Bahia, now the land of Candomblé. Here again it must be remembered that Afro-Brazilian religious syncretism, religious persecution, and slavery were traveling companions in colonial territories, so Minas stands out; after all, in 1733 Simão Ferreira Machado called Vila Rica, "for the circumstances of its nature, the head of all America; for the abundance of its wealth, the precious pearl of Brazil."[53]

By the 1780s, one in three Mineiros was a free person of color. Although slaves practiced calundú, blacks and mixed-race Brazilians born free (*forros*) and those who had purchased their freedom through manumission (*libertos*) were unhindered by the severe social limitations of the enslaved and better situated to lead and participate in calundú. African-born practitioners, however, may have been perceived as more authentic and spiritually powerful, and newly arrived slaves integrated into an oppressive system. Meanwhile, syncretism with Catholic and indigenous beliefs altered the role of African religiosity in the face of complex social change. Isolated areas often developed their own particular practices. For instance, healers from the rural São Francisco River district of Manga (today the river port city of São Romão) earned renown throughout northern Minas for an indigenous-derived divination and healing tradition that lasted into the twentieth century. These "mixed-race sorcerers" (*caboclo feitiçeiros*) of São Romão were common references in regional popular culture.

The War against Calundú

Authorities doubled down on the destruction of calundú social networks in a sort of religious and cultural genocide. The secrecy shrouding calundú speaks to this enveloping terror, to the danger *calundeiros/as* faced in maintaining traditions, and to the risks taken by white participants seeking healing and cures. Accounts of those condemned in Minas Gerais are found in the Inquisition records in Lisbon's Torre do Tombo National Archives, where testimonies offer proof that calundú flourished within a brutal slave system.[54] Identified in 1742 as a black *calundeira* living on the Antonio Pugas fazenda near Santo Antônio do Rio Acima, Isabel's singing and dancing of calundú with *feitiçeiro* Manoel Lobo Franco was part of a ritual aimed at "closing the body" from harm. In Sabará that same year, the *crioulo* slave Violante was accused of ritualistic dancing. In 1744, the black slave Francisco Axé faced the Inquisition for rituals including the use of a *chocalho* idiophone shaker. In Congonhas do Campo during 1745, Joana Jaguatinga, Manoel da Silva (both black), and mulatta Antónia da Silva were all denounced to the Inquisition for performing calundú, drinking chicken's blood, and other *feitiço*. Other victims included Felix, a black *calundeiro* who danced for divination (Catas Altas, 1755); an unnamed freed black woman, denounced for dancing in ceremonies (Nossa Senhora da Conceição dos Prados, 1759); and a freed black woman, Angela Maria Gomes, accused of dancing calundús and batuques with the devil (Itabira, 1760).[55]

It is worth considering the violence that awaited newly arrived enslaved Africans likely prone to continue their traditions in Minas Gerais. Punishments for simply using *curandeiro* medications could be brutal, with additional exorcism or chronically bad treatment awaiting. The slave Bernardo Pereira Brasil, found guilty of medicating himself with healing compounds taken from bones, received sixty lashes delivered by his owner.[56] The list of registered calundú infractions in Minas Gerais is long. The *calundeira* Luzia Lopes, a free, Brazilian-born black woman (*liberta crioula*), was severely whipped in the public square of the Serro Frio town of Conceição do Mato Dentro sometime after 1767.[57] In 1774, Ana Maria Mercês of Piedade de Paraopeba was denounced to the Inquisition for operating a calundú house (*casa de calundú*), where various acts of superstition and demonic pacts were practiced. She and Grácia, both blacks, were further charged for dancing with the devil; João Coelho, Antónia Angola, and Mónica Maria de Jesus for forming a procession that included calundú (near Sabará, 1775); slaves Roque Angola, Brizida Maria de Araujo, and other accomplices for calundú dances and rituals against Catholicism (Pitangui, 1777); Domingos, a freed black man, for calundú and dancing (São Brás do Suaçuí, 1779); the white slave owner Antonio Pereira and the black man Manuel for healing Pereira's slaves with calundú (Mariana, 1782); Francisco, of Mina, for his circle dance designed to heal another black man (Mariana, 1782); and the black man António Barbosa and the freed *crioula* Maria Lopes for calundús (Queluz, 1792).

This institutionalized religious violence appears alongside the historical arc of colonialism beginning with the 1446 Ordinances of King Afonso (Ordenações Afonsinas), Crown legislation governing black cultural expression in Portugal five years after the first enslaved Africans arrived in Lisbon. The very need for fifteenth-century promulgations suggests that black religious music expression was common, and threatening enough to warrant a legal framework of punitive social control. The Ordinances of King Manuel I (Ordenações Manuelinas, 1514) revised many of the 1446 laws. The 1603 Ordenações Filipinas of King Philip II of Spain (known as King Philip I when considering his simultaneous reign over Portugal) outlawed gatherings that included black music and dance. The language of laws controlling human trafficking, and of religious and cultural restrictions, is far removed from friendly literature such as the clever, playful poetry of Gregório de Matos e Guerra, which associated calundú with the Christian devil. Spared the fatal sentencing meted out to countless Jews and Muslims, *calundeiros* nonetheless risked fines, physical torture, and banishment, with the terror driving rituals further underground into a secrecy leading to generational loss and displacement of religious and healing knowledge. The fate of calundú, it has been stated, resulted from a combination of brutal oppression and increasingly syncretic forms of religious observance that competed with remnants of the banned practice: "In the realm of magic and religion, syncretism would ultimately prove itself uncontainable and ineradicable; it would forever bear the ambiguous mark of popular culture, which mixed the sacred and profane. Leaving behind it a trail of death, and horrific suffering, the long process of acculturation eventually merged sabbats, masses, and calundús."[58] Today's Aurélio Portuguese dictionary defines "calundú" as deriving from *kilundu* (a word commonly used in Angola), a supernatural being "that directs human destinies into a person's body, making them sad [and] nostalgic"; and as a synonym for *amuo*, a bad feeling characterized by silent moodiness. Calundú's fate was sealed when authorities associated it with "black magic" and *feitiço*, the latter a pointedly derogatory descriptor for non-Christian beliefs based on trance possession and related practices seen as deceptive, manipulative, and both emotionally and physically harmful.

The Demise of Calundú in Relation to Umbanda, *Candombe, Batuque,* and *Lundu*

African religiosity continued in Minas but was no longer documented by the Inquisition, an institution that was challenged and reformed by Pombal, and that ultimately closed its Brazilian shop in the 1820s.[59] Historical developments contextualizing the demise of calundú include, in addition to the Inquisition, the near-suspension of the importation into Minas of newly enslaved Africans between 1770 and 1820, curtailing the infusion of "fresh" African practices that may have invigorated calundú's presence in Minas Gerais as a parallel to Catholicism. This suspension clearly encouraged the transformational Brazilianization of those African traits, including music. Calundú's disappearance from the historical record as a specific, named practice in Minas Gerais corresponds with this record of oppression, but also with deep social and political shifts: the region's catastrophic economic decline, Brazil's emergence as an independent empire in 1822, the urbanization of coastal cities, and the social convulsions associated with the collapse of the monarchy. The resulting formation of the Brazilian republic in 1888 was shadowed by the abolition of slavery that same year.

Given calundú's historical importance, subsequent musical, religious, and healing practices may have absorbed or masked the tradition as it succumbed to persecution. What became of this legacy of music? Did calundú music carry a cultural inertia that influenced or joined other, established practices? Three genres of Afro-Mineiro sacred drumming in Minas Gerais emerge as likely candidates: the syncretic religions of Macumba and Umbanda, the candombe of the Black Catholic Congado tradition (not to be confused with the religious practice known as Candomblé), and the vestiges of spirituality in the otherwise secular galaxy of the batuque circle dance. Additionally, the popular colonial-era couples dance known as *lundu*, and its latter transformation as a sophisticated, imperial-era salon dance, lundu song, was likely a secular offshoot of calundú.

Elements of the parallelism that once characterized a strongly African religion defined by its independence from Christian practices, such as drumming, language, and dance, and that had been suppressed by authorities, survived as components of outwardly Catholic syncretic practices. José Jorge de Carvalho emphasizes that primary examples of creolized, syncretized, or hybridized Afro-Brazilian practices that continued to flourish include "*macumba* in Rio, *jurema* in Recife, *pajelança* in São Luís do Maranhão, *candomblé de caboclo* in Salvador, or, in more general terms, *umbanda*."[60] However, criticism of the very nature of syncretistic theory runs deep, for instance among Brazilian anthropologists examining black music and religion in Minas and the social conditions faced by cultural practitioners. Gomes and Pereira observe that "discourse on Brazilian religious syncretism must address the socio-historic conditions that enveloped this alleged symbiosis. In the specific case of blacks in Minas, this notion of syncretism did not, and still does not, correspond to an ontologically complete symbiosis."[61] From these and similar concerns, we can surmise that violence, fear, and cultural genocide were historical forces behind much so-called syncretism. A notion of syncretism presented as a naturally occurring product of unfettered interfaith dialogue, or willing amalgamation among equal social groups, is at best an absurd apology for cultural genocide. Simplistic notions of syncretism mask the hideousness of the worst type of social violence under slavery.

As Renato da Silveira notes, the term "calundú" was understood to be "synonymous with candomblé or Macumba" as it began to fall into disuse sometime during the latter half of the eighteenth century.[62] Calundú's decline thus occurred alongside the rise of hybrid religious practices that promoted Catholic references and imagery as they embraced African-derived music and drumming. It is probable that in Mineiro cities and the countryside, slowly changing from Portuguese colony to imperial Brazil, the earliest vestiges of mixed Afro-Brazilian religion such as Macumba gradually merged with and supplanted calundú's fragmented remnants. Other hybrid cults from Afro-Mineiro history include *canjeré* and *pemba*, the latter described as a religious practice in Minas Gerais "which is exactly midway between a *congada* and a modern *umbanda* possession cult."[63] The predominance of drum and percussion accompaniment to call-and-response chant structures in religions such as Macumba and other syncretic cults likely represents a stylistic connection to previous Afro-Brazilian religious practice. As calundú was driven underground and out of existence, these cults also absorbed the music and cosmologies of newly arriving enslaved Africans destined for the massive system of coffee plantations that came to socially dominate southeastern Brazil. The sometimes derisive term *macumba* is found in references to Afro-Mineiro religions variously mixed with Catholicism and practiced in early twentieth-century Belo Horizonte, the state's capital, which was planned and constructed in the 1890s. This was a period of unusually intense regional urbanization involving the first postemancipation generation of Afro-Mineiros.

In Mineiro author João Alphonsus's 1938 modernist novel *Rola-Moça*, Macumba, poverty, and blackness are the defining themes of social difference in depicting Belo Horizonte's first, turn-of-the-century favelas. The new, marginalized city dwellers both maintained and modified traditions, which were transformed by massive urbanization in a world ready-made for Afro-Brazilian cults such as Umbanda. Nationwide, the twentieth century witnessed the rapid growth of Umbanda, which became Brazil's most popular syncretic religion, with millions of followers, black, white, and brown. In 2010, more than 350 Umbanda centers proliferated throughout Belo Horizonte's metropolitan area.[64] In examining the Os Arturos community's Congado traditions of Black Catholicism in the Belo Horizonte suburb of Contagem, Gomes and Pereira characterize that area's tradition of Afro-Mineiro religiosity, arguing that Umbanda indicates the survival of an African community of belief: "In the past, Contagem's many slaves engendered the survival of diverse Black African communities of belief. Efforts by the Church and slave owners failed to hinder their development, a fact currently reflected in the area's significant number of Umbanda and Quimbanda houses of worship."[65]

There may be a historical connection between calundú's legacy of sacred drums and the candombe ritual drums still found in the region's Congado tradition, a popular form of Catholicism musically defined by drumming, call-and-response chant, and processional group dance. Candombe's highly regarded sacred drums, often stationary and hidden from the general public, are firmly associated with Congado's otherwise very public processional music and open worship, characteristics defining much of Brazilian popular Catholicism. The transformation of a violently oppressed calundú into an underground, increasingly secretive sacred ritual occurred within an ever-broadening cultural milieu of pan-Bantu ethnic roots, mixed-race offspring, and the general social and cultural mixing that characterized nineteenth-century Brazil. Candombe is clothed in both the myths of oral tradition, rich in symbolic legacies, and the social fabric of the highly documented presence of Catholic lay brotherhoods. Many generations of Afro-Mineiro brotherhoods defended the Atlantic creole Christian manner of celebrating the Virgin Mary, complete with African-derived drumming, dance, and song, and in doing so they could have easily absorbed the challenge to Africanisms as calundú was destroyed. Throughout the nineteenth century, newly arriving African slaves faced fewer opportunities to convey calundú-like beliefs and practices in Minas Gerais and instead faced a society channeling sacred musical practices into the Black Catholicism of candombe and into syncretic systems, the latter increasingly open to non-blacks. Meanwhile, batuque blurred the Western polarities of sacred and secular (see chapter 5). Eighteenth- and nineteenth-century observers dismissing the potential of sacredness in black, trance-based expression could relegate all of it to a willfully undiscerned, subaltern music that they freely termed "batuque." Today, the communities of Mato do Tição, Açude, and Os Arturos are still known for batuque drumming traditions.

Lundu: The National, Popularized Couples Dance

The final consideration with respect to the fallout from calundú's decimation lies with the secularized lundu, though this leads toward broad cultural developments beyond Mineiro borders. Portuguese folklorist Teófilo Braga controversially claimed that the word "lundu" appears in the 1514 Ordinances of King Manuel I, the sovereign who expelled Jews and Muslims from his kingdom and who protested "the dances of the blacks such as the batuques, charambas, lundus."[66] The Afro-Peruvian dance genre *landó* is said to have direct Angolan roots in a dance of the same name, suggesting that enslaved Africans brought landó/lundu to sixteenth-century Portugal. Regardless of these controversies, it is historically crucial to identify the term "lundu" as a truncated form of "calundú" used by Brazilian clergy in early eighteenth-century Bahia, a fact cited by James H. Sweet:

> In January 1715, Father Antonio Pires wrote from Bahia complaining about the proliferation of "Lundus." Seven months later, Father João Calmon noted that the Lisbon Tribunal was "very distant from this Bahia, where the witchcraft and merriment that the Negroes make, which they call Lundus or Calundús, are scandalous and superstitious, without it being easy to avoid them, since even many whites can be found in them."[67]

And, as historian José Fernando Saroba Monteiro has suggested:

> There was a greater acceptance of lundu [by Brazilian whites] than other cultural manifestations of the colony's blacks, especially the religious ones, the so-called calundús. "Kalundu" in the Angolan Antonio de Assis Júnior's *Kimbundo-Portuguese Dictionary* means "Spirit; being of the invisible world; magnetism," corresponding also to the calling ceremony of these spirits. The term "lundu" may originate from this term "calundú," which occurred not only in Brazil but also in Angola.[68]

In his study of race and music in twentieth-century Brazil, Marc Hertzman emphasizes lundu as "Brazil's first black or African national music. The word apparently derives from *calundú*, a Central African healing ritual featuring drums, scrapers, and a circle of adherents surrounding one or two leaders. Many of calundú's characteristic elements—collective gatherings, spirit possession, curing, percussive music, and dance—are also found in various Afro-Brazilian religions."[69] These clearly stated claims also cast light on calundú's remnants: the musical paths of secular dance created from Brazil's brutal cultural war against African healing practice, the documented demise of which throughout the eighteenth century chronologically dovetails with the rise of the use of the term "lundu." Through a cultural process that has never been fully understood or historically proven, (ca)lundu came to define a dance with a diminished role for drums and a greater role for the viola and the guitar's Western harmonic and melodic capabilities, leading to the lundu song of Rio de Janeiro salon culture at the end of the eighteenth century. Lundu is referenced in 1780s Lisbon as a Brazilian dance, naturally with no mention of calundú. In a letter penned that year, the Third Count of Pavolide (José da Cunha Grã Ataíde e Melo) compared the Brazilian lundu, danced by whites and *pardos*, to the Spanish fandango and the Portuguese *fofa* "The blacks ... dance and twirl like harlequins, and others dance with various body movements, which, though not the most innocent, are like the fandangos of Castile, the fofas of Portugal, and the lundus [danced by] whites and pardos of that country [Brazil]."[70]

The Portuguese poet Nicolau Tolentino de Almeida also referenced lundu dance, in 1780, a decade following the arrival in Lisbon of Brazilian mixed-race poet and *violeiro* Domingos Caldas Barbosa (1740–1800).[71] This musician had furthered stylistic appropriation in his lundu song by using rhythms associated with the originally rural, Afro-Brazilian lundu dance, fashioning stylized syncopations and expanding on the lundu-song style that had grown in popularity in nocturnal, 1740s Rio de Janeiro.[72] However, when Barbosa arrived in Lisbon to spread his courtly lundu song, the Afro-Brazilian dance known simply as "lundu" was already well known there, perhaps even correlated with the Luso-African dance styles associated with Lisbon's substantial African-descendent communities.

Music engendered calundú's healing and religious efficacy in eighteenth- and nineteenth-century Minas Gerais. Drumming, the invocation of spirit possession, and accompanying chants in various African languages and dialects were a performative cultural element that bound together religious beliefs shared by slaves, freed persons, and their descendants. The distinct cultural traits of music and language may be said to have exhibited an intellectual practice running parallel to the dominant religion of Catholicism. Music was highly incriminating evidence in testimony against *calundeiros* elicited in church hearings, testimony that was responsible for brutal punishments and for calundú's inevitable demise. Much testimony came from whites, some of high standing, proving that healing practices infused with trance possession involved broad sectors of Minas society. Some of calundú's cosmological tenets and performative characteristics may have been transformed or absorbed by syncretic cults, the candombe of Congado, and the increasingly secular batuque dance tradition. It is likely that popularized remnants of calundú developed into the couple's dance known as lundu. A plausible historical interpretation suggests that brutal oppression created an impetus for the hybridization of calundú practices deemed "too African." A complementary analysis adds that communities of African descendants, with traditions further challenged by poverty and isolation, engaged more readily in hybrid religions and popular Catholicism accommodated by Brazilian society. The Inquisition's dragnet, which brought down calundú, also captured in its trials the batuque dance, a pastime strongly associated in the eighteenth century with communities of African descent. In this paradigm of cultural change, secular dance was seen as the lesser of two evils, operating in the realm of popular culture. As calundú disappeared, batuque flourished along with the stylized lundu.

Chapter 3

Vissungo's "Songs of the Earth"

A Vanishing Tradition of the Serro Frio

In the early eighteenth century, enslaved miners in the Serro Frio mountain range of central Minas Gerais began enlivening their perilous work spaces and mountain communities with *vissungo* (Umbundu for "songs"). As Aires da Mata Machado Filho (1909–1985) shares in his seminal study of the genre: "In 1928, while enjoying vacation in São João da Chapada in the municipality of Diamantina, my attention was called to some songs in an African language, heard among those mining."[1] Today, this vocal style and repertoire have all but vanished from former strongholds in mountain hamlets in and around the vicinity of Milho Verde; and the remnants of its complex language of *falar Africano* are studied by contemporary linguists. Vissungo carried the most original regionalist link of all Mineiro music, as it was tied directly to the interiorized worlds of the miners who manually excavated the immeasurable tons of earth, gold, diamonds, and gems that provided Minas Gerais with its name, wealth, and reputation. While alleviating some of the drudgery and suffering that characterized forced labor, this vocal genre unique to Minas transformed social space and transcended the work song; it included funerary chants, ritualized incantations, and topical themes, empowering forms of resistance to social violence and daily hardships. The songs held a pan-African appeal among West and Central Africans and their Brazilian descendants, including *forros* and *libertos*, and were shared among the influx of enslaved workers forced to the Serro Frio.

It is also likely that in the secrecy of *quilombos*, as runaway slave communities dotting the region were known, ethnically diverse Afro-Mineiros nurtured vissungo and its associated *falar Africano* language, also known as the "dialect of the mines," Calunga, and Cafundó. It is in these musical and linguistic contexts that vissungo helped define historical strata in central Minas Gerais, one of the most populous sites of the eighteenth-century African diaspora. What once formed a cornerstone of regional culture, however, today verges on extinction, as former ways of life have long vanished. The music never engaged the outside world, let alone popular culture, as the field hollers of the American South influenced the blues, for instance. Mineiro historian Francisco Eduardo de Andrade writes:

> The *fundamento* [musical motif] ... is the feel of the text and its music of various songs, from what Mata Machado could translate, that reveal the themes composed for mining explorations: the road, discovery, the common grind of work, digging into the vein, drying the sluices, washing the stones, the intense work and conflicts among miners, the relations with the slaver and landowner, dealings with local businessmen and traders, life in the *quilombos* and the *sertão*. Furthermore, there are songs relating to desires that relieve hard work: the *quilombo* dweller's freedom, or love for one of the town prostitutes.... [T]here exists a *fundamento* that expresses an expectation of autonomy during the work shift and of the right to prospect for one's own sake.[2]

The small town of São João da Chapada to which Machado Filho refers above, where he completed much of his research on vissungo, sits at an altitude of almost 4,500 feet, twenty kilometers northwest of the colonial-era mining center of Diamantina, where he was born. In addition to books on linguistics and folklore, he wrote a history of his hometown, which was known as Arraial do Tijuco until 1831, when it was raised in administrative status to a *vila*; Diamantina's historic town center today is a UNESCO World Heritage Site. The locale began attracting miners following the discovery of gold in 1714, and then diamonds in 1729. Tijuco, and by extension the town of Serro do Príncipe (today Serro), about fifty kilometers south on the Estrada Real, became a highly protected mining zone of the Portuguese empire closed to outsiders, and vissungo developed as a unique genre within an isolated subregional culture. Between 1740 and 1771, the special district, overseen directly by the Portuguese court, became a legal and administrative fiefdom of diamond contractors that ended only when Pombal transferred supervision to the Royal Treasury in Lisbon. Regardless, a stream of runaway slaves joined clandestine miners (*garimpeiros*) at nearby sites, with many forming *quilombos* in the surrounding hills, settlements of freedom within the secured zone and its network of lucrative mines. Much to the chagrin of authorities, illegal mining extended throughout the frontier into the western *sertão* of the vast São Francisco River basin and beyond, and east of the Serro Frio mines into the so-called Forbidden Lands dominated by the Jequitinhonha, Mucuri, and Doce River basins, impassable rain forests, and increasingly embattled indigenous Natives defending their land.

Music, Instruments, Spirituality, and Language in the Vissungo Tradition

The sixty-five vissungo collected by Machado Filho include those describing laborious stages of the mining process, chanted put-downs, or "fines" (*cantos de multa*), funeral procession songs for carrying the dead (*cantos de enterro*), and various songs simply marking the time of day, with lyrics such as "It is morning / the hummingbird begins to sing / and the vulture is looking for a meal."[3] Another song was transcribed by Machado Filho as: "The sun is streaming in, let us leave with the work crew / I will start searching my stream for gold."[4] Some songs reflected a topical innocence drawn from the experiences of work gangs and itinerant miners; others contained sacred incantations and references to spells.[5] Composed of simple yet expressive melodic lines with a spirited musical motif, work songs were performed solo or in call-and-response mode whereby a lead vocalist (*mestre*), sometimes revered also as a charismatic spiritual leader, sang the callout (*boiado*), followed by an answering phrase by the responding chorus (*dobrado*). Marc-Antoine Camp, based on his fieldwork around Diamantina, describes the vestiges of vissungo he observed soon after the turn of the twenty-first century as "a form of ritualized communication, articulated as a vocal expression between speaking and singing." Camp continues: "Vissungo are expressed in a syllabic parlando with occasional melismatic ornaments and long sounds on the same pitch . . . individually remembered as oneness of sound, words and social use."[6]

Vissungo was known for improvisation, in terms of both melodic vocal invention and the flexible topicality of textual reference. French naturalist Auguste de Saint-Hilaire wrote of the diamond district in 1817, observing the slave-based mining system and describing how otherwise dispirited forced laborers entertained themselves with "choral songs from their land."[7] Work groups in these mines numbered at most a few dozen; they were smaller and more communal than in other colonial Latin American mining centers such as Colombia's massive slave-era gold-mining operations, where hundreds of laborers were forced together.[8] Rival groups often challenged one another musically, taking part in competitive renditions of the repertoire and improvised exchanges. Mining tools such as the sluicing pan (carumbé) and wooden, funnel-shaped bateia doubled as percussive musical instruments, and the iron field hoe (enxada) became a variably tuned, resonant metallophone. Though possibly unrelated, the enxada is still used as a percussion instrument that accompanies the dança cumbá in the Afro-Mineiro community of Mato do Tição near the town of Jaboticatubas, north of Belo Horizonte. The friction drum (angona-puita, or cuíca) and other drums were used in ceremonies marking leadership roles in work groups, linking to use of drums in other Afro-Mineiro practices such as Congado, batuque, and calundú. Though free laborers working the mines possibly played drums during daytime breaks, enslaved Africans would have played drums on work-free days, during evenings after work, and for funeral processions.

Some vissungo in Machado Filho's collection invoke African deities, with references to imbanda (also mbanda or embanda), nzambe, and ongira, Bantu terms for religious leaders and for God, with likely connections to calundú. Another regional religious practice known as cabula made use of Bantu words, such as engira, a ceremonial meeting of initiates.[9] As Roger Bastide notes: "The gods revered in vissungo included Zambiapungo (perhaps representing syncretism between Zambi, the great god of the Angola, and Opungo, the great god of the Congo), Angana-Nzambi, Calunga (the goddess of the sea and of evil spirits), and Cariacariapemba, who can be identified with the Christian devil."[10] The spiritual beings Curiandamba and Curicuca appear in lyrics to a vissungo transcribed by Machado Filho and recorded decades later by the great Brazilian singer Clementina de Jesus (on a 1982 LP discussed below): "Iáuê ererê aiô gumbê / Com licença do Curiandamba / Com licença

do Curicuca / Com licença do sinhô moço / Com licença do dono de terra"
(With the permission of the Curiandamba / of the Curicuca / of the young
man / of the landowner). In an analysis of Clementina de Jesus's recording,
José Jorge de Carvalho notes that the supernatural beings Curiandamba and
Curicuca were somewhat menacing powers demanding appeasement from
the community of believers. De Carvalho connects them to roles played in
other African-Brazilian religions by Eshu, Bara, and Legba, the trickster god.[11]

Machado Filho interpreted the words otchavi and Jomare as corruptions of the Yoruba orixá Oshumaré, referencing a member of West Africa's
pantheon of spiritual beings, suggesting that this was a vestige of the West
African "Mina" ethnicity, whose language, cosmology, and music had entered
a diasporic interplay of pan-African traditions in Brazil's mountainous interior. Overtly liturgical songs were likely chanted in non-work-related, ritualistic contexts, and, as with vissungo drumming, were likely performed in
the evenings and on work-free days. Some of these texts include syncretic,
Catholic liturgical devices such as the pade-nosso (Our Father), as in this
vissungo hailing the Congolese-Angolan deity Nzambe: "Otê! Pade-Nosso
cum Ave Maria / securo camera qui t'Angananzambê, aiô . . . / Aiô! . . .
T'Angananzambê, aiô! . . . Aiô! T'Angananzambê, aiô! . . . / Ê calunga qui
tom' ossema / ê calunga qui tom' Anzambí, aiô."[12]

A cultural heritage unique to this special zone of the African diaspora,
vissungo used a polyglot of Kimbundu, Umbundu, and Bantu-inflected,
creolized Portuguese particular to Minas Gerais.[13] The term crioulo often
described an enslaved African with skills in Portuguese. Diverse ethnic
groups were forced together, and some Africans became known as boçal (raw,
ignorant) due to their lack of Portuguese language abilities: falar Africano
emerged from this mix in the isolated, protected Serro Frio society in which
vissungo developed. Falar Africano is further characterized by the absorption
of lexical and grammatical aspects of West African Gbe and Mina-Jeje languages due to their notable presence in eighteenth-century Minas.[14] Machado
Filho's book ends with a very short chapter entitled "O dialeto crioulo de
S. João da Chapada" (The creole dialect of São João da Chapada), followed
by an annotated glossary of African-derived words, subtitled "Vocabulário
do dialeto crioulo sanjoanense" (Glossary of the creole dialect of São João
Chapada residents). Here, the author translated into Portuguese dozens of
terms still in use in the region at that time, noting that "we give below the
vocabulary and grammatical forms that Mr. João Tameirão suggested."[15]

Figure 3.1. *Lavagem do minério de ouro* (Washing gold ore), by Johann Moritz Rugendas, in *Voyage pittoresque dans le Brésil* (Paris: Engelmann et Cie, 1835). The image shows the laborious mining activities that formed the economic foundations of early Minas Gerais. By 1835, the year Rugendas published this and related images, enslaved Africans had been mining gold and diamonds in the region for more than 130 years.

Increasingly secretive even after slavery's end, falar Africano became a social space of resistance and protest, hosting an array of messages, coded or otherwise, in fluid reference to the ills of captivity, the oppression of authorities, and the hidden world of quilombos, suggesting more autonomous formations of Afro-Mineiro identities than previously theorized by historians.[16] "One of the black men still knew how to sing in his language," wrote beloved Mineiro novelist João Guimarães Rosa in the 1930s, in response to encountering a small Afro-Mineiro village in the hills among the isolated trails west of the mining district, echoing vissungo's survival into the twentieth and twenty-first centuries.[17]

Portuguese immigrant Antonio da Costa Peixoto arrived in Vila Rica during the early 1700s, looking to get rich. By the 1730s, he had compiled a dictionary of African words with Portuguese definitions, a manual designed for local slave owners that was also valuable to anyone interested in communicating across the cultures mixing in Mineiro cities, mining camps, and slave quarters (*senzalas*). In studying Peixoto's work, linguists today have confirmed that Mina-Jeje speakers of West Africa's Sudanese linguistic group were living in colonial Minas Gerais, alongside a small but increasing number of speakers of Bantu languages primarily of Congolese-Angolan origin. It is from this vast array of peoples and their descendants that vissungo emerged. Peixoto's dictionary already included the term *aglono* (from Angola), an early reflection of the gradual shift in Mineiro slave purchases from Bahia to Rio de Janeiro, with the latter's Portuguese contacts based in the Angolan ports of Luanda and Cabinda. In Brazil, Luanda became known as Aruanda, the land of the gods and ancestors for many of those helping to form a pan-Bantu presence in the New World. Northern and central Minas, including the Serro Frio, retained vestiges of West African influence. Vast numbers of marginalized free people of color, a demographic due partially to high rates of manumission in Minas, formed the core of the mobile population, occupying a central cultural place there and becoming increasingly influential. Well into the 1780s, when enslaved blacks accounted for more than 40 percent of the total Mineiro population, African-born blacks remained the most populous group, larger than Brazilian-born blacks and far outnumbering whites and those of mixed race. Vissungo flourished within the closed society of the secured mining area, yet an area resonating with the region's broader cultural developments.

Manumission and the Mixed-Race Society of Diamonds and Gold

Vissungo emerged from communities of workers both free and enslaved. Historians have argued that manumission was more prevalent in Minas than elsewhere in Brazil due to heightened and fluid economic opportunities brought by mining wealth, whereby slaves earned income they could apply toward the purchase of their own freedom, with many using payment installments known as *coartação*.[18] Some Brazilian scholars argue that across white colonial society in the post-Palmares (see below) gold rush boom of Minas Gerais, the widespread fear of slave rebellion and *quilombos* led to an increase in manumission rates as a social "safety valve" policy designed to avoid open rebellion and flight by offering some type of incentive for not fleeing. Legends abound of enslaved Mineiros being given their freedom in return for having discovered significant gold deposits or an unusually large diamond, and on occasion for denouncing a planned slave rebellion or reporting a serious security breach such as a slave possessing firearms. Manumission funds amassed by the dues-paying members of Catholic lay brotherhoods were greater in a captaincy stoked with mining wealth. Beginning in the 1770s, Minas's initial economic decline led to an increase in the manumission of male slaves as more owners sold freedom to their human assets in the face of economic crises, and the high monetary value of slave labor fell along with the price of manumission. The *decadência* induced a drastic decline of slave importation into Minas, which led to a more balanced gender ratio within black communities dominated by Brazilian-born blacks as early as the 1820s. Manumission was far more likely for mixed-race female children fathered by white slave owners, and offered far less frequently to African-born male laborers who may have managed to earn funds for manumission in their later years. Rafael de Bivar Marquese explains:

> Manumission in Minas Gerais obeyed a basic rule: the further removed from the transatlantic slave trade, the greater a slave's chances of receiving manumission. African men, the majority on the slave ships, hardly ever received manumission, though after one or two generations their descendants did.... [For consideration of granting manumission,] slave women were preferred to men, Mulattos to Negroes, Brazil-born to African, urban slaves to rural slaves, and many slave owners preferred to manumit babies rather than adults.[19]

Manumission was strongly connected to changing attitudes toward mixed-race children of slave owners, and the high rates of interracial reproduction. Royal decrees barring people of color from office, and limiting inheritances from white parents to mixed-race offspring, failed to deter this significant demographic shift toward *gente de cor*. By 1786, more than 40 percent of black Mineiros were free persons. In cities, towns, and fazendas, the offspring of blacks and whites began forming a majority well before the end of the eighteenth century. By 1821, close to 200,000 mixed-race persons and 52,000 blacks had been born free, almost doubling the total number of white Mineiros and surpassing the province's 181,882 slaves. In rural enclaves, mixed-race Brazilians formed the majority of a mushrooming population, continuously engaging and displacing indigenous groups. Traveling through Minas in the mid-nineteenth century, German-Argentine naturalist Hermann Burmeister noted a marked increase of mixed-race Brazilians holding important positions in towns and cities the deeper he penetrated the interior. Historian Emilia Viotti da Costa adds that, around the same time period, "[i]n towns far from the coast blacks and mulattos were police officers, judges, schoolmasters, and priests—something rarely seen in port cities."[20] Local needs arose for weapon-toting blacks in the military battalions of colonial and imperial Minas, and for the arming of slaves by slave owners and colonists for personal protection and the securing of property and businesses.

Colonial Minas Gerais joined neighboring Goiás in forming the world's most productive eighteenth-century gold-mining region. One of the Portuguese Crown's key representatives was the *guarda-mór*, who administered mining allotments called *datas* awarded to the first miner proven to have discovered gold in a particular location. In areas not effectively controlled by the *guarda-mór*, the right to mine fell via the simple code of first possession. One vast district known in the early eighteenth century for this lack of *data* administration earned the name Minas Gerais de Ouro Preto (General Mines of Black Gold). Even within Diamantina's nearly sequestered administrative zone, the socially and economically dynamic workforce that popularized vissungo included itinerant prospectors, both free and enslaved, known as *faisqueiros* (from *faiscar*, to glitter), who searched the gullies and canyons for alluvial gold flakes and small nuggets glittering in the many streams and riverbanks. Day laborers known as *jornaleiros*, either slaves or freed persons, were hired to seek out gold deposits outside of the *data* system of mine claims and its ancillary gold-mining regulations "green book." Finds made by the enslaved were handed over to owners, though historians widely believe that some enslaved *jornaleiros*, *faisqueiros*, and *garimpeiros* were allowed to accumulate gold for manumission.

As water flows downward, mining patterns in the mountains of colonial Minas Gerais spread uphill from the quickly exhausted alluvial deposits in and around streams. After the immediate riverine table was emptied by placer mining, eighteenth-century miners ascended surrounding slopes to ridges and mountaintop reaches. Vissungo followed them. Considerable numbers of autonomous adventurers, including black and mixed-race *garimpeiros*, settled in the hills and mountainous reaches of mining districts and became known as "residents of the hills" (*moradores dos morros*), sometimes avoiding control by colonial authorities. Some of these miners secretly engaged *quilombos*, the runaway slave settlements discussed later in this chapter. Those black, mixed-race, and poor white miners working outside established mining zones supervised by the Portuguese administration formed a large, illicit sector of clandestine trade in gold and diamonds. While in Diamantina in 1824, European visitor Georg Langsdorff wrote of the Pagão (Big Payout) mine, "one of the largest recently made discoveries":

> Some free blacks went there by chance to wash illicit diamonds. Two of them worked two to three months in silence and found great treasures. They engaged a third person and began to sell large stones. That attracted the public's attention; people flocked there en masse, because the area was not one prohibited by the Crown. The administration soon learned of this and sent in the army, where there already were about 1,000 miners, all diamond washings and mines were banned, and the government appropriated the site.[21]

Vissungo flourished too in the cracks of this mountainous frontier world, spaces forged by *garimpeiros* who furnished illicit stones to small-scale itinerant merchants known as *capangueiros*. Their underworld contacts also controlled export routes that handled large amounts of contraband gems, diamonds, and gold easily sold into the international black market. As the English traveler George Gardner noted regarding his travels through the Diamond District in the late 1830s:

> [Illicit diamonds] were mostly disposed of clandestinely to contraband dealers, many of whom used to hide themselves in the mountains by day, and at night, visit the huts of the slaves to purchase the stolen property; even the shopkeepers were deeply engaged in these illicit transactions.[22]

Gardner noted that the justice of the peace, "who was during the period of my visit one of the richest merchants in the city," made his fortune from contraband. More clandestine mineral wealth was smuggled north to Bahia via the São Francisco River and other northerly routes than the total amount officially processed by the Portuguese Crown. *Forros*, *libertos*, and some slaves were economically empowered by their mining skills, reputations for successful digs, and smuggling talents. In 1817, nearly a century after the first diamonds were discovered in Minas, Saint-Hilaire wrote:

> As the diamonds have become rarer [and] more arduous work is required to remove them from increasingly deep mines, only a few fugitive blacks will seek them at the edge of the streams. But if the *garimpeiros* are so few in number, there will certainly be smugglers who traffic diamonds stolen by the slaves in the various services.[23]

In contrast to those working the harsh, laborious mining pits, some free Afro-Mineiros emerged as highly qualified businesspeople partnering with white colonists, including nativist slave owners struggling against the hegemony of the Portuguese colonial authorities. In the eighteenth century, the city of Sabará provided "more widely available opportunities for autonomy for slaves than existed in large-scale plantation society economies elsewhere in Brazil or in other parts of the New World."[24] A small portion of wealth from gold and diamonds trickled down to a very few of the enslaved, subsequently fueling manumission, but also local sites of entertainment such as general stores (*vendas*), bars, and houses of prostitution, where patrons could enjoy drink-filled evenings. In this imaginative description, A. J. R. Russell-Wood emphasizes criminality and violence over quotidian routines of singing, music, and dance:

> These *faisqueiros* roamed the countryside and townships, prospecting and washing for gold in any likely spot. Once a week they returned to their owners to hand over the few grains of gold dust of the *jornaes*, or daily takings. Large numbers of such slaves on the loose represented a continual challenge to town councils and governors in the maintenance of law and order. . . . At nightfall such itinerant speculators congregated in the stores and taverns which flourished in the mining areas and became involved in brawls and knifings. Whores and unscrupulous storekeepers soon induced the *faisqueiro* to part with his *jornaes*.[25]

The Social Spaces of the Afro-Mineiro Work Song

Brazilian scholar Neide Sampião has suggested a broadening of vissungo's cultural scope to include more diverse song functions performed in a variety of everyday activities.[26] Although it is not known how vissungo-related song traditions may have traveled beyond the mines and funeral processions into other social spaces, it is possible that offshoots of vocal style and repertoire transformed and mixed with quotidian entertainment among marginalized classes populating the towns and cities of the Serro Frio. It was in these environs that enslaved metal- and woodworkers, shoemakers, carpenters, and other skilled craftsmen were often rented out by their owners (*escravos de aluguel*), or were allowed to engage clients as semiautonomous laborers known as "earning slaves" (*escravos de ganho*). A vast portion of their income was given to their owners. Some rental and earning slaves constituted a rare sector more common to Minas Gerais than other regions of Brazil: forced laborers with minimal yet regular income. A few escaped the daily supervision of their master, and fewer still managed to live outside the humiliation of the *senzala*. For these laborers, along with domestic workers, servants, and other urban laborers, public fountains (*chafarizes*), the primary source for household water and clothes laundering, were casual social nodes for daily activity and routine interaction. Work songs echoed throughout the daily public life of colonial and imperial-era Mineiro cities, where transporters (*carregadores*) and work gangs (*cantos*) were known for chanting while moving goods across town. Their voices mingled with the musical calls of street vendors, singing out their perfunctory jingles known as *pregões*.[27] Barbers in the booming cities and towns of eighteenth-century Minas were mostly Afro-Mineiros, and in their spare time they were known to pick up instruments and play a tune or sing. This work-related pastime was well documented in Rio de Janeiro, where nineteenth-century black barber-musicians are linked to the development of choro.

In the isolated São Francisco River port town of Januária in northern Minas, the adventuring British agent Richard Burton noted the chants of the many black laborers when he passed through in the 1860s: "The beach, as the river's edge was called, immediately brought about the spirit of an African marketplace, and the monotone singing of the blacks processing beans didn't diminish certain similarities to scenes from distant Zanzibar."[28]

Social mingling in bustling Mineiro cities such as São João del-Rei, referenced in the passage below, contrasted with that of the plantation-based social spaces of Brazil's coastal *latifundia*.

> Poor free persons and slaves frequented small businesses in search of entertainment, games, and drink. . . . In a society with few options for fun, hanging out on the street was a commonplace practice. The very architecture of the streets and houses favored public viewing of the lives of others. . . . However, the street was not the only space of coexistence between leisure and violence. Everyday neighborhood routines involved *vendas*, the *casas de negócio*, and *tavernas* frequented by diverse segments of local poor and slaves. . . . [S]mall stores were considered part of illicit activities, promoting suspect parties and gatherings, as spaces of disorder, in enabling furtive encounters and illicit relations, and allowing slaves to hang out at their newsstands. . . . [T]he small grocery became a space for collective leisure.[29]

Retail general stores (*vendas*, *lojas*, and *comissários*), which sold foodstuffs, dry goods, *cachaça*, and other items, were, like bars (*tavernas*) and some inns (*pousadas*), sites of music performances (such as batuque and viola) and cultural exchange available to an increasingly autonomous black population. These spaces represent a further distance from the mines where vissungo originated. Traveling to Vila Rica (now Ouro Preto) in August 1839, German visitor Ernst Hasenclever stopped in Capão do Lana, where the best inn was fully administered by free blacks. The inn's white owner lived in Vila Rica, leaving the free blacks in charge of a staff of enslaved workers.[30] Even as early as the first half of the eighteenth century, *vendas* and inns were places marked by a measure of independence for blacks, with some white shop owners and innkeepers entrusting forced laborers to help run their businesses. Needless to say, the routine gatherings of slaves, freed blacks, and other citizens at these venues offered rich possibilities for musical exchange, including work songs and their connections with developments in popular music making. Such scenarios challenged white Mineiro society, as Julio Pinto Vallejos argues:

> Because of this [situation], the colonial authorities found little success in their countless attempts to keep slaves out of stores and taverns, to restrict peddling outside the mining towns, and to limit the blacks' physical mobility in general. It became clear to them that the most stubborn obstacle to an

effective slave control lay in the complicity of white store- and innkeepers. This was sometimes strong enough for them to hide miscreant slaves, and in the most extreme cases even their weapons, within their premises. The profit motive also drove some whites to transact business with the quilombos, a practice that could only increase the government's exasperation.[31]

Vila Rica's Rua do Argel was noted for its many black-owned stores and bars; by the 1760s, there were several hundred such establishments, including those in the adjacent red-light district, many owned by free women of color.[32] This city coalesced in the conjoining of the predominantly black settlement known as Antônio Dias with the upper-class Vila Rica, which it bordered. Vissungo-like song traditions entering a broader popular culture beyond the workplace flourished in environs such as Rua do Argel, resonating with what Brazilian scholar Edison Carneiro, in distinguishing the Minas experience, emphasized was the importance of the colonial-era urbanization of semi-autonomous slaves.[33] While some forced laborers with a very small, sporadic income saved their meager resources for manumission, some others indulged to some degree in the entertainment-driven nightlife. In the nearby town São Caetano, an African-born *liberta* from the Mina coast, Maria da Costa, owned nine slaves and a successful restaurant and bar where guests danced the "fandango."[34] Even the daily routines of an autocratic slave society, filled with racist brutality and humiliation, offered some forms of limited mobility, with music providing social commonality for the least empowered. *Vendas* and drinking establishments were gathering places for serious events such as funeral services, as described by a bishop visiting Minas Gerais in 1726. Antonio de Guadalupe related how enslaved blacks marked such events, "gathering at night singing and playing instruments for their dead, joining together in stores and buying food and drink, later throwing leftovers as offerings into the grave."[35]

Another dynamic economic sector of Mineiro life revolved around market stalls operated by women of African descent (*negras de tabuleiro*, "black women of food stalls"), which were sometimes hubs of social activities including music. These women sold beans, rice, and collard greens (*feijão, arroz,* and *couve*), snacks such as coconut cakes and sweets (*cocada* and *doces*), and processed flour from manioc tuber, *mandioca*, borrowed from indigenous traditions. For the poorest, rarely did dried meat and cheese augment this menu. *Cachaça*, the sugarcane alcohol for which Mineiro producers are still renowned today, was a staple. The women often paid fees to property owners to set up their stalls close to mining sites, while others sold on public streets and *praças* (plazas). Some stall women were "rented" or "earning" slaves providing income for owners, with a few making a trickle of profit, which they typically applied toward manumission. *Negras de tabuleiro* were frequently denounced by the established business community, accused of prostitution and of inciting drunkenness and violence, and often scapegoated for the illegal diversion of diamonds, gems, and gold. Despite a spate of municipal laws aimed at limiting their activities in the 1760s, *negras de tabuleiro* survived, remaining integral participants in a complex economy and forming public social spaces hosting cultural pastimes.[36] These economically vulnerable women, and the marginalized workers engaged in vissungo and work-song culture, formed a dynamic subculture in a society dominated by colonial administrators and a slave-owning elite. Powerful oligarchs and "colonels" emerged from large-scale commercial farms, where they directed slave-based agricultural and cattle operations, and sugar mills (*engenhos*) that also produced *cachaça*. Profits and power grew from both forced labor and the large number of urban consumers in Minas Gerais, Brazil's largest domestic market for agricultural and dry goods, as well as for luxury items, until the 1808 arrival in Rio de Janeiro of the exiled Portuguese court headed by the Braganza royal family. Some towns grew around storefronts and *vendas* controlled by *fazendeiros*. More refined retail stores were located in a *fazendeiro*'s city townhouse complex, a marked verticality in the oligarchic socioeconomic structure whereby a single owner controlled mines, agricultural operations, food processing and fazenda warehousing labor, and retail locations. This flow of goods and loci of power were shadowed by the spread of cultural practices such as song traditions passing between the worlds of town and country, between work songs and their possible absorption into the landscape of popular music found in the public spaces of bars, taverns, inns, and *vendas*.

> In Minas Gerais, a popular culture was created based on values and beliefs both African and Portuguese. This popular culture could be seen in two ways. It was the way the servile population created its own society and culture. At the same time that it served as self-identification, it also served to create ties between the servile population and the society of free persons. Many whites and Portuguese not only accepted these values but participated in their formation.[37]

The *Quilombo* Heritage in Minas Gerais

Historian Carlos Magno Guimarães concludes that the large number of *quilombos* in Minas Gerais disproves once and for all the absurdities of those shabby theses claiming for the region "a gentle slavery, the harmonious relationship between masters and slaves, and the acceptance, by the slaves, of their condition."[38] The length of the colonial-era Estrada Real between Diamantina and Ouro Preto was a zone of African influence, particularly in small, mostly black Serro Frio communities associated with the *quilombo* heritage. Such was the case with runaway slave settlements in proximity to Diamantina, as noted by Machado Filho, and where vissungo traditions flourished into the twenty-first century in Ausente and Bau, *quilombo*-based hamlets close to the towns of Serro and Milho Verde, respectively. In collecting examples of the disappearing singing tradition in 1928, Machado Filho reminded his readers of the importance of *quilombos* in the Diamantina region:

> Surrounding the site today occupied by São João da Chapada, there were six famous *quilombos*: Caiambolas, Maquemba, one close to the Formiga stream, the *quilombo* of Antonio Moange, in Valvina, close to Macumba hill, one in Madalena, and another on the land of the Bezerra fazenda. . . . [*Quilombos*] were not rare in Minas. . . . These islands of separated, isolated populations, the remains of *quilombos*, or places chosen by the blacks to live tranquil lives, are common.[39]

Following years of onslaught by Portuguese colonial armed forces, Palmares, Brazil's largest and longest-surviving runaway slave settlement, in what is now the coastal state of Alagoas, fell in 1694. The settlement's collapse occurred within one year of the discovery of gold in Minas Gerais. The Portuguese's decades-long efforts to destroy the settlement served as a reminder to authorities and colonists in Minas Gerais of the threat from organized runaway slaves in the region's mountainous mine fields, where vissungo flourished. In surveying characterizations of Brazil's *quilombo* heritage, many of which center on Palmares (actually a network of settlements), Elizabeth Farfán-Santos mediates between two poles of interpretation. On one end is the positive portrayal of resistance, of heroism and valiant *quilombo* isolationism as a near-mythic kingdom upholding purely African values. On the other is the negative condemnation by authorities, in their paranoid fury, of alleged paganism, cancerous dangers, and the dystopian rot of Africanisms. The "Palmares effect," Farfán-Santos declares, has "led to the assumption that all blacks who resisted slavery were rebels bent on destroying modern European society in the fight to re-create an African one."[40]

No matter: slave insurrections and the rise of *quilombos* dot the history of colonial and imperial Minas Gerais. As early as 1719, coordinated uprisings in Ouro Preto, Ouro Branco, and Furquim resulted in the murders of slave owners. Subsequent accounts include what may have been myths regarding eighteenth-century revolts planned for Holy Week, a time during which many fazenda owners took part in solemn liturgies. The 1820 Portuguese constitution, resulting from that country's Liberal revolution and the Portuguese royal court's return to Lisbon from its Brazilian exile, was initially rumored to have clauses emancipating Brazilian slaves. Thousands gathered in various Mineiro towns to celebrate and learn more of this news, which proved too good to be true. In Santa Bárbara, near Catas Altas, a free black leader and landowner named Argoim, upon learning that there would be no emancipation, helped organize and speak for those slaves as violent rioting broke out in many towns, including Diamantina, Mariana, and Ouro Preto. Argoim became so well known in Minas that uprising participants became known as *argoins*.

Escape was rebellion. *Quilombos* formed a secretive yet significant social layer in which runaways were sometimes joined by embattled Indios (indigenous peoples), *caboclos*, mixed-race people, and a few poor whites forced into increasingly marginal lands. Archaeological work has revealed more than 160 eighteenth-century *quilombo* sites in Minas,[41] in addition to the hundreds of colonial-era *quilombos* defying the intrusion of authorities, estimated at 404 *quilombos* in proximity to 154 Mineiro towns and cities.[42] Primary *quilombo* regions of the eighteenth century, in terms of the sheer number of settlements, include those found near the juncture of the Araçuai and Jequitinhonha Rivers in the *capitania*'s northwestern region, and in the agricultural heartland of northern Minas, both areas far from the largest colonial urban centers. Smaller *quilombos* formed at the edges of colonial cities such as Vila Rica (Ouro Preto), Mariana, Tijuco (Diamantina), Sabará, Paracatu, and São João del-Rei, secretly engendering musical and religious culture as semiautonomous, liminal settlements. Others formed around coveted gold fields discovered by marginalized, clandestine miners and *quilombo* residents. In 1798, correspondence to Minas governor Bernardo José de Lorena from the city council of São José del-Rei emphasized the prevalence of *quilombos* throughout the state's central region, and the bravery of the town's past residents in combating them (the city's name changed to Tiradentes soon after the formation of the republic in 1888): "Throughout the surrounding wilderness are pagans and runaway blacks. Our town predecessors always struck back against the insults of these barbarians, until they were able to fight back against the Picada de Goiás and Campo Grande, destroying various *quilombos*."[43] The central mining district, with its wealthy network of gold-rich cities, accounted for a third primary *quilombo* area. Some modern-day Mineiro cities developed from *quilombos*, such as Bias Fortes in the Zona da Mata. Independent scholar Tarcísio José Martins of the Historic and Geographic Institute of Minas Gerais (IHGMG) has proposed a radical reconsideration of *quilombo* populations in the Campo Grande region of southwestern Minas Gerais. Dating to 1726, Ambrósio, also known as Tengo-Tengo and the "capital" of the Campo Grande network of runaway slave settlements,[44] was the largest *quilombo* in Mineiro history, an icon of resistance flourishing near the modern-day western Minas Gerais towns of Cristais and Ibiá. There, the African-derived language of Calunga remains in use in the twenty-first century.[45] Like an echo of Palmares, the Ambrósio settlement was finally overrun in 1759, following years of army assaults that had begun in 1743.[46] João Dornas dos Santos Filho adds:

> In the Captaincy of Minas Gerais, where mining gathered large numbers of black slaves, the insurrections were frequent, and already in 1759, Bartolomeu Bueno do Prado led four hundred men campaigning against several Quilombos near Campo Grande in the Rio das Mortes comarca, killing large numbers and taking prisoners. These were the remaining Quilombos where Gomes Freire de Andrada sent the *paulista bandeirantes* to ruthlessly decimate in 1746 ... [the *quilombo*] consisting of Indians and runaway slaves, and ruled by the black leader named Ambrósio, whence came the name Quilombo Ambrósio. It was the old Tengo Tengo Quilombo.[47]

Ambrósio and the greater Campo Grande network pocketed an area perhaps as large as twenty thousand square kilometers in the western and southwestern regions of Minas Gerais; an estimated fifteen thousand people lived in this twenty-five-settlement confederation, including Gondum, Calunga, Quebra Pé, Boa Vista, and Bambuí. Inhabitants of *quilombos* (called *quilombolos*, and in the colonial era *calhambolos*) carried on commercial trade with local Indians, isolated settlements of Paulistas, and European settlers. In the early nineteenth century during the *decadência*, this region witnessed a large-scale influx of economic refugees from the central mining district seeking new lives; they found opportunities in the family-based cottage industry of cotton spinning, manufacturing *panos de Minas*, the Minas cloth soon accounting for a large portion of the region's post–mining boom exports. The 1832 census reveals many Campo Grande fazendas with thirty to forty slaves per owner, with six owning more than one hundred.[48] *Quilombos* grew in number once again throughout the nineteenth century.

In his 2018 biography of internationally recognized "favela" author Carolina Maria de Jesus (1914–1977, b. Sacramento, MG), Tom Farias describes her family lineage and early twentieth-century living conditions in the *quilombo* Patrimônio near the small, isolated Triângulo Mineiro town of Sacramento.[49] Carolina's maternal great-grandfather had been enslaved in Cabinda, Angola, in the early nineteenth century and brought to Minas Gerais. His son, Benedito José da Silva (1852–1924), was emancipated in 1888 and eventually moved his family from Patrimônio to Sacramento, where he became a community leader active in the Brotherhood of the Rosary, Congado, and Folia de Reis festivities. The *quilombo* was a ramshackle hamlet that owed its existence to extreme racial inequality. The poverty-stricken network of predominantly black families scratched out an existence without public services, and lacked water and energy infrastructure. Residents dug wells and hauled water for daily needs. Aside from subsistence farming, work opportunities typically came in the form of servitude employment as domestic helpers in Sacramento and as farmhands, earning wages below the cost of living or laboring in exchange for goods and meager meals, without pay.

Fleeing to a *quilombo* constituted a complete act of resistance against the slave system, and these settlements served as a haven for cultural expressions celebrating that resistance. Although the facts are lost to history, they were likely sites of African-derived religious practices, capoeira, singing, and batuque, and a rich mixture of African-derived and Native Indio culture probably contributed to the spread of these musics to non-African descendants. In addition to the dominant presence of runaway slaves in these usually small settlements, Martins suggests that one factor contributing to the growth of some quilombos was the *capitação*, a highly controversial head tax meted out in Minas Gerais beginning in the 1740s obligating each person to pay their own "royal fifth": 20 percent of the amount of gold that person was estimated to have mined that year, determined by Lisbon, regardless of the individual's actual economic activities.[50] Countless impoverished residents fled, some to *quilombos*, or at least to rough-and-ready camps, in an attempt to avoid paying this significant amount. As multiracial, multiethnic communities, *quilombos* did not uniformly represent islands of pure, unadulterated Africanisms, and as Julio Pinto Vallejos comments:

[In Minas Gerais,] a numerous outlaw population could offer runaway slaves some measure of protection or complicity, especially when free blacks and mulattoes were already heavily represented in it. The ambiguity of the colonial police regulations, often lumping together "vagrants," Indians, slaves, mulattoes and blacks, is a good witness to the very real connections between these somewhat different problems. Likewise, those Indian nations who, like the Caiapós, put up a more sustained resistance to colonization, often found useful allies in the runaway slaves. It is probably no coincidence that some of the heaviest concentrations of quilombos were found in the Caiapó-dominated lands, or that the younger generations of quilombolas numbered a good quantity of black-Indian mestizos (*caboclos*).[51]

Inquisition testimony from 1747 reveals elaborate religious ceremonies, perhaps incorporating *acontundá* beliefs of the Courá peoples of Benin, held in a *quilombo* community roughly three miles from what was then the outskirts of Paracatu, a northwestern Minas gold city west of the Rio São Francisco. There, in her house of worship inspired by West African Mina culture, the African named Maria Josefa, speaking her native language while in trance, claimed the Virgin Mary and Saint Anthony as her parents, the latter, as she testified, having baptized her and sent her to earth. Maria had placed a pot of bean stew (*feijoada*) at the foot of the saint's altar, a dish traditionally served in honor of Ogun, an *orixá* who in the contemporary Candomblé and Xangô religious worlds of northeastern Brazil remains syncretically linked to Saint Anthony. Historian Luiz Mott states that "a few days after this sermon, five bounty hunters invaded the acontundá house of worship, scattered the attendees and abducted their objects of worship." In his two-volume study of the Mineiro interior, Ricardo Ferreira Ribeiro posits these remote, Mineiro examples of West African Mina culture in their "enormous similarity to the candomblés and xangôs of the contemporary Nordeste."[52] Today, a huge open-pit gold mine owned by a Canadian firm still operates close to Paracatu, an area surrounded by the still predominantly Afro-Mineiro communities of Amaros, Bagres, Machadinho, Porto Pontal, and São Domingos.

Vissungo after the Gold Rush and Slavery, into the Twentieth Century and Beyond

Vissungo survived remarkable changes in Mineiro society. In response to the economic decline of the *decadência* came a regional economic shift toward agricultural production for subsistence and export, and a significant drop-off of further importation to Minas Gerais of enslaved Africans. By the mid-1780s, slave shipments into Minas Gerais had practically ceased, with the population of forced laborers declining steadily and bottoming out around 1808. Meanwhile, free non-whites became a dominant demographic, and natural reproduction among the enslaved increased dramatically until the 1888 abolition.[53]

Yet gold and gem mining continued in mineral-rich zones, including the original mining district (*zona metalúrgica*). Bordering today's Belo Horizonte, and now the world's oldest active gold mine, Morro Velho hosted visitors in 1874 and 1885 who chronicled the vigorous singing of the miners. The French diplomat Count d'Ursey heard singing "from the very bowels of the earth," while American traveler Frank Vincent witnessed miners "singing a wild refrain, keeping good time with then heavy blows of their sledges.... They paused for a moment to salute our party with a double '*Viva!*' and then the banging, clanging, and strange though not unmusical singing continued."[54] While accompanying her husband, Richard Burton, the well-known British agent, explorer, and spy, Lady Isabel Burton made note of the chants she heard at the Passagem Mine in Mariana, near one of Minas's first sites of gold discovery in the 1690s:

> The miners were all black slaves. They were chanting a wild air in chorus in time to the strokes of the hammer. They work with an iron crowbar called a drill and hammer, and each one bores away four *palmes* a day. If they do six, they get paid for the two over. They were streaming with perspiration.[55]

Vissungo outlasted slavery, surviving both imperial-era Brazil's collapse and the rise of the Old Republic, transforming into a geographically isolated twentieth-century singing tradition. Labor-intensive manual mining had transitioned to mechanized, and then industrialized methods, displacing postemancipation laborers. The carrying of the dead in hammocks gave way to funeral processions with automobiles on paved streets. One can safely assume that as these contexts for singing gradually disappeared, and as the brutality of slavery became a thing of the past, so too did the knowledge and practicality of vissungo and the art of secretive *falar Africano*. Aires da Mata Machado Filho's 1920s research for his 1943 book *O negro e o garimpo em Minas Gerais* (The black man and mining in Minas Gerais), referenced at length at the start of this chapter, attests to both the survival of the genre and its demise: Machado Filho was concerned for the fragility of a dwindling pastime that would not last much longer.

On January 7, 1944, the remarkable Brazilian musicologist Luis Heitor Corrêa de Azevedo wrote from Rio de Janeiro to Harold Spivacke, the chief of the Library of Congress Music Division in Washington, DC: "With my next trip to Minas Gerais I shall expend the last money the Library allowed for our recording project."[56] Three years earlier, Azevedo had been invited by ethnomusicologist Charles Seeger to serve in Washington as a consultant to the recently founded Musical Division of the Pan-American Union, returning to Brazil six months later with field recording equipment and two hundred glass and aluminum recording discs. Ambitious field recording expeditions took him and assistant Euclides da Silva Novo to Goiás and Ceará during 1942–1943 before his Minas journey; he wrote: "It takes at least fifteen days to go from Rio to the North of Minas Gerais."[57] Azevedo then visited Machado Filho in Belo Horizonte, the year following publication of the Mineiro's seminal study of vissungo, where he also received advice on conducting fieldwork in Diamantina from Belo Horizonte mayor Juscelino Kubitschek.[58] During late January and February 1944, the team produced ninety-six acetate discs, including vissungo performed by José Paulino de Assunção, Francisco Paulino Assunção, and Joaquim Caetano de Almeida, one of which was a song for carrying the dead. Copies of the discs were later archived in Azevedo's Center of Folklore Research at the National School of Music in Rio de Janeiro (now the School of Music at the Federal University of Rio de Janeiro).[59] The originals were sent to the American Folklife Center at the Library of Congress, the sponsoring institution. A few of these recordings are available on the Endangered Music Project CD release *L. H. Corrêa de Azevedo: Music of Ceará and Minas Gerais* (1997), in the notes for which this author is acknowledged for his assistance.[60] This commercially available recording represents but a thin slice of the more than 130 separate recordings compiled by Azevedo and Novo, reflecting an amazing diversity of folk and popular genres capturing the vitality of Diamantina's musical world. Some of them are available on the *Hearing Brazil* YouTube channel.

With the disappearance of social institutions and customs contextualizing vissungo's original emergence in the Serro Frio, the song tradition and its *falar Africano* language has all but disappeared. In 1997, Ivo Silvério da Rocha performed three vissungo for a CD titled *Congado mineiro*, the first volume of a CD series titled Documentos Sonoros Brasileiros: Acervo Cachuera! The elderly musician has remained active for over fifty years in the Congado-related *catopê guarda* in the small Serro Frio region town of Milho Verde, on the mountainous, old Estrada Real between the cities of Serro and Diamantina (see chapter 6). Azevedo's 1944 vissungo recording in Diamantina featured singers who also provided *catopê* songs for that project. In 2008, Rocha was acknowledged with the granting of the Brazilian Ministry of Culture's National Popular Culture award. In liner notes to the 1997 recording, Paulo Dias shares that Rocha

> is one of the few remaining who know of the vissungo. These are songs inherited from the slaves that he learned from listening to residents of the neighboring black communities Bau and Ausente in the Diamantina region, when they transported their dead to the city cemetery. The first song expresses the pain and exhaustion of the bearers traveling many miles through the mountain pass; the other two, with some Benguela words, mark the moment when, close to the cemetery, the friends address the soul of the dead person, so that it can smoothly pass to the land of the ancestors.[61]

African-derived languages are still spoken in parts of Minas Gerais in the twenty-first century, and vissungo is referenced in contemporary academic Brazilian scholarship mainly through linguistic studies addressing the importance of African language survival in the state's central region. Ausente and Bau, small, mostly black communities of *quilombo* heritage close to the towns of Serro and Milho Verde, have been sites of recent linguistic research noting the gradual disappearance of vissungo traditions. The 2008 passing of Ausente resident Antônio Crispim (b. 1943) marked a particularly grievous loss. As with his friend Ivo Silvério da Rocha, this *capitão* of the Serro *catopê guarda* was also a living treasure of vissungo song.[62] Ivo and Antônio are featured in the short ethnographic films *Vissungo: Fragmentos da tradição oral* (directed by Cássio Gusson, Confra Filmes, 2009) and *Macuco canenguê* (directed by Pedro de Castro Guimarães, 2002), featuring the percussion group Tambolelê in the accompaniment of vissungo performances filmed at the Gruta da Silitri cave site of the Serro Frio.

Vissungo Revival in the National Afro-Brazilian Renaissance of the 1970s-1980s: Grupo Vissungo and Clementina de Jesus

Vissungo did not transform into a commercially viable song tradition, whether as a specific repertoire or as a valorized musical subculture, similar to the manner in which, for instance, slave-era African American worksong traditions from the southern United States inspired the blues at the dawn of the twentieth century. Nor did vissungo emerge as a widely known folk idiom that subsequently could have been tapped nationally by mid-twentieth-century Afro-Brazilian musicians searching for black music roots. This would have certainly been the desire of Abigail Moura (1905–1970), a remarkable musician who, in his twenties, left his hometown of Eugenópolis, Minas Gerais, to establish a music career in Rio de Janeiro. He ultimately founded the Orquestra Afro-Brasileira in 1942.[63] Under Moura's direction, the ensemble was limited to musicians of African descent and explored black identities in celebrating musical styles, instruments, and language defining the African-descendent presence in Brazil. If it had been known more widely on a national level, beyond Machado Filho's book and a few archived field recordings, vissungo, by virtue of its cultural value to Brazil's burgeoning black consciousness movement affecting politics and the arts, would certainly have joined the *maracatu*, batuques, *jongos*, and secularized songs of Umbanda and Candomblé liturgy championed by Moura. Around the time of the Orquestra Afro-Brasileira's founding, Moura was regularly attending services at Joãozinho da Gomeia's Candomblé *terreiro* in Rio de Janeiro's Duque de Caxias neighborhood, often in the company of Afro-Brazilian rights activist Abdias Nascimento and choreographer Solano Trindade. The three friends collaborated on theater productions and shared creative interests in exploring African-derived culture and progressive Afro-Brazilian causes.[64]

In 1975, vissungo inspired the founding of the Grupo Vissungo ensemble in Rio de Janeiro by vocalist and percussionist Spírito Santo (Antônio José do Espírito Santo). In updating Brazil's black music traditions with the Afro-Brazilian political consciousness of the times, and thus furthering the work of groups like the Orquestra Afro-Brasileira, Spírito Santo's ensemble embraced West African Afrobeat styles and explored contemporary contexts for both Congado and vissungo, performing, recording, and collaborating with filmmakers before disbanding in 1996. Grupo Vissungo joined Corner Club keyboardist and composer Wagner Tiso on the soundtrack for director Walter Lima's 1985 film *Chico Rei*, a dramatization of the legendary enslaved African who purchased his own freedom and became owner of the Vila Rica mine in which he had labored. Chico Rei is still heralded in parts of Minas Gerais as the mythical first king of the Congado (see chapter 6). The film's soundtrack songs "Quilombo de Dumbá," and "Chico reina" were performed by then eighty-four-year-old vocalist Clementina de Jesus (1901–1987).

Clementina's remarkable LP *O canto dos escravos* (The song of the slaves; Estúdio Eldorado, 1982) featuring fellow vocalists Tia Doca and Geraldo Filme, and percussionists Djalma Correia, Papete, and Don Bira, grew from the work of producers Aluízio Falcão and Marcus Vinícius de Andrade. The two producers crossed paths in the 1970s while working for Discos Marcus Pereira, and both had, independently of one another, become fascinated with vissungo through Machado Filho's *O negro e o garimpo em Minas Gerais.*[65] *O canto dos escravos*'s gatefold liner notes are straight from Machado Filho's introduction, and his permission was required for the recordings based on his published transcriptions found in the book. The 1982 album's fourteen tracks are labeled "Canto I" through "Canto XIV," with Clementina, Doca, and Filme singing together on track 1, then alternating as soloists through the rest of the album. "Canto II" is echoed in the 1985 *Chico Rei* soundtrack song "Quilombo de Dumbá," in which a young man fleeing to the Dumbá *quilombo* leaves behind weeping family and friends who are unable to join him.

Clementina was discovered at the age of sixty-two by producer Hermínio Bello de Carvalho as she performed folk and popular songs in a small Rio de Janeiro bar in 1963. Quelé, as she was known, became a star and a cultural treasure with emotive vocal timbres and an incredibly deep repertoire of samba, *samba-canção, jongo,* and sacred Afro-Brazilian liturgical songs. This led her to acclaim among Brazilians who heard in her music important links to an earlier repertoire of Brazilian popular music and sensed that she was a living connection to the rich heritage of African-derived performance practice. The singer's maternal grandparents, Isaac and Eva, had been enslaved domestic servants. Her biographers fancifully note the remarkable, only distant possibility that Clementina's paternal grandparents, Abraão and Tereza Mina, who fled from Minas Gerais to her birthplace of Valença, Rio de Janeiro, in the heart of Paraíba Valley coffee country, may have been related to a prominent African-born vissungo singer in the São João da Chapada community identified by Machado Filho in his 1943 treatise.[66] To link Clementina's paternal grandparents to vissungo singer Felipe Mina (Felipe Neri de Sousa) solely by surname is untenable, given the slave industry's common assignment of "Mina" as a surname to victims of Africa's São Jorge da Mina slave market. The Diamantina region of the Serro Frio was, like other regions of Brazil, likely home to countless slaves with the surname Mina, as the name was also an often erroneous "ethnic" designation for the West African "nation" (*nação*). What is true is that, between 1830 and 1860, many thousands of free African descendants like Abraão and Tereza Mina abandoned the mining districts of central Minas Gerais for work in Brazil's southeastern coffee plantations and in the cities of Rio de Janeiro, São Paulo, and the Zona da Mata of southeastern Minas Gerais. Clementina's cultural standing in Afro-Brazilian music history conjures a deep musical heritage in which sense she was a *mulúduri*, an heiress to the great pan-Bantu-derived oral culture in Brazil's southeast, "with the function of transmitting and perpetuating the ancestral songs of Mother Africa."[67]

Twenty-First-Century *Quilombos*

As vissungo disappeared as a cultural practice, the troubling heritage of postemancipation landlessness and contemporary social ills for most of Brazil's poorest did not. A living political resistance envelops aspects of the vissungo/*quilombo* legacy. Like hundreds of other territories of memory draped across contemporary rural and urban Minas Gerais, certain predominantly Afro-Brazilian enclaves are, in the twenty-first century, regarded by many as "remaining from *quilombos*" (*remanescente do quilombo*), "black lands" (*terras de preto*), "*quilombo* communities" (*comunidades quilombolas*), or "*quilombo* collectives" (*coletivos quilombolas*). Many fight for land ownership claims based on their slave-descendant heritage, and from within a federal legal system initiated by Brazil's 1988 constitution, the nation's first following the military dictatorship. Article 68 of the Provisional Act of the Transitional Constitution reads, "The remains of *quilombo* communities still occupying those lands are thus recognized as definitive property, and the State shall issue them respective land titles." This vague language was given more definition through subsequent federal laws and the establishment of agencies and partnerships designed to develop criteria and implement this complicated process. In 1988, the Ministry of Culture created the Palmares Cultural Foundation to promote the cultural, social, and economic values resulting from African-descendant influence on the formation of Brazilian society; in 2003, under President Luiz Inácio "Lula" da Silva, the foundation was tasked as the decision-making agency on granting titles to *quilombolo* status proposals.[68] Subsequent federal decrees articulated political action: Decree no. 3,912 (2001) attempted to regulate and stimulate claims for *quilombo* status without clearly defining a process, while no. 4,887 (2003) attempted to define racial and historical criteria for "remaining communities of *quilombos*" in these terms: "The ethnic-racial groups of remnants of *quilombo* communities are to be considered according to criteria including their historical trajectory, relationship to the specific territory, and the presumption of a black ancestry related to the resistance to, and the suffering caused by, historical oppression." This 2003 decree required the National Institute of Agrarian Reform (INCRA, founded in 1970) to register territorial demarcations in response to community proposals, and to create the Brazil Quilombola Program within the Secretary of Politics and Promotion of Racial Equality (SEPPIR), coordinated by the Subsecretary for Traditional Communities. These agencies worked for land rights, educational opportunities, improved nutrition, access to health care, and cultural recognition. Following the lead of other states, in 2005 Minas Gerais formed the Federation of Quilombola Communities of Minas Gerais (Federação das Comunidades Quilombolas do Estado de Minas Gerais, or N'golo), which works with the Palmares Cultural Foundation and INCRA to process community claims seeking land ownership and other benefits. By 2012, Minas Gerais was home to 296 mapped communities. Of the 3,644 such communities nationwide at that time, 1,820 were successfully certified for land ownership. By the end of 2018, more than 4,800 communities had submitted applications and were awaiting land titles. Elizabeth Farfán-Santos suggests that recent *quilombolo* movement strategies have grown from the racialized identities of black communities toward the documentation of contemporary cultural practices linked to inherited ancestry.[69] Musical heritage factors into land reform and cultural identity in the twenty-first century. Elected in 2018, and taking office in January 2019, far-right Brazilian president Jair Bolsonaro had long dismissed land rights issues, including Native claims and those of the *quilombo* movement. His first executive decree came on his first full day in office, on January 2, 2019, transferring the *quilombolo* project from INCRA to his newly formed Agriculture Ministry and placing all nongovernmental organizations under direct federal supervision by the Secretary of Government. Bolsonaro's reactionary stance toward progressive change has thus cast a dark shadow over the *quilombo* movement's goals.

Chapter 4

Sacred and Fine Art Music of the Colonial and Imperial Periods

From the intersection of Avenida Brasil and Avenida Afonso Pena in Belo Horizonte's busy Funcionários district near downtown, I am walking a short city block to meet Arnon Sávio Reis de Oliveira. He can speak firsthand of researching, conducting, and programming a repertoire known as *música colonial*. Although associated with the Minas baroque (*barroco mineiro*), the eighteenth- and early nineteenth-century composers who created this repertoire, collectively known as the Minas School or the "Mulatto" School of composers, were preclassical in style, having more in common with the opera-influenced homophonic textures of eighteenth-century Neapolitan composers than with the masters of polyphonic forms specific to the broader European baroque. Since 2003, Arnon has directed Coral BDMG (BDMG Chorale), an award-winning vocal ensemble that has performed throughout Brazil as well as in Paris, Germany, and Saint Peter's Basilica at the Vatican.[1] In addition to annual concerts at the quaint bandstand (*coreto*) at Belo Horizonte's Praça da Liberdade, and the elegant Our Lady of Lourdes Basilica, Coral BDMG began a long-term concert series project under Oliveira's leadership, bringing *música colonial* back to the towns and cities of the Estrada Real, the 1,630 kilometers of "Royal Road" linking the gold- and diamond-rich mountains to Brazil's coast. Since 2005, the "Coral BDMG on the Estrada Real" project has programmed dozens of concerts in the churches and cathedrals of more than sixty towns and cities located along these old colonial routes, including the illustrious, Golden Age urban centers of Ouro Preto, Mariana, Sabará, Serro, Diamantina, and Congonhas as well as the three musically rich cities of São João del-Rei, Tiradentes, and Prados in the Campo das Vertentes (Rolling Fields) region of Minas south of the central mining district.

"The repertoire of *música colonial* of Minas is best heard and performed in the small churches and cathedrals of the Mineiro interior, where there exist important *cidades históricas* [colonial-era towns]," Arnon states without equivocation, adding that those audiences dearly appreciate the return of this music to the heart of Old Minas.[2] The maestro emphasizes urban/rural dichotomies between Belo Horizonte's busy modernity and the tranquil world of the interior, such as that of his hometown of Sete Lagoas, roughly sixty kilometers northeast of the capital. The title of his ensemble's 2008 CD, *Coral BDMG na Estrada Real: A música colonial mineira em suas origens* (Coral BDMG on the Estrada Real: Minas Gerais colonial music in its origins), boldly advertises this premise and cultural undertaking, staking claim to an authenticity of place and regional musical identity. Some of the venues in these cities and towns are among the hundreds of architectural sites registered with the National Institute for Historical and Artistic Heritage (IPHAM). Works by hallowed names are sometimes performed in the cities where they once flourished: Padre João de Deus de Castro Lobo (1794–1832), Jerônimo de Souza Lobo (1780–1810), and Marcos Coelho Neto (1740–1806) and his son of the same name (1763–1823), from Ouro Preto and Mariana; José Joaquim Emerico Lobo de Mesquita (1746?–1805), born in Serro and active in Diamantina and Ouro Preto; and Manuel Dias de Oliveira (1745–1813), active in the Campo das Vertentes tri-city area of São João del-Rei, Tiradentes, and Prados. The *Ladainha* manuscript of Antônio Lopes Serino (no dates) was found in the church of Curral D'el Rey, which once stood close to where Arnon and I are now talking, in the small town that Belo Horizonte replaced in the 1890s. Little is known about these composers, and if their likenesses were once captured in drawings or paintings, those iconographic sources no longer survive.

The professional religious music of the Mineiro Golden Age was dominated by men of color, both free and enslaved, including, for example, the mixed-race musicians Francisco Mexia and Manoel da Costa Dantas, appointed consecutively to the prestigious Vila Rica chapel master position beginning in 1748.[3] In certain terms, these professionals specializing in European-derived fine art music competed as equals with whites in an exploitive slave society where such opportunities offered new horizons for mixed-race mulattos (also, *pardos*), who gained in social standing and in some cases formed multigenerational family legacies of music professionalism. As historian Kenneth Maxwell clarified, mixed-race composers were among the many *pardo* musicians, painters, and sculptors who "formed an urban artisan class which stood between the slaves and the white minority, which had become an influential native articulator, especially in the visual arts and music, of the distinctive character of the region."[4] With texts primarily in Latin, the region's characteristic sacred music was composed for Catholic calendar feast days and special rituals. While the best-known of the Minas School composers were free, mixed-race sons of white men and black or mixed-race women, many enslaved men joined the ranks of singers and instrumentalists alongside free musicians, rare opportunities for more favorable social position and livelihood that created new colonial-era contexts for racial politics and perceptions of race.[5]

The crucial roles played by lay orders in the fabric of music culture mark Minas Gerais as a unique Brazilian cultural region during the colonial period. As influential social institutions, racially segregated brotherhoods assumed many of the responsibilities of the first orders that were banned from Minas Gerais during the height of the gold rush, including the financing of new church construction and music services. In a society shaped by white authority, members of black and mixed-race brotherhoods were able to improve their status. The Minas School's liturgical music activities are linked to the mixed-race brotherhoods of São José dos Homens Pardos, a fulcrum of artistic and musical activity in Ouro Preto, including that of Aleijadinho and the notable painters Manoel Ribeiro Rosa (1758–1808) and José Gervásio de Souza Lobo (1758–1806).[6] By 1780, as Judge Teixeira Coelho wrote about the region, "those mulattos not thoroughly idle should find work as musicians, of whom there are many in the Captaincy of Minas, certainly more than the figures in the entire Kingdom of Portugal."[7] The training and livelihoods of these musicians developed from guild-like organizations known as *corporações* (organizations, associations), most of which were affiliated with brotherhoods. Many *corporação* directors were conductors whose private homes typically served as the group's headquarters, often functioning as a music conservatory where lessons and rehearsals were held.[8] The choral and instrumental repertoire they produced and rehearsed remained a cornerstone of the urban Mineiro musical experience. The story of fine art music in Minas Gerais starts with this functional, generally homophonic, preclassical style of sacred music composed from the mid-eighteenth century to the first quarter of the nineteenth century.

Francisco Curt Lange

During the economic decline of Minas Gerais, most of the parts and scores of this regional *música colonial* repertoire, including original manuscripts written in the composers' hand, were lost or misplaced, scattered across various Mineiro towns and cities, stored in church archives large and small, and handed down among the sometimes forgotten possessions of musical families.[9] Some communities maintained local performance legacies of their *música colonial mineira*, but the lost music remained forgotten and widely unknown to the general public well into the twentieth century. In Minas Gerais during the late 1940s, German Uruguayan musicologist Francisco Curt Lange (b. 1903, Eilenburg, Germany; d. 1997, Montevideo) began discovering treasures of manuscripts and historically valuable documents dealing with music.[10] In addition to research on the lives and works of composers, Lange's scholarship unearthed the grandeur and breadth of their musical activities, identifying Mineiro musicians among the pieces of a hitherto lost cultural puzzle who soon proved to have musically surpassed composers in the colony's other important religious centers in Recife, Salvador, Rio de Janeiro, and São Paulo. Of particular value were the accounting records of brotherhoods, churches, and municipalities detailing payments to professional musicians. In the late 1940s, Lange began publishing groundbreaking articles on *música colonial*,[11] which helped create a still thriving subdiscipline in Brazilian historical musicology dedicated to Mineiro music. From 1958 to 1960, he received UNESCO funding to research music in Minas Gerais. Now, published performance editions of *música colonial* carry their own modern-day narratives of rediscovery and survival, and shed light on this European-derived yet homegrown cornerstone of Mineiro musical identity.

The gold rush brought Portuguese folk and religious musical practices of the old regime to urban centers as well as rough frontier towns, settlements that initially developed without any effort to re-create family-based

Iberian society. This early stage of European-derived Mineiro music culture reflected the lay brotherhoods, colonial administration, and military garrisons, and the economic sectors supporting mining. Lange controversially claimed that a unique, regional musical style of *música colonial* quickly emerged, with roots in the earliest years of the colonial captaincy, following the War of the Emboabas (1706–1709). The new captaincy's first governor, Antônio de Albuquerque Coelho, conjoined the two closely situated settlements of Antônio Dias and Ouro Preto in 1710 to create the *vila* of Vila Rica d'Albuquerque (Ouro Preto). However, no documents prove that local composers were active there or anywhere in Minas Gerais at this time. *Vila* status ushered in municipal and parish administrative structures that grew into a city of twenty thousand by the 1740s, then one of the Western Hemisphere's largest settlements, close to twice the size of New York City at that time. Lange's notion of *mulatismo musical*, first promulgated in the late 1940s, which suggested that mixed-race composers here began producing a unique, nativist style of music, was echoed by international scholars such as Gerard Béhague.[12] Recent Brazilian scholarship has challenged the "mulatto style" hypothesis, that mixed-race Mineiro composers had collectively produced a particular Brazilian style indicating a unique regional, or national, character. For example, musicologist Rogério Budasz has suggested that Lange was overly influenced by Gilberto Freyre's nationalistic racial theories of Brazilian cultural development first set forth in the 1930s.[13]

In 1982, the seventy-nine-year-old Lange donated most of his collection relevant to Mineiro studies to the Museu da Inconfidência, Ouro Preto, dedicated to a failed rebellion for Brazilian independence that occurred in 1789 (fig. 4.1). Its holdings include furniture and other household belongings of the revolutionaries, a collection of works by Aleijadinho, and other rare artifacts defining the area's rich heritage. The museum is housed in what was the municipal building and jail (Casa da Câmara e Cadeia), an iconic example of late eighteenth-century Pombaline civic architecture, with thick stone masonry and a bell and clock tower facing Tiradentes Square, where a statue of the revolutionary hero for whom the plaza is named sits high atop a tall obelisk. Lange's donation combined with a wealth of other colonial and imperial-era manuscripts provided by various sources led to the creation of the museum's musicology section, coordinated initially by musicologist Régis Duprat.[14] Liturgical works by local composers were commonly performed in neighborhood churches in eighteenth- and nineteenth-century Minas Gerais.

Figure 4.1. The Inconfidência Museum in Ouro Preto commemorates the Minas Conspiracy revolutionary movement. This former municipal building and jail in late-eighteenth-century Pombaline style faces Tiradentes Square. In tandem with other institutions, the museum houses musical scores and manuscripts, and publishes editions of *música colonial* composed in Minas Gerais. (Photo by Jonathon Grasse.)

Many of these composers remain unknown, and a thematic catalog of 232 themes by anonymous composers was published by the Federal University of Minas Gerais in 1990.[15] Meanwhile, Lange's personal materials (library holdings, publications, recordings, musical instruments, correspondence, etc.) were moved to UFMG in 1995, becoming the Curt Lange Archive.

Between 1994 and 2015, the Museu da Inconfidência and the University of São Paulo published a series of four volumes of performance editions entitled Música do Brasil Colonial (see appendix 1). The works of Mineiro composers dominate the contents (eighteen of the forty-eight works are anonymous), and several pieces date to the imperial era of the nineteenth century. The scores reveal an array of two- and four-voice vocal arrangements of sacred texts mostly in Latin, a few a cappella but most accompanied by a variety of instrumental ensembles drawing from strings, winds, brass, and basso continuo. Some of the common instrumental groups are based on strings and may include paired valve horns (*trompa*) and/or paired flutes or oboes. Clarinetists may have read flute or oboe parts from transposed copies, and bassoons (*fagote*) could have read bass parts. Some of the string scoring is limited to two violin sections and bass (*baixo*, or *contrabaixo*), while a handful of scores feature the viola (the bowed stringed instrument, not the ten-string Brazilian guitar). The most elaborately scored work appearing in the *Música do Brasil Colonial* series is the brief antiphon in volume 3, "Hosanna Filio David" by Antônio Martiniano da Silva Benfica (184?–1905, b. Aiuruoca, MG), calling for full strings, flute, two clarinets, trumpet, tuba, two horns, continuo, and four-part choir.[16] There are no parts dedicated specifically to cello (*violoncelo*) in the editions, and it is assumed that cellists doubled the bass parts. The bass clef parts of the basso continuo would easily have been played by cello or contrabass. Keyboard continuo would have been played by harpsichord (*cravo*), organ (*orgão*), or in the later nineteenth century, the piano. Apparently, the guitar-like viola is thought to have been used as a continuo instrument when necessary (see chapter 7).

Back in the Madrigale choir's quiet Belo Horizonte rehearsal space, Arnon emphasizes the accessibility of this mostly homophonic music. "Emerico Lobo de Mesquita's Mass in F Major is likely the most often performed work of the period," he adds, noting that work's lyricism and its high place held among audiences and performers:

> [T]hose pieces come from a special moment in Brazilian history, before the arrival of the Portuguese court in Rio de Janeiro at the beginning of the nineteenth century, when Minas Gerais's wealth from gold mines enabled an entire sacred music culture in the churches and cathedrals of these towns and cities. While there was an opera house in Ouro Preto in the colonial era, productions were rather few. Instead, the music spectacles were to be found in churches, where masses were being composed for services, baptisms, and other functions. Along with the architecture and sculptures by artisans such as Aleijadinho, this is all work of the Mineiro people.[17]

José Joaquim Emerico Lobo de Mesquita: Icon of *Música Colonial* in Minas Gerais

Although important life details such as parentage and education remain a mystery, José Joaquim Emerico Lobo de Mesquita is the most important and well-known composer of the Minas School. Among his forty-eight verified works, there are only eight complete, or nearly complete, works by his hand.[18] Unsubstantiated claims state the year of his birth, in Vila do Príncipe (now Serro), as 1746; as a free mixed-race son of a Portuguese man and one of his enslaved servants, Joaquina Emerenciana, the legend continues, he studied music and Latin with Father Manoel da Costa Dantas, chapel master of the city's Matriz de Nossa Senhora da Conceição. No documented evidence of these claims exists.[19] Possibly by the age of thirty, Lobo de Mesquita moved north on the Estrada Real's Diamond Road from Vila do Príncipe to Arraial do Tijuco (now Diamantina), where he may have assisted in the installation of an organ at the Church of Santo Antônio and where he was likely hired as organist from 1783 to 1789. In Tijuco, he was a lieutenant in the Third Infantry of Pardos, though it is not known if he was employed as a musician or a soldier. At the end of the 1780s, he entered the three brotherhoods of Our Lady of Carmo, Our Lady of Mercy of the Crioulos, and Our Lady of Amparo, a list suggesting that this forty-something mixed-race musician was allowed to work among white members of the Carmo brotherhood.[20] During his time in Tijuco, he probably taught private music lessons.

Lobo de Mesquita moved to Vila Rica in 1798, likely for career opportunities awaiting a skilled organist, conductor, and composer, where he joined a thriving group of highly regarded church musicians. He was appointed conductor, and perhaps musical director, for the brotherhood of the Holy Sacrament (Santíssimo Sacramento), a duty otherwise reserved for whites, performing in the gloriously appointed cathedral of Our Lady of the Pillar (now the Basílica Nossa Senhora do Pilar). Construction of the original chapel began in 1696 and was completed by 1703, and the cathedral was lavishly refurbished twice during the first half of the eighteenth century. Lobo de Mesquita's Vila Rica was Brazil's wealthiest, most populous city, and the colony's de facto center of liturgical music composition, though the economic decline was in its second full decade. There, he likely met his generation's musical patrician, Marcos Coelho Neto (1740–1806), and his son of the same name (1763–1823); Florêncio José Ferreira Coutinho (1749–1819); and Francisco Gomes da Rocha (1754–1808), all illustrious composers.[21]

The church music of these composers contrasted with the fine art music performed elsewhere in the city. The Vila Rica Opera House opened in 1770, presenting *comédias*, *entremezes* and other theatrical plays, choreographed *bailes*, and religious displays.[22] Productions were a rich mix of original works in Portuguese, translations of non–Portuguese language operas, including works of unknown authorship (the most frequently performed), and works by Italian composers Carlo Goldoni (1707–1793) and Pietro Metastasio (1698–1782).[23] Plays by Jean-Baptiste Poquelin (Molière, 1622–1673) and François-Marie Arouet (Voltaire, 1694–1778) also graced the opera house stage. As the Vila Rica Opera House succumbed to neglect in the 1820s, the Teatro de Sabará was constructed in that gold-rich city in 1819 by Francisco da Costa Soares. The vitality of this eighteenth-century music scene led the Mineiro musician José de Torres Franco to publish a successful book on accompaniment in 1792, *Arte de acompanhar* (The Art of accompaniment), a publication indicating a good-sized market for musical instruction, and a rare accomplishment in view of the colonial-era ban on printing presses.

Though it remains unknown why Lobo de Mesquita left Vila Rica for Rio de Janeiro in 1800, it is fair to assume that limited financial resources had already marked the end of the Minas School. Gomes da Rocha filled his vacated position at the Pillar cathedral. In Rio, Lobo de Mesquita would have met, and perhaps worked with, José Maurício Nunes Garcia (1767–1830), regarded by many as Brazil's greatest colonial-era composer. Lobo de Mesquita died there in 1805, three years before the arrival in the city of the Portuguese royal court. Of his extant pieces, his Ladainha in F, several graduals, an antiphon, and *O Tércio* are the most frequently performed and recorded. Soon after performance editions of some of these works were made available in the 1990s, the Brasilessentia Grupo Vocal e Orquestra and the Ars Nova Coral of the Federal University of Minas Gerais made groundbreaking debut recordings.[24]

The three-generation legacies of the Castro Lobo and Corrêa Lisboa families centered in Vila Rica and nearby Mariana offer glimpses into lineages of important families active during the illustrious period of the Minas baroque.[25] Luíz Corrêa Lisboa (1737–1825) was a professional musician whose son, José Felipe Corrêa Lisboa (1770–1841, b. Mariana), is represented in Ouro Preto's Museu da Inconfidência archive with his composition *Variations for Flute and Piano*.[26] Some composers from Diamantina, Serro, Ouro Preto, and Mariana also participated in the region's secular salon culture, writing stylized modinhas and lundus for voice and piano. José Felipe's older brother, Luíz Vicente (1769–1825), and son, José Felipe Corrêa Lisboa Jr. (b. 1814), were also professional musicians in the Vila Rica/Mariana area. Performing at religious services, dances, and salons as well as teaching formed the basis for their livelihoods. Corrêa Lisboa Jr. assumed the musical directorship of the Catedral Basílica da Sé following the death of renowned Mineiro composer Padre João de Deus de Castro Lobo.[27] Castro Lobo's father (Gabriel de Castro Lobo, b. 1763) was a professional musician, while his grandfather, Manuel de Castro Lobo, was a registered musician in the Brotherhood of São José dos Homens Pardos sometime during the middle of the eighteenth century.

Less than ten kilometers from Ouro Preto, the city of Mariana houses another important music archive associated with *música colonial*. Located in the former Bishop's Palace near the city's historical center, the Museu da Música de Mariana opened its doors in 2007, after years of archival organization dating to the early 1960s, when Bishop Oscar de Oliveira began gathering and restoring old manuscripts previously kept in the Ecclesiastical Archives of the Archdiocese, an institution dating to the 1740s. Today, the museum's mission includes reconnecting history and culture to the people of Minas, its art education project reaching thirty nearby towns where musical groups and choirs are encouraged to include early music (*música antiga*) in their repertoire. Named the Don Oscar de Oliveira Collection, and registered by UNESCO as a Memory of the Latin American and Caribbean World, the archive was first organized in the 1960s with the aid of local musicians Vicente Angelo da Mercês and Anibal Pedro Walter. Among its more than two thousand manuscripts are Lobo de Mesquita's autographed original score of the 1783 work *O Tércio* and a book of plainchant dating to 1753 that once belonged to Mariana's first archbishop, Manuel da Cruz. The museum is now overseen by the Cultural and Educational Foundation of the Archdiocese of Mariana (FUNDARQ), which was also responsible for restoration initiated in 1982 of the rare Arp Schnitger organ housed in Mariana's Catedral Basílica de Sé. Arp Schnitger (1648–1719) completed the organ in Hamburg, Germany, sometime during 1701, and it was installed later the same year in Lisbon's Church of Saint Francis. King João V gifted the organ to the newly appointed bishop of Mariana in 1752, where it was installed the following year.

Listening to Arnon describe his choir's role in reaching Mineiros with this repertoire, I begin to understand his main point, which is also the simplest and most sincere: these works of the Minas baroque masters represent the authentic sound world of those majestic cathedrals and churches, architecturally dominating historical towns with their musically resonant, gold-leafed, sculpted interiors. Discovering and archiving the manuscripts, restoring scores, editing critical editions, and performing the music brings this notated, sonic culture back to life while acknowledging the composers' artistic and spiritual intentions. In stressing the importance of performances in these special places, in small towns and *cidades históricas*, Arnon reiterates that "Belo Horizonte cannot be the reference point for the historical identity of the state ... because it represents twentieth-century modernism based on the spirit of Brazil's emergence as a Republic. ... It is rather this network of towns in the interior that formed a layer of the Mineiro people." There also exists a sort of acoustic stiffness, he adds, in performing these works in modern concert halls and theaters. In further elaborating on this dichotomy, he describes the rural world of the *cerrado* landscape, the land itself, and the ways of life that shaped and constituted Old Minas, when and where a nucleus of colonial towns offered homegrown sacred music. "Those are our roots as a people," Arnon adds, noting the legacy of urbanism in colonial Minas Gerais and the role there played by European-derived Catholic liturgical music.

Guarding Liturgical Music Traditions in São João del-Rei, Tiradentes, and Prados

The wealthy cities of the central mining district were not the only places where liturgical music was composed in colonial and imperial Minas Gerais. With two full-time orchestras dating to the eighteenth century, São João del-Rei, the main city of Campo das Vertentes, still commands the title "City of Music," and the archives of its Orquestra Lira Sanjoanense and Orquestra Ribeiro Bastos are enriched by the liturgical music of local composers dating back over two hundred years (figs. 4.2, 4.3). The plaque at the entrance to the Orquestra Lira Sanjoanense offices reads: "The oldest active orchestra in the Americas." Parts for original liturgical music by local composers, the most famous and widely performed being Manuel Dias de Oliveira (1745–1813), were distributed among various ensembles in the nearby towns of São José del-Rei and Prados, handwritten manuscripts being the strict norm as printing presses were not allowed in the captaincy.[28] This region's first musicians arrived from the coast or from Portugal directly. But local-born blacks and mixed-race performers soon characterized the tradition, and it became rare to find white musicians.

In 1717, the governor of the Captaincy of São Paulo and Minas de Ouro, Dom Pedro de Almeida Portugal (the Count of Assumar), visited São João del-Rei, his arrival heralded in a civic ceremony with commissioned music performed by an ensemble led by Antonio do Carmo. That was followed

Figures 4.2, 4.3. Above: headquarters of the Orquestra Ribeiro Bastos; below: plaque for the Orquestra Lira Sanjoanense, São João del-Rei. The two orchestras date to the eighteenth century and help define São João del-Rei as the "City of Music." (Photos by Jonathon Grasse.)

by a *Te Deum* performed in the nearby main cathedral (*igreja matriz*).[29] Lange noted records of payments to musicians assigned to the governor's tour through Minas that year, including black musicians playing *choromels* (shawms). São José del-Rei and Prados soon followed with their own inchoate traditions of fine art music. Some of their chapels and cathedrals, like dozens of churches throughout Minas, house historically important archives as part of their musical legacies.[30] The bands and orchestras of mixed-race brotherhoods formed conservatories much like those in the central mining district towns, where conductors and ensemble directors refitted their private homes as music schools and rehearsal spaces. The vocalists and instrumentalists who received professional training there also performed bandas and secular music in public bandstands, at private clubs, and for social organizations. Unlike the guarded sacred music manuscripts, the secular repertoire was not generally preserved in archives. The banda tradition grew into a key cultural element in Campo das Vertentes.

Padre José Maria Xavier (1819–1887, b. São João del-Rei, MG) emerged as the province's primary nineteenth-century liturgical music composer, writing more than one hundred works. His maternal grandfather, José Joaquim de Miranda, founded a music ensemble in 1776 that later became the Orquestra Lira Sanjoanense. As an eight-year-old choirboy, Xavier was introduced by his uncle to the piano, music theory, violin, and clarinet. At twenty he completed *Qui Sedes*, his first mature composition, scored for bass voice and small orchestra. Contemporary Mineiro conductor Marcelo Ramos describes Padre José Maria's most widely recognized piece, an 1871 work for the Tenebrae, the "Service in Darkness" for Matins and Lauds of Holy Week (Semana Santa) "Because the city lacked an oboist, he replaces the oboe . . . with a trumpet in the melodic voice, with strings, flute, clarinet, and two horns. Violoncello and contrabass parts are duplicated in many passages, and the ophicleide, an obsolete instrument and forerunner of the tuba, is added in forte passages."[31]

Much of Xavier's output dates to his residence at the Our Lady of the Good Passing Seminary in Mariana, which he entered at age twenty-six.[32] His life maps historically to the continuing struggles of the region's economic decline, linking the past accomplishments of the Minas baroque to Brazil's imperial era and to the emerging realities of a new, republican Minas Gerais. Passing away the year before the collapse of the monarchy, the emancipation of slaves, and the formation of the republic, Xavier's life now appears submerged in those social changes. This is one reason he is celebrated so widely in Campo das Vertentes. Xavier's choral music was also performed at the 1872 Fifth Industrial Exposition of Minas in Juiz de Fora (Exposição Mineira União e Industria), acknowledging the composer's importance as well as that of the Zona da Mata city, then the largest in Minas and in close proximity to the cosmopolitanism of the imperial city of Rio de Janeiro. Juiz de Fora's Industrial Exposition of 1869 hosted another Imperial-era Mineiro composer of sacred works, Francisco Raposo Pereira Lima (1845–1905, b. Baependi, MG).[33] A tenor earning the nickname "Sabiá Mineiro" (*sabiá* is a singing bird) and who performed for Emperor Dom Pedro II, Lima also conducted, played violin and guitar, and taught piano during a career that took him to Rio de Janeiro. His works include seventeen masses, hymns, and pieces for Baependi's Holy Week celebrations. An autographed score exists for his *Cateretê*, a piece based on the popular dance and scored for female voices and orchestra. Today, the Federal University of Juiz de Fora (UFJF) boasts a decades-long commitment to *música colonial* through its Centro Cultural Pró-Música; in 1989, the university launched the International Festival of Colonial-Era Brazilian Music and Early Music.

At the dawn of the twentieth century, big changes surrounding the growth of Belo Horizonte included the arrival of foreign Catholic clergy as part of the church's renewed international effort to bolster its ranks.[34] The Campo das Vertentes tri-city area fought attempts to modernize their local liturgical services and repertoire. Local Tiradentes historian Olindo Rodrigues dos Santos Filho claims that the city's distance from Belo Horizonte enabled the continuation of local traditions: "In other places, Italian composers, who were Vatican officials at that time, began to dominate the rituals, but in São João (del-Rei) and Tiradentes . . . the musicians continued to use the scores by local composers."[35] In a collective resistance against the various modernization movements that began in the nineteenth century and reached their apex with the Vatican II reforms of the early 1960s, church communities in the regions of Campo das Vertentes and Sul de Minas successfully fought to retain local traditions of worship. Communities in the region fostered the continued performances of a repertoire of locally composed music, and a two-hundred-year-old traditional liturgy of Latin plainchant and longer ceremonies. This steadfast defense of performance and repertoire traditions in these and other towns is a point of regional musical pride. In the twenty-first century, thousands of Holy Week visitors flock to the tri-city network of São João del-Rei, Prados, and Tiradentes to participate in a two-hundred-year-old music tradition of local liturgical orchestras and religious calendar ceremonies including rare installations of the full Office of Tenebrae ("Service in Darkness") for Matins and Lauds. In 2009, Brazil's Instituto do Patrimônio Histórico e Artístico Nacional (IPHAN; the Institute of National Historic and Artistic Heritage) declared São João del-Rei's competitive church bell–ringing tradition during Lent a national intangible heritage. Suzel Ana Reily, in 2006 research detailing the defense of traditional liturgy in the Sul de Minas town of Campanha, writes that, in Minas Gerais, "based upon a baroque template, Holy Week, the main annual event throughout the former mining regions, came to epitomize Mineiro identity[,] and its production has provided a means of annually renewing the region's links with its glorious past."[36] It is remarkable that until the 1950s, a great majority of music education in this heartland of choral and orchestral music was accomplished through private teachers and family traditions: the first state-sponsored conservatory was founded only in 1953, the Conservatório Estadual de Música Padre José Maria Xavier (Father José Xavier State Music Conservatory), inaugurated by Governor Juscelino Kubitschek. The most influential of its first students was José Maria Neves (1943–2002), who went on to study and perform in Rio de Janeiro and France, returning to São João del-Rei with scholarly dedication to the city's music traditions, and to conduct the Orquestra Ribeiro Bastos. In 2006, the federal university system created a music department at the Federal University of São João del-Rei, joining the eleven existing state-run music conservatories in Minas Gerais.

Other Aspects of *Música Colonial*: Popular Music in Liturgy

By 1745, Minas Gerais had been divided into only 50 large parishes, a time when Portugal, at one-sixth the physical size, was organized into 3,987. The vast colonial captaincy grew to become Brazil's most populous, with a priest-to-parishioner ratio nearly twice that of coastal Brazilian captaincies. The Portuguese empire could not facilitate an orthodox church presence and banned the first orders from the region, leaving lay brotherhoods to organize most church activities. Of the eight administrative *vilas* (cities) created by Portuguese authorities in colonial Minas Gerais, only five were assigned official chapel masters, who were appointed by bishops and assumed professional responsibility for arranging performances and contracting musicians. These five cities, São João del-Rei, Sabará, Pitangui, Vila Rica, and Serro, each administered its own vast territory and an array of settlements situated at great distances.[37] The network of widely dispersed urban settlements and scarcity of church hierarchy challenged every chapel master's logistical ability to uphold the orthodox traditions of Iberian Catholicism and Council of Trent obligations. Chapel masters could not engage their entire constituency nor satisfy the needs of every religious service demanded of them. The situation led to the contracting and further subcontracting of professional and amateur musicians, resulting in comparatively unsupervised musical practices including the incorporation of secular and profane music. Meanwhile, due to the great number of black and mixed-race musicians looking for opportunities in professional and social advancement, many non-white musicians began filling positions, contrary to church and state laws and customs. While a distinct *barroco mineiro* cathedral-based culture flourished in the Golden Age, much of the musical practice in outlying parishes struggled to adhere to basic church doctrine. In a 1751 letter from the bishop of Mariana to Dom José I, the king of Portugal, the bishop disparagingly attributes inappropriate church music to mixed-race musicians:

> [There is] much profanity and indecency in the music sung in church festivities, in both lyrics and notes, because the musicians are almost all typically inadequate *pardos*. Also, the chapel masters take exorbitant fees through contracting musicians. . . . In order to avoid profanities and indecency, order a provision stating that if songs sung in churches and chapels are not performed in Latin, and if the notes are not in observance of the provisions of the Council of Trent, each district is to be inspected by a chapel master; and that the fees not be so excessive, as has become the rule.[38]

As musicologist Rubens Ricciardi states in his research on Mineiro composer Manuel Dias de Oliveira, the colonial-era musical practices of the Catholic liturgy "were more disordered or chaotic than can be imagined today."[39] Musicologist and leading *música colonial* scholar Paulo Castagna points to the sense of distance at which this busy yet scattered liturgical world of the Brazilian interior existed in relation to both church doctrine and issues of European musical styles:

> [Neither] cathedral regulations [nor] agreements with musicians contracted by brotherhoods and orders [defined] the style of the desired music, bequeathing this task to the chapel masters or to [those contracting music ensembles]. These musicians . . . did not always have access to all Tridentine liturgical doctrine [relating to Council of Trent commands of 1545–1563], [and they selected music] with or without the guidance of members of these institutions—principally in the musical repertoire received from Europe.[40]

Colonial Minas Gerais thus offered two ends of the orthodoxy spectrum, and perhaps everything in between: the grandeur of its sacred *música colonial*, studied and archived today and forming an increasingly important cornerstone of Brazil's original voice in colonial-era music, and "religiosity without religion," the often unorthodox, even profane practices of outlying churches, dominated by socially marginalized lay communities further challenged by great distances; the latter included classical music such as overtures and other festive works, popular music, and entertaining Afro-Brazilian genres. French sociologist Roger Bastide touches on the struggles within the brotherhood system and notes the racial discrepancies regarding worship music:

> In 1585, the pope sanctioned the establishment of brotherhoods of the famous Girdle of Saint Francis, white with three knots. [In the eighteenth century,] [t]he mulattoes of São João del-Rei, Sabará, Mariana, and Vila Rica seized the chance to organize chapters of this brotherhood in Minas since the Third Order was closed to them. The Tertiaries protested, not wishing to see people of color sneak into their white churches through the back door to hold celebrations "with guitars and drums [as the complaint to Lisbon stated] or participate in processions . . . as though they were no different from honest white people."[41]

The "guitars and drums" cited above indicate the extent of popularized, lay Catholic practices characterizing non-white, subaltern devotional worship. But the complaint focuses on racial and class boundaries more than the specific question of orthodoxy and music. These commercial agents, colonial administration functionaries, and writers and intellectuals with academic degrees conveyed their elite sentiment that people of color could worship however they wished, but that they should not be allowed to do so in a Franciscan church reserved for brotherhoods of the tertiary orders of Carmo and São Francisco. Furthermore, a solution would require measures issued from Lisbon, not from the local Franciscan authorities, as they were banned from the captaincy. Brazil's great history of popular Catholicism, as long displayed in the Folia de Reis tradition and Congado, has roots in Iberian folk Catholicism and Brazil's early trajectories of locally determined, non-orthodox practice.[42] Low rates of religious instruction among poor whites likely echoed similar conditions for the nonliterate, mixed-race lower classes, freed blacks, and enslaved laborers.

Nineteenth-century visitors to the Mineiro interior observed varied church musical practices, as Irish reverend Robert Walsh noted in 1829 in São José del-Rei,

The worthy mulatto priest . . . had received from a friend from Rio some English songs composed of peasant dances and marches of which the title's significance he does not understand. So, it was not to our surprise when during the religious service he errantly played "March of the Duke of York" and concluded his allegro with "Dance at Old Nick's House." To us it sounded extremely absurd and even profane. But not to him, nor the rest of his listeners, for whom the music did not arouse associations with such an idea. A dissident priest once noted there was no reason that Satan should monopolize all the good music.[43]

German-Argentine botanist Hermann Burmeister noted during his visit to church services in Congonhas during 1851:

On solemn occasions a choir is organized, which meets in the balcony above the entrance, [and] there is the playing of Strauss waltzes, popular melodies, batuques or lundus, the overture of one or the other opera and anthem of the Mineiros . . . but no note of sacred music is heard.[44]

Some Catholic festival day processions were understandably ripe for alternatives in musical style, content, and delivery due to the popularity of such variations among socially marginalized laypersons, the isolation of the communities, and lax church oversight. That is how Auguste de Saint-Hilaire noted São João del-Rei's Ash Wednesday celebration of 1819, where he found the procession to be an irreverent mix of singing clowns and near-respectable Catholic formality. The local priest shared his disapproval of the superficial religiosity of the festivities.[45] Sometimes, local priests supported or engaged in profane celebrations during church calendar events, as notes José Ramos Tinhorão regarding "festive priests of Minas" who transformed Catholic traditions such as the Espírito Santo processional into a "true carnival parade."[46]

Baroque Festivals: Vila Rica's Triunfo Eucarístico

From above the cathedral of Our Lady of the Pillar's entrance, light pours through clear glass, illuminating the nave's sumptuous interior, beckoning the Ouro Preto faithful into one of Brazil's most richly appointed churches—an elaborately designed ten-sided interior bathed in gold leaf, ornamental gilded sculpture, and paintings. The massive altar alone is said to be covered in four hundred kilograms of gold. This is where Lobo de Mesquita carried out his duties at the very close of the eighteenth century. Following the completion of a 1733 renovation, this baroque church was the center of a famously elaborate, two-day-long festival known as the Triunfo Eucarístico (Triumphant Eucharist), an example of what historian Camila Santiago describes as the "baroque soul's hunger for playful festivity, sharpened by the region's enormous wealth derived from gold."[47] The pomp of the Triunfo Eucarístico presented music, theater, and dance along with Masses at the Rosary and Pillar churches, coupled with stunning displays of the state power of the Portuguese court. The spectacle accompanied a solemn transfer of the Holy Sacrament back to the Pillar cathedral from the church of the Rosary of the Blacks, where it had been sheltered during renovations. Floats, parading dancers, and richly costumed actors depicted the cosmos, the four winds, the sun, moon, planets, and constellations, bringing to city streets a theater of the Catholic universe governed by church hierarchy and the majestic scope of power projected by Portuguese king Dom João V (1707–1750).

The Pillar cathedral belonged to the elite whites of the Holy Sacrament brotherhood. Blacks, whether free or enslaved, were allowed only to stand in the rear passageways. Yet the black brotherhood of the Rosary was far more integral to the Triunfo Eucarístico than simply having housed the holy sacrament and participating in the procession. Competing in rivalrous manner with other brotherhoods, as was common, Rosary blacks contributed funds, constructed a road between the two churches for the processions, and paid for the Lisbon printing of Simon Ferreira Machado's account of the festival the following year, "redefining the triumph by turning the celebration of the Eucharist into an act of self-celebration," as historian Lisa Voigt suggests.[48] The historical record of black musicians' presence in these events is valuable as evidence of such racial inclusion, whereby participation by low-social-status Mineiros in elite-brokered festivals was made possible by the institution of the brotherhoods. A Luso-Iberian festivity best exemplified during Dom João V's reign, the celebration's fireworks, theatrical displays, and sumptuous costuming expressed both monarchic power and, through "royal patronage," the solemnity of the church: the Vatican had for over two centuries delegated to Portuguese rulers the control of the church within the kingdom. Lisbon's monarchic authorities needed a show of state and church power in Minas Gerais, a theatrical display complementing the force of the

Portuguese Inquisition and its small army of prosecutors and familiars. The Triunfo Eucarístico helped establish religious control where a dragnet was in the process of selectively crushing African-derived practices such as calundú and attacking the secular batuque dance. Another elaborate baroque festival illustrating the mid-eighteenth-century pomp and power of church and state was the Áureo Trono Episcopal (Golden Episcopal Throne), welcoming Bishop Dom Frei Manuel da Cruz to the recently created bishopric of Mariana in 1748. The public procession included a local *caboclo guarda* of the Congado tradition (see chapter 6). As mentioned in chapter 2, during Bishop Cruz's first year in office, he ordered the public whipping of two black slave women accused of pacts with the devil, one being Rosa Maria Egipcíaca da Vera Cruz.

Choromeleiros of Minas Gerais

Accounts of the Áureo Trono Episcopal and Triunfo Eucarístico have brought to light what historian Elizabeth Kiddy cites as "the best known example of the rosary brotherhood participation in public celebrations from the first half of the eighteenth century."[49] Celebrants paraded draped in white silk robes, some carrying gold- and diamond-fitted statues of Our Lady, Saint Benedict, and Saint Anthony of Categero (Carthage). Forming a small yet impressive part of their procession through Vila Rica's cobblestone streets were eight gallantly dressed black musicians playing the double-reed instrument known as the *choromel* (shawm) in alternation with a bugle player. The *choromeleiro* tradition, with partial roots in the Iberian troubadour heritage, was transplanted from Portugal to Minas, where the term eventually applied generically to an array of ensembles composed mostly of mixed-race musicians. Iconographic sources from sixteenth-century Portugal reveal formally dressed black musicians performing with *choromels* and other wind and brass instruments. Thirteenth-century Galician Portuguese codices known as the *Cantigas de Santa Maria* reveal iconographic details of *choromels* of an earlier Iberian era. In colonial Minas Gerais, trained instrumentalists retained hopes of achieving professional status in their manumitted freedom. In 1717, the recently appointed governor of the newly created Captaincy of Minas Gerais was assigned such professional musicians for his tours. Documents note that when the Count of Assumar began his residence in Vila Rica, "six black pages and four *charmeleiros*" were put at his disposal to distract His Excellency.[50] As Reily states, brotherhoods hired ensembles of black *choromel* players (*ternos de choromeleiros*) and drummers (*tambores*)

> to collect donations for their festivals, to play during processions and to pro-
> vide street entertainment between the religious ceremonies of the festivals.
> Although these musicians generally had limited formal musical training, they
> played by ear, and some became quite accomplished. Often the musicians
> used by the brotherhoods were rented to the association by their owners.[51]

Francisco Curt Lange suggests that certain enslaved musicians were "expert" players, contradicting the above suggestion that black *choromeleiros* had only limited training. In Lange's research on *choromeleiros* and church accounting records, he relates that with regard to celebrations ordered by Governor Luis da Cunha Menezes in Vila Rica during 1786,

> in private, closed places, there were musical groups brought together consist-
> ing of *charamelas* (*choromeylleyros*, as they say), and various types of wind
> instruments, but all integrated with instruments designed for classical music.
> The strings (violins, violas, cellos, and double basses) were added not only
> in theatrical plays but also in open festivities with alternating choral spec-
> tacles, always praised for their quality. The *choromeleiros* constituted very old,
> Portuguese troubadour traditions from the "time of the kings."[52]

Lange stresses the slave status of some of the musicians in further discussion of the Mineiro music culture:

> The popularity and frequent occurrence of the *charamelas* in the social life of
> Minas are illustrated by the purchase made by Capitão-Mor Henrique Lopes
> in 1717 of "three black *choromeleiros* costing four thousand cruzados," join-
> ing the orchestra, musical groups, and choirs to improve the reception of
> Governor Dom Pedro de Almeida in his travels through Minas Gerais. These
> musicians [black *choromeleiros*] were always dressed in finery "of Berne fabric
> with matching linings" according to the chronicle. These slaves were expert
> players of diverse wind instruments, and their cultivated repertoire belonged
> to the fine art music of the day.[53]

Although the *choromeleiro* was a backbone of colonial-era music in Minas, the region's post–gold rush economic decline led to the collapse of the profession. Precious funds for ranks of trained musicians slowly vanished. This local subculture was then also challenged by the relocation of many skilled, free musicians seeking opportunities in the growing cosmopolitanism of early nineteenth-century Rio de Janeiro. Later in the nineteenth century, economic and demographic shifts favoring coffee plantation culture in Sul de Minas prompted the development of slave-based fazenda bands. This destiny of the *choromeleiro* heritage is outlined by Tamara Elena Livingston-Isenhour and Thomas George Caracas Garcia in their history of Rio de Janeiro's urban popular music known as choro, a truncation of *choromel*:

> [There is] substantial historical evidence documenting the musical instrumentation employed in the choromeleiro, [and] its development in the interior state of Minas Gerais. . . . Choromeleiro came to mean a group with charamelas [shawms] as well as the musician who played the instrument. Over time, the term came to designate any musician, regardless of instrument, who played in an ensemble that included charamelas. Eventually the flute supplanted the charamela as the wind instrument of choice; because the charamela was loud and suitable only for playing outdoors, the versatility of the ensemble increased with the permanent addition of the flute. Even after the charamela had become obsolete, any instrumental ensemble with a wind instrument was called choromeleiro, including the choro *terno* [group] of flute, cavaquinho, and guitar.[54]

Although Lange's overly ambitious notion of *mulatismo musical* falls short of the claim that the Minas School created its own distinct style of liturgical music, the musicologist's groundbreaking research held a spotlight on the racial politics of colonial culture. As the *choromeleiro* tradition offered professional opportunities and livelihood to Afro-Mineiros, the Minas School also illustrates Brazil's skin color spectrum of racial divide. Brokering exceptions to whites-only laws that governed professional music, lighter-skinned Brazilians of color were deemed "more white than black" and were allowed opportunities and financial success. While black brotherhoods guarded professional music performance opportunities for their members, few Africans or African descendants with dark skin (those Afro-Brazilians known as *pretos*) were allowed to ascend to the positions of composer or musical director. This racialized social schema based on phenotype and the presence of white parentage, in which lighter-skinned mixed-race Brazilians slowly gained entry to upwardly mobile social opportunity, complements the harsher aspects of racial politics correlating blackness to African-derived beliefs and practices actively repressed by state and church authorities.[55] However, gradually emerging throughout Brazil, including in Minas during its time of economic decline, were multiracial civic and military bands (bandas) that developed institutionally as a secular, increasingly democratized alternative to the Golden Age lavishness of the Mineiro church experience.

Bandas: Military and Civic Bands, Fazenda Bands, and the Empire of Coffee

As Minas Gerais faced a long-term economic downturn after the 1760s, civic and military bands composed of wind, brass, and percussion instruments gradually displaced *choromeleiros* in the performance of formal, composed music. The cultivation of learned, notated music remained, too, in the salon-based repertoire of imperial-era modinhas. Arguably, these secular bands also partially assumed the spotlight from the sacred repertoire of preeminent regional liturgical composers in locales where their works were either lost or fell into disuse. It was during this long period, leading to Lange's discoveries in the 1940s, that many of the manuscripts and records of the region's liturgical treasures fell into obscurity. Formal musical band organizations (*corporações musicais*) and musical societies (*sociedades musicais*) gradually inherited the mantle of fine art music from the *barroco mineiro*, accompanying a rising bourgeoisie and dominant class during the imperial reigns of Dom Pedro I and his son, Dom Pedro II (together, 1823–1889).[56] Bandas became the core public experience of *música erudita* (erudite music, a common term in Brazil for classical music). In this sense, the region retained a stratum of musical culture associated with learned society, and bands began speaking to a broader imperial-era citizenry, cultivated among amateurs rather than professionals due to the region's harrowing economic decline. This was a transition of sorts, in the realm of trained musicians and fine art music, from the sacred to the secular, from the performers of the colonial church to the civically minded, more racially inclusive bands appearing in public squares and for events marking imperial rule. Civic and military bands drew from all racial backgrounds and socioeconomic classes within the growing cultural arena of the European-derived band ensemble.[57]

The first eighteenth-century military bands in Minas were assigned to the mixed-race colonial regular army, the militia and auxiliary troops who secured gold fields, roadways, and settlements. These bands typically consisted of some variation of trumpets, fifes, clarinets, bassoons, and drums. Membership in such bands was known on occasion to have led to a salary and opportunities to arrange or compose music.[58] The illustrious Minas baroque composers Lobo de Mesquita, Gomes da Rocha, and Dias de Oliveira each served in the militia.[59] In 1802, colonial authorities decreed that each infantry regiment include a band to perform for civic and religious events, and commemorations of important buildings. Countless small towns and cities featured at least one plaza bandstand. Nationwide, early nineteenth-century army and National Guard bands continued to recruit mostly black, mixed-race, and poor white musicians from rural areas, this during the period when the Portuguese royal court fled Napoleon and relocated to Rio in 1808.[60] Queen Maria I of Portugal and the prince regent (later Dom João VI), and their court of more than 14,500 people, had retreated from Napoleon's invasion and fled Lisbon for Rio de Janeiro in November 1807. Brazilian ports were then opened to foreign shipping, and the colonial capital of Rio de Janeiro became the seat of government, where the Portuguese Crown remained until the Liberal revolution of 1820, after which Dom João VI returned to Lisbon. For thirteen years, Rio de Janeiro was the court and administrative center of the global Portuguese empire.

The official military band that honored the royal family's arrival in Rio was augmented by the Portuguese Royal Marines Brigade Band (Música Marcial da Brigada Real da Marinha de Portugal), from which later emerged Brazil's Naval Marine Band. Bands were quickly created for the court's infantry and cavalry regiments.[61] An increasingly cosmopolitan Rio de Janeiro reshaped Brazil's musical identity in countless ways as the Braganza family's arrival was a foreshadowing of imperial Brazil, bringing a musical court life that bolstered the colonial-era military music of the former colony and soon to be empire. The royal family encouraged a music scene in Rio de Janeiro that eclipsed the decades-old legacy of Mineiro fine art music, creating a magnet for skilled musicians and composers. Between 1808 and 1821, the number of royal court musicians in Rio quadrupled from fewer than twenty-five to more than a hundred, including singers, instrumentalists, choir directors, and conductors.[62]

Brazil's socially inclusive, racially-mixed band tradition was reinforced by imperial design, and these ensembles began to ween from purely military function and repertoire, assuming wider roles in fine art music repertoire. Civic music association bands in urban centers developed apart from National Guard bands, first created in 1831. The new Brazilian monarchy supported military bands, while civic bands were often maintained by religious brotherhoods. Until the founding of Belo Horizonte's Orquestra Sinfônica in 1925, bandas were the only musical ensembles in Minas to receive government support. Imperial-era bands and music associations in Minas, including small string ensembles known as *liras*, proliferated throughout the nineteenth century, playing at the bandstands of public parks, at official festivities, during civic events, and for religious ceremonies.

Brazil's nineteenth-century band instrumentation typically included flutes, fifes, clarinets (including the *requinta*, an E♭ clarinet), cornets, trumpets, trombones, baritone horns, and tubas. Percussion sections featured bass drum, snare drums, various field drums, cymbals, triangle, and *prato* (a plate scraped and tapped with a knife). Traditional to the brass section into the early twentieth century was the now defunct ophicleide, a bass-register-keyed bugle invented in the early nineteenth century and later replaced by the tuba. A spin-off of formal band ensembles was the *charanga*, a small band playing popular music with these same instruments, discussed below in the context of traveling circuses. Conductors and musical directors became influential trendsetters by providing listeners with organized, large-ensemble musical experiences in the Mineiro heartland. The *marcha* and *marchinha* were associated with what was known as regiment music (*música dos regimentos*) and the martial traditions of the first half of the nineteenth-century.[63] The *dobrado* (*pasodoble*) is a binary form subgenre of the march, the up-tempo "double" with contrapuntal lines and a rich, symphonic approach to arranging for concert and symphonic bands. Throughout the remainder of the 1800s, the *marcha* and *dobrado* developed also within popular contexts, primarily as dance music in diverse genres such as the *rancho* and *pastoral*; European forms such as the waltz, polka, and mazurka; and other processional types later associated with carnival, before being nudged from the spotlight by the early twentieth-century urban samba.

Writing in early 1860s Diamantina, the British explorer Richard Burton noted how band music highlighted what he considered an otherwise dull social life: "As usual in the Brazilian interior, the city is guiltless of club, cafe, Mechanics' Institutes, Christian Young Men's Association and Mutual Improvement Societies, except for musical purposes; the bands, however, are all things considered, good."[64] Bandas of high caliber proliferated throughout the historical cities of the Mineiro interior, supported by societies and associations, the military, and other civic groups. The repertoire of the still extant Banda Carlos Gomes, discussed in chapter 8 below, included classical scores such as excerpts from *O Guarani*, an 1870 opera-ballet by Brazil's greatest Romantic-era composer, Antônio Carlos Gomes (1836–1896); Wagner's *Tannhäuser* (both performed during Belo Horizonte's inauguration); Viennese waltzes by the Strausses; and works by other well-known European composers. Photographs of turn-of-the-century Belo Horizonte bandas reveal mixed-race ensembles sometimes dominated by blacks.

Fazenda Bands

Fazenda bands developed from orchestras whose musicians were also forced laborers on large coffee plantations, some of which were located in the Sul de Minas and Zona da Mata subregions. By the mid-nineteenth century, coffee had supplanted sugar as Brazil's main export, and plantation owners promoted their special interests through national legislation governing slave labor and land rights, and by manipulating political decisions at every level. Wealthy coffee barons (*comendadors*) of the Paraíba Valley and other areas in the states of Rio de Janeiro, Minas Gerais, and São Paulo soon came to form Brazil's class of ruling oligarchs, who brokered the abdication of Dom Pedro II and the rise of the republic. Yet railroads had not yet penetrated the interior, and large coffee fazendas were often isolated affairs, the epicenter of life for many hundreds of people working and living in proximity to the core agricultural activities of planting, maintaining, and harvesting crops. Enslaved musicians performing sacred music and secular entertainment were both functional elements of plantation life and displays of wealth by rural elites. James Fletcher and Daniel Kidder published a rare and insightful account of a slave orchestra at the Soledade fazenda in Sul de Minas (becoming in 1901 its own administrative district called Soledade de Minas):

> The Comendador told us that he had his "own music now." . . . We desired to hear his musicians, supposing that we should bear a wheezy plantation-fiddle, a fife,

and a drum.... An hour after vespers I heard the twanging of violins, the tuning of flutes, short voluntaries on sundry bugles, the chattering of trombones, and all those musical symptoms preparatory to a beginning of some march, waltz, or polka. I went to the room whence proceeded these sounds; there I beheld fifteen slave musicians,—a regular band: one presided at an organ, and there was a choir of younger negroes arranged before suitable stands, upon which were sheets of printed or manuscript music. I also observed a respectable colored gentleman (who sat near me at dinner) giving various direction. He was the maestro. Three raps of his violin bow commanded silence.... [T]he orchestra commenced the execution of an overture to some opera with admirable skill and precision.... But the next piece overwhelmed me with surprise: the choir, accompanied by the instruments, performed a Latin mass. They sang from their notes, and little darkies from twelve to sixteen years of age read off the words with as much fluency as students in the Freshman year.

The plantation's chapel was the center of religious activity. Liturgical music augmented the duties of musicians and fazenda bands, who also played programs of secular music for the purpose of regular entertainment.

While at supper we were regaled by waltzes and stirring marches, among the latter "Lafayette's Grand March," composed in the United States. [Later] I was awakened by a servant, who informed me that the orchestra was about to play the *Brazileiro* in honor of O Senhor Comendador's guests; and in a few minutes the band, with the addition of big drum, little drum, and cymbals, startled the early birds by the national anthem of Brazil.[65]

The demand for accomplished slave musicians led to the establishment of music schools, which were often run by Jesuit priests. Many *fazendeiros* kept business and political ties in Rio de Janeiro and were influenced by urban trends and fashions, "including music, and their bands were expected to play the latest urban songs and dance music at rural parties.... [The *fazendeiros*] demonstrated their wealth in many ways ... [including] the size and ability of their bands."[66] In carrying the torch of fine art music, fazenda bands simultaneously emerged as catalysts in the development of Brazilian popular music. Dominated by blacks, fazenda bands constituted another source for the urban choro music tradition emerging in Rio de Janeiro during the latter half of the nineteenth century; Junior Callado (1848–1880) is regarded as the iconic driving force behind the genre. During the second half of the nineteenth century, Rio de Janeiro composers Anecleto Medeiros (1866–1907) and Chiquinha Gonzaga (1847–1935) adapted European dance forms to a contemporary, Brazilianized band repertoire of *xotes, polcas, marchas, valses,* and *dobrados.*[67]

Circus *Charangas*

Nineteenth-century traveling circus tent shows created significant musical venues, and they often contracted local wind, brass, and percussion players for their *charangas,* another professional opportunity for instrumentalists.[68] From the 1830s well into the 1900s, traveling circuses brought entertainment to disparate Mineiro towns and cities. Moving from place to place with ox carts, these road shows journeyed over the old, precarious roads of imperial Minas. The Chiarini circus visited São João del-Rei and other Mineiro cities as early as the 1830s; performers were described as masters of gymnastic arts, dancers of fandangos and castanets, and rope balancers. Locals eager for entertainment welcomed the transformation of *praças,* empty lots, and clearings at the edge of town into rare, illuminated spectacles. This was good business for touring groups such as the Circo Zoológico Brasileiro, Spinelli, Pavilhão Circo Zoológico Francês, Casali, Circo Sotero, and Circo Eqüestre. Belo Horizonte, with its regional centrality and growing population, was a profitable destination well into the twentieth century. *Charangas* whipped up potential audiences by playing in advance of opening night, serenading the town with classical and popular music arrangements. Circus perform-ers, primarily clowns, played viola and *violão* while singing popular songs between acts by jugglers, acrobats, and animal trainers. Singing clowns such as Eduardo das Neves and the Mineiro Benjamin Oliveira became widely known stars skillfully performing traditional modinhas, the latest songs from Rio de Janeiro, and *canções reportagens* (news songs).[69] They were trouba-dour-like messengers predating the rise of radio. Citing an 1893 article in the Barbacena, Minas Gerais, newspaper *A Folha,* Regina Horta Duarte describes the music of the circus, including singing clowns and *charanga* bands:

> Often their dialogues mingled with madcap singing accompanied by a lit-tle band consisting of trumpet, piccolo, sax, bass, bass drum and cymbals.

The musicality of the clown's performance generously extended the nights of circus spectacles. A few moments before the start of the show, the band animated the audience's entry, "rustling the air." After everyone was seated, the musicians entered the bandstand, "constructed over the tunnel to the ring's backstage." . . . [P]iccolos and trumpets played triumphal marches to the arrival of the performers: "the master, with frizzed hair and a coat decorated in medals, greeted the public while wielding a whip; the artists, dancers in costumes, did cartwheels, the strong man and the trapeze acrobat sported tough arm and leg muscles through their clothing, the clown with a red-tinged face made comical reverence."[70]

Duarte continues:

Music was not confined to the performance's opening. Throughout the spectacle, it accompanied the numbers, creating and reinforcing emotions. In the presentation of difficult aerialist jumps, "when the entire audience was focused," the band, "in a slow waltz and amid whispers, made a sonorous background." Ending the act, "a galloping march style" invaded the circus, as the running horse exited the ring, followed by the "beautiful girl" who rode and performed all sorts of stunts, "earning applause and sparking desires in the hearts of the young men, some married." The most touching moments would often be evoked along with the sounds that surrounded them. A boy, watching the "dance of the giant," would never forget the "special music" performed during those magical moments.[71]

Classical Music in Minas Gerais
Following the Economic Decline

Throughout the Mineiro interior, young musicians interested and able in classical music typically gained homespun amateur training from a parent or older family member, or learned music from the dwindling number of private teachers marking the region's past urban experience. In the second decade of nineteenth-century Minas, more than 330 teachers (*professores de arte da música*) officially registered with the confraternity of Saint Cecília.[72] Successful amateur composers and performers maintained separate professional activities and livelihoods, and musicians in larger towns and cities engaged regional salon culture as they enlivened the soirées and bailes in private homes with modinhas, lundu songs, and opera arias. Like the growing banda tradition, modinha-based salons represented another secular move away from the region's diminished cultivation of sacred *barroco mineiro* repertoire. Although strongly linked to urban popular culture, both modinhas and lundu songs kept one foot in the world of classical music, as nativist styles and forms tended to by Brazilian composers who notated their work. The modinha ("short song") was the Brazilian answer to the light French chanson, sentimental poetry set to lyrical vocal melodies accompanied by keyboard, viola, or guitar.[73] Volume 4 of the Música do Brasil Colonial series published by the Museu da Inconfidência is dedicated to modinhas, lundus, and other secular salon-style works associated with the imperial period; the volume features several modinhas by Manoel Severo Figueiredo Netto (1825–1893, b. Diamantina), among others. The viola had a place in the fine art music of the eighteenth- and nineteenth-century salon culture of the coastal cities, where imperial Brazil's aristocracy hosted European music and gentrified stylizations of Brazilian modinhas and lundu songs. This was the audience of Rio de Janeiro–born Domingos Caldas Barbosa (1740–1800), the mixed-race poet and *violeiro* who later championed his innovative secular songs and instrumental style in Lisbon's royal circles. The published modinhas and lundu songs of Brazilian composers following Barbosa's style are still performed in recitals and concerts, as instrumentals and as art songs performed with bel canto vocal technique. Barbosa incorporated the viola into his innovative lundu salon songs in Rio de Janeiro during the Golden Age of Minas Gerais. He performed for the upper classes a sophisticated derivation of an already established rural lundu dance genre that had attracted viola players as accompanists to singers and dancers, a genre that was experiencing a transitional stage of urban popularization.[74] Modinhas composed by Mineiros can be found in archives also housing sacred works from the region.

Economic decline was a primary cause of the demise of the Minas School of liturgical composition. But it was not the only blow to the region's Golden Age of learned music culture. It was at this point when Mineiros seeking a formal musical education relocated to Rio de Janeiro to attend the Conservatório de Música, founded in 1841. This school became the Instituto Nacional de Música in 1890, following the founding of the republic (and is now the Federal University of Rio de Janeiro School of Music). Musical life in nineteenth-century Rio de Janeiro flourished with an array of imperial-era theaters, visiting European professors, performers, and ensembles, including touring operas and theater groups. The city was Brazil's imperial capital, a powerful, neutral municipality (*município neutro*) politically independent from the administrative province of Rio de Janeiro. An increasing number of Brazilians who graduated from the formal music institutions in Rio would begin seeking further training in Europe, primarily Italy.

Leaving Arnon's rehearsal space, I reflect on the contemporary Brazilian musicians and scholars dedicated to understanding and interpreting region-defining slices of the Mineiro past. The repertoire of conservative Catholicism, seemingly lost for a century and a half, reemerged as a historical legacy almost magically in the middle of the twentieth century, and appeared in practical performance editions and recordings decades later. A rediscovered treasure was somehow lifted out of history by Francisco Curt Lange and others, and today is admired for its rarified beauty and religiosity, associated simultaneously with the refined art of *música erudita* and the near folk-like *música colonial* from the Mineiro interior. There, in the architectural splendor of historical cities, far more works by anonymous composers, whose names are lost to time, also breathe again. Although Suzel Ana Reily here speaks of the religiosity of the local liturgical traditions she studied in Sul de Minas, her words arguably apply generally to a regional sensibility developed over time, when "discourses linking the cultivation of high art to social distinction developed and the preservation of the baroque legacy came to represent the discerning tastes of the Mineiros. . . . [G]ood taste coalesced around the legacy of the gold era, defining regional identity."[75] The rise of Belo Horizonte would mark a modern break with the Mineiro past, symbolizing an independent republic's turn away from colonial and imperial epochs, the new city assuming its place of regional centrality after the fall of slavery. The fine art legacy of Minas Gerais would find a new home here. Now, walking back through the bustling Funcionários district to Avenida Afonso Pena, I turn my ear to listen, ready for a new Hearing of Brazil that will require an understanding of Belo Horizonte as a city of music.

Chapter 5

Batuque

The percussion-driven batuque circle dance arrived in Brazil with enslaved Central Africans and became a national pastime attracting participants across racial and class lines. This chapter considers batuque as an Afro-Mineiro tradition indicative of the region's social development, foregrounding it against the national backdrop, in which the dance played a pivotal role in the formation of samba. Its associated spiritual beliefs and modes of ancestor devotion helped facilitate communal resistance to both slavery and the socioeconomic marginalization of free persons. Drumming propelled the circle dance and its transformative effect on social spaces, bringing Brazilians together while mediating individual and collective memory in festive celebration. Throughout its more than five-hundred-year presence in Brazil, batuque has been beholden neither to a religious calendar nor a ritual orthodoxy, spreading so widely throughout colonial and imperial Minas that some nineteenth-century foreign travelers mistakenly assumed that enslaved Mineiros were allowed to dance, play music, and sing while working, reinforcing the myth that Brazil had developed a more humanized system of slavery. As a creolized mainstay in colonial and imperial Brazil, the dance in various forms slowly became popularized across social and color lines as a recreational entertainment celebrated in public streets and squares, private homes, taverns, and stores. While batuque grew to complement the Afro-Mineiro legacies of calundú, vissungo, Congado, and capoeira, what emerged as an

African-derived expression increasingly embraced by non-blacks character-izes Brazilian popular culture's changing attitudes toward race.

The most detailed published description of a pre-twentieth-century batuque dance in Minas Gerais was written by visiting botanist Hermann Burmeister somewhere near Mariana in 1851:

> The batuque is danced with two to four people, each having the right to include spectators in the dance. It consists of hip movements and simple steps; their bodies walk, jump, and shimmy, each pair trying to stay as close as possible to each other without touching. Sometimes they stamp their feet, clap their hands, or snap their fingers, for which the women have a remark-able ability. . . . When a man and woman dance, the tempo is often more moderate and the movements more decent, especially if there are strangers among the spectators.[1]

Dances of many types, including the quadrille and the Iberian-derived fan-dango, enlivened Mineiro society after the region's first gold rush settlements were established at the dawn of the eighteenth century. Yet in the nineteenth century, batuque is the musical activity most frequently cited by European and North American botanists, geologists, and engineers chronicling their expeditions in imperial Minas. The dance's popularity has been revealed in private and official letters exchanged among colonial and imperial admin-istrators in Minas Gerais, in the wording of laws and ordinances, and in the historically valuable, sometimes detailed records and testimonials in church archives. These sources tended to criminalize batuque, portraying it as a dance associated with blacks and African-descendant communities, yet transitioning toward more diverse racial and socioeconomic groups that had begun embracing the free-spirited pastime. Despite its associations with segregated, marginalized classes, and its erratic criminalization by church, municipal, and colonial authorities, batuque became an accepted cultural currency increasingly enjoyed in burgeoning colonial-era cities such as Vila Rica. Musicologist Fábio Henrique Viana notes:

> Despite attempts to repress [the dance] throughout the eighteenth century, "batuque was danced almost every night," and during work breaks, particu-larly taking advantage of church holidays. By the end of century, the dance had finally been accepted by the Vila Rica elite, whose "ladies, who were once

not allowed to say the word," became "calm spectators of this extremely free dance without anyone being surprised."[2]

On a national level, batuque rhythms emerged as nativist Brazilian musical expressions thematized in late nineteenth-century works by Rio de Janeiro fine art concert music composers such as Alexandre Levy (1864–1892) and Alberto Nepomuceno (1864–1920). They appropriated and adapted popularized Afro-Brazilian dance music styles as what was by then a nationalist point of pride among their elite circles. This ascendance of social status for a folk practice previously associated with the lowest classes of society was also facilitated by the generalized use of the term "batuque" for a variety of Afro-Brazilian dances such as *caxambú, quimbête, coco, calango, sarambeque,* and *sorongo,* all genres encountered in Mineiro cultural history. Other dance genres such as *cateretê* (discussed in chapter 7) had evolved from nineteenth-century Afro-Mineiro practice; *cateretê* was seen as a key to African-descendent cultural resistance in Minas and other southeastern black communities.[3] Some practitioners within the batuque popular dance galaxy also danced the lundu, a secular couple's genre that arguably emerged from the fragmented practices of calundú and that was eventually appropriated and adapted by Brazilian elites as the gentrified, urban salon-based lundu song beginning in the latter part of the eighteenth century. Mixing fandango with dances from Portugal and Africa, lundu choreography set itself apart from batuque's free-form improvisations, a process also seen in the development and popularization of samba beginning around 1850, discussed below.

Looking for Batuque's Past

The term "batuque" originated from a Bantu term for an Angolan dance, *butuco* or *batuco,* conflated with the Portuguese verb *bater* (to hit), and further resonated with *bateria,* a term for percussion ensemble. Non-Bantu corruptions of the word's original meaning grew to apply to various African-derived dances, likely originating in late fifteenth-century Lisbon, where black dances (*bailes de pretos*) enlivened public festivities and Catholic processions such as the Corpo de Deus.[4] Through the dance's early, ubiquitous presence in Brazil, ritualized Afro-Brazilian religious sects in Rio Grande do Sul became known as *batuque,* and in Belém, Pará, several thousand kilometers to the north, the term references the houses of worship of syncretic religious sects. In fact, though valuable in historical descriptions, often unreliable vagaries surrounding the word "batuque" in historical literature make it suspect. Rather, what were batuque's functions, instrumentation, and musical and dance styles as described in these accounts and documents, and how did batuque relate to social development in Minas Gerais? For certain a circle dance accompanied by percussion, little is known about batuque's specific historical development in terms of dance styles or formal musical practices.

Batuque's possible origins in African fertility rites likely engendered early European notions of lascivious sexuality in the pelvic thrusts of the *umbigada*, the choreographic touching of the navels by male and female dancers (from the Portuguese *umbigo*, navel) frequently cited by Brazilian, Portuguese, and other observers in their descriptions of batuque. Brazilian scholar Edison Carneiro (1912–1972) noted in his studies of Bantu culture the touching of bellies as a Central African dance tradition, and the continued use in southeastern Brazil of the phrase *batuque de umbigada*.[5] Thirteen-year-old Alice Dayrell Caldeira Brant of Diamantina (pen name Helena Morley, 1880–1970), wrote in her diary on December 9, 1894:

> I gobbled up my dinner and went to the senzala. I swear I never saw such a wonderful party. There are only three Blacks at the chácara now who came from Africa: Bemfica, Quintiliano, and Mainarte. They sang songs from their land, turning round and round and clapping their hands and then bumping bellies with the women. The Blacks from here are jealous of the old ones who know the African songs and who dance with more spirit.[6]

It is necessary to disentangle two historical modes of (mis)interpretation that intertwine batuque's heritage, both complicated by the fragmentation and misunderstandings caused by the social ravages of slavery, racism, and colonialism. The first concerns the nature of an original batuque, perhaps as an African fertility rite, and its subsequent stylistic and functional transformation into a social practice fracturing under the violence of slavery. Batuque, after having lost some connection to its specific, original social function and stylistic denotation, became a hybridization of spiritual embodiment and quotidian entertainment, a wedding of celebratory collective memory with compelling, locally determined music and dance traditions. Dislocation from its origins led to a broadening of its functions, an inclusive range of musical styles and instrumentation, and admixtures of quasi-sacred and secular experiences that blurred Western notions of religiosity and entertainment. A second historical mode of (mis)interpretation emerged from negatively racialized discourse, bigotry's dismissive judgments, and cultural ignorance among European and Brazilian observers who constituted the cultural outsider viewpoint and who documented Afro-Brazilian music prior to the twentieth century. Many such observations, as valuable as they might be for certain historical details, often degenerate into sweeping, pejorative judgments and assumptions, misidentifying social functions through what could have been willful disregard. Most social outsiders simply dismissed the seriousness and sacredness of black expression, reducing such percussion-based music and dance, and their use of African languages, to a purposefully undiscerned, subaltern cultural background, undeserving of careful description.

Batuque and Samba in 1860s Minas Gerais

A brief consideration of samba's tangled nineteenth-century origins sheds light on Mineiro cultural history. During the early to mid-nineteenth-century rise of southeastern Brazil's coffee economy, the demand for domestic forced labor brought both African- and Brazilian-born slaves south from the economically depressed northeastern provinces. Meanwhile, a huge increase of newly enslaved Congolese Angolans began entering the Mineiro subregions of Campo das Vertentes, Sul de Minas, and Zona da Mata. The coffee boom generated a newly imported slave population larger than that of the prior colonial era, and within two generations it far surpassed the total number of enslaved Africans sent to the territory that became the United States. Between 1826 and 1850, at least 733,000 slaves were shipped to "Brazil South of Bahia," mainly to the Sudeste coffee latifundia.[7] Roughly half of the Africans shipped to Rio de Janeiro during the 1820s continued directly to Minas,[8] where forced labor was also needed to slash, burn, and clear-cut the once mighty Mata Atlântica rainforest acre by acre, fazenda by fazenda, to make way for new coffee fields and to produce lumber and fuel for new towns and the region's fledgling iron foundry furnaces: iron ore emerged to replace gold as the region's primary mining sector and principle raw export material.

The imperative use of the word "samba," shouted by batuque dancers in this burgeoning southeastern subculture, suggests that enslaved Central Africans introduced that term to Brazil within contexts of existing batuque performance.[9] A Bantu term for navel, *semba*, suggests the nineteenth-century emergence of rural samba's distinct trajectory from within the orbit of batuque's *umbigada* choreography. This southeastern melting pot of batuque likely helped spawn samba during the second half of the nineteenth century, a scenario differing wildly from the widely held theory that samba originated strictly in Bahia and traveled to Rio de Janeiro with postemancipation blacks, where it emerged as a popularized style around the turn of the twentieth century. A revisionist history posits samba, as a term designating a mannerized dance, as having possible origins in the rural polyglot of southeastern batuque dance cultures. Brazilian writer José Ramos Tinhorão dates the earliest Brazilian documentation of the word "samba" to 1859, in the northeastern state of Ceará, stating that "this transformation from the chaotic batuque of the early colonial period, to circle dances with some choreographic order, with the name samba, must have happened in a rural area."[10] Only eight years following this earliest known documented use of the term "samba" in Brazil, the word was used in Minas Gerais by visiting English agent Richard Burton in his 1867 description of a festive, mixed-race dance in Saco Grande:

> A small crowd [was] preparing for the samba, that is, passing the "Holy Saturday" and perhaps the "Holy Sunday" with dance and drink. The men carried shotguns in their hands and knives in their belts—proof that they were not willing to be recruited [to dance]. The women were dressed up as if for a gala—their lustrous hair colored blood red; but of the dozens of them, none were entirely white.[11]

It would not have been impossible for a stylized dance recently developed in the northeast to have spread from Ceará to Minas Gerais in a few years during the middle of the nineteenth century. It is a safe assumption that the samba to which Burton referred during his time near Mariana would have featured the stylized dance of the same name. Equally probable was that he chose to use the term "samba" (rather than batuque, lundu, *festa*, or baile) because he heard others using it. That is, Burton would not have appropriated the word from some previous experience and then unilaterally applied it to a dance he later witnessed. In his extensive writings about his travels through Minas, Burton never used the word before, or after, this 1867 anecdote.

The origins of samba aside, it is the nature of batuque, and its place in Mineiro and Afro-Mineiro history, that is of most concern here. Though rightfully connecting samba to batuque practice, Tinhorão's characterization of the latter as "chaotic" is problematic in its dismissive rush to distinguish its improvisational aspects from the since valorized and nationalized choreographic traits of the samba style. Although improvisation within locally determined, free-form batuque can be fairly characterized as having lacked a consistently mannerized, stylized choreography, its nonstandardized spontaneity likely defined its staying power: the "chaos" to which Tinhorão refers was really a rich array of African-derived dance and music aesthetics, modes of collective memory, and vitally creative, improvised performance practices. This free-form style of batuque was elemental in its stockpile of musical antidotes to slavery's brutality and dehumanization, and to the social marginalization of people of color in twentieth-century Brazil. Rather than representing merely a lack of style (thus inimitable by cultural outsiders, namely urban whites), batuque presented a wellspring of improvised corporeal and oral communication both topical and spiritual, remaining a fresh, expressive cultural form. Yet samba's rise to a nationalized style diminished the value of batuque both as a dance and as a historical reference to a tradition, which now appears as a mere cultural backdrop to the national pastime. With respect to this discursive, cultural devaluation of batuque as a result of samba's rise, and its subsequent loss of meaning for Afro-Brazilians, Carlos Sandroni states that batuque no longer referred to a particular dance, and therefore "this generic sense of the word [batuque] was valid until the start of the twentieth century, when, as we will see, the word 'samba' became more commonly used."[12] But what of the actual practice of batuque, and its meaning to Afro-Mineiro communities since?

In its own way, samba as a black music tradition shares aspects of batuque's fate in this ongoing dialogue about Afro-Brazilian identity and nationalized appropriation. In the mid-1980s, Brazilian sociologist Renato Ortiz spoke to the rise in popularity of North American soul music among Afro-Brazilians during the 1970s, and to the painful issues of music and black consciousness in view of samba's nationalization, an envelopment potentially damaging the music's authenticity as an Afro-Brazilian tradition.

Here lies the potential "emptying" of samba's cultural meanings with regard to Afro-Brazilian identity.

> The construction of a mixed-race national identity [in Brazil] makes it difficult to discern the boundaries of color. Promoting samba as a national music, which effectively it is today, empties its specificity of origin as a black music. When black movements [respond by] claiming [American] soul [music] to affirm blackness, what is being done is an importation of symbolic material resignified in the context of Brazilian nationalism. It is true that soul does not overcome the contradictions of class, . . . but it serves better to express anguish and racial oppression than does samba, which has been nationalized. The problem faced by black movements is how to reclaim the various cultural manifestations of color, which are often marked with the sign of Brazilianness. Since blacks themselves also define themselves as Brazilians, the process of cultural reframing becomes problematic.[13]

In light of this consideration, an original sense of batuque remains in some contemporary Afro-Mineiro communities precisely because it is *not* samba: batuque's "chaos" is its cachet, a spirit of performance that nationalist discourse, in its spotlighting of samba, has branded as too African, too black, or perhaps too low-class and unrefined. Batuque's "chaos" is the placenta of samba's birth that broader Brazilian society either disregarded or could not commodify or assimilate as a nationalistic idiom. The performative values of inventive spontaneity (the "chaos"), arguably a set of African-derived stances within a positive batuque identity among Afro-Brazilians, were difficult for others to appreciate. The free-form spontaneity and improvised mannerisms of batuque were not absorbed and popularized, as was the style of samba, due in great part to elements of a performative attitude transcending choreographic mannerisms, and not easily copied by whites. Yet batuque flourished with its own aesthetic despite the entertainment industry's commercial inability to profit from it, and despite the culture clash that deemed African-derived sensibility as "chaos."

Meanwhile, the term *batucada*, derived from batuque, came to designate the outdoor, roots-music drum circle of Rio de Janeiro's earliest urban samba, before 1910. Although samba was being recorded by 1917, the inability of early recording technology to capture the dynamic spikes of *batucada*'s percussion instruments without distortion led to a decade of softer arrangements, transferring that energetic rhythmic language to other instruments responsible for melody and harmony, such as the guitar, piano, and wind instruments. This occurred as vocalists entered samba circles as primary links between audiences and a burgeoning commercial galaxy. The first electromagnetic recordings of the late 1920s allowed studio microphones to more clearly record *batucada* by including the *surdo*, *pandeiro*, and other percussion instruments, finally bringing an authentic energy and urban samba's timbral roots in samba-of-the-hill (*samba de morro*) to recordings, and to radio airwaves. This engendered the so-called Estácio sound of the 1930s, referring to Rio de Janeiro's influential Estácio de Sá samba school (*escola de samba*). Subsequently, this *batucada* essence was often left out of the gentrified, commercial samba-song (*samba-canção*) that developed further during the 1930s via commercial recordings and radio broadcasts aimed at Brazil's middle class.

Finding *Batuque* in Old Minas

That the term "batuque" became synonymous with drumming had its drawbacks, adding confusion to the historical record and arguably furthering the negative contexts of dance's social functions as they were described in outsider documentation. Father Manoel Lescura Banher wrote to the bishop of São Paulo about black music he heard in Sul de Minas during his November 1786 visit to Silvianópolis, near Pouso Alegre. He described Congado as marked by "the always horrible use of the batuques."[14] Traveling in Minas during 1824, Georg Langsdorff foregrounded his disapproval of "noise" in his undiscerning narrative of lodging at a fazenda near Lagoa Santa, just north of modern-day Belo Horizonte:

> Today is a holiday. A large group of blacks made a ruckus all last night until four in the morning, with singing, dance, and music, in homage to the arrival of the priest. Like everyone else, he was hardly able to sleep. As the blacks did not have to work today, they were able to rest. They did not hesitate to stay up all night chatting around the campfire singing, dancing, and making noise.[15]

Ostensibly to honor a priest's visit, these festivities coincided with a holiday, allowing many blacks a chance to stay up all night for a musical gathering labeled as "a ruckus" and "noise." Although the true intent of this dance will never be known, it is not unreasonable to suggest a range of possibilities, from innocent partying to liturgical observance. Who was the priest? If a Catholic priest, then the celebration may have been in readiness for a special Mass for the black *irmandade*, or a festive preparation for a particularly sympathetic clergyman. The priest referred to by Langsdorff could have belonged to a syncretic African-derived religious practice. The "noise" may have been religious in nature, perhaps a liturgical rite.

Passing through Sul de Minas in 1818, Austrian naturalists Johann Baptist von Spix and Carl Friedrich Philipp von Martius noted their distaste for the "obscenity" of batuque: "Sometimes there also appear dancers dressed as women. Despite this dance's obscene features, it has spread throughout Brazil, preferred everywhere by lower-class people who do not stop themselves despite the church's prohibition. It appears to be originally from Ethiopia, introduced in Brazil by African slaves, like many other habits."[16]

The hardships of slavery and the ethnic complexity of pan-Bantu Mineiro society led the dance toward secularization and cultural fragmentation, as anthropologists Núbia Pereira de Magalhães Gomes and Edimilson de Almeida Pereira explain:

> In Minas Gerais, we have reference to various forms of the same dance: batuque of Our Lady of the Rosary, the crib *batuquinho*, *batucão* of weavers. This aspect of Afro-Brazilian dance in our state requires a large study through research and documentation in the field. . . . There is a distinction between sacred batuque and profane batuque that seems to connect at the origin of the dance. . . . [B]atuque transformed from the sacred dance that it was, to a profane dance. The change came from the dance being transplanted, and therefore [it became] unrelated to the original context, which would have had its own, full meaning. The alteration of the function suggests that batuque, formerly a fertility rite, has been transformed into a recreational dance.[17]

Here, the batuque of Our Lady of the Rosary refers to patron saints' brotherhoods, with the Virgin Mary being the most favored patron saint of blacks. The diminutive *-inho* makes the crib *batuquinho* a "little batuque" children's song. The augmenting suffix *-ão*, of the *batucão* of weavers, references a work song with many participants.

Batuque Instruments: Drumming in Minas Gerais and a Borderland's *"Batuque* Zone"

Drums still serve as batuque's lifeblood, and secular drumming is a primary musical legacy batuque bequeathed to Brazil. By the mid-eighteenth century, Brazilians had begun using the term generically for black dances, including those lacking loud percussion instruments. Traditionally, cylindrical, conical, and footed drum shapes have been made variously from hollowed tree logs (*tambores de tronco*; the word *tambor* is discussed below), from bounded slats fashioned into a barrel-type construction, or from thinner, bent wood rolled into shape and fixed with metal or leather rings and nails. Cowhide drumheads played with hands, sticks, or both are typically fitted using nails, but also ties and wooden wedges, or laced rope. Such drumheads are tuned by heat if fixed with nails, otherwise using wedge or rope tension to tighten skins. A circle dance closely related to batuque, *caxambú*, is named after its largest primary drum (from the Congolese *cachá* [drum] and *mumbu* [music]), a hollowed-out tree section topped off with a cowhide drumhead. The term appears very early in colonial Minas Gerais, in a document in the Arquivo Público Mineiro mentioning the musical activity of "African Negroes" in 1717, reporting that the slaves "sing melancholy songs in the Bantu dialect: they invoke the protection of the *orixás* through dances like the *caxambú*, accompanied by rattle and foot stomping."[18] The word *caxambú* was prevalent enough in Sul de Minas for it to be used in the naming of a town, and for the trade name of a widely distributed bottled water produced in the Circuito das Águas (Water Circuit), a region celebrated for its mineral water, spas, and regional tourism. *Tambu* is the simple corruption of a generic Portuguese word for drum, *tambor* (perhaps one also conjoined with *mumbu*), and is a term still used in Minas Gerais. Dating to the nineteenth century, the rare *tambu* drums of the Serra do Cipó community of Açude are a set of three footed vertical drums featuring nailed, heat-tuned heads (fig. 5.1). These prized musical instruments are still used for both sacred candombe ceremonies and secular batuque dances.

Batuque's tall standing drums of conical design were sometimes termed *atabaques* by nineteenth-century observers. The grouping of three drums is an ideal format for traditional Afro-Brazilian sacred and secular ensembles. The great religious sects of Candomblé, Xangô, Tambor de Mina,

Figure 5.1. The *tambu* drums of the Açude community, one of several culturally important Afro-Mineiro enclaves in the Serra do Cipó region, also including Jequitiba, Mocambeiro, and Mato do Tição, that have maintained music traditions such as *candombe*. (Photo by Jonathon Grasse, 2015.)

and Babassué typically feature trios of graduated-sized sacred drums augmented by handheld percussion of contrasting timbre such as struck bells, clapper bells, and metal or woven shakers of various types. This also may have been the ideal drum ensemble for the once prevalent calundú practices in Old Minas, and for forms of Umbanda and Macumba that emerged from calundú's colonial-era repression. The rhythms and sound worlds of sacred ensembles call forth the spirits for trance possession religious practices, and the anthropomorphic assignment of father, mother, and child is often attributed to this drum trio, or family. Longer, deeper-pitched drums were laid on the ground and straddled by the player. In the early 1820s, Maria Graham wrote in Rio de Janeiro of "drums made of hollow trunks of trees, four or five feet long, closed at one end with wood, and covered with skin at the other. In playing these, the drummer lays his instrument on the ground and gets astride on it, when he beats time with his hands to his own songs, or the tunes of the gourmis [lute]."[19] Five similarly straddled, horizontally placed *tambu* drums appear in a rare photograph of a Congado ceremony being staged for a visitor's benefit at the Morro Velho mine in 1867, near present-day Belo Horizonte (fig. 6.4). The stationary *tambu* seen in this photo were not used for the ambulatory Congado's parading *cortejos* (entourage) but perhaps rather for stationary Congado events such as the election of the local King of Congo (as described below), the ritualized raising of the ceremonial banner, or the esteemed but often secretive candombe ceremonies. Twentieth-century studies of the so-called batuque zone northwest of the city of São Paulo confirm that the word *tambu* was still widely used for this long drum, also rested on the ground and straddled by the player. Brazilian musicologist Rossini Tavares de Lima began studying batuque ensembles in this area in 1946, and much later Austrian ethnomusicologist Gerhard Kubik followed suit.[20] Against the horizontal *tambu* leans the smaller, footed *quinjengue* drum (also known as *candongeiro*). A third ensemble member strikes sticks (*matracas*) against the long side the *tambu*. This São Paulo batuque drum ensemble is completed with a shaker such as the metal cone *guaiá*, or the quieter basket rattle known as an *angóia*. The Minas Gerais border, amid coffee latifundia, is less than eighty kilometers away from this São Paulo "batuque zone," and it is probable that this core batuque ensemble so well studied in São Paulo was formerly more widespread across the rural southeast. Over two thousand kilometers to the north, the *parelha* ensemble of the northeastern dance genre *tambor de crioula* in São Luis, Maranhão, mirrors these southeastern batuque ensembles, featuring a very similar long drum upon which rests a smaller drum, with a third player striking the long drum with sticks also called *matracas*.

Over the course of many generations, the social and functional variations of batuque probably led to more diverse instrumentation. Maintaining exclusive ensembles of three drums likely proved an unnecessary luxury for casual batuque practitioners, whose lack of resources necessitated the use of other instruments in informal settings. Drums were joined, or replaced when necessary, by handheld idiophonic percussion such as scrapers made from notched wood or bamboo (*reco-reco*), bead-covered gourd rattles (*xequerê*), and shaken instruments of woven basketry, wood, or metal such as the *chocalho* and *guaiá*. Johann Moritz Rugendas's 1820s etching *Batuque* depicts a circle dance accompanied only by handclaps (fig. 5.2).

Further widening the historical criteria of batuque instrumentation is German painter Franz Xaver Nachtmann's early nineteenth-century lithograph *Die Baducca, in S. Paulo*. Though probably depicting a lundu dance, this work reveals a notched wooden scraper and an ambulatory xylophone known as marimba, an African-derived instrument that fell out of use in

Figure 5.2. Depiction of the batuque dance by Johan Moritz Rugendas from *Voyage pittoresque dans le Brésil* (1835). The entertaining circle dance gradually brought together Brazilians of all colors and classes despite attempts by authorities to ban the pastime.

Brazil.[21] Stringed instruments provided melodic contour, percussive verve, and harmonic background to solo and call-and-response vocal forms developing within the Afro-Brazilian circle dance tradition, which absorbed into its musical world the ten-stringed viola and the guitar's strummed and plucked rhythmic patterns. Roles for viola and guitar in African-derived dance accompaniment remain an important legacy in Brazil's development of song genres such as lundu and samba. The viola remains a core instrument for other historical Afro-Mineiro dance types, including the *cateretê*. Another harmony instrument, the *sanfona* (accordion), appeared in Brazil during the 1850s and acculturated into southeastern dances and popular Catholic religious processions. Vocalists adept at spontaneous, topical lyrics fueled the intensity of circle dance traditions with songs and recreational banter. Singing provided a perfect arena for social commentary, exaltations of community traditions, social lamentations, invocation of ancestral spirits, and good tidings. With harmonic accompaniment provided to singers, dance traditions found their characteristic rhythms and cultural weight appropriated by song forms defining new folk idioms, salon-based Brazilian genres, and twentieth-century popular music.

Historical, Public Spheres of Batuque

Batuque transformed public and private social spaces. Nowhere in Minas did batuque contrast more with Western norms and the tastes of social elites than in cities, where the aristocratic social calendar revolved around the church services of white brotherhoods, fine art salons in elite private homes, and formal productions of European-derived theatrical works and operas. Ouro Preto, Mariana, Sabará, São João del-Rei, and Juiz de Fora were the largest Mineiro cities throughout the imperial era, as cities in the southern half of the province, below the nineteenth parallel, continued their growth. In the eyes of Mineiro elites, batuque was, despite its creeping popularity across class lines, associated with the vast numbers of the poor, including mixed-race people and whites, and understood to be a music produced and consumed at the socioeconomic margins. During French botanist Auguste de Saint-Hilaire's first sojourn through Minas in 1817, he stopped in the town of Barbacena along the Estrada Real's busy Caminho Velho linking Rio de Janeiro to his destination of Vila Rica: "Barbacena is celebrated among *tropeiros* for the large number of mulatta prostitutes . . . and with them they dance batuques, those lascivious dances that we cannot mention without shame and that have become natural in the province of Minas."[22] Eighty kilometers east of Barbacena in the Mineiro town of Ubá, Saint-Hilaire again took historically valuable note of black dancers, musicians, and singers of the batuque. The description below references the *pandeiro* frame drum or *adufe* (referred to as a tambourine), the *reco-reco* scraper idiophone, and the "beating" that signifies the use of drums:

The creole Negroes [blacks able to speak Portuguese] danced batuques, while one of them played on a kind of tambourine and another, rapidly sliding a small rounded piece of wood along the transverse notches of a stout stick, produced at the same time a noise rather similar to the rattle. In another corner of the yard some Mozambique Negroes formed a circle in the middle of which sat two or three musicians who began beating in strict time on small and not very loud drums. The dancers accompanied them with their songs: they jumped as they went round and round in the same direction, and each in time round their movements became livelier. Knees bent, fists closed, forearms upright, they moved forward on prancing feet, and gave all their limbs a kind of convulsive shaking which must have been extremely tiring for men who had been working the whole day long.[23]

Saint-Hilaire traveled from Barbacena to Vila Rica, attending a formal dinner at the palace of the provincial governor, Dom Manuel de Castro e Portugal, where guests dancing contradances and fandangos wore contemporary Parisian fashions.[24] Three years prior to Saint-Hilaire's visit, German naturalist G. W. Freireyss had also stayed in Barbacena, where, the evening before his journey to Vila Rica, he wrote: "[W]e had, until late at night, dancing and all the noise it made directly above our room."[25] And, like Saint-Hilaire, he arrived in Vila Rica to find European-derived music entertaining the same governor. Freireyss witnessed a performance by "mediocre" mixed-race actors of an unidentified work at the Teatro Municipal Casa de Ópera.[26] He, too, noted batuque's social prominence and cultural influence in Vila Rica's street life of 1814:

> Among the festivities, the Brazilian batuque deserves mention. The dancers form a circle to the beat of a guitar, and a single dancer moves into the center, then advances toward a person of the opposite sex and touches belly to belly [*umbigada*]. At first, the slow beat of the music gradually increases, and the dancers are replaced after each *embigada* [*sic*], and this continues throughout the entire night. One cannot imagine a more lascivious dance than this, also because it has many enemies, especially among priests. Thus, for example, a priest refused absolution to a parishioner, thus ending the dance, but with great displeasure of everyone. There is still batuque danced in Vila Rica, at big parties and in the presence of many ladies who cheer wildly. It is rare to see other dances [than batuque] in the countryside. However, in cities the English dances are almost taking over batuque.[27]

Notable in this account is the guitar's presence (although it could have been a viola), more proof of this instrument's rise in popular music forms associated with Afro-Brazilian innovation. The final comment, on the surge of English tastes in Mineiro dance habits, reflects the opening of Minas Gerais to foreigners at the dawn of the imperial era. However, while valuable evidence of the presence of contradance traditions, the claim of English dances "overtaking" batuque is exaggerated wishful thinking on the part of a Eurocentric chronicler. More telling is the suggestion that it was those social groups already prone to European trends, namely whites and wealthy members of the mixed-race communities, who were adopting English dance styles in place of their previous batuque activities. Importantly, Freireyss clearly indicates that batuque was danced across color lines. In September 1821, the English mineralogist Alexander Caldcleugh also noticed the foreign influence of English dances in Vila Rica, while contrasting the wealth of the governor's palace with images of economic decay in the city streets:

> The poor now have dominion over all of Vila Rica. The streets are full of beggars, many of them sick and asking for handouts, but if in good health pan for gold in the streams as well as from the charity of the city's wealthy. At night, there was a dance at the palace, crammed with people and too hot. The English quadrille predominated the entire evening. I had another opportunity to observe how thin are the women of Minas.[28]

Vendas, Bars, and Public Venues of Batuque

Porto da Estrela, at the mouth of the Inhomirim River on the north shore of Guanabara Bay (today part of the city of Magé in the Rio de Janeiro municipality), was the location of the Praias Mineiras (Miner's Beaches), the main hub and bustling staging area for travelers and import-export facilities servicing Minas Gerais from the Rio de Janeiro coast. From this steamship terminal connecting the area to the city of Rio de Janeiro, an inland road linked Porto da Estrela to the Estrada Real near Petrópolis, the location of the emperor's palace. In 1854, Porto da Estrela became the terminal for Brazil's first railroad, the Estrada de Ferro Mauá, which ran to the foothills below Petrópolis. There, while preparing for his October 1843 research expedition to the Mineiro interior, French naturalist Francis Castelnau commented that, "upon mounting our horses, there appeared a band of neighborhood revelers, with musicians at the front making deafening noises. They had just celebrated their Sunday at a *venda*, as was their custom."[29]

Vendas, bars, and restaurants were dynamic locales of music exchange. The English minister Robert Walsh relates a story of casual, everyday music-making in 1829, at a *venda* near Congonhas in central Minas. He does not describe a batuque but rather a young boy playing the monochord musical bow of African derivation known as the *berimbau*, a ubiquitous instrument now long associated in Brazil with capoeira. Arriving at Chapada do Mato at noon, Walsh and his party were eventually served by an eccentric, rude woman at the *venda*. He describes in detail the "extremely rustic instrument" the boy played as they drank coffee out on the veranda, writing that it produced three or four melodic notes that would otherwise have been used to accompany a song or dance. "He was so shy that when we praised his music he blushed under his skin. This was perhaps the first time in his life that a white man had complimented him. We said goodbye to our rude hostess and hurried to cross the hills of Ouro Branco, which stood now before us."[30]

Traveling in Minas Gerais during December 1816, Saint-Hilaire spent the night in a rancho on the New Road leg of the Estrada Real linking Rio de Janeiro to Vila Rica. He left an account of a *venda*, describing the place as a hangout for drinking, informal parties, and popular music:

> Nothing can compare to the confused and discordant noise that frequently reigns in *vendas*: no one connecting to what goes on around them—this one dancing the *sapateado*; the other one lazily leaning against a wall singing a barbaric song in an out-of-tune voice while accompanying herself on an even more barbaric instrument. As *venda* owners, many lower-class Portuguese from Europe began earning their wealth.[31]

Establishments such as *vendas* were important public meeting places, established social spaces spreading popular music and customs. In colonial and imperial Minas, those traveling the interior included mule train drivers, slave convoys (*comboios*) led by a slave driver (*comboieiro*), cattle horsemen (*vaqueiros* and *cavaleiros*), and oxcart drivers (*boiadeiros*). These were the free, rural poor who, regardless of race, began forming the backlands stock of the mobile, interior Mineiro population. Before the rise of Belo Horizonte, Mineiro towns were like "cells within rural protoplasm" throughout the nineteenth century, with fazendas forming important, intermediary nodes linking agricultural society with the towns and cities they supported.[32] Self-sufficiency became an emblem of Mineiro identity during and after the *decadência*, contrasting with the cash crop export economy of plantation-based coastal Brazil. It was the network of long-established urban centers, the towns and cities providing fazendas with a domestic market, and the bolstering of exports to coastal cities that led to increased Mineiro self-sufficiency following the gradual decline of mineral wealth. If nineteenth-century life in the countryside was a challenge,

Mineiro cities and towns during the *decadência* offered perhaps only a slight advantage to a struggling populace.

The French naturalist Alcide d'Orbigny traveled the Caminho da Bahia (Bahia Road) south into Minas Gerais along the São Francisco River, spending part of 1832 visiting the isolated northern reaches of the province. He remarked that, among few diversions, the population enjoyed batuque, "a dance imported from Africa and that had become nationalized," although he found it too indecent to describe.[33] In the northern Minas *comarca* (county) of Rio São Francisco, beyond the gold and diamond fields, where cattle and agriculture empires marked the ascendance of a colonial-era local elite, a vast population of free people of color made their livelihoods in remote settlements that were in proximity to the three main towns of Montes Claros, Januária, and São Romão, each barely approaching a population of four thousand even by 1920.[34] It was in the São Francisco River port of Januária where world traveler and British agent Richard Burton sensed parallels with the spirit of an African marketplace. Though the percentage of blacks in northern Minas was half that of the mining district, the *comarca* nonetheless boasted a popular culture deeply imbued with African-derived practice. As in other parts of Minas Gerais and Brazil's broader southeastern region, batuque had developed into a northern *sertão* point of pride by the nineteenth century. Amid the political turmoil following Emperor Dom Pedro I's abdication in 1831, nativist revolts against Portuguese monarchism seethed with populist activism organized by elites and anti-Portuguese radicals (*exaltados*) willing to incite the lower classes, including freed persons of color. Local *exaltados* harnessed batuque's popularity as a litmus test for nativist Brazilian identity. The transformation from banned pastime to proud emblem of Brazilianness (*brasilidade*) is sensed in the account below, in which Judy Bieber describes a mob attacking the home of a Portuguese merchant in Montes Claros:

> The throng invaded Loredo's home and demanded that he dance the batuque, an energetic and sensual Afro-Brazilian dance.... The ringleaders highlighted their Brazilian-ness by engaging in Afro-Brazilian practices such as the *batuque*, in contrast to the staid culture of local Portuguese residents.... [The nativists] further demonstrated their acceptance of Afro-Brazilian customs by practicing the *jogo de buzios*, a Yoruba-derived form of divination. In an era that associated European cultural norms with power and status, participating in Afro-Brazilian customs represented a bold statement of identity.[35]

Such identity stemming from Afro-Mineiro music and dance tradition is not surprising, since these local practices were widely recognized elements of the area's broader popular culture. Yet Bieber's point is not lost: despite proving itself elemental to popular Brazilian character, batuque was not considered high class, to be sure. Also, Bieber's reference to Yoruba practices attests to the West African legacy in northern Minas, a remnant of the region's connection to the Bahian slave traders the previous century. East of Montes Claros, where Mineiro rivers flow fast toward the Atlantic side of the Serra do Espinhaço, the isolation and poverty of the great Rio Jequitinhonha Valley is synonymous with northeastern Minas. The river runs six hundred miles from its headwaters a few miles west of the old mining city of Serro through northeastern Minas and across Bahia to the coastal town of Belmonte. Today, this is the valley of hunger, one of the poorest regions of Brazil. The importance of batuque traditions in contemporary Afro-Mineiro communities here is substantial: a style attributed to African-descendant communities in the Jequitinhonha Valley is still believed to have originated in this region of Minas.[36]

Batuque in the Zona da Mata and Sul de Minas Subregions

Crossing the isolated interior of Sul de Minas in 1818, Spix and Martius made note of rural batuque in a town near the São Paulo border:

> In Estiva, a lonely farm with vast, magnificent fields surrounded by isolated mountains, residents were celebrating, dancing the batuque; they rarely hosted foreign travelers, and invited us to witness the amusements. The batuque is danced by a man and woman who snap their fingers while making unrestrained movements and pantomimes, approaching and moving away from each other. The main charm of this dance, for Brazilians, is in the artful spins and pelvic contortions; they exaggerate almost as much as the fakirs of the East Indies.[37]

The regions known as Zona da Mata and Sul de Minas carry an agricultural heritage of coffee latifundia, dairies, and cattle. Decades following the exhaustion of the gold and diamond mines, a nineteenth-century coffee boom brought a new, massive influx of enslaved Central Africans to Minas Gerais. Most of the 733,000 slaves shipped to Brazil between 1826 and 1850 went to labor in the coffee latifundia of the southeastern interior of Minas, São Paulo, and most famously Rio de Janeiro's Paraíba Valley. The gradual decline in the number of incoming slaves beginning in the 1850s, until the emancipation of 1888, also marked a gradual lessening of ethnic rivalry among African descendants in Minas, the rise of the so-called *bantolização* ("Banto-ization"), and complex processes of creolization as Brazilian slaves by the tens of thousands, sold by their owners in the northeast facing economic vulnerability, entered the cultural dynamics of the southeast.

In May 1865, Swiss-American naturalist Louis Agassiz and his wife, Elizabeth, traveled northwest from Rio de Janeiro to visit the coffee fazenda of Mariano Lage, near Juiz de Fora in the Zona da Mata. The Harvard professor's entourage crossed the heavily forested Serra do Mar using what existed of a new road linking Petrópolis to Juiz de Fora, encountering some of the French construction company's German laborers. In Switzerland many years earlier, Agassiz had been hired by Spix and Martius to describe and classify the Brazilian fish the two naturalists had brought back to Switzerland in 1820. He was an ardent proponent of human polygenism, investigating human races as separately created species put on earth by God, and he subjected humans to a classification system not unlike that of the fish he studied. This anti-Darwinist's subscription to the standard scientific racism of the day contrasted with the boldness of what was then his own, groundbreaking theory: that the earth had once gone through an ice age. The founder of glaciology marveled at the geological splendor of Minas. Agassiz's time at the coffee fazenda also had its musical moments. As he remarked on an evening's events "An excellent dinner awaited us at the little hotel just opposite, the door of which is shaded by two stately palms; and with a ramble in the neighboring grounds of Senhor Lage, and a concert by a band of German musicians, consisting of employees on the road, our day closed,—a day full of pleasure."

Later in his stay, Agassiz witnessed a colorful celebration, a batuque dance that enlivened the festivities of Saint John's Day (Festa de São João):

> We rode home in the evening to a late dinner, after which an enormous bonfire, built by the negroes in honor of the Eve of St. John, was lighted in front of the house. The scene was exceedingly picturesque, the whole establishment,

the neighboring negro huts, and the distant forest being illuminated by the blaze, around which the blacks were dancing, accompanying their wild gestures with song and drum. Every now and then a burst of fireworks added new brightness to the picture.[38]

Mariano Lage, the Brazilian engineer overseeing the road construction, had joined in the Minas coffee boom years earlier, directing his slaves in clearing the ancient rainforests; in the planting, maintenance, and harvesting of coffee trees; and in the processing and transport of the beans to Rio de Janeiro. Coffee fazendas were home to work songs, though few of them are known. Agassiz noted:

> It was the harvesting season, and the spectacle was a pretty one. The negroes, men and women, were scattered about the plantations with broad, shallow trays, made of plaited grass or bamboo. . . . Little black children were sitting on the ground and gathering what fell under the bushes, singing at their work a monotonous but rather pretty snatch of song in which some took the first and others the second, making a not inharmonious music.[39]

Mineiros played a role in the transformation of batuque into a more widely engaged, social pastime. Francisco de Paula Ferreira de Rezende (1832–1893, b. Campanha, MG), minister of Brazil's Supreme Court and a provincial vice governor, left an indication of batuque's prevalence in the city of his birth in Sul de Minas. Brazilian scholar Regina Horta Duarte cites his memoirs in her study of circus and theater life in nineteenth-century Minas Gerais; she writes that batuque's

> staying power, despite prohibitions, can be seen in the mid-nineteenth century, when a memoirist narrates a curious event. Despite claiming that the batuque was danced only by "low and ordinary people," one Mineiro from Campanha [Rezende] noted the frequent participation of "good people" and "careless priests" who do not back down "even before the greatest scandal." He had met a religious man who was not only a devotee of the dance, but one who "behaved with such an indecency and an extravagance" the author was too ashamed to describe. . . . The batuque ended up being a lure "to many good people," as in the case of one police officer, who upon receiving a complaint of an evening batuque, arrived at the scene with the intention of arresting all

participants. However, instead of intervening he joined in "as the most furious of dancers," going at it "the rest of the night."[40]

Rezende's emphasis on authority figures underlines not only their complacency with respect to the spread and acceptance of batuque but also their direct, joyful involvement. If batuque in eighteenth-century Minas was seen as a type of dangerous African socialization imperiling elites, its nineteenth-century profile transitioned toward a broadly popular pastime enjoyed by non-blacks, including whites of higher class standing. Batuque's social emergence included a presence in some local churches: the German-Argentine botanist Hermann Burmeister was in Francisco Rezende's hometown of Campanha in 1853, where he casually noted the frequent use of nonsacred music in church services, including batuque:

> In the church . . . litanies in Latin are not understood, and the music, although an attraction for many, is a rare thing. On solemn occasions, a choir is organized, which meets in the balcony above the entrance; there is the playing of Strauss waltzes, popular melodies, batuques or lundus, the overture of one or another opera, and the Mineiro anthem.[41]

In Rio de Janeiro State's famous Paraíba Valley coffee fazendas, just beyond the Mineiro border, *caxambú* dance was often referred to as batuque, including a playful, vocal component of these festivities known as *jongo*.[42] Late nineteenth-century laws in some Paraíba Valley municipalities required police permits for batuque celebrations, while other laws prohibited its practice in city streets. A "king" and occasional "queen" of *caxambú*, wearing idiophonic anklets known as *nguizu*, directed the sessions as they, too, danced. The dance circle was joined by participating slaves, who repeated the *jongo* riddle sung by the leader, clapping their hands and swinging to the drummers' patterns known as the *batida* (beat). Other *jongueiros* were encouraged to introduce their own rhyming textual riddles and answers. Participants took advantage of the opportunity to slyly denounce their oppressed situation and slave society at large.[43] *Caxambú, jongo*, and batuque survived in small, marginalized Afro-Brazilian communities such as Rio de Janeiro's Fazenda São Jose in the Paraíba Valley town of Santa Isabel do Rio Preto. Perhaps sixty kilometers from the Vassouras coffee fazenda studied by Stanley Stein, the community is even closer to the Minas Gerais border.[44]

Batuque's Spiritual Path

In chapter 2 on calundú, batuque was presented as a historically spiritual practice having possibly absorbed calundú's drumming and some degree of its religious efficacy. It is worth noting again that ritualized Afro-Brazilian religious sects in Rio Grande do Sul are known as *batuque* while in Belém, Pará, the term references the houses of worship of syncretic religious sects. Transformations from its African roots toward a reconfigured popular culture in the New World never completely overshadowed batuque's spiritual dimension as a celebration of ancestral lineage. The dance's power regarding spiritual embodiment, invocation, and identity of place flourished, for example, in the late nineteenth century in fazendas surrounding the village of Curral D'el-Rey, the site for Belo Horizonte, where batuque's role in both formal and casual religiosity may have cushioned African descendants from the blow of losing calundú. Here, batuque flourished among communities associated with the Black Catholicism of Congado that came to characterize the region mapping to what is now the Belo Horizonte urban sprawl of six million people. Leda Maria Martins comments that on this region's expansive Fazenda Pantana, "there was a small chapel. It was there where for a long time slaves probably celebrated the Reinado do Rosário. The batuques ... were performed in the *senzalas*, or in the forest shade, resuming with what remained of their cultural origins and of their rites and divinities."[45] Today, in Serra do Cipó communities less than ninety kilometers from the Fazenda Pantana location, topical batuque songs about love and life experiences join those performed during Festa Junina (the June Saints' Days celebrations) and in proximity to sacred festivities of popular Black Catholicism such as candombe. Danced throughout the night, or after holiday ceremonies, batuque rhythms and drum timbres are musical links to ancestors and collective memories. Yet these are not ritualized ceremonies. Batuque is among the varied musical practices found also in the nearby Afro-Mineiro community of Mato do Tição within the municipality of Jaboticatubas, where it has been studied by Núbia Pereira de Magalhães Gomes and Edimilson de Almeida Pereira. Here, topical lyrics are accompanied by drums, percussion, and viola. The links between past and present are fluid and elemental to contemporary batuque:

The batuque of Mato Tição is not a religious feast in the sense of the ritual celebrations of Our Lady of the Rosary, São João, or São Benedito. There is no ceremonial lifting of the mast, and the songs are not of the character of the other sacred rituals. Lasting until dawn after the holiday ceremonies, or on any occasion, people gather to dance the batuque. The songs express the games and conquests of love, and the joys of coexistence. The *sapateado* dance accompanies the singers. Amid laughter, body language shows blacks as heirs of a common lineage: in Mato Tição this is a special treat, for batuque rhythms are those of ancestors. Its realization eases the tensions associated with sacred rituals: the unity of the assembly maintained by the desire to witness the best dance steps. The syncopated rhythms of the songs, the guitar and the percussion instruments accent the plasticity of the dancer's bodies. In batuque, the recreational spirit adds to an ethnic heritage, constituting links between past and present.[46]

A perhaps similar batuque practice exists in the urban Os Arturos community in Contagem, an industrial city in the middle of Belo Horizonte's vast metropolitan area. Here are familial links to nineteenth-century fazenda slaves who lived throughout the area. Their batuque is utilized during weddings and birthdays, typically late in the festivities following samba, *forró*, and other popular, entertaining dances. In these instances, batuque's African heritage marks a more serious celebratory atmosphere, requiring what community members call bringing "the feeling" (*por sentido*).[47]

Past Criminalization of Batuque

Inquisition hearings prosecuting calundú also encouraged the identification of batuque practitioners caught in the ecclesiastical dragnet. Suspicious colonial authorities, fearing batuque's cultural empowerment of slaves and other socially marginalized people, further framed the dance as having challenged European-derived sensibilities and Christian morality. "When witnesses in the ecclesiastical visits [of eighteenth-century Minas Gerais] denounced batuques, they did not refer to African religious practices but saw batuques as a suspect and dangerous activity that enabled Africans to recreate forms of sociability prevalent in their homelands."[48]

Batuque was feared as a possible mask for conspiratorial meetings during the decades-long influx of newly enslaved Africans, when mining town strife between slaves and owners was periodic. Music and dance heightened elite apprehension of revolt and runaway settlements. And as this observation of batuque in Ouro Preto of the 1750s suggests, drums were seen as weapons. An ordinance stated that

> small parties of blacks, mulattoes, and *carijós* perform[ing] on Sundays and holy days should . . . be dispersed by patrols of six men and one sergeant, organized expressly for this purpose. The argument [of this ordinance] was that "great disorders" were born of these batuques, which often degenerated into quarrels and injuries. It is significant that the drums were to be destroyed by patrolling guards, which in a way equated them with weapons.[49]

Batuque's power of cohesion among the masses was threatening enough to Mineiro authorities that some municipalities passed laws banning the dance. The ample documentation of batuque's criminalization by church and Crown suggests the very popularity of a burgeoning music culture among a growing spectrum of Mineiros, including whites of the propertied class and some clergy. Recalling the discussion of the vague, generalized use of the term "batuque" earlier in this chapter, some of these records, and the language of municipal codes, can be interpreted as having used the word to describe all gatherings of blacks involving any type dance and music. Indeed, Maria Conceição Rezende points to the criminalization of black dances, particularly batuque, as a major source of documentation: "In colonial Minas, [in] documents including the 'ordenações' and the 'Extravagant Laws of the Kingdom,' the allusions are often to the 'danças de negros' and to the 'bailes dos pretos,' and especially to the 'batuque.'"[50]

In the testimony of eighteenth-century investigative hearings by the archbishop of Mariana known as the *Devassas eclesiásticas*, batuque is cited as a secular dance. The 1734 northern Minas case of the *crioula forra* Violante Coutinha (a manumitted, Brazilian-born woman of color) documents batuque's historical role as popular entertainment distinguished in this case from sacred ritual.[51] Coutinha was denounced for "dancing and making calundús," an overtly religious practice then being rooted out by the church. The informant, shoemaker Manuel Antunes de Carvalho, testified that he had previously witnessed blacks gathering at Coutinha's home *only* for batuque.

Here, the comparatively innocent, routine batuque entertainment contrasts with the ritualized seriousness of private, ceremonial calundú more zealously prosecuted by the church. Similar testimony suggests associations between batuque practitioners and sacred calundú, indicating distinctions between sacred and secular. However, in the Caminho Velho town of Brumado (now Entre Rios de Minas), north of São João del-Rei, a well-known *feitiçeiro* named Calundúzeiro (which is also the term for a practitioner of calundú) is identified as hosting "corrupting" batuques in his home.

> African elements were generically present in a case in Brumado in 1764, in which a black *feitiçeiro* by the name of Domingos Calundúzeiro was denounced for corrupting the slaves of the parish who assembled in his house for *batuque* dances. On one occasion, Domingos had been seen curing a slave girl owned by Manoel Freire. During the ritual, Domingos was surrounded by a quantity of blacks with three or four of them playing drums.[52]

Both church and Crown denounced batuque regardless of its perceived secular or sacred function. The following *postura* (municipal act) promulgated against the dance by the Chamber of São José del-Rei (later Tiradentes) in May 1829 refers to a broad framework of social contexts for the dance.

> Prohibited are the infamous and pernicious dances called batuques, be they in public or in private, day or night, as they are opposed to the dogmas of Our Lady of Religion and public morality, and through the terrible consequences that repeatedly has happened with such a dishonest pastime; any person of either sex, quality, or condition that is found to be participating in this dance will be imprisoned for ten days even if not caught in the act; the same penalty is to be given to the owner of the house in which the dances were held.[53]

The wording above clearly indicates that the dance was practiced widely and frequently enough to be "infamous," which can be interpreted as acknowledging the dance's pervasiveness across racial and class lines. Many references to batuque on the plantations of Brazil's coastal latifundia emphasize Sunday performances limited to slave quarters (see below). However, written in the context of an urban environment, this *postura* does not identify batuque as a Sunday event but rather as a dance freely practiced at the whim of the townspeople, by men and women, both day and night, in public and in private homes and properties. The *postura* further suggests that batuque represented a level of autonomy for blacks and other marginalized classes, thus threatening authorities and offending white elites. The law does not specify any particular social demographic (blacks and slaves, for instance); the reference to property owners suggests a broader popularity of batuque affecting any "quality" and "condition," free persons and the moneyed class included. Whites of any social standing were thus ostensibly subject to prosecution. Batuque was framed as "dishonest" by authorities perhaps due to its proximity to spiritual practice and "magic," and to the quasi-heretical practice of using music and dance for fortune-telling, healing, and the "closing of the body" to misfortune, as found in calundú. Such laws carried the threat of fines and imprisonment yet could not stem the dance's popularity, as the galaxy of batuque dance and music expressions entered into wider popular use.

The Count of Arcos (Marcos de Noronha e Brito), the governor of Bahia from 1810 to 1818, famously discussed batuque as a cultural institution to be manipulated by Crown authorities to foment ethnic rivalry among the *nações* (ethnic nations) of enslaved Africans. Here, the governor argues against an outright ban of the dance on Bahia's sugarcane plantations. Perhaps many of the Minas Gerais authorities weighing the cultural persecution of batuque considered similar arguments. In the end, the governor's words attest to the power of batuque in the shaping of Brazilian society, at least as a force recognized by authoritarian cultural outsiders such as white elites.

> Seen through the government's eyes, [batuque] is one thing; seen through the eyes of individuals, it is something quite different. The latter believe that the batuques infringe their dominical rights, either because they want to employ their slaves in useful work even on Sundays, or because they want to station them before their doors on these days of rest as a way of showing off their wealth. The government, however, sees the institution of the batuques as something that obliges the blacks unconsciously and automatically to revive every week the feelings of mutual aversion instinctive in them since birth, which are nevertheless gradually extinguished in their common suffering. These feelings may be regarded as the best guarantee of the security of the great cities of Brazil. If the different "nations" of Africa were totally to forget the furious resentment which by nature has divided them, if the Agomé were to become the brothers of the Nagô, the Gêgê of the Hausa, the Tapa of the Ashanti, and so on, a tremendous and inescapable danger

would descend upon and destroy Brazil. And who can doubt that suffering has the power to create fraternization among its victims? Thus, for the government to stand in the way of the only possibility of dissension between blacks would amount to indirectly preaching their union. This could only have terrible consequences.[54]

Some Contemporary Aspects of Batuque

In the latter half of the twentieth century, professional folkloric and commercial music groups referenced batuque as a genre, style, and ensemble type relating to, and reclaiming, an African-derived heritage. For example, Batuque Afro-Brasileiro de Nelson Silva was founded in Juiz de Fora in the early 1960s. At times featuring up to sixty members, this music and dance troupe performed in various Mineiro towns and cities, having been founded in the context of the Arte Negra movement's focus on traditional Afro-Brazilian music, dance, and art as instruments of positive social change.[55] The Batuque Afro-Brasileiro ensemble may have been inspired by bandleader Abigail Moura (b. 1905, Eugenópolis, MG; d. 1970, Rio de Janeiro), whose Rio de Janeiro–based group Orquestra Afro-Brasileira released the seminal LP *Obaluaye* in 1957, and *Orquestra Afro-Brasileira* in 1968, the latter featuring the compositions "Rei N'aruanda" and "India," described respectively as a "batuque with orchestra and chorus" and a batuque with its first part "sung in the African language of nhegatu."[56] Broad application of the historically ambiguous term includes its synonymous use today for popular dance and drumming, as for instance in the title of *axé* music star Daniela Mercury's 1990 hit song "Batuque," about a couple meeting at a neighborhood samba-reggae dance. Batuque is today a popular synonym for drumming also because drums and percussion serve as the circle dance's lifeblood.

There still exist predominantly Afro-Brazilian communities in Minas Gerais fostering batuque's links to previous generations, where the dance's functions can range from casual entertainment to the calendar of popular Catholicism, including the Festa Junina, or June Saints' Days, and the Feast of the Divine (Festa do Divino). In several Serra do Cipó communities north of Belo Horizonte, and in those south of the city in the Paraopeba River Valley, batuque is promoted as a traditional culture attraction.[57] In the Verde Grande and Gurutuba River Valleys far in the north of the state, batuque and other dance traditions such as lundu, *samba de roda*, and capoeira remain important localized customs in some of the many black communities identified as contemporary *quilombos* (*comunidades quilombolas*). The semantic reassignment of the term *quilombo* (runaway slave community) has been adopted by many dozens of communities in twenty-first-century Minas Gerais, part of the nationwide *quilombo* land rights movement that began at the end of the 1980s. With roots in eighteenth-century *quilombos*, the Gurutubanos area is home to a conglomeration of over thirty settlements where close to six thousand live, where batuque is a couple's circle dance and a primary, drum-based music form.[58]

Percussionist and community activist Reinaldo Santana Silva adopted the nickname Reibatuque as a play on his name's etymological connection to "king" (*rei*) and batuque, furthering the living tradition in his Paraopeba River Valley home of Marinhos southeast of Belo Horizonte. There, economically impoverished residents have maintained Congado groups as well as a carnival celebration initiated by Reibatuque's parents in the early 1960s. Home to eighty families, Marinhos joins nearby Sapé, Rodriguez, and Riberão as a group of *quilombo* communities in a valley network of African-descendant settlements officially registered with the Brazilian government between 2007 and 2011. Reibatuque and others organize drum-based music and dance for educational workshops and to attract visitors to the community, where batuque is a cultural calling card for supportive outsiders and local tourists beckoned to participate in Marinhos's economic survival. To these ends, the community has created two projects, the Café (a community gathering place serving food and coffee, open to visitors) and "Batuquenatividade," another play on the term "batuque" designed to encourage young residents to value and celebrate African-descendant traditions.[59] In the heart of old Belo Horizonte, batuque is just one of the activities celebrated in the annual Canjerê Festival of Minas Gerais Quilombolo Culture, held during May at Praça da Liberdade and sponsored by the state energy agency (Companhia Energética de Minas Gerais, CEMIG), the Instituto do Patrimônio Histórico e Artístico Nacional, the Centro de Documentação Eloy Ferreira da Silva (CEDEFES), the Fundação Cultural Palmares, and local, state, and federal cultural ministries.

Chapter 6

Congado in Minas Gerais

*The Feast Day of Our Lady of the Rosary
and the Election of a Black King*

Colorful public worship of the Virgin Mary and patron saints performed by lay communities has long been a cornerstone of popular Catholicism in Brazil. Congado processions in Mineiro cities and towns, and in other parts of Brazil, help form a festive celebration known as the Reinado (Reign), or by variants of the title Festa do Reinado de Nossa Senhora do Rosário (Feast of the Reign of Our Lady of the Rosary).[1] The Reinado, symbolic in many ways of a five-hundred-year-old Luso-African legacy (see appendix 2 for a historical outline), is a locally determined ritual that typically begins with a ceremonial raising of flagpoles for patron saint banners (*levantamento de mastros*) that launches several days of communal festivities and banquets. Events may include the ambulatory prayer rituals of *novenas*, "payments of promises" to patron saints (*cumprimento de promessas*), and an ornately costumed ritual procession of drum-accompanied public worship, with dances and call-and-response praise songs known as *cantigos*, and chants (*canticos*). Festivals sometimes incorporate a special Mass designed in the 1970s (Missa Congo), and a reenactment of the 1888 "Golden Law" of emancipation in which, during a mock slave auction, a theatrical "freeing of the captives" is celebrated. The Reinado's "crowning" also refers to the election, or observance, of a king and queen of the Congo (*rei e rainha do congo*) chosen from the local community, a link to both colonial-era religious conversion practices in Portugal and the colonizer's earliest Central African missionization campaigns. These popularized forms of Catholicism surrounding Congado have been termed a "mythical Afro-descendent religion in Brazil."[2] The Reinado may include both festive and solemn theater involving a royal couple, traditionally of African descent, and their court of appointed officers and dignitaries, whose dramatized dances and plots resonate with unique Black Catholic cosmologies and Luso-African oral history:[3] "The black man came from far away / Came from Angola, from the Congo / To the mines of Minas Gerais."[4]

In this sense, the royal couple's parading entourage, or *cortejo* (cortege), includes chosen individuals of status, rank, and position, all within the theme of a royal court, conveyed in this song excerpt addressing the passing of the crown to a new royal couple in Jatobá, Minas Gerais: "You surrendered [the crown], sir / You surrendered, lady / You will receive [the crown], sir / You will receive, lady / The crown of the Virgin Mary."[5] African-derived musical, textual, and corporeal aspects of the Reinado tradition sensually embolden *congadeiro* identity, allowing forms of resistance to flourish as a vernacular, fluid system of oral traditions sometimes including a sprinkling of Central African, Bantu, and creolized liturgical texts. *Guardas*, a term for Congado's core music ensembles discussed below, retain individual client links to patron saints to whom they remain devout. Congado communities historically descend from racially segregated Catholic lay brotherhoods dedicated to the Our Lady of the Rosary; or to one of several other patron saints of blacks (*santos pretos*), including São Benedito (Saint Benedict "the Black" or "the Moor"), Santa Efigênia (Saint Iphigenia of Ethiopia), and Nossa Senhora das Mêrces (Our Lady of Mercies); or to lesser saints such as Balthazar, Domingos, Lourenço, and Anthony. Patron saint banners (*bandeiras*) front each parading *guarda* and are objects of devotional affection.

Within public arenas of streets, plazas, and churchyards, Congado's devotional expressions during processions reveal symbols of survival and resistance particular to Afro-Mineiro heritage, creating locally determined modes of collective memory. Its praise song repertoire of lyric poetry exhibits verse and rhyme schemes of four-, six-, and eight-line strophes, with notable free forms resulting from improvisation and intertwining with traditional guiding principles maintained by devotees through communal discourse.[6] Augmenting praise songs to Our Lady and patron saints, and those reflecting the sacred poetry of holy kings, other textual themes capture the genre's rural

Figure 6.1. *Festival of Our Lady of the Rosary*, a watercolor completed sometime during the 1770s by the Luso-Italian military engineer and artist Carlos Julião (1740–1811). The image conveys the colorful Afro-Brazilian festival's formal costuming and ceremonial pageantry.

past and include agricultural and harvest rituals such as weeding ceremonies. Congado's more playfully spontaneous dance components emerge from batuque's Bantu-derived aesthetics, which negotiated a historical relationship with church rituals groomed by colonial Luso-Brazilian society. Processions dominated by pounding drums and call-and-response praise songs retain aspects of ancestral worship and the observance of symbolic *pretos velhos* (wise, old black men), whose knowledge and survival skills are carried in the busts and statues of elderly, white-haired Afro-Brazilian men.[7] The percussion orchestra's magical timbres herald the transformation of public spaces, with parade routes often visiting the private homes of important individuals, churches, and other noteworthy places. From a Congado song text we find that: "The people of the Congo are brave / The king of the Congo has arrived / He came from Luanda with his entire group";[8] and from another emerges a definitive shard of oral history: "The black man came from far away / Came from Angola, from the Congo / To the mines of Minas Gerais."[9]

Guardas: The Musical Groups of Congado

Groups of Congado musicians, singers, and dancers are known as *guardas* (less often *ternos*), with processions including up to seven different *guarda* types: *catopê, moçambique, congo, candombe, vilão, marujada,* and *caboclos,* each symbolizing elements of locally determined devotional oral traditions.[10] Few festivals feature all, or even most, of these *guarda* types. An eighth *guarda* known as *cavalaria de São Jorge* (Saint George's horsemen) has fallen into disuse, almost disappearing from the tradition. In Minas, the highly respected candombe, regarded as the sacred mythological source of Congado Mineiro, rarely participates directly in processions and is discussed in more detail below. Under the direction of a captain (*capitão*), each *guarda* retains locally determined functions within the procession. *Guardas* might be further delineated in name and category by gender, such as a *congo feminino* or a *moçambique masculino*. Children, adolescents, and the elderly regularly participate, underscoring the familial, communal nature of the oral tradition through which local practices have been passed down through generations.[11] Like the king's royal crown, an important ritual object is the ceremonial scepter (*bastão*) belonging to an older captain, a powerful symbol historically linked to the sculpted wooden *milhanga* of Central African religions such as the Lupambulu sect active near the mouth of the Congo River,[12] and among the Bakongos and Cabindas, who artistically and delicately craft richly worked and ornamented *bastões*.[13] The *bastão* remains a potent relic representing group identity through the community's older *congadeiros*, primarily the captains, and music "masters" (*mestres*) responsible for the performative integrity of this sacred oral tradition. *Congadeiros* acknowledge as points of pride the spiritual legacy entrusted to captains and kings as specialists in the continuation of ritual and community heritage. As Leda Maria Martins notes in her study of Congado in Jatobá:

> Prepared by the captain, the *bastão* contains herbs, beads, and seawater, and is also consecrated at the altar during a religious ceremony. A sign of strength and wisdom, it represents the power of its bearer, who must guard it and honor it with propriety.... They are reminiscent of African craftsmanship in the carving of wood and in the masks and totems.[14]

Within this rich oral tradition, *guardas* appear in an origin myth widely shared among *congadeiros* based on the rescue from ocean waves of the Virgin Mary and the baby Jesus by African-descendant drummers, symbolically binding Our Lady of the Rosary to Afro-Brazilians. The *marujada, guarda* in naval regalia, represent colonial-era Portuguese sailors, who, like the "Indian" *caboclos* dressed in feathery, Native-inspired costumes with bows and arrows, were unable to call the Virgin Mary to safety from the ocean waters. Often a stand-alone event found outside of the Congado world, *marujada* is a maritime-themed version of the medieval Iberian dramatic dances rooted in reenactments of the Reconquista in which Christians battle to victory against Moors in full naval regalia. As widely performed folk Catholicism, *marujada* is popular even in the isolated interior of Minas Gerais, as described by Hermano Vianna and Beto Villares in their notes on 1990s recordings made in northern Minas "Some of the members of the Montes Claros Marujada have never seen the ocean. Many of them are unaware that battles fought by Christians against Moors form the basis of their playful display. But none of this diminishes the excitement with which they fight sea battles in the middle of Guimarães Rosa's *sertão*."[15]

Marujada became a tangential *guarda* of Congado, fulfilling the origin myth in its representation of Portuguese sailors who fought the naval battles of the Reconquista, or searched at sea for Our Lady. Filipe Gaeta comments:

> The dances of the *marujeiros*, of Portuguese origin, related to the life of the sailors in their travels at the time of the discovery of new lands such as Brazil. [The dances] became popular in Minas Gerais from the beginning of the 18th century, brought by Portuguese to the region during the gold rush. Along with use of fife and *pipiruí* (popular name given to fife players in Conceição do Mato Dentro), *marujada* became of fundamental importance to the Reinado festival in Conceição do Mato Dentro. . . . The dance was appropriated by blacks for their festivals in honor of Senhora do Rosário, and assumed senses and meanings linked to this practice. Thus, the Feast of Nossa Senhora do Rosário has elements of Portuguese and African origin; it is important to note that these elements were reinterpreted by blacks in Conceição do Mato Dentro.[16]

As the legend of this Congado myth continues, the Virgin Mary emerged from the waves only when beckoned by the candombe's enticing drumming and praise songs imbued with Bantu text. Depending on the telling of the origin myth, a particular musical instrument, such as the *tamboril* frame drum or the *ingoma* log drum, is said to have beckoned Our Lady from the ocean waters, garnering ritualistic weight for that instrument. By way of this foundational story, *guardas* perform expressive and narrative roles within a loose hierarchy of spiritual efficacy.

Figures 6.2, 6.3. Depiction of a Congado procession, *Festa de Nossa Senhora do Rosário, padroeira dos negros* (The Feast of Our Lady of the Rosary, the patron saint of blacks), by Johann Moritz Rugendas, in *Voyage pittoresque dans le Brésil* (1835). The pomp and circumstance of the king and queen of Congo are shown complete with *caixa* (drum), *pífano* (fife), *gaita de foles* (bagpipes), and the lamellophone known as a *quissanje* among other names.

Figure 6.4. A Congado in Minas Gerais, by Ruy Santos, 1876. Seen in the inner circle of participants are five men each straddling what are likely *tambu* drums, placed horizontally on the ground. This performance method was similar to that of batuque.

Figure 6.5. *Encenação de uma congado* (Staging of a Congado), by August Riedel, 1868. In addition to the king of Congo and his ambassadors, viola players can be seen to the far right and left of the group.

The notion of liturgical drum patterns calling to the Virgin Mary echoes the pan-African belief in communicative drum and percussion timbres calling directly to the gods and ancestors of the spirit world. Likewise, the West African *orixá* Yemanjá, widely worshipped in Brazil, is associated with the sea, rising from the waters (as does the Virgin Mary in this origin myth) to join in the possession trances of the Afro-Brazilian Xangô and Candomblé sects. The candombe drum's display of power and attraction to the Virgin Mary may have echoed the liturgical calling forth of *orixás* with sacred rhythms. The drums, as visual and sound icons, historically emerge as symbols of religiosity bridging diverse African origins and valorizing performance aesthetics. The origin myth also establishes Congado's de facto cultural elevation of percussion music and call-and-response chants: Our Lady of the Rosary's celestial presence as the patron of blacks emerges in spiritual conjunction with African-derived music and performance aesthetics. In Minas Gerais, *congadeiros* wear the rosary as a ritual object of devotion. As the story is told, the Virgin's tears fell in witnessing the brutality of Brazilian slavery, with each tear dropping onto the rich soil and creating a new life in the form of a seed. Sorrow watered the struggling plants, one variety becoming known as *lágrimas de Nossa Senhora* (Our Lady's tears). It is from the bead-like seeds of this plant that *congadeiros* make their rosaries of ritual power.

According to some *congadeiros*, the *guarda* name *catopê* is a corruption of *quatro pés* (four feet), referencing how slaves fleeing their owners crawled on all fours to avoid being sighted. The dance associated with *catopê* thus represents to some the shape shifting of the slave's flight to freedom. As with the many origin narratives of Congado, the *vilão* (villain) has multiple explanations. One is that the word stems from the Portuguese dance of the same name. Another has its origins in the late nineteenth-century social fallout of the "Golden Law" (*Lei Aurea*) of May 13, 1888, freeing slaves: "villains," some claimed, were those who in the eyes of whites opposing emancipation celebrated in the streets loud enough to signal the end of slavery to those hiding in the surrounding *quilombos* and squatter camps.[17] The *congo guarda* often is placed at the front of the procession to attract attention and announce the *cortejo*. The *moçambique* sometimes appears as the most important *guarda* due to its role in accompanying the crowned principals. A praise song from the *congo* and *moçambique guardas* states: "Hail Mary in heaven / with the rosary in hand / contemplating the mysteries."[18]

Congadeiros worship publicly during processions, exhibiting devotional spoken prayer (*oração*) as personal, humble supplication, or as an individual prayer identifying with a particular saint. Praise songs remark on the history, nature, and gratification of patron saint relationships with the group or community. *Guarda* banners depicting the group's saints are displayed at the front of the procession and are often touched or kissed by members of other *guardas*, and by spectators. Within this array of religiosity occurs ceremonial, obligation-fulfilling "payment of promises," exchanges of statements and gestures among participants acknowledging social hierarchy and reciprocity. Almost all of this ritual occurs in public streets, plazas, and churchyards, and in front of private homes, which become parallel social spaces transformed by a religiosity hybridized by African-derived performance practice. Congado's storytelling is wrapped in the sound worlds of drums, shakers and vocal timbres, an orchestra of insistent sounds redefining public space. *Guardas* also perform for special events, the Day of Kings on January 6 (Reisado), and feast days of other patron saints.

Candombe: The Most Sacred of *Guardas*

Though strongly associated with patron saint festivities, candombe retains strong links to ancestral worship and other personalized contexts such as the "payment of promises," and is often performed separately from Congado processions.[19] Candombe is further linked to the June festivals (Festa Junina) celebrating the church calendar days of four Catholic saints: Saint Anthony, on June 13; Saint John, on June 24; and Saint Peter and Saint Paul, on June 29. The less-public, sometimes secretive candombe is regarded by many *congadeiros* as the original, most sacred *guarda*, which may descend partially from the absorbed remnants of non-Catholic, Afro-Mineiro religious practices such as calundú.[20] As Paulo Dias has commented,

> Candombe takes place preferably in sacred places such as brotherhood chapels, yards of older black communities, at the foot of crosses, or churchyards. In some places, the candombe goes out into the streets following the *congo* and *moçambique guardas*. It is danced in commemoration of the patron saint Our Lady of the Rosary or other patron saints—Santana, Santa Cruz—as a ritualized appeasement, or marking events of great religious significance.[21]

Today, candombe is practiced in communities that form a geographic arc through the counties surrounding Belo Horizonte in central Minas: Açude,

Mato do Tição, Os Arturos in Contagem, Jatobá, Matozinhos, Ribeirão das Neves, Justinópolis, and others.[22] In Mato do Tição, the candombe drums known as Crivo, Santana, and Requinta receive blessings as vessels of communication with community ancestors.[23] The Mineiro towns of Fidalgo and Mocambeiro host parading candombe *guardas* that join other *guardas* in street processions: footed drum players carry their instruments, periodically stopping to play in preestablished locations along the parade route. Some contemporary scholars have noted an isolated candombe cultural zone in central Minas:

> In Minas Gerais, candombe is observed in the region north of Belo Horizonte until Serra do Cipó. . . . The candombe, perhaps the most Bantu of the Congado, is a type of closed society for blacks of the Our Lady of the Rosary brotherhood who desire to be Christians without having to stop being Bantus. Ancestors are remembered to the rhythms of old, sacred drums. . . . Zambi (the God Creator) is with them. In many cases, candombe appears as *jongo* or *caxambú* [nonliturgical circle dances associated with blacks in the Sudeste].[24]

This region has further been identified, by anthropologist José Jorge de Carvalho among others, as having maintained a certain remoteness among communities known for candombe:

> As a cultural form, the candombe is a spectacular case of socially constructed remoteness within a framework of deep musical interrelationship. Matição [also spelled Mato do Tição] is a village quite protected from the outside world, especially from the central institutions of the state: very poor formal education, no television, a minimum access to radios, inaccessible dirt roads, very few economic activities apart from subsistence agriculture and some handicrafts. Yet . . . Matição shows a high degree of integration and contact, probably over hundreds of years, with other Afro-Brazilian traditions of the area.[25]

The Serra do Cipó lies at the southern end of the Serra do Espinhaço and is partially protected as a national park (Parque Nacional Serra do Cipó), with watersheds flowing west to the Rio São Francisco and east to the Rio Doce. The highland *cerrado* brushland here once met what had been the massive Mata Atlântica's western edge, the rainforest once covering a large swath of Minas's southeastern zone. The Diamantina–Ouro Preto leg of the colonial-era Royal Highway, the Estrada Real, a segment known as the Diamond

Road (Caminho dos Diamantes), runs through the Serra do Cipó. During the slave era, *quilombos* dotted the mountainous landscape surrounding these towns and hamlets, and like the rest of Minas, they faced a postmining economic decline. In the twenty-first century, research has revealed widespread manifestations of Congado-related musical practices throughout *quilombo* communities (*comunidades quilombolas*), a term appropriated to describe a number of marginalized black and mixed-race communities, some of which are remnants of runaway slave villages.[26] Here, the cultural and religious heritage of local ancestors is seen as a distinct, collective tie to the rich legacies of African-derived drumming, dance, song, and language within the Afro-Mineiro traditions of Black Catholicism. Several of Minas's highland interior communities fostered candombe as a Reinado specialty, and as a component of saints' day celebrations.

The spiritual powers of ritualized drums are invoked in an origin myth for a particular set of rare *tambu* drums constructed in the nineteenth century (fig. 5.1) that are still used in candombe festivities held by the Açude community in the Serra do Cipó, home to roughly sixty residents, some of whom performed with Milton Nascimento's Tambores de Minas project (see chapter 9). In 2004, Brazilian president "Lula" da Silva awarded the Medal of the Order of Cultural Merit to residents of Açude for preserving candombe. Writer and journalist Afonso Capelas Jr. relates:

Immediately after the prayer in honor of Our Lady of the Rosary, there is a short procession to the yard where the *tambus* are resting beside the fire, so that the leather stretches into the desired tone. Suddenly someone crosses the yard dressed as a bull, chasing and scaring people with his run. Half an hour later, the *tambus* are tuned and then played by three men of the community, and candombe begins to pierce the night. A human circle forms around the drummers, and a *candombeiro* enters the center to sing. The verses are short, fired off defiantly. The themes vary from religion to love and routine events. Often the *candombeiro* improvises his song, and the circle of participants answered in chorus with traditional verses from the time of slaves. Dancing and swirling the body frantically, as if in a trance, the *candombeiro* turns the space inside the dance circle to another participant. Anyone, of any age—even those who do not belong to the Açude community—is always welcome to participate. The party continues until dawn, when cake, *fuba*, and *broa* [corn dishes] are served for guests. But the fuel for *candombeiros* is really *cachaça* accompanied by manioc cookies. "It serves to relax, but is not required," says Dona Mercês [Maria das Mercês Santos, matriarch of the Açude religious community].[27]

Equally important to candombe's spiritual efficacy are African *mandinga* beliefs augmenting the Black Catholic origin myth in which the candombe drums call forth the Virgin Mary and baby Jesus from perilous ocean waves. Açude's legendary *tambu* carry the mythical power revealed in this passage describing the nineteenth-century owner of the contemporary community's enslaved ancestors, the slave master living in the nearby Cipó Velho fazenda, which still stands:

> The main story related to the candombe in the Serra do Cipó says that the slave batuques always took place in the early evening after work in the fields. The blacks of the Cipó Velho fazenda gathered to dance to the *tambus*, even though it was not to the liking of the white owner. One day, irritated by the noise coming from the slave quarters, the master ordered the foreman to end the party, burning the *tambus*. But the smoke released by the drums penetrated the big house, bothering the owner for hours. Almost suffocated, he imagined that it was a curse commissioned by the blacks. Startled [in fear for his health], he ordered the slaves to build new drums, believing that only in this way would the spell be annulled. This was done, and the *mandinga* faded.[28]

The Açude candombe heritage is illustrated in a 2004 documentary film, *Candombe do Açude: Arte, cultura e fé,* and a 2012 documentary film, *Tá caindo fulô . . . Tambús de candombe de comunidade do Açude,* which feature extensive footage of *tambu* drum performances.[29]

Drums remind contemporary audiences of candombe's African-derived principles. This ritual's trio of sacred drums is sometimes collectively referred to as the *terno de candombes.* The tall, footed, conical drums carved from tree trunks are often given the names, widest to narrowest, Santana, Santaninha, and Jeremia or Chama.[30] Santana (Santa Ana/Saint Anne) is recognized as the Virgin Mary's mother and thus the grandmother of Jesus Christ. Santana is also a patron saint of miners. In nearby Jatobá, *congadeiros* perform candombe on drums known as Gomá, Dambim, and Dambá. Recalling the African association of *ngoma* drumming and healing, it is worth noting that "Gomá" is likely a corruption of this word. The cowhide skins of the candombe are often nailed to the wood. This ancient, polygenetic goblet drum design is common throughout disparate regions of sub-Saharan Africa, characterizing for instance the *bulup* dance drum of the Kuba peoples of the Congo, and other types in Malawi and Mozambique. The footed drum types common to the Brazilian *jongo* and batuque genres of the rural Sudeste are known as *quinjengue, candongueira*, or *joana*.

Candombe ensembles from the central Minas tradition might further include the *puíta* (a friction drum also known as *cuíca*), the *caixa* barrel drum, and the *guaiá* woven basket shaker. The *cuíca* is known throughout Brazil and is found in a wide range of genres, from carnival samba to mainstream commercial MPB hits. The variously sized instrument's uncanny, voice-like groan, created by rubbing a stick attached to the underside of the drum's single membrane and located inside the shell, can be made to produce subtle rhythmic variations; an expressive, accomplished player can tonally manipulate the drum by depressing the skin with their free hand, thus raising and lowering the pitch. Another term for this friction drum is *onça* (jungle cat). Typically, this dance and music style retains an additional, ritualized connection to the spirit world of Afro-Mineiro ancestors and their lands of origin. It is in this sense that candombe can be performed outside the context of Congado. In Açude, functions include the "paying of promises" (*pagamento do promessas*) to a patron saint. However, there are few claims to common practices among all the candombe communities of central Minas. In the urban Os Arturos community, located in the Belo Horizonte suburb of Contagem, candombe is a private ritual within the Reinado festival. Geraldo Arthur Camilo, leading elder of Os Arturos and direct descendant of the community patriarch (Arthur Camilo Silverio, mentioned earlier), confirms the legend positing the candombe drum as the sacred instrument responsible for rescuing the Virgin Mary from the ocean waves.[31] During the 1990s, some outsiders were allowed to observe the Os Arturos candombe event. But community elders later decided to close it off to nonmembers, fearing a loss of spiritual force.[32]

Congado Instruments: The *Tambores de Minas*

The closing song of a Reinado in Jatobá includes the lyrics "If death does not kill me, *tamborim* / If the land does not eat me, *tamborim* / I will return next year, *tamborim*."[33] Instruments supporting the feast of Our Lady of the

Rosary were never authoritatively fixed or prescribed by an orthodox body. The procession seems to have always required a combination of drum-based propulsive dance rhythms and idiophonic shakers, timbres transformed by ritualized contexts into mystical sound worlds. An anonymous witness chronicling a festivity in 1730 Portugal noted:

> [O]ne has never seen so peaceful a feast with so many blasts: there was a sequence of minuets, and many descant singers on their parts, [and] the blacks of the Rosary making a well-concerted dissonance with guitar, *gral*, violin, and playing the horn by the *cumbe*. . . . [F]or at the same time they played among them *pandeiros*, stones, *arranhol*, board-shaped guitars, cocoa violins, whistles, *berimbau*, and rattles.[34]

Loud, open-air drums played along procession routes have earned the moniker *tambores de Minas*. Today, *congo* and *moçambique guardas* parade with low-register, rhythmically interlocking drums known as *caixas* or *tambores*. Carried by shoulder straps, these large, cylindrical drums are typically made of wood, have double-headed cowhide skins, and feature laced rope tension, or metal rod assembly tuning. In the past, *caixas* would have resembled other ambulatory drums constructed from hollowed-out tree trunks, such as those of the influential *ingoma* family of African-derived drums. Many of today's *caixas* are factory made with metal bodies and plastic heads, like those of the modern *surdo* drum of samba fame. They are played either with two mallets, long-handled beater mallets with hide-covered or fabric heads; or with curved wooden sticks. The construction, performance, and maintenance of traditional wood and skin *caixas* are points of pride; these drums are a core of percussion-heavy accompaniment anchoring call-and-response praise songs and creating distinct patterns of repeated rhythmic ostinatos known as *padrões rítmicos*, with interlocking resultant rhythms called "answering and marking" (*caixa de esposta* and *caixa de marcação*), all further embellished with ornamental flourishes known as *floreios*. A third percussive voice, often a *caixa de repique*, initiates "chiming-in" pattern variations called *resposta*.[35]

Brazil's treasure of African-derived music has produced varied, regional uses of musical terms, including *ingoma*, widely used for drums; to designate cultural space or a group of instruments, performers, or dancers; and as an adjectival expression for a "very good" performance.[36] The nineteenth-century founder of the Os Arturos community in Contagem, near Belo

Horizonte, Arthur Camilo Silverio, is known as the "father of the drum" (*dono de ingoma*).[37] *Guardas* from community to community throughout Minas may feature from two to four or more *caixas*. Patterns referred to as *marchas* by some *congadeiros* are shared in variant forms throughout the region and are further distinguished by variations in *caixa* rhythms.[38] Re-created through imitative oral tradition, rhythmic patterns retain essential characteristics meeting each *guarda's* functional and aesthetic standards. The rhythms known as *marcha lenta*, *marcha grave*, and *marcha dobrado* each have a place in ritualized sequences. In a July 1996 field recording made in Ribeirão das Neves, Minas Gerais, for instance, *caixa* players from both the *congo* and *moçambique guardas* of the Rosário de Justinópolis join to play a *marcha grave* (roughly seventy beats per minute) during the *festa's* important opening ritual of the raising of the banner.

The *tamboril*, a small, rectangular, double-sided frame drum held by a handle, appears in in some versions of the seminal origin myth: its special sound coaxed the Virgin Mary and the infant Jesus to shore, thus ascribing symbolic power to that instrument.[39] The *tamboril's* simple, box-like wood-and-hide construction is typically festooned with colorful ribbons and metal disc jangles, and like other instruments it is often adorned with the rosary. The skin is nailed to the wooden frame and struck with a short, thick stick. Also known by the variant *tamborim*, the *tamboril* here described is closer in sound and appearance to the antiquated Iberian *adufe* frame drum (from Arabic *al'duf*) than to the small, circular *tamborim* of the modern-day *batucada* percussion ensemble associated with samba and carnival.

The *canzalo* (also *canzale*) is a notched wood or bamboo scraped idiophone rubbed with a stick and known elsewhere in Brazil as a *reco-reco*. Typically, there are multiple *canzalos* in the same *guarda*. The traditional *canzalo* is held vertically and rested against the player's shoulder, its materials creating a more subdued, mellower timbre than the metal, mass-produced *reco-reco* (*industrializado reco-reco*) also used by some *guardas*. The variously designed metal *reco-recos* found in *guardas* include those identical to types readily heard in samba and *carnaval baterias*. As with the shaker instruments discussed below, the *canzalo* player produces variations of accented patterns within a constant subdivision of the beat. *Pantangomes* are circular metal shakers of various sizes, some with welded handles, held horizontally at chest level with both hands. Several *pantangomes* can grace a single *guarda*, providing continuous timbral strata of shimmering metallophonic accents. Other shaker instruments may include the *meia-lua* (half-moon), *guaiá*, *maraca ganzá*, *chocalho*, and *xequerê*. *Gungas* are metallophonic anklet shakers requiring accented stepping and marked kicking of the lower leg to activate the sound, adding to the corporeal aspect of the processional music. *Guizos* are very similar but strapped higher up the leg, just below the knee. Dance movements activate *gungas* and *guizos*, augmenting the march-like progression of the procession's gentle, simple gait. As a praise song states, "Sing and dance, creole / with the power of God."[40]

In addition to these core percussion instruments, *congadeiros* have welcomed the viola, guitar (*violão*), *bandolim*, saxophone, and clarinet. Some Reinado festivities feature brass bands and variations of small mixed ensembles composed of winds, brass, and percussion from the band tradition. The *sanfona* (accordion) sporadically joined Congado following its introduction to Brazil by Germans immigrating to Rio Grande do Sul and its subsequent spread to the northeastern region by soldiers returning from the Paraguayan War of 1864–1870, where it became essential to *forró* and *baião*. The *congadeiro* Sinval, from Bom Despacho, Minas Gerais, refers to instrument making and the magical divination of the *mandinga* tradition: "It was a thing made with a lot of *mandinga*; we had a certain time to enter the forest to cut the wood, kill the animal, and make the drum."[41] Recalling his sixty years as a *congadeiro* in his rural hometown a day's journey east of Belo Horizonte, Bené shared with researcher Patrícia Brandão Couto insight into instruments of the *congado* and *moçambique guardas* from the 1930s onward:

> In the *congo* there was the *caixa*, *adufo*, and *canzalo*, what today is called the *reco-reco*. All the instruments were made from the forest, where we went to compose the batuque. We didn't have the *sanfona*. The *pandeiros* we have here now we would never have dreamed of. . . . The first *pandeiros*, do you know what they were made of? We used empty cans of guava paste, punctured holes in the side, and screwed in bottle caps, and there: we made a *pandeiro*. . . . today we just attach ribbons [to modern *pandeiros*] to make them pretty! We had a *tambourinho* also. What *capitão de congo* walks without a *tambourinho*? [also known as *tamboril*]. The *caixa de guerra* was made of wood, rope, and hide from a bull or cow. But in the early years, they were made with leaves of the yam plant. . . . Today, the *congo* has viola, *cavaquinho*, *sanfona* . . . some even have a banjo! The *moçambique* [however] is almost the same as it used to be: *caixa*, *gunga*, *patangona*, and *meia-lua*, but they cannot change, right? They have to be the same—as when Our Lady accompanied them.[42]

Flutes of the *Pífano de Congado* in Rural Northern Minas Gerais

A rich heritage of wood and cane flute instruments grace regional Congado styles in parts of the Serro Frio region and in the more isolated north and northeast of Minas Gerais including the Alto Jequitinhonha. Northern Minas *pífano de congado* exists in cultural and geographic proximity to Brazil's northeastern region, where *pífano* traditions (flute, fife) flourish, primarily the *banda de pífano* featuring two or more transverse flutes and drums such as the *zabumba*. The Congado ensembles of central and northern Minas have thus been referred to as the Mineiro version of the northeastern fife bands, though both echo medieval Portuguese genres. Iconography from the thirteenth-century *Cantigas de Santa Maria* (Canticles of Holy Mary) illustrate bagpipes, and two individuals each simultaneously playing a small drum and end-blown flute. The *Cantigas de Santa Maria* are attributed to Alfonso X "The Wise," king of Castile and León, and include 420 musically notated poems written in Galician-Portuguese, many featuring miniatures illustrating pairs of musicians performing on various instruments. Many eighteenth-century Portuguese immigrants settling in Minas Gerais originated from northern Portugal, where traditional religious-folk ensembles called *gaiteiros*, associated with local patron saints' day celebrations, consisted of bagpipes (*gaita de foles*) with snare drum and bass drum (*bombo*). Common to northeastern Portugal, a solo performer known as a *tamboleiro* simultaneously plays drums and the end-blown *flauta* translated as "shepherd's flute."[43] The *adufe* square frame drum is a staple instrument in eastern Portugal, where it is played by women in accompaniment to popular religious songs. Though the *adufe* was generally displaced by the *pandeiro* in twentieth-century Brazil, a close relative known as the *tamboril* appears in contemporary Congado Mineiro.

The *pífano de congado* of northern Minas Gerais brings insight to Congado's most often cited iconographic source, an 1820s etching by Johann Moritz Rugendas. This German artist, known for his valuable documentation of nineteenth-century Brazilian life, depicts in his etching *Festa de Nossa Senhora do Rosário, padroeira dos negros*, the *caixa* drum, *pífano*, *marimba*, and *gaita de foles* accompanying a procession in Ouro Preto (fig. 6.2 and 6.3). The etching places Old World Luso-African instruments in Minas while presenting some of the cultural roots of *pífano de congado*. The term *marimba* was often historically used in Brazil for the lamellophone, formerly known there as *quissanje*; the instrument descended from the great

African traditions of *mbira,* or *sanza.* A much earlier work, Carlos Julião's 1776 *Coroação de um rei nos festejos de reis* (Coronation of a king in the Festival of the King), depicts a portable gourd resonator xylophone (also known as a *marimba*), and a female participant playing a transverse flute among the parading orchestra of natural horn, viola, *caixa, pandeiro, adufe,* and *canzalo.* Portable resonator xylophones were used in some *guardas* of coastal São Paulo as late as the 1950s.

Daniel Lima Magalhães's ethnomusicological studies of *pífano de congado* in northern Minas examine large subregions of the state, including the towns and surroundings of Conceição do Mato Dentro, Serro, Alvorada de Minas, and Diamantina; to the east and north, Minas Novas, Capelinha, Taiobeiras, and the Rio Pardo de Minas region; and in the valley of the Jequitinhonha River including the Alta Jequitinhonha and the Minas Gerais–Bahia state border area.[44] Some of the larger towns in this northern Minas region east of Montes Claros, such as Grão Mogol, grew from eighteenth-century illicit mining settlements; near the confluence of the Araçuaí and Jequitinhonha Rivers, the town of Araçuaí emerged as a regional center for gemstones. Here, in local Congado honor guards (*guardas de honras*), flutes join large *caixa* drums in northern Minas Reinado traditions (*pífanos e caixas nas festas de Reinado*) in which six-hole, transverse *pífanos* (sometimes *pífaro* or *pife*) and end-blown vertical flutes known as either *gaita* or *canudo* enliven *pífano de congado* processions.[45] The village of Sucuriú hosted the Spix and Martius expedition in 1818. This Alta Jequitinhonha settlement twenty miles northeast of Minas Novas, since renamed Francisco Badaró, was already home to a thriving *pífanos e caixas* music tradition utilized for the São João celebrations of the still very popular Festa Junina:

> When we entered the camp at sunset, there began to resonate the strident resounding of drums and flutes and the penetrating sounds of *canza*, the bursting of firecrackers announced the solemnity of São João, celebrated mainly by blacks, with extravagant merriment. The formalities of black religious practice are observed with such fervor that they take the lead over the whites, allowing them in many circumstances to the take the lead in a certain way.[46]

The northeast of Minas is also home to ensembles of bamboo flutes known as *bandas da taquara* with an almost exclusive connection to Congado, named after the variety of bamboo used to make the flute.[47] *Taquara* flutes are known in other parts of Minas Gerais dating back to the colonial era; Englishman John Luccock described them in 1818 when he heard some local musicians one night in Lagoa Dourada, on the Estrada Real's Caminho Velho north of São João del-Rei "A few black musicians came to our inn, and one of them played the *flautim* [piccolo] while another played guitar. It was nothing to disregard; the third had made for himself a passable instrument, something like a flute from a section of *taquara*."[48]

"They Danced a Curious Step": Three Nineteenth-Century Accounts of Congado

With a dearth of descriptive accounts, early eighteenth-century Congado in Minas Gerais is known primarily through lay brotherhood documents such as charters and financial accounts detailing payments to musicians and clergy for a sung mass, a *Te Deum*, or a sermon. Priests and church officials were sometimes known to enter communities only to perform fundamental sacraments such as funerals, weddings, and baptisms. Historically important descriptions begin to emerge with the travel literature of visiting Europeans invited by the emperor to tour Minas.

Spending Christmas 1843 in Sabará, the French naturalist Francis Castelnau describes an election of the king of the Congo on December 27:

One of the windows of the salon allowed us to enjoy a unique spectacle; I refer to the big festival during which blacks meet for the election of a king of Congo. As done every year, this extravagant carnival bestows on the elected great influence over his comrades. The scene was very curious, remarkably mixing recollections of the African coast with Brazilian customs and religious ceremonies. At first, the king of Congo, in the company of his better half, arrives to occupy one of the chairs placed beforehand for use in his court. Both are magnificently dressed, bearing solid silver crowns and gold scepters. . . . A thing worthy of repair, the king brings a black mask, as if afraid that the permanence of his forefathers' natural color had faded. The court, whose costumes mix all colors and fancy embellishments, sit on either side of the royal couple; they enter after a multitude of other characters, the most considerable of which are undoubtedly great captains, famous warriors, or powerful ambassadors from afar, all attired in the fashion of Brazilian savages, with large tufts of feathers, cavalry sabers, and arm shields. In this tumult mingled national dances, dialogues between people, between them and the king, or king and queen, and simulated combat with every kind of somersault worthy of trained monkeys. The funniest thing was when a black man masqueraded as white, dressed in the red uniform of an English soldier; carrying a guitar, he was accompanied by an orchestra, so to speak, of the native type. The darkness eventually fell over these characters, who wanted nothing more than to be part of the confusion.[49]

In examining this account, we can say that the guitar could easily have been a viola, as Sabará was home to a vibrant viola luthier community. The "native" orchestra was likely a selection of African-derived drums and percussion just as "national" dances references in all likelihood African-derived practice. "Simulated combat" refers to battle action theatrically depicted in the procession, or may even reference capoeira, the ludic fight dance of Brazilian/Angolan origin: capoeira practitioners were known to have participated in Congado processionals in the nineteenth century. Commissioned by Louis Philippe, France's last king, Castelnau spent five years traveling from Rio de Janeiro to Lima, Peru, with a botanist and taxidermist. While the account and chronology may have been accurate, such Congado elections were not typically celebrated in late December, although today this is done in the Serro Frio town of Conceição do Mato Dentro and other small towns in Sul de Minas. The event may have been staged for Castelnau's benefit, or perhaps the details were taken from the author's previous experience and fancifully inserted into his Sabará timeline. Although he described Congado's cast of characters and reenactments of war scenarios and diplomacy, the king's "black mask" hints at the role of Baltazar from the *máscaras de Santos Reis* (Holy King masks) of the Folia de Reis tradition. The king of Congo is not known for wearing a black mask in the Congado tradition.

Castelnau's "extravagant carnival" is echoed in a description by another European observer, suggestive even of Congado's links to the premodern carnival practices that were developing in the nineteenth century. In June 1851, Hermann Burmeister made note of elections for a king of Congo in Lagoa Santa, less than twenty miles from the heart of today's Belo Horizonte. Peter Lund, mentioned in these comments, later made the 1863 discovery in nearby caves of the ten-thousand-year-old human remains of what became known as Lagoa Santa Man.

[In Lagoa Santa,] the big festivities of Our Lady of the Rosary begin on June 8. . . . Slaves choose among themselves a king and a queen, and always from among legitimate slaves, not from the free blacks also participating. The royal couple appoints ministers, princes, and princesses, knights and ladies of the Court, and others of the new Court. These dignitaries adorn themselves in the best way possible, using old blankets and uniforms, footwear silk and everything else they can find, prizing most the ornaments of real gold and diamonds. At Dr. Lund's house, I saw his butler's daughter sporting on her arms and neck chains of gold of considerable value, and also earrings. On these occasions, participants help out one another: parents the children, the oldest the teens, but only members of the Court are presented with jewelry. The king uses a crown of golden cardboard and a scepter, while the queen is presented with a jewel-encrusted tiara. Accompanied by his entire Court, the king parades through the town to the sound of a music band in a procession both solemn and joyful, with banners and singers, and approaches the church to receive the blessing of the priest. The procession continues, later finishing with a great feast. The queen's patron usually pays the feast expenses, and other costs of the church are covered by funds obtained through a collection. The party continues into the night with dances and parades to torchlight, continuing until the revel slows and the participants are overcome by fatigue and sleep. Then life returns to normal: the king removes the crown, the queen takes off the tiara, the dignitaries undress their showy uniforms, and jewelry is returned to the coffers. During the festival, of little interest to the whites, and of great importance for blacks, no one accepts work offers even when promised a fortune. Spectators are not lacking; whites, mulattoes and blacks hear, for days, the monotonous hum of hundreds of voices. The celebration for Our Lady of the Rosary is the biggest of the year in the life of the poor slave.[50]

Here, Burmeister emphasizes the Reisado's carnivalesque atmosphere, an observation echoed by later commentators connecting Congado to secularized carnival parades. Behind the scenes, benefactors (slave owners, members of elite brotherhoods aiding their Catholic brethren, and locals of importance) supplied luxury goods and other material and financial support, although whites in general showed "little interest." This assistance was in addition to fundraising efforts by black Catholic brotherhoods, organizations already beholden to religious patrons of the white establishment for some forms of financial support.

While accompanying her husband, Sir Richard Burton, at the Morro Velho mine bordering modern-day Belo Horizonte, Lady Isabel Burton commented on a staged Congado celebration at the mining headquarters:

[T]he slaves gave us an Indian representation of Indians of a war-dance, and fight. They were dressed in war-paint and feathers. The King and his son were enthroned on chairs, and the courtiers came and seated themselves around on the grass, the attendants carry[ing] umbrellas. First there was a council. The King was dissatisfied with his Minister of War, who was seized and brought before him. Then the Minister made a speech in his own praise. Then here was a fight, in which a captain took everyone prisoner, and gave the swords to the King. Then the Minister was poisoned by the enemy but cured by a nut which the King gave him. Then all the captives crawled on the ground like snakes to the King's feet to do him homage. The King's jesters were great fun. They had a gong and bells and tom-tom and sang and danced at the same time. They danced a curious step—little steps in which they adhered to a peculiar time.[51]

Here, "Indians" (a *caboclo guarda*) and court intrigues are cast in the light of the king's magical healing powers, which beg comparison to indigenous and sacred African healing rituals of powerful sorcerers. The living king-sorcerer of Congado mediates the threat of fatal illness and death, juxtaposing the two cosmological worlds of the living and the dead.

Music and Ritual as African Parallelism in Popular Catholicism: Drums, Dancing, and the King of Congo

Catholicism, its adoption by Africans and their descendants, and the manner in which it was taught and practiced among the enslaved in Minas Gerais, did not necessarily represent a full displacement of African-derived cosmology and methods of worship. James H. Sweet comments:

Catholicism and traditional Kongolese beliefs remained discrete cosmologies because their ends were vastly different. Christian revelations, when they occurred, demonstrated and validated the power of a largely unknowable, mysterious, otherworldly God. And this most often required blind faith—communion with an idealized apparition dwelling in the heavens. Kongolese revelation, on the other hand, was a dialogue between the living and the world of the spirits, including the spirits of ancestors, whose powers and foibles were familiar and well known, in real life as well as in death.[52]

In considering Atlantic creole Christianity, Kalle Kananoja theorizes that many enslaved Africans, unlike most Europeans, made less of the conflicts between Catholic and African cosmologies.[53] However, it is obvious that most Afro-Brazilians during the slave era had little choice but to adopt new perspectives on religiosity in the face of systemic violence, as seen for instance in the Inquisition's brutal repression of calundú practices in Minas Gerais. From its inception, Congado accommodated African-derived musical traits and creolized belief systems, with these alternatives to orthodox practice in some ways mirroring popular Catholicism in its broader growth in Brazil regardless of race, class, and region. Primary African beliefs included a cosmology explaining and accounting for social roles and differences; the human soul as an eternal force; and spirit-imbued worlds of the living and of the dead, the latter populated by the active souls of ancestors whose influence mediates healing and divination.[54] There are detailed differences between cosmologies such as the "knowable," available gods and spirits of the Congolese, and the "unknowable" God of Christianity; the daily revelations of the spiritual world to the laypersons in Congolese cosmology, and the super-rare, miraculous revelations brokered by hierarchical figures distancing the layperson in Christianity. In critiquing the notion of religious syncretism in black brotherhoods in Minas Gerais, Gomes and Pereira repudiate claims of a syncretic "symbiosis" of cultural traits of Europeans, Africans, and Native Indians.[55] Historically, some Congado practices in Minas included African cosmological beliefs and ritualized interaction with natural forces, including the use of *mandinga* and amulets, divination, healing, and liturgical song praising African deities. Laura de Mello e Souza states: "[T]he slaves' Afro-Catholic syncretism was a reality that ended up merging with the maintenance of 'primitive' African religious rites and myths. St. Benedict was worshipped, but so was Ogum."[56] Proof of this rests in some white, elite attitudes toward Congado. Late twentieth-century ethnographies in Sul de Minas reveal stigmatized associations by town elites between this processional practice and Macumba, denying the Reinado its Catholic due while interpreting African-derived cultural expression as "black magic."

Today, the Black Catholicism particular to Congado Mineiro still mediates hybridized African-derived performance practice and cosmologies clearly framed within Catholic structure with strong admixtures of fundamentally Christian beliefs. Ultimately, the Virgin Mary and her rosary transcend the role of a divine heroine granted to blacks by Christian tradition. Reconstituted in colonial and imperial Minas Gerais, and bolstered with African beliefs, the brotherhood of the patron saint became a primary social institution. The most obvious form of parallel ritual was the election of a black, "African" king, an activity associated with West Central African descendants, leading to outsider views of the festivities as profane. In Minas Gerais, nineteenth-century provincial laws protecting the election and countering edicts passed against *congadeiros* during the Pombaline era resulted in the regional stamp of Congado Mineiro. Elizabeth Kiddy has noted:

> The acceptance of the Reinados of the blacks by the lawmakers, and thus the elites, of Minas Gerais also demonstrates that the celebration had become part of the society and culture of local Minas Gerais. This acceptance of the Reinado in Minas Gerais diverged from the tendency of provincial lawmakers elsewhere in Brazil during the same period . . . [and] demonstrates the continuation of a pattern from the eighteenth century of white interest, and even participation, in Afro-Mineiro activities. . . . Rosary brotherhoods, therefore, were able to continue public celebrations—increasingly using the financial backing of white patrons—that linked them, as Africans of many ethnicities, to their own past and reinforced their unity as a community of blacks in Brazil.[57]

Congado's Social Roots in Minas Gerais

Linked to Luso-African traditions found in other parts of Brazil, Congado in Minas Gerais reconstituted itself among the colonial-era community-based religious brotherhoods that developed with little direct control and participation of the local church parish. The social institution of the brotherhood was designed by church doctrine, absorbed into Crown law, and kept in place in Brazil by white elites, colonial and imperial authorities, and slave owners. They molded behavior and class distinctions yet also accommodated some degree of African-derived aesthetics and cosmologies. In this sense, culturally powerful yet politically marginalized black brotherhoods, seen as a distinct social opportunity by their members, were also ambiguous social institutions creating unique social spaces of resistance. A popular Catholicism of the liminal classes, Congado Mineiro flourished in the eighteenth century as slaves and freed persons maintained lay versions of the ceremony, resulting in a quilt of vital yet fragmented profiles reflecting local needs, more individualized religiosity, and varying music styles. This tradition distinguished public life in slave-era Minas Gerais, bringing together socially marginalized participants through devotional traditions.

With owners responsible for the education of the enslaved, a lack of printed material for religious instruction and catechism was the norm. Religious education for the few enslaved Africans and their descendants actually given the opportunity was purged of notions of equality and human rights and rather emphasized humility, docility, and the punishments awaiting those lacking such characteristics. They were often excluded from the civilized, family-based practices that religious society offered others, denied for instance the right to serve as baptismal godparents. In Minas, blacks were allowed into mixed-race churches yet were typically forced together into segregated sections. Afro-Mineiros faced repressive measures enforced by the Portuguese Inquisition and *Devassas eclesiásticas* against calundú and other African religious beliefs, a broad campaign of social violence that drove those practices underground and channeled many Mineiros of African descent toward participation in Christian organizations. For some of these African-born and Brazilian-born blacks, social bonds among brotherhoods grew strong with belief in the spirit world and ancestor worship, accommodating diversity and difference and channeling community among ethnicities forced together by slavery.

The eighteenth-century Jesuit writer André João Antonil critiqued Catholic teachings among Brazilian slave populations and emphasized the importance of allowing a parallel, African-derived religiosity in popular, folk Catholicism. He encouraged the Reinado festival, the crowning of the king of Congo during the feast of Our Lady of the Rosary, and the adoption of patron saints for blacks, and called for the legitimization of the cult of Saint Benedict. The Portuguese Crown, however, cared little for such inclusion, or for the education and religious instruction of the mostly nonliterate free poor. The regional social impact of this distance between religion and religiosity was greatly magnified by the banishment from colonial Minas Gerais of religious orders, which occurred in 1720.[58] The policy applied to most priests and other church officials in a high-stakes game of political and financial control over the region's mining wealth. The long distances separating parishes greatly impacted even the chapel choir directors responsible for music in those churches and their ability to maintain liturgical tradition. More than fifty segregated brotherhoods existed in colonial Minas Gerais, relatively independent of direct church control, each with its own devotional focus and membership requirements.

Some of these social aspects of religiosity and religious organization leads historian Renato da Silva Dias to surmise that "the political control [of slaves and the poor] via religion suffered many drawbacks in Minas."[59] That is, while the social structuring of Minas Gerais grew through castes, ranks, corporations, and guilds, as it did in the rest of Brazil, this society of "estates" (*sociedade estamental*) placed more influence in the hands of local, racially segregated brotherhoods as institutions sponsoring cultural events such as the Reinado. Notions of Catholicism as a form of blanket political and spiritual control over the Afro-Mineiro population, and as a belief system responsible for the wholesale displacement of African-derived cosmology, lack efficacy due if only in part to these conditions. Glaura Lucas points out:

> In Minas Gerais . . . brotherhoods reflected social relations and differences in a society that emerged marked by tension and insecurity. . . . [I]n their devotional celebrations to Our Lady, blacks were permitted to include certain African rituals such as the coronation of kings and queens, and the right to use percussion instruments in the performance of their music and dance.[60]

Congado's significant use of African-derived cultural expressions flourished as a result of these factors, particularly the expulsion of church orders, a development that allowed black brotherhoods more aesthetic independence in public displays of devotion. Afro-Mineiro brotherhoods, in their belief systems and in their mounting of processions enriched with drumming, chant, dance, and costume, enjoyed this type of independence from direct church control. Brotherhoods reflected and generated colonial society's racial segregation through strict membership rules and restrictions based on race, social position, legal status, and income. Congado developed a regional iconicity in the social niches of socioeconomically marginalized communities

Figures 6.6, 6.7. Twenty-first-century *congadeiros*, Ouro Preto. (Photos by Jonathon Grasse, 2015.)

of people of color, creating local conditions for vernacular permutations of resignified church doctrine and orthodoxy.

Black brotherhoods in Minas assumed greater responsibility for a wide array of local activities, including the hiring of priests to direct doctrinal activities, officiate Mass, and complete other services in parish churches. Routine church activities were often the responsibility of laypersons, who also raised funds for religious celebrations. Sometime before 1728, the archbishop of Rio de Janeiro, while on a pastoral visit to the Mineiro interior, banned blacks from entering the church in Conceição do Mato Dentro, leading Afro-Mineiros there to construct their own using donations from Jacinto de Barros, the black wife of the white *capitão* Manuel Correa de Paiva. Black *forros* and slaves constructed their own churches dedicated to Our Lady of the Rosary and other patron saints of blacks, and many refurbished examples dating to the eighteenth century still stand today in Diamantina, Ouro Preto, Sabará, Mariana, Conceição do Mato Dentro, and other towns. In Mariana, the founding stone of the church for Our Lady of the Rosary of the Blacks was set in a 1752 ceremony attended by the bishop and county judge (*ouvidor*).[61] The Crown barred the entrance into colonial Minas Gerais of the Sacred House of Mercy brotherhood (Santa Casa de Misericórdia), an

Figure 6.8. Congado *guarda* entering the Padre Faria Chapel, Ouro Preto. (Photos by Jonathon Grasse, 2018.)

institution responsible for hospitals and burial services throughout Brazil. Only in Minas Gerais did brotherhoods possess their own funeral bier and manage the burial of their brethren. Grave sites within a church, underneath flooring or on the grounds, were reserved for brotherhood members, and such cosmologically significance entombment remained prized locations.[62]

Further Historical Developments of Congado in Minas Gerais

In 1872, Brazil's priest-to-parishioner ratio was roughly 1:4,202, while in Minas this ratio was doubled, and closer to 1:8,062. In addition to the geographically challenged province parishes, the system was hampered by chaotic administration: of Minas's 179 parishes, 126 belonged to the bishop of Mariana, 21 to Bahia, 18 to São Paulo, 7 to Goiás, 6 to Pernambuco, and 1 to Rio de Janeiro.[63] Amid this crazy quilt of diocese oversight, Congado's religiosity, while allowed, was rarely met with church acceptance and was widely misrepresented by cultural outsiders, elites, and church orthodoxy as being mere folkloric entertainment—secular, carnivalesque pageantry. Historical changes would exacerbate the strained relationship between church and *congadeiros*. The collapse of the Brazilian monarchy and the founding of the first republic in 1889 brought an end to the Luso-Brazilian Crown's royal patronage of the Catholic Church (*padroado real*), an end to the marriage between state and church. During Brazil's first republican government, brotherhoods began losing prestige and influence, coinciding with the end of slavery and the rise of dominating social institutions such as political parties and labor unions. As Richard Graham notes "The principles of equality and individualism undermined the appeal of the irmandades. With their decline, the opportunity to have a voice and be consulted by authorities disappeared. Irmandades had never spoken for all blacks before the state, but in the nineteenth century, they now spoke for no one."[64]

Perhaps as part of the church's lessened role in Old Republic policies (namely in education), an increasingly conservative Vatican began to disavow Reinado rituals. The music and dance that characterized Congado were deemed too African, and the genre, long a product of lay believers without church supervision, was relegated by many twentieth century commentators to the category of staged folklore. Beginning in 1932, Congado was prohibited by Belo Horizonte archbishop Dom Antônio dos Santos Cabral, with the city's police chief, Carlos Prates, entrusted to keep tabs on black communities violating the order.[65] It has been well documented that during the 1950s, church intervention led to the banning of the Reinado in the western Mineiro city of Divinópolis, in just one example.[66] Today, two statewide agencies help administer congadeiro interests, the Federação dos Congados de Minas Gerais (Centro das Tradições do Rosário em Minas Gerais), and the Associação dos Congadeiros de Nossa Senhora do Rosário do Estado de Minas Gerais (ACMG). In June 2014, the ACMG celebrated their first Cortejo de Cultura Popular (Popular Culture Congado Procession) in the Santa Efigênia district in conjunction with the City of Belo Horizonte. The event also honored João Lopes, the *mestre* and former *capitão-mor* of the important Irmandade de Nossa Senhora do Rosário do Jatobá, a district within the metropolitan area.

In the eyes of Crown and church, brotherhoods for the marginalized and slave populations were to preserve the social hierarchy and never to directly promote racial or class consciousness. The creation of confraternities was not a liberal measure nor seen as a contradiction of colonial rule and slavery on the part of the Portuguese rulers. Though certainly not promoted by authorities, forms of racial and class consciousness grew nonetheless from the injustices and social strains created by slavery and the unfair treatment faced by *forros* and *libertos*. What resulted was a significant sociocultural milieu developing within the brutality of the slave system yet in some ways beyond the control of slaveholders, Crown, and church. Congado—its performative Africanisms, its brotherhood-based arena for absorbing pan-African cosmologies, and its communal nature—thus symbolized resistance and survival. In this vein, *congadeiros* created and defended their Atlantic creole Christian manner of celebrating the Virgin Mary, and they still create ritualistic spaces of resistance in which divine presence is invoked in a dual embodiment calling forth cultural forces. In her introduction to Gomes and Pereira's book *Os Arturos: Negras raízes Mineiras*, Monique Auigras posits Congado in Minas Gerais as a long-standing form of social resistance:

> White priests organized the Brotherhood of the Rosary to create a frame for "black men" and to ensure their abandonment of "witchcraft." The batuque dance had been forbidden, but during the feast of the Rosary dance and song were allowed. Blacks then invented songs, and since they did not know how to "speak correctly," took advantage to pass messages: "Look at the language of Angola, look, nobody understands." In fact, there were those who understood, but they were seen as nobodies in the eyes of the powerful. The Congado is both a festival and a challenge, including calls for prayer and for the fight: "Wake up, black man, you need to wake up." It is a staged display and not an open war.[67]

The Chico Rei Legend: The First King of Congado

Cornerstone legends locating the mythical roots of Congado in Ouro Preto form a poignant oral tradition, positing five hundred years of Luso-African Catholic practice within a framework of Afro-Mineiro legacies. Vacuums created by slavery's catastrophic trauma to collective memory necessitated local links to a regionalist past further groomed by Mineiro geographic isolation and social fragmentation. Broader, transoceanic narratives of Congado's rich historical record (see appendix 2) were challenged by brutal reality, and its living heritage, its links to ancient Congolese kingdoms and the international politics of early European expansion, were displaced by an oral tradition foregrounding Ouro Preto neighborhoods and a celebration of a single man's conquest of slave society. The Chico Rei legend tells of a historically factual Vila Rica slave who had once been an African king, and who purchased his freedom to became the first *rei do congo*. Historians suggest that Chico Rei was born as Galanga sometime before 1715 in the Kingdom of Congo, where he became a warrior-king and priest of the god Zambi-Apungo. He was captured along with his entire extended royal family by Portuguese slave traders. Then possibly as young as twenty-five, Galanga and only one of his sons survived the Atlantic crossing on the slave ship *Magdalene*, which arrived in Bahia in 1740. There, the ship's entire cargo of slaves was purchased by Major Augustus, the owner of the Encardideira mine in Vila Rica. Given the name Francisco (Chico), he saved enough gold to buy his and his son's freedom. The freed slave continued saving his gold, purchasing Encardideira. Gradually, the legend continues, Chico Rei bought the freedom of many local slaves sharing his specific Congolese ethnicity, becoming known once more as a "king," complete with civic acknowledgment during his lifetime by the governor-general of Minas Gerais, Gomes Freire de Andrade. Most of those he freed joined the Santa Efigênia brotherhood, making them perhaps the first brotherhood of free blacks in Vila Rica. They founded and constructed the city's Church of Santa Efigênia, still standing on a prominent hill, Alto da Cruz, home to active Congado communities. Chico Rei's son, Muzinga, purchased land in the nearby Paraopeba River Valley region, where their descendants likely remain.[68] In 1950, the city of Ouro Preto renamed the Encardideira site the Chico Rei mine.

Tarcísio José Martins has controversially argued that the only document suggesting Chico Rei as the first King of Congado is a questionable footnote in Diogo do Vasconcelos's 1904 book *History of Old Minas*.[69] Martins notes that among the innumerable iterations of the Chico Rei myth in novels, short stories, film, and articles, no scholarly historical research or evidence is presented to support the legend. The argument is that, with documentation of Chico Rei having been the "first *rei do congo*" absent from the historical record, Vasconcelos was likely to have simply repeated tales from the oral traditions of the city's *congadeiros*.

Social memory and historical sense are not lost in the Chico Rei legend of the origins of Congado, but rather replaced in the oral tradition by new symbols valorizing the regional tableaux of the survival and social ascendance of Afro-Mineiros, some of whom maintained the Congado tradition. Since 2008, during epiphany week, the Ouro Preto Congado of Our Lady of the Rosary and Saint Iphigenia parades with visiting Congado *guardas* in a Reinado festival, the Congado parade following a route from the Santa Efigênia church in the Alto da Cruz neighborhood "in the direction of the Chico Rei mine." On the festival's previous day, the hometown *guarda* holds its own procession in the opposite direction, down a steep hill to the early eighteenth-century Padre Faria Chapel, in a subdistrict of the same name (fig. 6.8). The Santa Efigênia church sits dramatically atop one of Ouro Preto's many hills, in the heart of the hosting group's community; it was constructed by slaves between 1733 and 1785 and partially funded by Chico Rei. In 2016, this festival, titled the Faith that Sings and Dances, attracted a dozen Congado groups invited from many Mineiro regions (in 2020, thirty-five *guardas* participated).[70] The event is a popular Catholic festival, dedicated to the Virgin Mary and the group's patron saint, Iphigenia of Ethiopia, two figures joined in worship through a nearly equally passionate devotion to Chico Rei. A spectacular display of public devotion to Catholic icons, the festival's embrace of the Chico Rei legend also contests Brazil's prevailing racial injustices in a theatrical "desegregation" of the old city's streets and landmarks, a marking of cultural territory. Although the procession's spiritual destination is the Chico Rei mine, the gates to the Church of Our Lady of the Conception, a stone's throw away, serves as a picturesque compromise: the masses of musicians, dancers, and spectators would overwhelm the narrow street running past the Chico Rei mine entrance. The pageantry links iconic physical locations symbolizing one of Minas's primary modes of regional identity: gold mining and spectacular colonial-era architectural cityscapes now protected by UNESCO.

The Alto da Cruz and Padre Faria districts of Ouro Preto's eastern edge were originally a distinct village known as Antônio Dias, founded at the dawn of the eighteenth century. It was near Antônio Dias that gold was discovered in 1697, and the village became home to the working poor as well as a community frequented by the enslaved. Antônio Dias bordered Vila Rica, Portugal's wealthy, colonial gem in the New World. Today, the parade route traverses what were these two worlds, one of poverty-stricken black workers and the other a picture postcard of a cultivated colonial city reflecting the European elegance of political and social power. At play in the festival is also the social space of freedom, Chico Rei's freedom and the promise of

manumission, the figurative grounds for the Reinado's contemporary commemoration. "Space" is here a very telling, physical, cultural territory, a social
arena of confrontation etched into history and into notions of collective
difference. Music's formative spatialities created by the Reinado tradition,
and its Congado processions, confront histories of difference and legacies of
hope while expressing and celebrating African-influenced forms of Catholic
religiosity. These Afro-Mineiro communities have emerged from a particular
frontier of the African diaspora.

In 2020, Mauricio Tizumba (b. 1957, Belo Horizonte) was the honorary
leader of the Faith that Sings and Dances festival, leading a ceremony commemorating a two-hundred-year-old cast-iron Reinado flag (*bandeira for-
jada a ferro*) discovered very recently in the Padre Faria Chapel. Tizumba
came of age in Belo Horizonte as a struggling musician, actor, and playwright,
and he embraces unique Afro-Mineiro traditions in his search for politically
conscious dimensions of Congado.[71] One of the region's most respected *congadeiro mestres*, Tizumba regaled Belo Horizonte theater audiences in his role
as Chico Rei a few weeks after the festival, in his staged musical play, *Galanga:
Chico Rei*, produced in the Grand Theater of the city's Palacio das Artes.

Chapter 7

The Viola in Minas Gerais
Rural Dreams and Urban Realities

As a musical instrument and cultural symbol, the viola has forged a mystical life while helping to sound Brazilian identity. Its five double-course strings grace recordings and performances of music both old and new with a metallic timbre often conjuring the rural past. Throughout its centuries-long journey in the hands of popular and folk musicians in both city and country, the instrument also known as the ten-string viola (*viola de dez cordas*), "country hick" viola (*viola caipira*), "wire" viola (*viola arame*), and Brazilian ten-string guitar appeared regularly in musical salons of the colonial and imperial-era aristocracy. In eighteenth- and nineteenth-century homes of the well-to-do, the viola shined in the small chamber ensembles integral to music soirees, where art song genres of modinha and lundu song flourished, a repertoire still performed in the twenty-first century. It is the namesake of Bahia's *samba-da-viola* genre and prominent in the storytelling *repentista* tradition of Pernambuco and other northeastern genres. The viola is heralded for its "country music" roots in *música caipira* and original *música sertaneja*, and still accompanies Congado and other widely practiced processionals of popular Catholicism such as the Folia de Reis, Festa do Divino, Folia de São Sebastião, Dança de Santa Cruz, and Dança de São Gonçalo. Since the 1970s, the instrument has speared a movement loosely known as *música viola*, or *instrumental de viola*, with its exceptionally skilled viola players (*violeiros*) fusing fine art sensibilities with sophisticated musical forms and techniques, diverging from the roots music from which it draws inspiration. Examining the instrument entails exploring the historical soul of rural Minas Gerais and its urban representations in twenty-first-century Belo Horizonte, where players expand on tradition and contemporary luthiers conserve and innovate while maintaining a musical heritage. After considering the viola's place in the region, I conclude this chapter with a descriptive account of Belo Horizonte's first Viola de Minas festival.

The term "viola" was used in fourteenth- and fifteenth-century Italy for several types of guitar-like instruments, and it was the Portuguese word for the small, five-course instruments made by sixteenth-century Lisbon luthiers such as Belchior Dias. Violas visually similar to Dias's, some of which were less than half the length of the modern classical guitar, are depicted in colonial-era Brazilian iconography. The viola's so-called natural tuning is one of several regional tunings and echoes that of the baroque guitar, its European cousin. Later, the fuller-sized "Spanish" guitar with six single strings became known in the Luso-Brazilian world as the *violão* ("big viola"). Jesuits brought the viola to Brazil in the mid-sixteenth century, where it was introduced in adaptations of indigenous dances appropriated by missionaries for the catechism of local Natives. Such roots in colonial-era religious lessons can still be located in viola *caipira* repertoire, as in the song "Barca nova" (New boat), claimed to be one of Brazil's oldest: "Let's go see the new ship / it fell from the sky to the sea / Our Lady [the Virgin Mary] will be on board / her little angels rowing."[1] Colonists, the clergy, Native Indians, and later enslaved Africans were eventually exposed to the instrument, either in proximity to colonists on the coast or in isolated agricultural settlements in the hinterland.

From this southeastern mission subculture of the 1500s emerged the *cateretê* dance, rich in association with the viola, which developed into a secular line dance common to nineteenth-century coffee fazendas in Minas's Zona da Mata and Sul de Minas subregions.[2] *Cateretê* song is characterized by a lead and responding vocalists (*mestre* and *contramestre*) accompanied by a pair of *violeiros* in call-and- response vocal arrangements, hand clapping, and foot stomping. It is the origin of today's *catira* dance of *caipira* culture, which still employs the viola as the sole accompaniment instrument. *Cateretê* grew throughout the nineteenth century in the Brazilian southeast, joining batuque, lundu, and other popular music and dances originally associated with socially marginalized non-whites in Minas Gerais. The viola frequented these Afro-Brazilian circle dances described in nineteenth-century Minas travel literature, with lundu remaining a notable dance genre in *viola caipira* repertoire.

The spirit of exploration and journey marks the legacy of an instrument strongly linked to colonization and the gold rush. Of the primary viola types common to colonial-era Portugal, the *viola braguesa* (from Braga), *viola toeira*, and *viola beiroa* made it to Brazil,[3] brought by Portuguese immigrants pouring into mining towns during the eighteenth century. In other Brazilian backland regions, viola bodies were ingeniously fashioned out of solid pieces of *maciça* and *buriti* wood, or with necks attached to gourds.[4] Previous to the gold rush, seventeenth-century *bandeirantes* with the help of coastal Tupi Indians sporadically trekked along hinterland paths long established by Natives, creating the Caminho Geral do Sertão (Backlands Road), which ran north from São Paulo into the wilderness that became Minas Gerais. Fernão Dias Pais's *bandeirante* group famously traversed the region between 1674 and 1681, with some frontier people remaining in small settlements, some of whom who later discovered the gold and gems of Portuguese America's El Dorado. The Native American population's violent decline, which began in the seventeenth century, also preceded the gold rush, a result of enslavement by the *bandeirantes*, disease, displacement, and sporadic warfare.

The *Caipira* and the *Sertão*

The creole offspring of white men and indigenous women were known as *caboclo*, with Paulista descendants further comingling with the isolated demographic. Twentieth-century Brazilian folklorist Luis da Camará Cascudo defines *caipira* as "a man or woman of little education not living in a city. A rural worker, of the riverbanks, of the seashore, or of the *sertão*. They are also called *caboclos*, *jeca*, *matuto*, *roceiro*, *tabaréu*, *caiçara*, or *sertanejo*, depending on the region."[5]

Some of these terms for the rural poor remain highly pejorative. Telling is *caipira*'s etymology: Tupi for "those who cut the trails/clear the forests" (*caa* = forest, *pir* = cut).[6] The original *caipiras* were the hardened laborers controlled by *bandeirantes* as they colonized the Mineiro interior. Today, the notion of *caipira* culture, though proudly embraced in nationalist and regionalist discourse, is often associated by mainstream urban Brazilians with the inferior social status of the uneducated rural masses. The rural interior of Sul de

Minas, São Paulo, and portions of Paraná and Mato Grosso are considered the *caipira* region, and its inhabitants are often referred to as *caipiras*.[7]

Sertão is a truncation of *desertão*, a vast uninhabited place, a "big desert." Northern Minas Gerais is the southern boundary of Brazil's great drought-prone northeastern *sertão*, stretching from parts of Goiás and the interior of Bahia to Ceará and Piauí, a region dominated by shrub-like vegetation known as *caatinga*, which is leafless during the dry season. A *sertanejo* (an inhabitant of the *sertão*) generally refers to a Brazilian from this region. West and north of Minas's central Serra do Espinhaço (Spine Mountains), tens of thousands of square miles of the state's *grande sertão* represents a transition zone between the semi-arid *cerrado*, the central Brazilian plateau's dominant scrubland landscape (also known as *chapada*), and the remnants of the great Atlantic rainforest that once stretched to the coast. The Mineiro *sertão* is celebrated as a vast poetic space in song, and by writers native to the region such as João Guimarães Rosa, whose novel *Grande Sertão: Veredas* remains a landmark of twentieth-century Brazilian literature. The *sertão's* mythical aura grew from the earliest, most Eurocentric days of the Portuguese empire, when such expanses were portrayed as godless and lawless, regions without faith or promise, home to allegedly cannibalistic pagans. The Brazilian *sertão* fulfilled the original European colonial vision of an inhospitable zone far from Western-style settlements, distanced from civilized ideas; a place where the devil did his work. Premodern rural life remains an elemental theme of *música caipira*. Brazilian historians Angela Botelho and Carla Anastasia describe the *sertão* of eighteenth-century Minas Gerais as "a place of amazing wonders, the devil, and a refuge for Indians and bandits[;] . . . like other backlands of immense Portuguese America[,] a stage for the collective and interpersonal violence of those enshrined in history."[8] Renowned contemporary *violeiro* Paulo Freire (b. 1957, São Paulo) addressed the iconic power that the *sertão's* natural wonders hold over the instrument: "The viola carries the world. An apprentice *violeiro* looks for meaning in the rural backwoods, in what he's learned throughout the days and by nights living with nature. Suddenly he is immersed in her rhythms and mysteries. Inevitably, he is taken over completely by the viola."[9]

Predating the gold rush, explorers from Brazil's northeast created the Caminho da Bahia (Bahian Road) following the Rio São Francisco south into Minas Gerais from the interior of Pernambuco and Bahia, the latter home to Salvador, the capital of the colonial government until 1763. The north-flowing São Francisco is a river highway known as O Velho Chico (the

Old Chico, "Chico" being a nickname derived from "Francisco"). In Minas, settlers from Bahia and Pernambuco created cattle empires dotting the São Francisco River basin west of the central mining district. River laborers including boatmen (*remeiros*) and their families formed a unique backbone to this slice of the *caipira* world, where incoming tonnage shipped from Bahia and Pernambuco met outgoing Mineiro exports delivered to river ports by oxcart from all over the Mineiro *sertão*. São Francisco ports and markets at Pirapora, São Romão, and Januária were major crossroads of the backlands, nourished by the river waters, the massive cattle ranches, and the commerce and exchange of traded goods. Independent-minded *sertanejos* of northern Minas were famously involved in the Sedition of 1736, an anti-Portuguese populist revolt echoed by the urban, elite-brokered, and equally ill-fated Inconfidência Mineira (Minas Conspiracy) fifty years later.

If there is a pure, authentic musical gesture of this hinterland, it is the *aboio*, the melodic vocal cry of the *vaqueiro*, the cowboy's musical shout. As immigrants and slaves began flowing into the gold fields, *tropeiros* were loading up their mule trains (*tropes de muares*) with goods in Rio de Janeiro, São Paulo, and other coastal locales. *Tropeiros* and Portuguese immigrants brought the viola into the mining towns and fazendas of early eighteenth-century Minas, where they delivered, sold, exchanged, and purchased goods, traveling along roads where commodities sold for higher prices and returning to Rio de Janeiro and São Paulo loaded with Mineiro products.[10] Starting out from Porto da Estrela near Rio de Janeiro on his 1819 trip to the sources of the São Francisco River in Minas's southwestern Serra da Canastra, French naturalist Auguste de Saint-Hilaire noted violas among the *tropeiros* arriving from northern Minas with 130 mules laden with cotton.[11] A year earlier he had traveled through the central regions of Minas, observing:

> The *tropeiros* of several caravans when drawing nearer to one another share conversation, relate their travels and love adventures, and sometimes one charms his neighbors by playing a viola and singing one of those Brazilian arias that have so much grace and sweetness. Everything goes with order; and otherwise they rarely converse, and rather talk to each other with a delicacy unknown in Europe among men of the lower class.[12]

As Minas was settled outward from the central mining district, powerful landowners coalesced into a rural oligarchy, creating a strong-arm system known as *grande fazenda*. Many large enterprises combined multiple operations whereby a single *fazendeiro*, or colonel, pursued mining, sugar production, cattle and pork processing, or diverse agricultural crops, simultaneously running retail markets in nearby towns and cities, where some kept upscale homes and printed their own newspapers.[13] Within sixty kilometers of Belo Horizonte, the main houses of the enormous Bom Jesus do Amparo and Boa Esperança fazendas still stand, the latter constructed at the end of the eighteenth century around extensive gold mines and ironworks, which was then home to more than 1,200 slaves. Influenced by the country estate styles of northern Portugal, these structures were, like other economically successful fazendas, rural palaces.

Violas were proud possessions even in the more isolated, often hidden layers of rural fazenda culture—the simple houses of subsistence farmers and the modest, rural enclaves of marginalized agricultural laborers beholden to landowners. In the countryside, parcel farming (*parceira*) and sharecropping (*meiação*) allowed some rural poor known as *agregados* to live on fazendas. Free persons, including poor whites, were enveloped in a stratified and exploitative rural order in which squatting became an increasingly limited option. Economic opportunities decreased for those whose family networks lacked access to jobs, education, or benefactors with political power. Quilombo-based Afro-Mineiro communities surviving the slave era dotted Minas, but their residents remained isolated or only partially integrated with surrounding towns and settlements. The historical arc of Mineiro *caipira* communities throughout the *sertão*, though dominated by mixed-race *mestiço* culture, perpetuated the marginalization of blacks and *caboclos*. Meanwhile, unacculturated indigenous peoples were pushed eastward, killed off, or forced into reservation-type communities. Well into the 1940s, parts of the Mineiro interior remained a frontier subject to landgrab settlements and squatting, partially due to an oppressive social system that led to high rates of migration and subsistence farming as long as the soil permitted cultivation.[14]

The Viola in Old Minas

The viola regularly appears in travel literature published by nineteenth-century foreign visitors to Minas Gerais. In 1818, having traveled northeast from Campanha toward Lavras in the valley formed between the Serra Capivari and the Serra Ingai, Spix and Martius noted at the Fazenda do Corrego dos Pinheiros: "The countless sons of the house struggled, meanwhile, to entertain with unpretentious, national songs, accompanied to the sound of the viola."[15] In addition to fazenda environs, the viola was a regular with city folk, including women, and used as a pastime by the enslaved, and thus it was found across socioeconomic, gender, and racial lines. While visiting the Estiva fazenda near Vila Rica during the early nineteenth century, Spix and Martius note the viola in an evening batuque dance:

> Almost everywhere we arrived in the evening we were met by the buzzing sound of the guitar [the metallic ringing of the viola], to whose accompaniment people sang or danced. At Estiva, a lonely ranch with marvelous broad fields surrounded by distant mountains, the inhabitants were engaged in dancing the baduca [batuque]. . . . It often goes on for several hours on end to the monotonous chords of the guitar [viola], sometimes alternating with improvised vocals or with folk songs.[16]

The travelers further capture the viola's widespread use in Afro-Mineiro batuque circle dances: "Harsh at times, the monotonous chords of the viola sound for whole hours without interruption; or alternating with improvised songs and national modinhas, whose subjects correspond with their rudeness."[17] Advertisements for the capture of runaway slaves published in local newspapers documented the instrument's use among the enslaved population, as in José Drumond's 1883 notice in Ouro Preto's *Liberal Mineiro* detailing the runaway slave Adão's viola skills.[18]

John Mawe, the first European traveler officially welcomed to investigate the Mineiro interior by the prince regent, Dom João, arrived in Diamantina in 1808. There, the Englishman remarked that too few pianos had made the trip from the coast to this great city, where ladies enjoyed playing the viola with plenty of feel and grace, echoing the instrument's presence in coastal aristocratic circles.[19] Perhaps some of the first violas appearing in Diamantina were transported there by Ismael Pinheiro de Oliveira in 1733, who brought them from the central mining district town of Sabará, where they were likely made.[20] Pulling into the small Minas town of Rio Preto in early August 1839, German traveler Ernst Hasenclever made note:

> Now I will be able to draw a marvelous nocturnal, tropical landscape in the vibrant colors of this little town, of the river and the mountains in the moonlight, where adorable figures move in exotic dances to the sound of the voluptuous viola. . . . In time to the violas one could also hear the mule's braying

melodies, and in the unseen movement in the brush, the sound of fat pigs cavorting in the dirt.

The following week, Hasenclever's party arrived at an inn in Barroso, where he showed his notebook of drawings to others as they rested the animals: "The evening is beautiful; we light a small fire on the veranda and tell our stories, [and] to the sound of a viola they sing sad songs with languid eyes and rough voices until I say goodnight."[21] In eighteenth-century Minas, the viola also appeared in celebrations of the Holy Spirit in the town of Nossa Senhora da Cachoeira:

> Accompanying the float meandering through town walked Father Lourenço Ribeiro and Father Pedro Antonio playing the viola with laypeople, among them Cônego Angola and the priest Padre Manoel de Bastos, bringing along in the same float a free creole woman of Vila Rica named Vicência, dressed as a man and singing "O Arromba" and other earthy songs, causing a completely notorious scandal.[22]

Still today, in some backland environments, the viola is linked to beliefs of supernatural forces and the devil; Brazilian anthropologist Luzimar Paulo Pereira states that "stories of pacts with the devil are important topics of musical, social, and religious life of violeiros in the north and northwest of Minas Gerais."[23] Here among rural practitioners in the Mineiro sertão, it is widely believed that the best violeiros receive advanced musical skills directly from God: those acquiring such musicianship by other means do so through a ritualistic pact with the other side (*pacto-com-o-outro-lado*) carried out, for instance, at the gravesite of a deceased violeiro. Writing about the eastern edge of the state, scholar and virtuoso violeiro Ivan Vilela (b. 1962, Itajubá, MG) reminds his readers:

> We remember well the fieldwork conversation with a resident of the Serra do Caparaó dividing Minas Gerais from Espírito Santo. He told us that it was a commonly known fact in the region that *violeiros* kept small *manfarros* [devils, or evil imps] imprisoned in bottles. The more of the little devils kept, the greater the *violeiro*'s power with his instrument.[24]

Concern for supernatural harm (*malinagem*) caused by rival performing groups within the Folia de Reis tradition underscores the mysteries and legends surrounding the viola in places such as the hinterland town of Urucuia in northwestern Minas.[25] Some term this vast expanse of brushland the *cerrado mineiro*. The small town of Urucuia, farther from Belo Horizonte than from its namesake river's origins in the *cerrado* of Brazil's central plateau (*planalto central*), is only one of many cultural hotbeds of viola roots tradition in the state's northwest. Here, traditional music accompanies the Urucuia River as it snakes east, flowing into a remote stretch of the Rio São Francisco.

The viola's "*caipira*" characterization was championed by early twentieth-century folklorists, voices from Brazil's nascent culture industry, and nationalists promoting sociopolitical concepts of authenticity and heritage linked to vestiges of Brazil's rural past. This was a world increasingly marginalized by urbanization and industrialization during the first stages of the southeast's twentieth-century modernization. Brazilian musicologist Elizabeth Travassos has portrayed the viola as an Iberian artifact repackaged by urban modernity as "backwoods."[26] It is worth noting that the guitar, not the viola, became integral to choro, a uniquely Brazilian popular urban music taking form in 1870s Rio de Janeiro. The viola's role as an urban instrument of poets and learned salons vanished as it transitioned toward the *caipira* cultural concept emerging from the urban-industrial southeast's modernist social prism.[27] Its distinctive timbre transformed into the nostalgia-laden lyricism of *toadas* (folk melodies) wedded more to idealizations of the countryside that evolved in the twentieth century. The instrument thus stood in contrast to burgeoning urban, popular music styles such as the guitar-dominated choro and samba. In the meantime, in the Mineiro heartland, *sertanejo violeiros* and countless so-called *maestros analfabetos* (illiterate maestros), it was said, created their own repertoire.[28]

Rare Instruments from the Mineiro Past: The *Violas de Queluz*

By the end of the eighteenth century, many of Rio de Janeiro's viola luthiers had coalesced on Rua de Violas in the Praias de Mineiros neighborhood of Porto da Estrela. The coast's wet, hot tropical climate proved difficult for luthiers, as did the interior central plateau's arid environment hundreds of kilometers inland. Better climatic conditions grace the town of Conselheiro Lafaiete in the less humid Serra do Ouro Branco (White Gold Mountains) of Minas Gerais. A village of indigenous Carijós there was transformed by local gold discoveries in the 1690s, and later became the Estrada Real town Campo Alegre dos Carijós. Known as Queluz between 1790 and 1934 (when it was renamed Conselheiro Lafaiete), the town attracted the Salgado and Mereilles families from Portugal, who established significant luthier workshops there in the nineteenth century. In 1867, after departing the Morro Velho mine for her return trip east to Rio de Janeiro, Lady Isabel Burton passed through Queluz and wrote:

> We left Holaria at nine, and came to Quelsez [sic], a long village with shops and a few decent houses. I stopped at the shop of a Portuguese Jew to look at violas. We then rode along a rather pretty and level road, where we met mules and tropeiros, which indicated that we were joining the civilized world again.[29]

Earlier during the same journey, she noted in the hamlet of Rio das Pedras (now Acuruí, less than ten kilometers northeast of Itabirito):

> These good people sang songs and glees, and danced Minas dances for me to the native wire guitar, snapping their fingers and beating time with their feet....At ten I retired to try and sleep, leaving them to continue their festivities, but what with the excitement of the day, and the still twanging guitars on the other side of the partition I could not succeed.[30]

The Salgados crafted instruments in Queluz between 1880 and 1930 (figs. 7.3, 7.4). The family patriarch played for Emperor Dom Pedro II and constructed two custom instruments for him after he passed through Queluz in the 1880s. Dark wood inlay (*marchetaria*) of flowery, delicate arrows, bells, circular branches, and the finely wrought cow shinbone designs on fingerboards, headstock, and bridges became trademarks of local luthiers. Through innovative design and quality materials, Queluz shops became Brazil's best, and they added pioneering acoustic improvements to the aesthetic beauty of well-crafted pine, cedar, and spruce tops, and the now world-renowned *jacarandá* (Brazilian rosewood) for fingerboards and other parts. The Queluz name reached beyond Minas Gerais, with clients clamoring for personalized inlays and increasingly artistic designs. The instruments are now a recognized cultural treasure, with collectors, festivals, and research projects promoting them with regional pride. Like pre–World War II Martin steel-string acoustic guitars in the United States, the Queluz violas of the 1920s are highly sought after. Some have been refurbished and put into use, for instance José de Souza Salgado's 1908 specimen expertly restored by Sabará-based luthier Virgílio Lima, and played by Rodrigo Delage on his self-released CD *Viola Caipira Instrumental*. The renown grew with a wider market, and several of the area's family-based cottage industries produced many fine instruments into the 1930s, after which less expensive models mass produced in São Paulo factories dealt Queluz luthiers a blow. Eduardo Braga de Souza, the son of José de Souza Salgado, made his last *viola de Queluz* in 1969. Inspired by the Queluz heritage, the Rodriguez family of luthiers of Baldim, near the Serra do Cipó, began producing hand-made violas in the 1970s. José Leite Fonseca, an instrument builder active in Rome, began constructing violas based directly on Queluz examples in the late 1990s.[31]

Twentieth-Century Viola Narratives

Myriam Taubkin, curator of the Brazilian Memory Project (Projeto Memória Brasileira) and producer of the collection *Violeiros do Brasil*, recalls: "The viola crossed my path when I settled in rural Minas Gerais. The viola is an important instrument in various regions of Brazil, such as São Paulo, the hinterlands of the northeast, some parts of the south, and in central Brazil. But Minas Gerais has generated the majority of *violeiros*."[32]

In the rural southeast, the viola and guitar entered the twentieth century as a team. They accompanied vocal duets (*duplas*) in songs of the Festa Junina (including Saint John's Day), the religious music of small churches, Folia de Reis processions, and widely performed folk music of cowboys, oxcart drivers, and rural folk of the Mineiro interior including *cururu*, *cateretê*, and *cana verde*. *Moda de viola* (viola song) arose as a generic term for repertoire performed by a vocal duet singing in thirds accompanied by viola, with an optional guitar. Rio de Janeiro, São Paulo, and later Belo Horizonte swelled with early twentieth-century immigrants from rural communities with enduring associations with such genres. Today, this repertoire has gained the label "roots music" (*música de raiz*) to further distance *música caipira*'s proud lineage from the trendy strains of the commercial *música sertaneja* industry. This music of Brazil's south-central interior emphasizes the sentimental pathos of loss and isolation, and the freedom associated with rustic simplicity, setting off urban experiences in sharp contrast. Notions of *caipira* authenticity connect to the backlands spirit, echoes of the suffering of the marginal horseman, the *tropeiro*, and the agricultural laborer (*lavrador*), while inviting the *sertão*'s natural wonders: the sun and moon, rolling-hill landscape, and flora and fauna. The fazenda, too, remained a primary backdrop to the viola's *música caipira* songbook. Rivers, boats, paths, roads, oxcarts, mule convoys, and trains provide the Mineiro regionalist themes of travel, lost love, escape, and dialogue with the outside world.

These old Mineiro symbols of contact with the outside world, and of the travel required to conquer long distances between hinterland locales, still remain in some form though they are fading. Geographic vastness and isolation envelope the troubadour-like image of viola-playing songsmiths (*caipiras cantatores*) mapping to life in small towns, wandering on Mineiro roads, and commenting on the wilderness. The viola today is also laden with symbolism of places of contemporary subjugation, both personal and social, and weighted with a forlorn awareness of forgottenness. Songs about farmers, cowboys, and lonely figures of the interior project feelings of loss for the traditional ways of life transformed by the market economy, industrial agribusiness, and a political world that has betrayed the *caipira*. The song "Canto de vaqueiro" (Cowboy song) depicts the life of a cowboy, drinking from a wide river flowing through the scrub brush, who plays a viola that "will carry [his] heart."[33]

Country roots music waited nearly thirty years for its own studio time following Brazil's first commercial recordings in 1900. Only in 1929 did Columbia release Cornélio Pires's set of 78 rpm recordings *Danças regionais paulistas* (Regional Paulista dances), considered to be the first *música caipira* records. They helped transform *cururu*, *cateretê*, and *cana verde* into commercial song forms. Pires was possibly the first to label these styles collectively as "caipira" as he attempted to illustrate musical traits shared within this nascent genre in his 1910 book *Musa caipira*.[34] The sentiments, instrumentation, and music styles were ripe for popularization through more advanced production techniques, commercialization, professional songwriting, and lyrics reflecting social change and the older ways now increasingly isolated by development and notions of progress. Subsequently, this music became the soundtrack for city-bound *ruralistas* looking for work as they drove the twentieth century's most intensive urbanization movement, including those flooding into Belo Horizonte.[35] *Música caipira* also resonated with nativists searching for independence from the tidal wave of urban modernity overtaking many of Brazil's folk traditions, offering a counter to the racist stereotyping of rural *caboclos* such as that by the bigoted yet influential writer José Bento Monteiro Lobato. With radio broadcasts proliferating, what came to be known as *música caipira* was quickly enveloped and propelled by its own commercial success and the explosive growth of its sentimental offshoot *música sertaneja* (music of the inhabitants of the *sertão*), popular with rural immigrants in large Sudeste cities.

By 1950, the commercial *música caipira* genre was fortified by the Zé Carreiro and Carreirinho *dupla* recordings on Continental, a label already responsible for the meteoric rise of Tonico and Tinoco *dupla* starting in 1944. The commercial musical cousin of *música caipira*, *música sertaneja*, since the 1950s a product of mass urbanization and north-to-south migrations of the working poor, gradually redirected the sound of country music to that of a commodified electric rock band format. For several decades one of Brazil's most widely sold popular music forms, *música sertaneja's* modern production aesthetic has gone far in displacing the image and timbre of the viola's atmospheric presence. Developing quickly since the 1970s, *música sertaneja's* commercial "country" music has grown distinct from roots *caipira* with an increasingly disparate audience drawing from laboring migrants, students, and rising middle-class youth searching for Brazilian musical identities contrasting rock, samba, and MPB. *Sertaneja universitária* (university student country music) is a yet more distilled, sentimental pop form slickly marketed since 2010 to upper-class Brazilian youth. Still today one crosses a series of borders when leaving the city and entering the countryside. Yet music as a style, recording, idea, or other disembodied notion is a master of migration less hindered by borders. Music relates to space with fluid mediation through which individuals and groups experience transformational processes of memory and belonging, but also of transcending boundaries, of crossing over to other places, of forgetting, leaving, and departing. The *caipira* songbook, the *cancioneiro caipira*, protects its memories, myths, and poverty in its battle with the perhaps overly successful urban sphere of Belo Horizonte, what Marshall Eakins terms the "megacephalia," modernity's "giant-headedness" draining the countryside of soul and rural authenticity, arguably betraying the promises of rural development.[36]

Zé Coco do Riachão: The Hero *Violeiro* of Twentieth-Century *Música Caipira* in Minas Gerais

In 1979, Carlos Felipe, a journalist for the newspaper *Estado de Minas*, received an audiotape in his Belo Horizonte mailbox, one poorly recorded yet revealing a moving performance of folk music.[37] The recording was of sixty-eight-year-old Zé Coco do Riachão (José dos Reis dos Santos, 1912–1998), sent from northern Minas by Mineiro *violeiro* and popular culture scholar Téo Azevedo (later, a 2013 Latin Grammy winner).[38] Zé Coco was born east of the Rio São Francisco port city of São Romão, in Brasília de Minas, isolated among these backlands stretching from the arid northeastern hard-luck *sertão* to the *cerrado* scrub brush of the southeast. In characterizing the music's social origins, Felipe characterized northern Minas as a "cultural kaleidoscope" of migrant-fed crossroads, home to Zé Coco's universal regionalism.[39] Raised by a luthier father, he began at the age of eight playing viola melodies, *modas* and *toadas*, of the Folia de Reis tradition that helped define the boy's musical world. The family moved to the equally isolated, tough town of Bela Vista (now Mirabela), seventy rough kilometers north of Montes Claros, on a lonely road much later developed into Federal Highway BR135.

Coming of age during the Great Depression, Zé Coco was in his teens when the first *música caipira* 78 rpm records were released. He worked as a cabinet maker, carpenter, shoemaker, ironworker, *carro de boi* (oxcart) driver, and mandioca mill operator while composing, developing multi-instrumentalism, and establishing his luthier skills. He ultimately settled in Montes Claros, maintaining a luthier workshop producing exceptional violas, the folk fiddle known as *rabeca* or *violino caipira*, guitars, cavaquinhos, and *pandeiros*. He played them all while managing to learn the *sanfona*. According to Ivan Vilela, Zé Coco would say that young *violeiros* afraid to hold a snake between their fingers as an initiation to the instrument could instead rub into their hands the fat taken from a *sucuri* or *jibóia* snake. Municipal markets throughout northern Minas sell small bottles of these snake oils, which are still used as folk remedies for tendonitis and muscle aches.[40] Zé Coco's role in the viola's legacy throughout the *sertão* resonates with the cultural powers the instrument has increasingly wielded as a symbol of the rural past, his name heralded as a that of legendary musician, a treasured link to the old ways. His masterfully crafted violas remain highly valued cultural objects that keep a regional tradition alive. Like a few of his fellow northern Minas *violeiros*, he wrote and played lundus, the secular couple's dance genre likely rooted in Afro-Mineiro calundú, in a repertoire that includes the waltz, mazurka, *maxixe*, *corta jaca*, and forms associated with the *repentista*'s dueling challenge verses (*desafios*) such as the *guaiano* and *calanga*. All of these types appear on his recording *Vôo das garças*, a project realized a few years before his death, which includes his song "Arubu cinnamon": "I am the king of viola players / With me, no one can play fiddle / I am a bull on the viola."

Luthiers and *Violeiros* at the Mercado Novo in Belo Horizonte

For over thirty years, luthier Orlando França had been running his Orlau stringed instrument repair shop in Belo Horizonte's labyrinthine Mercado Novo (fig. 7.1). He passed away after my visit in 2013. There are no upscale boutiques or trendy fashions here, a block from downtown's busy Praça Raul Soares. Inexpensive eateries and repair counters for local wage earners ring the building's street-level exterior, facing crowded bus stops and ever-worsening traffic. The plain-looking building's windowless facade features sections of open-air, honeycombed brick. The first floor's poorly lit produce wholesaler stalls join an out-of-the-way luncheonette for workers, with the second floor a rough amalgam of printing presses, pipe fitters, and machine shops. The place is alive and buzzing with commerce. The upper level's busy loading area has a truck ramp slicing down through the building to Avenida Olegário Maciel; the dark hallways on this level empty into a large, noisy central corridor with a two-story high ceiling. França's shop is on this level, and his motto is printed on the sign above his small storefront: "Pontualidade e Perfeição" (punctuality and perfection). For sale are a few nylon- and steel-string guitars, and violas hanging from the wall. In various stages of repair are perhaps a dozen guitars and violas in cases tucked away in a small room off the hallway behind the store.

Eighty-something Orlando "Orlau" França is hustling about behind the counter, consulting with an assistant and two customers. He sits to play a recently repaired viola. Everyone in the shop seems pleased, the instrument's owner smiling with expectation. The old man quietly strikes up a tune, staring past me into the corridor, filtering out the Mercado Novo's clanging workaday sounds. He concentrates on fingering and picking; his body gently rocks, his head slightly moving in time. A big black hat covers his downturned face. Like most *violeiros*, he works the strings with his right hand using a slip-on thumb plectrum and forefinger: thumb strumming and plucking downstrokes across the lower-register strings, forefinger brushing precise upstrokes across the top strings. The tune is absolutely melancholy, ripe with a forlorn nostalgia; those in earshot grow hushed and pensive, as the old man lets out a slight grin. At tune's end there is complete silence before he starts up a cleverly phrased waltz, just as the central corridor grows busier and louder. Within the dark hull of the *mercado*, total joy floats about from this quixotic little tune. Spotting my camera, an unfriendly security guard approaches, gesturing, and aggressively warns me not to photograph the building interior. As he walks away, one of Orlau's assistants quietly dismisses him as a fool, suggesting that I return the following day for the Saturday morning gathering of *violeiros* who will meet a few steps away at the Vincente Machado Sala de Viola next to another small stringed instrument shop called the Violão de Ouro (Golden Guitar). Orlau has finished his test drive and hands the viola to his customer, another instrument ready for merrymaking.

Returning the next morning to this small corner in the middle of the big city, I see a few players with instrument cases and their friends slowly wandering in, quietly chatting and claiming the few chairs set up in a narrow walkway in front of the *sala de viola*. For no charge, and for no pay, they play *música caipira*, sing, and hang out, sharing their passion for viola as a common bond. Among these men of all colors between perhaps twenty-five and seventy years of age are rugged faces and hands of laborers, and others who are likely white-collar workers or professionals. Among the waves of twentieth-century modernization changing and crippling the old agrarian routines of life that gave rise to much of this repertoire, *violeiros* and songwriters working in the *música caipira* vein have continuously reinvented themselves as neo-cowboys (*novos-caipiras*), a term I loosely apply to those with a hand in urban re-formations and representations of *música caipira* here in the twenty-first century.[41] Importantly, these urban, sometimes middle-class, nonrural *novos-caipiras* stand apart from the excessively commercial *música sertaneja* that is increasingly insensitive and irrelevant to its own *caboclo* and *caipira* roots. Their viola continuum's lonely poetry of rural isolation and sentiments addresses the problems of urbanization and the advent of mechanized agriculture.

Figure 7.1. The late Orlando "Orlau" França's viola shop at the Mercado Novo, Belo Horizonte. The shop and clientele were a home for weekly *roda de viola* sessions. (Photo by Jonathon Grasse.)

During the twentieth century, Belo Horizonte mushroomed, as did the incredible success of electrified, commercial *música sertaneja*. But the irony of urban cowboys, if it ever existed here, has long faded, as the rural memories and passionate channeling of backwoods aesthetics have always been welcomed in urban Minas. Belo Horizonte is, after all, a provincial capital, a headquarters for all things culturally Mineiro, playing a constant role in juxtapositioning new with old, sleek modernity with rustic nostalgia. The Mercado Novo has transformed into a curiously rural social space with its own country vibe. Straight shots of *cachaça* are slyly offered to me at ten in the morning, and I get my chance to ask a few questions of a fellow named Rodrigo, who seems to be helping set things up. He grins and offers me a chair. His precise answers come between quick, short sips of drink, and he shares that a few teachers will be attending today with some friends and students. I see that about twenty people have arrived, all men. Some are sporting *vaqueiro* attire, including cowboy hats, simple neck scarves, plaid shirts, and boots. There is a serious air, almost subdued, and people are talking quietly among themselves. Several musicians start tuning up: the classic pairing of viola and guitar wistfully accompanying voices harmonized in thirds characterizes the backwoods songbook. Double-course violas of even moderate quality can be difficult to keep in tune. Rodrigo assures me that the music will begin in thirty minutes or so. City grit is giving way to a friendly social space hosting and representing the poetics of the rural past.

This gives me a chance to visit one of Orlau's sons, Luiz Alberto Neves França, in his own Mercado Novo luthier shop bright under fluorescent lights and only a bit larger than the claustrophobic front display area where he hangs a few of his handmade violas. He gets right to showing me his woodworking tools and several of his works in progress. Curved wood braces rest next to a nearly completed instrument with dark wood marquetry, or inlay work (*marchetaria*), on the lighter-colored top piece. He quickly produces an X-Acto knife set carefully housed in a small, blue metal box, the razor edges used to hand-carve thin wood ornamentation (*laminas da madeira*) fitted into equally precise shapes cut into the light beige surface of the *marupá* wood top. This beautiful "white" wood, also known as *caxeta*, grows in the Amazon's Xingu region. Intricate *marchetaria* is also exemplified in a fine rosette (*mosaico*) encircling the rim of the viola's sound hole. A light, yellowish cedar wood (*cedro-rosa*) is often used for tops. Luiz Alberto says that the raw Brazilian jacaranda he shapes into various instrument parts comes from Bahia and Mato Grosso, mostly rescued from demolished structures and buildings. He cuts each metal fret, placing them into the fingerboard made of jacaranda, a hardwood into which he also fits *marchetaria*; the rich, dark texture sets off position markers of pearl-like inlays. Another viola resting against the far wall has a clean, blank fingerboard ready for fretting. It is a deep, chocolate brown jacaranda with dense, almost black grains. The luthier shapes other pieces of this rare wood into the mustachioed bridges, the back, and the sides. This viola's sides feature a rare bi-tone grain that Luiz Alberto claims is derived from the outer portions of the tree, with the complex shadings and contrast of new and old growth in the same piece. For the viola's back, he uses the darkest, most well-cured and aged wood from the tree's center. The cattle bone bridge saddle and nut are pale white. Very thin yet dense and flexible decorator plastic with a mother-of-pearl sheen is ready to cut into binding strips to finish the edges. The shiny brass assembly of tuning heads and white-tipped pegs he screws onto the headstock are purchased wholesale down the street at the Serenata music store, one among several specialized music shops in a block-long music retail zone on the other side of Praça Raul Soares. Picking up a recently completed viola, Luiz Alberto tunes up, strumming and picking a brief melody. The instrument rings out, resonating well and projecting that familiar, shining viola timbre full of metallic, upper harmonics. Throughout our discussion, traffic noise from the street below periodically drifts in from the end of the corridor, where the building's massive honeycomb cinderblock walls are open to the outside chaos of the city. Squealing brakes and the hum of surging truck and bus engines punctuate the luthier's fond, thoughtful playing of the viola he made by hand. After his last notes fade to silence, I ask if any of his children have grown fond of the instrument, as future performers or luthiers. He shrugs, cracks a smile, and answers that they really just like to play video games.

Back at the *roda de viola* now spilling out of the Vincente Machado Sala de Viola, two musicians in *vaqueiro* shirts and felt and leather cowboy hats start up a tune. They sing in tight harmonic thirds. The *violeiro* picks out upper-position, higher-register melodic voicings, a couple of open strings ringing out, the nylon-string guitarist rhythmically strumming fully voiced chords. They stop briefly to improve the viola tuning, starting up again a song referencing a moonless night and the sorrows of long-lost love. The intimate audience surrounds the salon's small interior, seated in slight, frail folding chairs filling up the narrow hallway. They are certainly part of this, witnesses to the evocations of simple *fazendeiros*, tenant farmers, and lonely women who leave their even lonelier *sertanejo* men among symbols of the *sertão*'s stunning natural world. Transported participants embodying the ideals are meeting Brazil's past halfway. They are all here for visions of a vast, rural interior, for a poetry about what has been forgotten. This morning, their strummed and picked music drifts up into the upper reaches of the vast, high-ceilinged corridor, mixing with some faint radio chatter and a distant, thin sound stream of tinkling metal coming from a far-off machine shop, where a choir of old and new sounds disappear. Overcoming the *mercado*'s boisterous work routine, these Saturday morning listeners seem to make nothing of what I hear as distracting noise, perhaps a sound metaphor for the social confrontations facing *caipira* expression and the authenticity of its cultural legacies. But this performance space is as real as it gets: the tough environs of *música caipira*'s industrial relocation that began decades ago.

Virgílio Lima's Luthier Shop in Sabará: Twenty-First-Century Instruments for the New Masters of *Música Viola*

A few days before my Mercado Novo visit, I examined violas for sale at the recently opened Serenata music store on Avenida Getúlio Vargas, close to Belo Horizonte's Savassi district. Here among the factory-made instruments by Giannini, Casa del Vecchio, and Rozini were the least expensive models manufactured in China. Since the 1990s, the numbers of *violeiros* have grown. Large ensembles known as viola orchestras sprouting up in Minas, São Paulo, and elsewhere reflect this tide of rediscovery, a flourishing of "things *caipira*." These are certainly indications that *violeiros* are on the rise: but lesser-quality, inexpensive violas challenge the viability of some luthiers producing hand-made instruments. Would Zé Coco have been able to survive competition from Chinese factories? The complete antitheses to cheaply made, imported violas are the highly sought-after, museum-quality instruments handmade by master luthier Virgílio Lima (b. 1958, Sabará, MG) in his shop above the scenic colonial-era city that is his hometown (fig. 7.2). My friend Bruce was more than willing to drive there on his day off: Sabará is only a few kilo-meters away from Belo Horizonte, centered on the spot where, early in the eighteenth century, gold was discovered near the Sabará River's entry into the slow-moving Rio das Velhas (River of Old Women).

We make it to Lima's Vila Esperança neighborhood through the circuitous cobblestone streets of Sabará's hills. With a humble kindness characterizing so many Mineiros, the luthier welcomes us to the quiet inner space of his bright workshop, with a vista of the beautiful three-hundred-year-old town. Here, he makes just over twenty instruments per year, with a waiting list to last into the next decade. Since the 1980s, Virgílio has been counted as one of Brazil's primary viola luthiers, successfully confronting the instrument's troublesome design and intonation issues. He pioneered advanced construc-tion techniques and researched higher-quality material in creating instru-ments technically worthy of demanding professionals and the challenging repertoire of the instrumental *música viola* genre. The Mineiro's foundation in luthier studies came from a dedicated, late-1970s apprenticeship with the *nipo-brasileiro* (Japanese Brazilian) Shigemitsu Sugiyama, a luthier from the legendary Masaru Kohno's Tokyo shop. After moving to São Paulo in the early 1970s and working briefly in the Giannini factory, the Japanese immigrant

Figure 7.2. Master viola luthier Virgílio Lima in his Sabará workshop. Lima emerged as a leading innovator and instrument builder in the 1980s, settling in a picturesque colonial town with important historical roots in viola production. (Photo by Jonathon Grasse, 2015.)

began building instruments later adopted by Brazilian classical guitar legend Turíbio Santos; MPB stars Chico Buarque, João Bosco, Paulinho da Viola, and Toquinho; and others. After studies with Sugiyama, Lima spent years creating new approaches to viola construction, sometimes in collaboration with *violeiro* and fellow Mineiro Roberto Corrêa (b. 1957, Campina Verde, MG). This phase of his career included experimenting with string gauges and tensions to create violas with improved intonation, and those optimized for certain tunings.

Today's *música viola* of the concert halls, executed by studiously accomplished musicians, some of whom are classically trained guitarists, at times seems to echo the instrument's role among Brazil's innovative poets and musicians of the past, whose courtly modinhas and lundu song graced eighteenth-century Rio de Janeiro's salons and Lisbon's royal court. Twenty-first-century Brazilian ensembles dedicated to restoring the viola to its place in fine art music, such as Anima, Lira d'Orfeo, Banza, and Quadro Cervantes, have incorporated the instrument as an authentic voice in arrangements of Luso-Brazilian chamber music, such as that of Rio's famed imperial-era salon culture. This was the world of Rio de Janeiro–born Domingos Caldas Barbosa (1740–1800), the poet and *violeiro* who later championed his innovative secular songs and instrumental style in Lisbon's royal circles. The published modinhas and lundu song of Brazilian composers following Barbosa's vein are still performed in recitals and concerts, as instrumentals and as art songs performed in bel canto style. Barbosa incorporated the viola into his innovative lundu salon song during the Golden Age of Minas Gerais, and championed among the upper classes a derivation of the already established rural lundu dance genre that had attracted viola players as accompanists to singers and dancers, then a genre experiencing a transitional stage of popular urbanization. Yet as a harmonic accompaniment instrument for this richly lyrical repertoire, the viola lost its place to the harpsichord, piano, and *violão*—the Spanish or French guitar, as the modern six-string guitar was known in nineteenth-century Brazil. The 1808 displacement of the Portuguese court from Lisbon to Rio de Janeiro brought to Brazil wider uses of the *violão*, and an eventual association of the viola with rustic, rural social practice. During that century, the viola gradually became associated with the lower socio-economic classes, with the piano to be found in more prosperous homes.[42] Discussing Barbosa's important use of the viola, and of the modinha's and lundu's strong association with that epoch of Rio de Janeiro nightlife, José Ramos Tinhorão cites Joaquim Manuel de Macedo's 1870 novel *As mulheres de mantilha* in suggesting that the instrument had lost its aristocratic shine a century earlier, in the story's setting of 1760s Rio de Janeiro:

"Lundu again!"—exclaimed a beautiful girl, standing up and taking the viola.

"Why not the harpsichord? The harpsichord is nobler, fitting for a nice country house and ballads; the lundu is plebeian and is wedded to the viola, the instrument of the common people."[43]

Anima has collaborated in performances and recordings of some of this repertoire with master *violeiros* Ivan Vilela and Paulo Freire. A replica of a 1769 viola found in Capivari, Minas Gerais, handmade in the 1990s by luthier Roberto Gomes in São João del-Rei, was played by Anima's Gisela Nogueira.[44] Lira d'Orfeo features "viola *caipira*" in their 2008 recording of arrangements made from eighteenth- and nineteenth-century lundu and modinha. Classical guitarist Nicolas de Souza Barros joins Renaissance and baroque guitars with viola in his performances with the Brazilian early music group Quadro Cervantes, in repertoire ranging from the medieval period to the Brazilian songbook of the nineteenth century dominated by lundu song and modinhas. Colonial-era letters describing musical performances in Brazil indicate a broad role for the viola in what constituted elite musical life. In the realm of European-derived fine art music, the harpsichord (*cravo*) became part of the colonial sound world, with the viola sharing that plucked keyboard instrument's timbre rich in upper harmonics. Virgílio Lima has likened viola timbres to those of the harpsichord, with others, such as Vilela, claiming that the viola may have been used in Minas as a continuo instrument in the performance of baroque-era chamber music recitals executing chords in the realization of figured bass accompaniment.[45]

Some *música viola* practitioners are also composers venturing into new harmonic and formal territories, crossing traditional boundaries and bringing the instrument into concert halls and universities, where it attempts to translate its significant cultural weight. Tavinho Moura, a highly skilled original composer and accomplished *violeiro*, is discussed in chapter 9. Although allying themselves with, and drawing from, traditional music associated with *música caipira*, most performers of *música viola* remain concerned with instrumental virtuosity (though some also sing), challenges to compositional structures and techniques, and the rich projection of quality concert stage instruments that stay in tune. "Refined," "erudite," "fine art," and "classical" are some of the descriptors Brazilians have applied to *música viola* in parsing the genre from its roots in *música caipira*'s folk traditions with which these *violeiros* ally themselves in unique ways. *Música viola* players sing less often than more commercial popular performers, render folkloric references through original compositions and virtuosic technique, and bring contemporary interpretations in their elaborations of the *caipira* galaxy. *Violeiros* such as Renato Andrade (1932–2005, b. Abaeté, MG), whose 1977 recording *A fantástica viola de Renato Andrade na música armorial mineira* pushed the viola to its instrumental limits,[46] and better design and materials were necessary to launch *música viola* in its sophisticated mixture of popular, folk, and classical elements. The Brazilian government sponsored Andrade's concert tours abroad, promoting the viola's music styles and sound. A few Brazilian masters of the classical guitar began adopting the viola either as a side instrument or as a newly dedicated instrument for concert performance, and a market for higher-quality violas materialized. The best violas for this genre began appearing only in the late 1980s, claims Lima: "They sound great, very vibrant, and stay in tune far better than any viola ever stayed in tune before." Of the eleven *violeiros* featured on Myriam Taubkin's 2008 *Violeiros do Brasil* project, the nation's best, four are playing instruments made by Virgílio during the 1990s.

Today, artistically elevated uses of the viola indirectly spotlight how the instrument's role in rural *caipira* and Afro-Mineiro legacies contrast with its place in salons. *Violeiros* of the caliber of Renato Andrade and Roberto Corrêa are no longer so rare. The Paulista Paulo Freire, inspired in part by the poetic visions of the Mineiro interior in the novels of João Guimarães Rosa, relocated to the isolated northwestern Minas town of Urucuia, studying viola for two years with local practitioners. Freire's first solo CD, *Rio Abaixo: Viola brasileira* (1995), was awarded Brazil's prestigious Sharp Award for new recording. His primary teacher in Urucuia, Manuel de Oliveira, later released his own CD, entitled *Urucuia* (2006). Freire published and recorded a range of materials and songs bringing to light this regional viola culture, attracting other *violeiros* from the big city such as Rodrigo Delage. Virtuosi from Minas such as Ivan Vilela have established academic positions for the viola at major universities, where the instrument's roles in Brazilian musical culture are studied in depth. Born and raised in Sul de Minas and today a professor of music at the University of São Paulo's School of Communication and the Arts, Vilela begins his 1998 album of original music for viola, titled *Paisagens*, with his composition "Prá matar a saudade de Minas" (For the killing-off of the longing for Minas), an homage to his own homesickness for the region's musical landscape. *Paisagens* features Luiz Henrique Fiaminghi playing a *rabeca* made by Zé Coco, and Ricardo Matsuda playing a guitar built by Virgílio Lima's mentor, Shigemitsu Sugiyama. Vilela's viola on this recording was made by Virgílio in his quiet workshop overlooking Sabará, in the heart of Minas. One of the walls in Virgílio's workshop is covered with tools, and cluttered with storage compartments filled with violas at various stages of completion. He brings over a thin rectangular piece of jacaranda sliced from a railroad tie, adding: "One of those railroad ties is enough wood for ten violas." This jacaranda *violeta* is very stressed from its many years of compressed wear and weathering, supposedly making it a great resource for luthiers. Wood brokers scavenge for fine, old-growth wood from house demolitions, discarded furniture, and railroad works, which are some of the only legal sources for protected specimens such as jacaranda. Setting the small piece down on his worktable, he delicately scrapes off a super-thin surface area to reveal a beautiful grain. He then dips a small applicator brush into a jar of oil and swathes the newly exposed jacaranda layer. A rich, deep burgundy grain blooms with beautiful patterns where there had only been a plain, dry surface before. "There are fifty species of jacaranda growing in Minas Gerais," he says, holding the now jewel-like piece at different angles in the light streaming through the window overlooking Sabará, "but their woods are similar in mechanical characteristics—and each is protected by law." The color variants among jacaranda types are a trove for Brazilian luthiers, with *baiano* (Bahian rosewood) being the most sought after. That species is nearly extinct, having practically disappeared from Minas along with the remains of the Mata Atlântica rainforest. "Three-hundred-year-old trees are the best. And artificial cultivation does not produce high quality wood for us." Virgílio sets the small piece of glistening *violeta* wood down on his table. "The jacaranda must grow in its own jungle setting to produce the molecular characteristics we are talking about." Some recently dismantled homes in Sabará proved a treasure of fine woods for his luthier projects.

During his journey through Sabará in 1824, the German naturalist Georg Langsdorff noted the viola makers on a fazenda near Bom Retiro, a town now called Roça Grande:

> Two free black men that live here work as carpenters. They make wheels for cotton spinning among other things, such as violas, a type of *citara*. These artisans buy old, European pine boxes and use the wood to make these instruments. A common viola sells for five to eight *patacas* [silver coinage terminated in Brazil in the 1830s].[47]

A century later, Sabará of the 1920s boasted forty luthiers working on and around what became known as Rua das Violas. Virgílio Lima is continuing

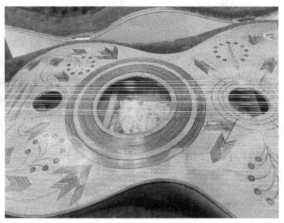

Figures 7.3, 7.4. Two rare violas de Queluz from the Max Rosa collection, constructed by the Salgado family in the early twentieth century. An accomplished luthier based in Nova Lima, Rosa helped spearhead a renaissance in appreciation for the handmade violas from Queluz, Minas Gerais. (Photos by Jonathon Grasse, 2015.)

a Mineiro cultural legacy particular to this city. Since the mid-1980s, he has been making the best violas in Brazil, though he would never make that claim. As *música caipira* scholar Rosa Nepomuceno states, "Violas made in Minas have always been famous."[48] All of this attention to the instrument and its music breathed new life into the legends and mysteries of the Mineiro viola makers of Queluz.

Max Rosa, a student of Lima's 2007 luthier workshop, is sharing with me the cream of his *viola de Queluz* collection, case by case, bringing each new treasure into the small showroom of his modern luthier shop in Nova Lima, an old town bordering the southern edge of Belo Horizonte's mountain escarpment, the Serra do Curral. Though he specializes in building steel-string guitars, Rosa is an expert on historical viola construction in Minas, particularly the *viola de Queluz*. He undertook many long road trips throughout the state's central region in search of specimens, leaving his home before dawn, following dirt roads, and simply asking anyone and everyone in small towns and settlements about possible violas and names of *violeiros* in the area. During one early search for rare violas, Max by chance met a fellow who had recently cleared out his late father's belongings: a 1920s Queluz viola was still in the dumpster. The young luthier gladly took the banged-up instrument back to his shop for restoration, the incident sparking what has proven to be his life-long passion for collecting and restoration. Max opens a case revealing a particularly old instrument dating from the 1880s; its *marchetaria* includes the customer's initials, *J.R.P.*, in fine bone decorations. Other instruments reveal, instead of a single, large sound hole, between two and five.

Max soon discovered that another Mineiro collector was also searching the countryside for old violas. A resident of nearby Betim, and also a *violeiro* and composer, Claudio Alexandinho caught the bug in the late 1980s, and he now owns a collection of more than 150 rare violas including many fine Queluz specimens. Max and Claudio remain leading participants in the post-1990 resurgence of interest in the once-again-famous Mineiro tradition of violas, a rediscovery Max says was slow in coming considering the importance of the legacy to Mineiro cultural identity. Seminars, expositions, and journal and newspaper coverage have revolved around the activities of Max and Claudio and created a resurgence of wider interest in this regional cultural legacy. If rare violas still sit undiscovered in the countryside at this point, they might remain there forever. A peak of scavenging by collectors lasted from 2006 to 2009, a few years during which such picking seems to have cleaned out the treasures, contrasting with the (roughly) 1950–1990 period during which, Max claims, there was little documented interest in the *viola de Queluz*.

Belo Horizonte *Excursión*: The Instituto Brasileiro de Viola Caipira's First Festival Mineiro da Viola, 2013

With a friend, I am catching a taxi in Belo Horizonte's Mangabeiras district to attend the first Festival Mineiro da Viola, a state-wide competition with prizes awarded for both original songwriting and performance. Earlier in the week, I purchased tickets at the SESC Palladium box office, a major performance venue in downtown Belo Horizonte created by the Serviço Social do Comércio (SESC), a publicly funded yet private institution. Organized by the Instituto Brasileiro de Viola Caipira (IBVC), the first-of-its-kind festival is being held in the Palladium's biggest auditorium, the Grande Teatro. The

IBVC engages local viola-based organizations throughout Minas Gerais, such as Uberlândia's Festival Nacional de Viola de Cruzeiro dos Peixotos (FENACRUPE), originally based in the Cruzeiro dos Peixotos neighborhood of this city of over six hundred thousand in the western section of Minas known as the Triângulo. FENACRUPE's *viola caipira* festivals routinely draw audiences of more than ten thousand in a region where agriculture and cattle industries dominate. One of the IBVC's founders, Pedro Lemos Barbosa, underlines the importance of the viola to the statewide musical scene by emphasizing the 2013 festival's search for ten finalists representing divergent regions of the state, each vying for a winner's pot: first-, second-, and third-place finishers receive prizes of R$5,000, 3,000, and 2,000, respectively. The SESC showcase reveals the centrality of Belo Horizonte as a magnet for regional culture, and though the Festival Mineiro da Viola is no power grab of the viola, not an attempt to claim from the rest of Brazil a regional exclusivity of the instrument, the city stands as a natural host for a celebration of the instrument's iconic status to Minas. During the months leading up to the 2013 festival, ninety participants from all over the state submitted online entries through the IBVC website, each recording evaluated by a group of notable judges, and all meeting the requirement that their song reference Minas in their lyrics or song title. Online voting was also opened up for fans, in recognition of the instrument's broad community of supporters. The festival's long-term goal is to recognize new talent while bringing together Mineiro styles and performance techniques, a process acknowledging the viola's deep cultural presence that also maps its hinterland expanse. As Barbosa commented on the festival's website: "Each region plays a different viola style, and we try as much as possible to consider all of them."

After filing through the Grand Theater's entrance in a long line of attendees, we stream into a well-appointed concert hall. A prominent and simple Festival Mineiro da Viola banner, incorporating the red triangle of the Minas Gerais state flag, hangs prominently upstage, flanked by tastefully dramatic drapes, which will be bathed in a palette of solid, gem-tone colored lights throughout the night. The house is comfortable and the audience large considering that this first Festival Mineiro de Viola is being held on a weekday night in August. Many in the audience sport rural, cowboy wardrobes. Stage right finds the MC and his podium sharing space with a prominent IBVC sign, "Bringing viola culture to you," aided by two circular photos, one of a close-up left hand fingering a viola, the other of a luthier fashioning a viola

Figure 7.5. Encore: Finalists of the first Festival Mineiro da Viola, the SESC Palladium, Belo Horizonte, 2013. Contestants came from diverse regions of Minas Gerais, competing with their original compositions for viola and various ensemble formats. (Photo by Jonathon Grasse.)

frame. A bullet-point list promotes the institute's activities of research, lectures, meetings, projects, luthier classes, and workshops. The MC warmly and enthusiastically introduces each judge, and their small group quickly fills a table in the stage left wing: local viola star Chico Lobo, percussionist Carlinhos Ferreira, producer Tadeu Martins, folklorist/journalist Carlos Felipe (the *Estado de Minas* writer assisting in the rediscovery of Zé Coco), and radio host Múcio Bolivar, whose show *Trem caipira* (*Caipira* train) has aired on Rádio Inconfidência for more than twenty years. Stagehands and a live sound reinforcement crew will accommodate various ensemble types and their unique sound needs. Among the ensembles are percussionists playing shakers, rattles, and drums of many types, including traditional-looking *caixas* and a *tambor*. One band features a prominent flute part, and another boasts a lead female vocalist who plays no instrument and wears pants, not a skirt like the other female participants. Several groups feature electric bassists. Some ensembles present a combination of nylon- and steel-string acoustic guitars as accompaniment to the featured viola. The vocals are handled by a lead singer, who is sometimes in frequent or constant tertial harmonization by at least one other vocalist who is likely to be playing an instrument as well.

The competition continues for two hours. It will become apparent that each performing group has a rooting section of friends, family, and fans, some traveling from all corners of the state to cheer on their *violeiros* in the big-city festival. Signs are hoisted along with the shouting, chanting, and screaming of performer and band names, ratcheting up the enthusiastic atmosphere, a cross between a battle of the bands, a music recital, and a civics class on regional pride. Here, the focus is not on flashy virtuosity but on the subjectively tasteful qualities showcasing the viola. The top prize winner, singer-*violeiro* Guilherme Faria, renders his song "Velho Chico" in a solo performance, an homage to the São Francisco River, "Old Chico," the soul of the northwestern Mineiro *sertão*. The festival finale features regional *violeiro* star Chico Lobo and his trio of electric bass and multi-instrumental percussion as a solidifying headline act. Moving beyond formality and the competition's mild tension, this closing encourages the audience to let off steam, to sing along. All of the competition participants are on stage in a large semicircle behind Lobo, leading the auditorium in a rousing, heartfelt *toada*, ending the festival with applause for all of the performers, a collective gesture emerging from across the Mineiro interior (fig. 7.5). For too brief a moment, a musical instrument, passionate musicians, and their fans have all come together. The viola is Brazil's gift to itself, and Minas shares in this magic.

Chapter 8

Belo Horizonte Nocturne
Subtropical Modernism, 1894–1960

Leonardo José Magalhães Gomes, writing about the vast, sweeping changes of the twentieth century, posits music as an emergent character of Belo Horizonte, stating:

> The demolition of the village [Curral D'el-Rey] and the construction of the capital represent in the field of music the end of the colonial tradition and the beginning of a new musical culture that, with the passage of time, brings about a convergence of local, regional, national, and international currents, the catalytic action of which results in the city having its own musical characteristics toward the end of the twentieth century.[1]

With an ever-blooming sea of new high-rise apartment buildings, thick traffic jams, and an expanding sprawl of urban squalor, Belo Horizonte in the second decade of the twenty-first century approaches the three million mark, its greater metropolitan area of thirty-four municipalities boasting close to twice that number. The new, belle époque state capital was the Mineiro answer to the Brazilian republic's founding in 1889, the young nation's first planned city, designed originally for two hundred thousand residents and horse-drawn transportation. The modern city symbolized social and political transitions away from imperial rule and the slavery era, and its quiet optimism distanced inhabitants from the region's post–mining boom economic decline, then still fully evident in struggling *cidades históricas*. "The great metropolis was the daughter of modernity's rational design, [and] granddaughter of its master, conservative colonialism," states Bruno Viveiros Martins in his study of the Clube da Esquina popular music collective and its home city.[2] Work on what was first named Cidade de Minas (Minas City) began in 1894, where stood the small Arraial do Curral D'el-Rey (Village of D'el Rey's Corral). Today, the downtown district's majestic Boa Viagem Catedral towers where the Curral D'el-Rey chapel once welcomed worshippers. Exploring the Brazilian interior for five years during the early eighteenth century with a team of botanists sent by King Louis Philippe of France, London-born naturalist Francis Castelnau described the mountains that became iconic of Belo Horizonte: "The town of Curral del-Rei is pleasantly situated in the middle of the woods. From the windows of the house is revealed a magnificent panorama of mountains belonging to two different chains."[3] Of course, material difficulties mean poverty of the "interior," as the vast outlying subregions of Minas Gerais gradually became known in their relation to the new city. He wrote of his brief January 1844 stay in nearby Betim, "We witnessed a sung Mass in honor of Saint Sebastian, the music, without being good, was better than expected. In short, we see each day, taking into account the material difficulties that beset the residents of the interior, the state of civilization here is well underway."[4]

BH, as the city is also known (in Portuguese, the letters, *be-agá*, are pronounced "bay ah-gah"), stares back through time to the historical social spaces of regional music found throughout the Mineiro interior. Many of these places and their social contexts have long been transformed by the tides of progressive change, development, and decay, eclipsed and replaced by new surroundings and social values. Belo Horizonte's birth came in the early years of the Old Republic (1889–1937), a period of nearly fifty years launched by the abdication of Emperor Dom Pedro II and brought to an end by the centralizing forces of Getúlio Vargas's coup and subsequent "New State" (Estado Novo). The former provincial capital of Vila Rica, in the 1740s one of the largest and most prosperous city in the Western Hemisphere with close to twenty thousand inhabitants, was now called Ouro Preto and entering a second century of decline. Belo Horizonte was a phoenix of sorts, rising from the ashes of the imperial era and from the dust and gravel of two centuries of a frontier civilization built on fazendas, the time-worn historical towns of Old Minas, and mining (including that of the new gold, iron ore). From those cities, small towns, and rural enclaves, Belo Horizonte's new residents brought their nineteenth-century repertoire of popular music such as modinhas, *serenatas* (nocturnal street serenades), *toadas*, and humble ditties. In the new city, this array of sacred, folk, and popular song retained complex ties not just to the Mineiro interior and layers of regional imperial and colonial society but to cities and towns along the Brazilian coast, and to both Portugal and Africa.

The urban core of architect Aarão Reis's city plan was designed for political and administrative functions of the state, industrial and commercial processing, basic services, and smaller business operations; this core was surrounded by suburbs and outlying zones set aside for country homes (*situs*).[5] Curral D'el-Rey's surrounding large fazendas such as the Pantana, Jaguára, and Jatobá were home to perhaps thousands of formerly enslaved laborers, now free, as Belo Horizonte took shape. Many Afro-Mineiros remained in the area following emancipation, either staying where they worked, settling in rural hamlets, or moving to the city's new favelas (hillside slums). Other newly freed people of color were drawn to Rio de Janeiro. As the nearby rural oligarchy also splintered from both economic hardships and new opportunities, many large properties were sold off into parcels. Some local communities of impoverished, formerly enslaved Mineiros situated therein survived and remained in place. Within a few years of the city's construction, two districts had already become "invasion areas" or "areas of irregular occupation," home to more than three thousand slum dwellers. These first favelas, such as Leitão, have long since been dismantled and redeveloped.[6]

Afro-Mineiro musical traditions nourished by fazenda laborers who maintained their religious practices, music, and dance for generations were integral elements to the urbanization engulfing central Minas Gerais: batuque, Congado, and, as a link to the long-lost calundú religious practice, both Umbanda and Macumba. Settled by the poorest beginning in the 1920s, Morro do Papagaio (Parrot Hill) was eventually formed by five communities coalescing over ninety years into a favela of seventeen thousand, sitting today in close proximity to the city's most valued residential real estate. Compounding the ill-prepared inclusion of socially marginalized former slaves and their descendants, the original city plan lacked adequate housing even for construction workers, forcing many low-income laborers to settle in ramshackle structures along with squatters.[7] In 1896, two thousand Italian workers employed in the construction of Belo Horizonte threatened to strike when their compatriot railroad workers in nearby Sabará rioted over poor work conditions. The state militia had to intervene.[8]

Bandas in BH

A passionate slice of the city's early musical profile was its continuation of nineteenth-century banda traditions, including performances of popular and fine art concert music at private salon parties. The pastime was transplanted from surrounding *cidades históricas* to the new city. The musical arrangements conducted by maestro José Nicodemus de Silva with the city's Banda Militar came from his own collection of quadrilles, waltzes, and polkas entitled *A rainha da festa*, published in Ouro Preto in 1881. It is believed that many of these pieces were played in the Clube Belo Horizonte and other salons by the Banda da Brigada Policial, also directed by Silva.[9] I discuss the link between bandas and fine art concert music as illustrated by this conductor, who also played cello, below. In December 1897, the city's ceremonial inauguration was held at Praça da Liberdade, a celebration featuring performances by the Sociedade Musical Belo Horizonte's band, formed the previous year by Alfredo Camarate (d. 1904). A Portuguese architect in town for the many opportunities to shape the city, Camarate was also a flutist, composer, and music critic, engaging the city's first generation of classical music lovers.[10]

The band was composed mostly of Italian construction workers and was soon renamed the Banda Carlos Gomes (Sociedade Musical Carlos Gomes Banda) after Brazil's greatest Romantic-era composer, Antônio Carlos Gomes, who had died in 1896.[11] The ensemble that became Banda Carlos Gomes had debuted two years earlier, in Curral D'el-Rey's old chapel of the rosary, that settlement's last remaining architectural remnant. Two months after the new city's inauguration, the banda played in a commemoration of the Brazilian army's victory in the bloody Canudos campaign, during which the last vestiges of Antônio Conselheiro's settlement in Belo Monte, Bahia, was destroyed by federal troops.[12] This concert may have taken place in one of three venues accommodating large ensembles: the Teatrinho Provisório (constructed 1895), the Clube Recreativo Bello Horizonte (using an archaic spelling; 1894), or the Clube Esportivo de Dezembro (1895).[13] These were theaters that also saw performances of the Lira Mineira civic band, formed in 1895 by Otávio Barreto de Oliveira Braga.

Figure 8.1. The bandstand in the Parque Municipal, Belo Horizonte. Public plazas and parks are not complete without a *coreto* (bandstand), a testament to the historical and cultural importance of municipal, military, and neighborhood bands. (Photo by Jonathon Grasse.)

Considered to be the city's first proper theater, the Teatro Soucasseaux was completed in 1899 and soon competed with the existing Teatro Paris. Both venues featured in-house orchestras.[14] Cidade de Minas was optimistically renamed Belo Horizonte (briefly Bello) to commemorate the dawn of the twentieth century, as it absorbed the music played in its salons, cafés, little bars, streets, and plazas. In 1909, the Teatro Soucasseaux reemerged as the Teatro Municipal, and in 1942 transformed once again, becoming a movie theater, the Cine Metrópole. According to Maria de Oliveira:

The [Teatro Municipal's] inaugural program on October 21, 1909, presented the show *Magda*, staged by the Nina Sanzio Company, directed by the consecrated *mineira* actress, who had had success in Europe, and which incorporated the Italian actress Eleonora Duse. Many foreign companies visited this theater year-round, with production teams complete with singers and conductors, choir, ballet, scenery, wardrobe, and technical staff, as the new capital could not yet offer such services.[15]

Under the leadership of Henrique Aristides after 1906, the Banda Carlos Gomes performed most of their concerts at the newly constructed bandstand of Praça da Estação, the Beaux-Arts train station that still stands, fully renovated in the twenty-first century. Official military bands, such as that of the Federal Army's Fifth Battalion, performed at government and military events, and for parties at Belo Horizonte's finer salons; they competed with the bandas of the First and Second Battalions of the Military Police, which had relocated from Ouro Preto.[16] The city remained under continual construction into 1915, by which time suburbs such as Calafate, Lagoinha, and Floresta had mushroomed despite lacking basic services. Fervent Lagoinha Catholics addressed these and other community issues by raising funds to build a church and support an orchestra and girls' chorus; by 1914, they had formed the mixed-race Corporação Musical Nossa Senhora da Conceição, later the Banda da Lagoinha.[17] The group, founded by Manoel Arranjo, survived for ninety years through local donations, illustrating the close relationships some music organizations had with the church and its religious festival calendar.[18] Neighborhood bands flourished throughout the young city, such as Fanfarra, formed by Italian immigrants in the 1920s.[19] By 1930, three additional bands of note had formed in Belo Horizonte: Santo Antônio, Santa Cecilia, and Euterpe Horizontina.[20]

Since the late 1990s, a total of 216 civilian and military bands (*agremiações musicais*) have paraded with arrangements of hymns, marches, polkas, and popular songs in the Serviço Social do Comércio's Minas Gerais Band Meeting representing all regions of the state and held in Belo Horizonte. In November 2014, the sixteenth annual parade was held in and around Praça Floriano Peixoto, attracting eleven bands from all over the state including four from Belo Horizonte. With colonial-era roots, the Belo Horizonte band tradition still thrives in the twenty-first century.

The Rise of Belo Horizonte's Classical Music World:
Salons, Conservatories, and Concert Halls

Mineiro musicians throughout the nineteenth century had only dim prospects for local formal music training with professionals, and those interested in classical repertoire lacked opportunities. Brightening this scenario was the growth of Belo Horizonte, where salon music such as modinha and lundu grew in popularity along with performances of European-derived classical music, sometimes referred to in Brazil as *música erudita* (erudite music). This cultural landscape changed with the rise of elite culture's taste for live music, the need for skilled musicians in theaters and cinemas, the emergence of music schools, and a general demand for amateur and professional ensembles. The lyrical gestures of modinhas and art music genres such as the Italian aria were performed in salon programs by amateurs and a few touring professionals accompanied by piano. Like the aristocratic circles of imperial-era coastal cities and São Paulo, early twentieth-century Belo Horizonte salons were limited to members and guests of private social clubs such as Violetas, Rose, Edelweias, Elite, and Belo Horizonte.[21] The Clube Rose boasted an all-female mandolin ensemble that was directed by Esther Brandão, the governor's wife. These invitation-only chamber concerts, mixtures of classical and popular music, were organized, funded, and attended by professionals, upper-level government functionaries, academics and intellectuals, engineers and industry leaders, local business elites, and the clergy. As Magalhães Gomes comments on Belo Horizonte's nascent classical music scene:

> The salon culture created a market for scores, sheet music, and other music publications: in the clubs founded and maintained by lovers of the arts . . . small chamber groups generally formed by amateurs realized their musico-literary soirees in large rooms as impromptu concerts. With pianos, clarinets, flutes, violins, and cellos, they performed the modinhas, maxixes, tangos, lundus, toadas, marches, and other genres representing salon music inherited from the Empire. They also incorporated waltzes, arias, art songs, sonatas, polkas, romances, [and] nocturnes from works imported from Europe.[22]

Pianeiros hired to play popular music, and *pianistas* specializing in classical repertoire, stood apart from one another, though both could find sheet music and scores at Casa Machado Coelho e Companhia, Belo Horizonte's best downtown music store.[23] It was there where Edison phonographs (*phonógrophos*) first appeared in the city in 1898, and four years later the Casa Edison recording catalog presented Xisto Bahia's version of the lundu song "Isto é bom," Brazil's first commercial recording. While Brazil's popular and classical music worlds never experienced the levels of anxious separation that they did in Europe and the United States, socialites and status seekers in a young Belo Horizonte kept their distance from lower socioeconomic classes. In the meantime, cinema and the phonograph were technologies as new as the city, and they spread increasingly diverse music to wider audiences regardless of their background. In discussing social contexts, Magalhães Gomes notes that during this time in Belo Horizonte, "[t]he guitar was a marginal instrument that had not yet entered the houses and venues frequented by high society. It was found in the bars and in the houses of the simplest people, where at any moment someone would play it alone or as accompaniment to a modinha, lundu, *seresta*, or *toada*."[24] Belo Horizonte's first professional classical musicians performed for the Clube das Violetas in the downtown Palacete Steckel (Steckel Palace) before the end of the 1890s. The most noted included cellist and conductor José Nicodemus de Silva, pianist Carlos Barrouin, conductors and composers Francisco Flores (1860–1926) and José Ramos de Lima (also a pianist, b. 1866, Itajubá, MG), and pianist and composer Francisco Valle (1869–1906, b. Juiz de Fora). Valle moved to Rio de Janeiro as a young man, later studied composition with César Franck in Paris, and returned to Europe again after receiving financial support from the Minas Gerais provincial government. Resettling in Brazil, he visited Belo Horizonte as a concert pianist. His father, Manuel Marcelino do Valle (1839–1903), was born in Rio Preto, Minas Gerais, near the provincial border with Rio de Janeiro, and attended the most important music institution in the country, Rio de Janeiro's Imperial Conservatory of Music. The elder Valle was awarded a silver flute by Emperor Dom Pedro II for his virtuosity in that instrument.

Francisco Flores was born in the small Zona da Mata town of Mar de Espanha, less than twenty kilometers from the Rio de Janeiro border.[25] Following Imperial Conservatory studies in clarinet, conducting, and composition, he worked as an organist, directed bands, and taught music theory before moving in 1901 to Belo Horizonte, where he founded the Escola Livre de Música. In 1912, he was named director of the Banda da Força Pública do Estado. In 1916, the short-lived Sociedade de Concertos Sinfônicos (Symphonic Concert Society) grew out of Flores's Orquestra Sinfônica de

Belo Horizonte. The year Flores arrived in the city, Cuban cellist Manoel Acosta was invited there by painter and businessman Frederico Steckel, whose Palacete Steckel competed with the Grand Hotel as a concert music venue.[26] Support and organization for some of these productions came from local writer Arthur Lobo's Jarindeiros do Ideal literary circle of academics, lawyers, and members of the city elite.

Concert highlights illustrate the city's blossoming of formal performing arts. A turn-of-the-century newspaper review of the Concertos Populares concert series noted: "For the first time, we heard in this city some examples of music completely new to our public, among them the *Ária de Marília* and the opera *Tiradentes* by Manoel Joaquim de Macedo."[27] Macedo (1847–1925) had been the concertmaster of the Covent Garden Orchestra of London before returning to Rio de Janeiro in 1871, and he was soon selected by Emperor Dom Pedro II as the music director of the royal chapel.[28] His nativist opera *Tiradentes*, with a libretto by regarded Mineiro poet and author Augusto de Lima (1859–1934), celebrates the iconic leader of the Inconfidência Mineira in a regionalist echo of Brazil's nineteenth-century nationalist trends. An April 1904 concert presented by the short-lived Clube Schumann included Macedo's nativist-themed symphonic poem based upon the life of Old Republic hero Floriano Peixoto, which shared program space with a work by José Ramos de Lima. Club Schumann was Belo Horizonte's answer to Rio de Janeiro's imperial-era Clube Mozart and Clube Beethoven (founded in 1867 and 1882, respectively), and São Paulo's Clube Haydn, music associations promoting high-society concerts and recitals. The remarkable musician Dinorá de Carvalho (1896–1980, b. Uberaba, MG) was just one of Brazil's concertizing pianists who made Belo Horizonte stages and salons regular tour destinations. Moving to São Paulo as a child following her father's death, she studied and concertized in France and Italy, and later founded Latin America's first all-female orchestra. Her compositions were performed at festivals.[29]

Pattápio Silva (1880–1907) was the nationally recognized heir apparent to Junior Callado (1848–1880), Brazil's greatest nineteenth-century flutist and first choro master. Both musicians died young. Silva's poverty-stricken childhood in the Zona da Mata town of Cataguases did not foreshadow his later success at Rio's newly renamed Instituto Nacional de Música (National Institute of Music, previously the Imperial Conservatory of Music). His output as a composer and recording flutist mark him, like Callado, as a virtuoso of both classical and popular forms. Silva's 1904 Belo Horizonte appearance came soon after his performance for President Afonso Pena in Rio's presidential palace (Palácio do Catete), and his first Odeon label recordings.[30] Laís Corrêa de Araújo remembers:

> Of the music events in Belo Horizonte during the earliest years of the twentieth century, one of the most important occurred in 1904 featuring the flutist Pattápio Silva, accompanied by various local musicians. The duo formed by brothers Branca and Stael de Carvalho also frequently performed in the salons, in recitals, or accompanying visiting concertizing musicians.[31]

By World War I, the Rose and Violetas social clubs had faded, replaced in social importance by the Clube Belo Horizonte, which carried the torch of the young city's disappearing salon tradition. The emergence during the 1920s of professional classical music ensembles such as the Sociedade de Quarteto de Belo Horizonte nourished the city's fine art scene.[32] An April 10, 1921, review appearing in the *Minas Geraes* newspaper notes a Sociedade de Quarteto de Belo Horizonte concert performance featuring works by Mendelssohn, Antonio Bazzini, and Pablo de *Sarasate*. There, pianist Inasinha Prates, violinist Carlos Ascherman's string quartet, and twenty violinists "both ladies and gentlemen" performed Camille Saint-Saëns's *Le Cygne* and Schumann's *Reverie* in unison, with piano accompaniment.[33] A decade later, as the Great Depression settled in, Belo Horizonte journalist Jader de Oliveira noted in his memoirs:

> The city's finest salon always was, and continues to be, that of the Automobile Club, since 1929 in the Vetusto Building on Avenida Afonso Pena at the corner of Alvares Cabral . . . visited by Edward, Duke of Windsor (Prince of Wales) and his brother George (the future king of Great Britain) in April 1931.[34]

Cinema Orchestras of the Silent Film Era

The proliferation of cinema houses provided several decades of livelihood for trained pit orchestra musicians accompanying silent film. Cinemas joined salon recitals and bandas as opportunities for professional musicians, first offering live music accompaniment to mask projector noise, then shifting to emphasize action, moods, and emotions on screen. The first public screening of a motion picture in the Americas, in New York City, occurred the year before Belo Horizonte's inauguration. The Barucci Company began showing films in Belo Horizonte's Teatro Soucasseaux in 1905.[35] The city's first dedicated cinema theater was the Teatro Paris, screening its first film in 1906, followed by the Cinema Teatro Comércio, both boasting orchestras by 1908.[36] Six major movie houses had opened before the end of 1915, each competing for entertainment dollars with some type of live music ensemble.[37] In 1915, Ary Barroso, who would become a famous songwriter, played piano as a twelve-year-old in the Cinema Ideal movie theater in his hometown of Ubá, Minas Gerais.[38] Belo Horizonte resident Celina Albano years later recalled these cinematic spectacles:

> They all had the same ritual: the room darkening to the sound of an enveloping melody, and a heavy curtain opening to reveal a silvery screen in the center of the stage reflecting glowing lights that dominated the spectator's eyes for two hours. But each cinema had its own music at curtain opening; for the Pathé it was "The Legend of the Crystal Mountain."[39]

The first feature-length "talkie" film, 1927's *The Jazz Singer*, spelled the demise of the silent era, and Belo Horizonte's first talkie screened in 1930. Prerecorded music now entered Mineiro lives via phonograph recordings and film soundtracks. The city's professional musicians thrown out of work by technological progress also faced the onslaught of the Great Depression, although radio would quickly pick up slack by hiring musicians for live studio broadcasts. In the meantime, some former cinema house musicians found assistance with the União dos Professores de Orquestra (Union of Orchestra Professors), founded and directed by composer and flutist Fausto Assunção (1892–1956, b. São José del-Rei, MG). He had left Minas for Rio de Janeiro following his early music studies in São João del-Rei, his hometown's neighboring city, which is still known in Minas as the "City of Music." After graduating from Rio's National Institute of Music, where he received a Gold Medal as the school's top flutist, Assunção moved to Belo Horizonte and became a professor of flute at the Minas Music Conservatory, now the Federal University of Minas Gerais's School of Music. He composed more than a dozen original works between 1923 and 1950.[40]

The Rise of Public Concerts and Music Schools

Soon after Belo Horizonte's inauguration, the First Battalion of the Military Police band performed concerts and dances of waltzes, polkas, schottisches, tangos, and opera excerpts in the Grand Hotel's large banquet rooms and at the Steckel Palace. Formal yet less exclusive concerts open to the public were produced in public spaces such as the auditoriums of the Senate and the Deputies Chamber of the state government, such as the Concertos Populares concert series, created by violinist Antônio Sardinha and conductor Francisco Flores. These performances included fundraisers for the Escola Livre de Música (Free School of Music).[41] This school, founded by Flores in 1901, presented choir and band concerts under his direction in the Teatro Municipal.

In 1926, the elegantly designed and prominently located Music Conservatory opened on Avenida Afonso Pena (fig. 8.2), where it remains today under the protection of the state agency of patrimony known as the Instituto Estadual do Patrimônio Histórico e Artístico (IEPHA). The conservatory was conjoined with five other institutions of higher learning to form the public Universidade de Minas Gerais in 1927.[42] There, in the late 1920s, an advanced piano student would likely have studied with Brazilian virtuoso Fructuoso Vianna (1896–1976), born into a family of amateur musicians in the old gold town of Itajubá, Minas Gerais, in the Serra da Mantiqueira foothills less than seventy kilometers from the tri-border with Rio de Janeiro and São Paulo States. Vianna studied with piano teacher Antonina Bourret, also from Itajubá, before relocating to Rio de Janeiro at age sixteen, where he befriended Heitor Villa-Lobos and subsequently launched an international career.

In 1922, German-born violinist Carlos Achermann, and conductor and clarinetist Francisco Nunes (1875–1935, b. Diamantina), founded the Orquestra de Concertos Sinfônicos de Belo Horizonte, the city's first professional orchestra concert series open to public audiences. By that time, Achermann had founded his string quartet, the Quarteto Achermann. Francisco Nunes came from a musical family. His father, Francisco Nunes Netto Leão, was a composer of sacred music, active mostly in Rio de Janeiro, where he died in 1896. Born in Taquarassu, Minas Gerais, his brother, José Maximo Nunes, was also a composer and orchestral conductor, dying in Rio de Janeiro in 1921. Francisco Nunes was raised in Rio de Janeiro, attending the

Figure 8.2. Belo Horizonte's Music Conservatory opened on Avenida Afonso Pena in 1926 and soon joined the public Universidade de Minas Gerais (later the Universidade Federal de Minas Gerais). The building still functions as part of the UFMG's Music Department. (Photo by Jonathon Grasse.)

Figure 8.3. The Francisco Nunes Theater in Belo Horizonte's Parque Municipal was commissioned in the 1940s by mayor Juscelino Kubitschek, who later became governor of Minas Gerais and president of Brazil. The theater's namesake was one of Belo Horizonte's most important classical musicians during the 1920s–1930s, directing the Minas Music Conservatory and conducting the first professional orchestra in the city to perform for public audiences. (Photo by Jonathon Grasse.)

Instituto Nacional de Música, where he studied clarinet and met the school's renowned director, nationalist composer Leopoldo Miguéz. Nunes became the institute's clarinet professor before returning to Minas Gerais in the 1920s, where he assumed the director's position at the newly formed, state-sponsored Minas Music Conservatory (Conservatório Mineiro de Música). Conservatory faculty included among others Hostílio Soares, Mercedo Moreira, Ester Jacobson, and Elviro do Nascimento. Vocalist Asdrúbal Lima, who had relocated from Rio de Janeiro, initiated opera, theater, and choral groups and productions in Belo Horizonte.[43] Also from Rio de Janeiro, Nunes brought new members of the conservatory's growing music faculty, including pianists Pedro de Castro and Fernando Coelho, and violinist George Marianuzzi, who went on to briefly direct the highly regarded orchestra of Belo Horizonte's state-run Rádio Inconfidência. That station was broadcast from downtown's Feira Permanente de Amostras building, a few floors away from the luxury establishment Restaurant da Feira, where classical music recitals featured the likes of soprano Cristina Maristany and pianist Alexander Brailowsky in the early 1930s.

Belo Horizonte emerged as a de facto regional music center, a vital social space for state-supported fine art music education and chamber and symphonic music performance, gradually attracting musicians and conductors trained in Rio de Janeiro, São Paulo, and Europe. The Minas Music Conservatory soon boasted the Sociedade de Concertos Sinfônicos de Belo Horizonte; as mentioned above, Nunes directed the state's first government-sponsored orchestra, and his name would grace the theater constructed in the Parque Municipal Américo Renné Giannetti in the 1940s (fig. 8.3), a project initiated by mayor Juscelino Kubitschek (served 1940–1945). Known as "Mayor Hurricane," Kubitschek oversaw massive renewal and development in the city, matching improvements in the cultural sphere, including the 1944 creation of the Escola de Belas Artes (School of the Arts) in the Parque Municipal, for which he hired one of Brazil's leading painters, Alberto da Veiga Guignard (1896–1962).[44] This new cultural landscape offered a welcome change to a region that had forced nineteenth-century Mineiro musicians and artists to pursue advanced training and professional careers in Rio de Janeiro, São Paulo, or Europe. Four notable musician-composers born within a decade of Belo Horizonte's construction flourished there: Elviro do Nascimento (1890–1980, b. Uberaba, MG), Flausino Rodrigues do Valle (1894–1954, b. Barbacena, MG), Hostílio Soares (1898–1988, b. Visconde do Rio Branco, MG), and Luís Melgaço (1903–1983, b. Dores da Indaia, MG).[45] Following training in Uberaba, Nascimento relocated to Belo Horizonte, where he met Soares and studied with Nunes at the Minas Music Conservatory, and where he later directed the city's Military Police band. Among other orchestral, chamber, and vocal works, Nascimento composed the regionalist *Suite Mineira* for orchestra in 1936. While practicing law in Belo Horizonte, Valle was an accomplished violinist, composer, and musicologist whose work as concert master for several orchestras balanced his varied publications on Brazilian music and his compositions (Valle's *Ao pé da fogueira* was recorded by violinists Jascha Heifetz and Zino Francescatti). Melgaço's three-act opera *Catuíra dos Araxás*, with a libretto in the Tupi language, joins the composer's long list of vocal works, in addition to his catalog of over three hundred notated bird songs.

Two important Mineiro concert musicians of the following generation who also trained in Belo Horizonte were Milton Antonia da Cunha (1922–1989, b. Itinga, MG) and Roberto de Castro (1931–1975, b. Belo Horizonte). Cunha, a cellist, composer, and conductor, founded and directed sacred choral groups and created the Juiz de Fora Conservatory Chamber Orchestra. Castro was a composer and conductor, whose cellist mother and composer-professor father had instructed him in harmony, counterpoint, and composition, preparing him for advanced studies in Italy. Upon returning to Minas, he joined Belo Horizonte's newly formed Madrigal Renascentista, founded in 1956 by one of Brazil's greatest conductors, Isaac Karabtchevsky (b. 1934, São Paulo). Castro later founded several choral groups for which he conducted and also composed.[46] John Wirth summarizes the city's development near mid-century:

> That Belo Horizonte was becoming the new focal point for regional culture was not so obvious, even in the 1940s, when it was a city of almost one-quarter million. . . . [T]he basis for a true urban center was being formed. Conceived as a political capital, the city's commercial and light industrial base began to support a society more diverse than that of the politicians and functionaries who were the first to settle. It became a medical and educational center, also a garrison town, and this encouraged and attracted the middle classes. Working-class districts sprang up. . . . The tree-lined streets of jasmine and magnolia, the neat middle-class bungalows, the blue sky studded with thunderheads gave a fresh, open aura to this growing but still provincial city.[47]

A few foreign-born nationals professionally trained in European fine art music relocated to Minas Gerais. French composer and conductor Fernand Jouteux (1866–1956) studied with Jules Massenet at the Paris Conservatory before visiting Brazil in 1894, ultimately relocating to Garanhuns, Pernambuco. In 1934, during a concert tour throughout Brazil designed to raise funds for the premiere of his four-act opera *Os Sertões* (composed between 1912 and 1925), Jouteux conducted his music in Tiradentes with the Ramalho Orchestra and Concert Band. He resided in Sabará during 1940. At the age of ninety-five, he finally heard the premiere of *Os Sertões*, in Belo Horizonte, where soon after he died. His original French libretto was translated into Portuguese by Celso Brant.

Arthur Bosmans (1908–1991, b. Antwerp) was a self-taught violinist who earned a place in the Symphonic Orchestra of Mons at the age of twelve.[48] Later a professional conductor and composer, he fled Belgium at the onset of World War II, arriving in Rio de Janeiro in 1940, where he continued his conducting career with the help of Heitor Villa-Lobos, who

> enabled him to adapt Brazilian folksongs, and this activity facilitated his integration into the music scene of Brazil. In 1941 and 1942 he conducted the

Orquestra Sinfônica Brasileira and the Pro Musica orchestra. In this period, he also started teaching composition and instrumentation at the National Conservatory in Rio de Janeiro as well as composing music for Brazilian films and a ballet, *Visiones de la guerra*.[49]

Like the painter Guignard, Bosmans was invited to Belo Horizonte in 1944 by mayor Juscelino Kubitschek, who had recently spearheaded both the creation of the Orquestra Sinfônica and construction of the city's Teatro Municipal that would later carry Francisco Nunes's name. As a conductor, composer, and professor at the School of Music of the Federal University of Minas Gerais, Bosmans distinguished himself in the capital's fine art music society. In European concert hall appearances, he conducted works by Brazilian composers such as Francisco Mignone, Edino Krieger, Lorenzo Fernández, and Radamés Gnattali. In 2009, Bosmans's former UFMG student Oiliam José Lanna conducted the Orquestra Sinfônica de Minas Gerais in a concert commemorating the centenary of his late mentor, a program that included the Belgium-born composer's *La vie en bleu*, *Sinfonietta lusitana*, *La rue*, and *Trois valses*, performed in the Palácio das Artes's Grande Teatro, a complex that opened in 1970 adjacent to the Parque Municipal.[50]

Mineiro pianist Venício Mancini met conductor, pianist, and educator Sérgio Magnani (1914–2001) in Rome during the early 1950s, and convinced the Italian musician to relocate to Belo Horizonte. Conducting the city's leading orchestras and opera performances throughout the 1950s and 1960s, Magnani also played piano for the Ars Concordia Trio with cellist Atílio Ginocchia and violinist Leonidas Autuori. Magnani was an influential educator and tireless promoter of classical music, leading Verdi's *Requiem* in 1999 for his last concert in Belo Horizonte.[51] By 1950, four orchestras specializing in Western fine art music had been founded in Belo Horizonte: the Orquestra Sinfônica de Belo Horizonte, 1944; the Orquestra Sinfônica Estadual, 1948 (both conducted by Bosmans), the Orquestra Sinfônica da Academia de Policia Militar, also 1948; and in 1950, the Orquestra Sinfônica Mineira.[52] Some of the support for these activities, and for bringing visiting foreign artists to perform in Belo Horizonte and other Mineiro cities, came from the Sociedade de Cultura e Artística de Minas Gerais. The SCA was initiated in 1947 by the influential medical professor, politician, and respected cultural philanthropist Clóvis Salgado.[53] Today, his foundation (the Fundação Clóvis Salgado) still facilitates many diverse musical performances, and in 1976 it helped found the Orquestra Sinfônica de Minas Gerais. A new orchestra, the Orquestra Filarmônica de Minas Gerais, was founded in 2008, and in 2015 it moved from the Parque Municipal's Palácio das Artes into the new Sala Minas Gerais, designed by architect José Augusto Nepomusceno and located in the Barro Preto district's new Estação da Cultura Presidente Itamar Franco. The orchestra's opening program in their new venue included Camargo Guarnieri's 1958 orchestral work *Suite Vila Rica* commemorating the historical Mineiro city.

The Bohemian Zone

Praça da Estação (Station Plaza) is Belo Horizonte's old railroad station and adjacent plaza, today beautifully restored and home to wide-open public spaces and a museum. It was completed in 1894 as the end of the line for a twenty-kilometer rail extension from nearby Sabará that delivered materials for Belo Horizonte's construction. During the twentieth century, this central district changed as the city mushroomed. By the 1930s, Praça da Estação was the unofficial border of Belo Horizonte's downtown bohemian zone, hopping with live music, cheap hotels, and bars such as the Bar dos Aliados and the Bar do Ponto. Vera Chacham wrote of these small yet culturally important places, positioning Belo Horizonte as a city of memories and lamenting the 1959 demolition of the building housing the Bar do Ponto, its loss defining nostalgia while symbolizing for Chacham the shrinking of public life in the Mineiro capital.[54] Such places became symbolic of the city's public memory. The city's growth in the 1940s entailed the demolition of select buildings from the original 1894 construction. The loss of the Bar do Ponto and other such cafés, as part of a modernist replacement of the earlier belle époque architecture, challenged the collective memories of city residents. Such places had already become iconic of *belohorizontean* public experience. In successive decades, the city's population doubled twice: 1950, 352,724; 1960, 693,328; and 1970, 1,255,415.

Music for the nightlife once filled cabarets such as the Mariana, the Capitólio, and the Montanhez; other jazz orchestra nightclubs; and small, modest dance halls known as *dancings*. The Orquestra Montanhez still exists, with big band jazz specializing in mid-twentieth-century dance hall repertoire. Madame Olympia's famous establishment Éden rounded out the red-light district. "Montanhez danças" and "Cabaré mineiro" are 1970s-era songs by Corner Club artists Tavinho Moura and Murilo Antunes that celebrate the atmosphere of these bohemian environs and posit the collective urban memory of a musically infused history of the city and its dwellers.[55] Márcio Rubens Prado notes: "This profusion of addresses was the destination and refuge for bohemians, intellectuals, students, musicians, and gays. . . . Men searched these streets and places for drink, to debate the latest issues, to hear music, and chat with the women."[56] In these clubs, it was necessary for a single guy to buy a dance with a working girl, a *dançarinha*, in order to hear the large jazz groups, often copying North American big band styles in addition to charts written by Brazilians drawing from a growing array of sambas, *marchas*, jazz, and bolero-influenced styles. Madame Olympia, a Spaniard newly ensconced in a Parisian-style salon catering to the city's men who could afford her girls, later opened the Palácio de Cristal cabaret featuring musical stage shows.[57]

The hard life of most professional musicians in the city meant staking a claim at Ponto do Músicos (Musicians' Point), a strip of downtown sidewalk on Avenida Afonso Pena. There, waiting musicians met those seeking to hire groups for bailes (dances), *horas dançantes* (parties), and carnival-related events. Professional musicians from the generation born in the 1930s such as bassist Paulo Horta, guitarist Chiquito Braga, Célio Balona, and many others paid their dues at Musicians' Point, brokering gigs and building reputations. In the 1960s, young members of the Corner Club collective also relied on this method of getting hired for gigs (see chapter 9). Simpler bars (*barzinhos*), and some smaller clubs such as the Chanticler and the Mariana, featured less formal performances of popular music. By the 1950s, such venues provided professional opportunities for local musicians to play a wide range of popular entertainment including tangos, boleros, North American jazz, and of course the extant Brazilian songbook of samba, *samba-canção*, and regional styles such as *baião* and choro. The bohemian district was the setting of *Hilda Furacão*, a widely read 1991 novel by local writer Robert Drummond (1933–2002) portraying a debutant's fall from grace into a life of prostitution during the late 1950s and 1960s. The story was later adapted into one of Brazil's most watched television miniseries. As Rubens Prado reminisces: "The orchestras and small groups of the Montanhez were remarkable schools, where, under the direction of band leaders such as Delê and Osvaldo Castilho, studied and shined names such as Célio Balona, Hélvius Vilela, Serrinha, Túlio Silva,

Bié Prata, Mauro Coura Macedo, Erasto Meniconi, and dozens of others."[58] Rubens Prado further recalls the Montanhez as the center of Belo Horizonte's bohemian zone, where the club opened in 1930 in place of Dona Olympia's 1920s showcase *salão* (large salon):

> In the back, on a stage three or four steps up, was where the orchestra sat. Or better, the orchestras alternating in unforgettable performances. Created in the style of American big bands, really deserving the name *orchestra*, they had brass, wind, string, and percussion sections—very complete. The most memorable and most admired orchestras were directed by Castilho and Delê, two musicians of supreme competence, elegance, [and] sociability, and zealously demanding of their players in the areas of musical performance and attire. One piece that stays in my memory: Carlos Gomes's "O Guarani" played by Castilho's orchestra in samba rhythm that made the room swarm. Many years later I learned that this spectacular arrangement was authored by another of Brazil's musical legends, Radamés Gnattali. When the orchestra was on break, a smaller group kept the dancers occupied, typically a trio of piano, bass, and guitar.[59]

Two *Sambistas* from Midcentury Belo Horizonte

Rômulo Paes and Mestre Conga (José Luíz Lourenço) emerged as the Belo Horizonte's first prominent carnival music figures.[60] Paes hailed from the Sul de Minas town of Paraguaçu, born in 1918. His father, Waldemar Tavares, accepted a philosophy of music professorship at the Minas Music Conservatory and moved the family to Belo Horizonte. A cousin of *samba-canção* legend Ary Barroso (1903–1964), the young Paes became a radio broadcaster and staff singer by 1935, but never appeared on a recording. He was promoted to the position of artistic director for Rádio Guarani before directing Rádio Mineira. In his twenties he began a composing career, specializing in carnival sambas and *marchinhas*, eventually penning close to 150 songs that competed with those of the city's other carnival composers such as Jair Silva, Jadir Ambrósio, Aníbal Fernandes, and Gervásio Horta.[61] Local studios were used for regional releases of carnival songs during the last two months of each year. Belo Horizonte's most famous midcentury carnival composer and radio personality, Paes was feted with a landmark plaque in the downtown district's Rua Bahia. It reads, "A vida é esta, subir Bahia e descer Floresta" (Life is this: to ascend to Bahia and to descend to Floresta), meaning that the bohemian life of Avenida Bahia in the city's downtown district, with the nightlife of clubs, bars, and the Grand Hotel, was uphill from his home in Floresta, where he would return every evening to after-hours clubs and ultimately his residence. Those all-night parties at the Hotel Floresta needed plenty of musicians.[62] Across the Arrudas River, beyond the rail station's Praça da Estação, the *bairros* of Santa Tereza and Floresta were known for their late-night destinations for bohemians and serenades. Neighboring *bairro* Lagoinha was home to the after-hours establishment Bar do Coelho (Rabbit Bar), which "was frequented by big names of popular music, such as Sílvio Caldas and Cyro Monteiro—all guided there by Rômulo Paes."[63] Wander Piroli remembers musicians Mário Pandeirista and Nelson Gonçalves at the Coelho, recalling that the establishment "would open its restaurant at eleven to feed all the night owls with its homemade hot meals."[64]

The Golden Age of *samba-canção* witnessed the polished production of nationally recognized performers, songwriters, and a hit parade with growing audiences made possible through recordings, live performances, and especially radio, particularly Rádio Nacional, broadcast out of Rio de Janeiro. Of local flavor were the Paes hits "Minha Belo Horizonte" and "Mineiro bom." His list of works include *samba-canção* and carnival *marchinha* recordings on various national labels by singers Dalva de Oliveira, the Anjos do Inferno, Valdomiro Lobo, and Marlene, among others. In the 1950s, he wrote nationally recognized songs in the *baião* style popularized by Luiz Gonzaga, who recorded one of his works. With no high-quality recording studio in town to meet the standards of Brazil's top labels (Belo Horizonte's first major studio was Bemol, founded in the 1960s), Paes arranged a session in Rio de Janeiro for Isnard Simone's recording of his 1957 RCA hits "Se você chorou" and "Ai tá certo." Paes later entered politics, becoming a councilman for the city of Belo Horizonte.

A singer, dancer, and composer, Mestre Conga emerged as one of Belo Horizonte's original kings of samba beginning in the 1940s, and he was later acknowledged as the city's pioneer of carioca-style samba (*samba-enredo*).[65] Born José Luíz Lourenço in 1927, one of ten children of *sanfona* player Luíz Balduino Gonzaga and Cacilda Lourenço, he moved at the age of six with his family to Belo Horizonte from Ponte Nova in the Zona da Mata. He was raised in the Congado Mineiro culture, a musical background and education augmented by *batucada*, samba, and the *calango* circle dance tradition. In their new Belo Horizonte neighborhood of Vila Brasilina, later known as Sagrada Família, he gravitated toward the salon dance–style crazes that were developing at a time when the public carnival parades (*desfiles*) were banned. During World War II, the death of his father forced him into working at a textile factory. The teenage Mestre Conga frequented the original Clube do Barro Preto, leading to his recruitment into the percussion section (*bateria*) of Surpresa, one of the city's best samba schools (*escola de samba*). He soon was performing with other groups and in 1940 received the title "Citizen of Samba," elected in a competition sponsored by the Associated Newspapers of Assis Chateaubriand.[66] Mestre Conga became the youngest and most notable *bamba* of the city's samba subculture, and in 1950 he founded his own samba school, Grêmio Recreativo Escola de Samba Inconfidência Mineira, with whom he paraded from 1950 until 2010.[67] Word spread of his compositional flair, such as the samba hit "Lágrimas sentidas," and his mastery of old-style rural samba, and he was recruited to appear in Gino Palmisano's 1952 film *Alvorada de Glória*. The film was shot in Rio de Janeiro, to where he relocated for two years. Upon his return to Belo Horizonte, he organized a carnival composers' group, convincing carnival organizers to adopt the carioca carnival pastime of theme-based *samba-enredos* and *desfiles*. In 1954, the premiere Belo Horizonte carnival theme was the Inconfidência Mineira's legendary revolutionary leader, Tiradentes. In 2013, a biographical film heralding the *sambista*, *Mestre Conga: O inconfidente do samba* by director Chiquinho Matias, premiered at the SESC auditorium. In 2014, the elderly musician was still performing with the Velha Guarda de Samba (Old Guard Samba) and dance workshops.[68] And at age ninety-three, Mestre Conga was feted during Belo Horizonte's 2019 carnival.

Radio

The first local station in Belo Horizonte, Rádio Mineira, had its inaugural broadcast in 1927, five years after the introduction of the technology to Rio de Janeiro.[69] Rádio Inconfidência (using the eighteenth-century nativist revolt as its namesake) was taking up two floors of downtown's Feira Permanente de Amostras building when its first broadcast hit the air in September 1936.

For that occasion, eight cars navigated the dirt roads from Rio de Janeiro to deliver Brazil's reigning samba stars for a spectacular live broadcast: Orlando Silva, Nuno Roland, Dalva de Oliveira, Herivelto Martins, Sebastião Pinto, and Morães Neto. Silva returned to Belo Horizonte the very next month for Rádio Guarani's inaugural broadcast.[70] A fourth, smaller station began serving the city in the 1950s, Rádio Itatiaia. Jader de Oliveira's memoir refers to ensembles known as *regionais* (s. *regional*): "Rádio Inconfidência grew rapidly, and successfully adapted the same style of varied programming found on Rádio Nacional. They had orchestras, *regionais*, theater, [and] singers."[71]

With the onset of mass media radio and phonograph recording, these versatile orchestras and ensembles flourished, capable of playing arrangements reflecting Brazilian genres and tastes, including regional and popular musical styles from the Nordeste as well as Brazilian choro, samba, bolero, jazz, and concert music orchestrations. *Regionais* directed by such midcentury luminaries as Garoto, Benedito Lacerda, and Luperce Miranda accompanied the top singers on radio broadcasts and recordings dedicated to these popular genres. Like other radio stations and record companies, a few Belo Horizonte stations featured their own in-house *regional*. The conservatory established in the late 1920s provided Belo Horizonte's radio stations with instrumentalists and conductors for classical music repertoire.[72] At the peak of radio's influence, three types of orchestras were required: *típicas*, which played tangos and other popular styles; *regionais*, such as those specializing in Brazil's array of regional popular and folk-based styles; and *orquestras de salão*, specializing in classical music. Deluxe auditoriums hosted audiences, guests, and performers at Rádio Guarani and Rádio Inconfidência, with the latter's main theater seating 1,500.

Local singers performing live on Belo Horizonte radio stations in the 1940s and 1950s could potentially become regional stars and record when possible. But they could not make a living as professional musicians in Minas. Crooner Gilberto Santana rejected an invitation by national star Francisco Alves to relocate to Rio de Janeiro to further the former's career and remained in Belo Horizonte, where he became a dentist while pursuing his recording and performing dates. Other prominent Mineiro musicians considered moves to Rio de Janeiro, for example Luíz Claudio (b. 1935, Curvelo, MG), bringing his guitar, voice, and love for the *serenata*, modinhas, and the music of Minas to Rádio Inconfidência in the early 1950s. He began at that station, but not as a soloist; he had earlier been a member of the trio Trovadores do

Luar, in 1948. When he turned solo, his first performances were in English. His first record from 1952 on the Sinter label featured "Fim de semana" (by Rômulo Paes and Nilo Ramos) on side A, and on side B, "Primavera em Setembro" (by Kurt Weill, arranged by André Rosito). Claudio became the most widely recorded Mineiro singer of the 1950s, and his career flourished after moving to Rio. As a composer, Claudio attracted as illustrious partners famed Mineiro authors Carlos Drummond de Andrade, with "Viola de bolso," and João Guimarães Rosa, with "O galo cantou na serra."[73] "Viola de bolso" extolls the cultural power of the Mineiro viola player, whose simple tunes, neither strong nor beautiful, yet recall the past and the "beloved present [with] friends, images, [and] landscapes."

Pampulha Casino

A midcentury modernization development in suburban Belo Horizonte, the Pampulha Casino was designed and constructed beginning in the 1930s; the effort was led by Governor Juscelino Kubitschek (1902–1976), modernist architect Oscar Niemeyer (1907–2012), and landscape architect Roberto Burle Marx (1909–1994). In hindsight, Pampulha was a warm-up for a bigger act: by the mid-1950s, Kubitschek was president of Brazil, building with Niemeyer the nation's then ultramodern federal capital, Brasília, sited in the tiny, newly founded Federal District at the western border of Minas. The Belo Horizonte development grew both as an attraction and as a vital, functioning part of the city: a manmade lake surrounded by groomed, upscale residential areas, a yacht club, a regional airport, and the nearby Federal University of Minas Gerais. The architecture and mosaics of the undulating Saint Francis of Assisi Church are now protected by UNESCO, an iconic landmark and twentieth-century modernist repackaging of the conservative symbol of Minas: the church. A casino complex, long since transformed into an arts center, capped off Pampulha's original architectural development, known as the Conjunto Arquitetônico da Pampulha.[74] Completed in 1943, the casino had an ironically short life as a center of chic nightlife in the city: at his wife's request, conservative Brazilian president Eurico Dutra (in office 1946–1951) quickly outlawed gambling throughout the nation. During its nearly three years as a functioning casino, its stage attracted international stars including theater and film diva Elvira Ríos, Mexico City's contralto bolero singer famous throughout Latin America. More importantly, the casino was a crucial professional opportunity for local musicians who too quickly returned to rely on gigs in the downtown clubs and cabarets once it closed.[75] An art museum since 1957, the "casino" once again hosts musical events. The nearby Mineirão football stadium hosted the city's rival football clubs Atlético Mineiro and Cruzeiro. The stadium has also served as a rock show venue attracting international acts such as Paul McCartney, Metallica, and Black Sabbath.

The casino's flourish jibed with the Golden Age of Brazilian big bands, supper club *samba-canção*, and postwar vestiges of the Jazz Age: Severino Araújo's Orquestra Tabajara, Fon-Fon's orchestra, Radamés Gnattali's orchestra, and the big band orchestra led by Zacharias. Local bandleader Delê (José Braz de Andrade, 1916–1980) struggled to form an orchestra to perform there but finally won a contract; as he recalled:

> Once opened, the casino hired two orchestras, that of the American conductor Colma and Rio Cândido Botelho, who was sponsored by Getúlio's wife, Mrs. Darcy Vargas (the wife of Brazil's president, Getúlio Vargas). At this time, I already had the intention of improving my professional life. So, imagining myself playing at the casino, I gathered a group of musicians and quickly formed an orchestra. To get an idea of how badly paid musicians were at that time, if we played in a place like Montanhez, we earned 20 cruzeiros per night. At the casino, the salary was 100 to 120 cruzeiros per night.[76]

Luíz Claudio is a good example of a local musician who missed out on having a supportive night spot such as the Pampulha Casino. So, too, is Francisco "Chiquito" Andrade Braga (1936–2017, b. Belo Horizonte), an influential guitarist who later mentored Corner Club legend Toninho Horta, Juarez Moreira, and many other young Belo Horizonte musicians. Both Horta and Moreira went on to international careers in jazz. Braga's father, José Raimundo, was also a guitarist with whom the boy played the smaller, plucked stringed instruments such as the *violão requinto*, cavaquinho, and viola at markets and fairs. Chiquito acquired his first electric guitar in the mid-1950s from his older brother Daniel while coming of age in the city's Padre Eustáquio neighborhood. Influenced at a young age by the music of Ravel and Stan Kenton, he developed rich, jazz-influenced guitar voicings and chordal-type playing, developing the harmonic language for which he became known. In his teen years, Braga was already playing professionally through his Musicians' Point contacts and accompanying singers Tito Madi and Clara Nunes (1943–1983, b. Paraopeba, MG). At the age of twenty-two, Braga was invited to tour with Elizeth Cardoso soon after her recording of the 1958 watershed LP *Canção do amor demais* featuring the bossa nova pioneer João Gilberto on guitar. In 1966, he moved to Rio de Janeiro to work with Moacir Santos, pursued an illustrious career playing with dozens of the top names in MPB, and composed music for television.[77]

By the late 1950s, large, expensive dance orchestras playing big band arrangements in nightclubs had already been losing out to smaller groups.[78] Clubs such as the Buchecha, Sagarana, and Boate Sukata hired more economical ensembles for their bossa nova chops, knowledge of standards, and versatile jazz combo versions of international hits. The Grand Hotel in downtown Belo Horizonte was torn down in the late 1950s, replaced by a new cultural anchor and haven for nightlife, the gargantuan Edifício Arcângelo Maletta, or simply the Maletta.[79] Composer and keyboardist Pacífico Mascarenhas (b. 1935, Belo Horizonte), another of the city's high-profile musicians and member of the Savassi district's *turma* (social group) of serenaders and writers, responded quickly to the bossa nova revolution. He released one of Brazil's first independent LPs in 1958, going to Rio de Janeiro with singer Marcus Vinícius and Paulo Modesto's band to record it.[80] He formed the group Conjunto Sambacana in the early 1960s with fellow Mineiro Roberto Guimarães, maintaining a presence in the Belo Horizonte music scene for decades, including support in 1964 for a younger pair of talented musicians from Três Pontas who became mainstays of the Corner Club collective discussed in chapter 9: Milton Nascimento and Wagner Tiso.

Another hardworking influential bandleader at the time was Célio Balona (b. 1938, Visconde do Rio Branco, MG). The Conjunto Célio Balona was a magnet for fresh talent playing Brazilian styles, boleros, cha-cha-chas, Cuban music, and North American jazz. Balona's groups performed at Belo Horizonte's top venues and did a weekly broadcast on local station TV Itacolomi.[81] Such gigs provided livelihood and exposure for up-and-coming players of jazz, classical, rock, and other global styles alongside their own traditions. Other leading musicians at this time included Paulo Modesto, Gilberto Santana, and pianist Túlio Silva, the latter two former members of one of the city's biggest acts, Delê's large dance orchestra.[82] Before launching the Corner Club collective with their many Mineiro collaborators, Milton Nascimento and Wagner Tiso earned gigs with this older generation, particularly Mascarenhas and Balona. In addition to its own, fast-paced growth, Belo Horizonte would be rocked by the violent political fallout of the 1964 military coup, labor unrest, and the winds of the international youth-culture revolution brought by rock 'n' roll and political consciousness. Alluding to the city's next generation, that of the Corner Club, Bruno Viveiros Martins writes:

> Belo Horizonte was the point of departure for the creation of a new musicality that carried on a stretcher the baroque density of the songs of religious festivals; that played with tearful melodies of nighttime *serestas*; that flirted with the imprudent acrobatics of jazz; that loved bossa nova's harmonious guitar beats; that wrapped itself in the mixed cadences of Latin American song; that accompanied the rhythmic batuque of Congado and allowed itself to be carried away by the electric delirium of rock guitars.[83]

Chapter 9

Regionalist Themes in the Songs of the Corner Club

Emerging in Belo Horizonte during Brazil's eclectic popular music scenes of the 1960s, singer, songwriter, and guitarist Milton Nascimento (b. 1942, Rio de Janeiro) spearheaded a collective of musicians and poets that became known as the Corner Club (Clube da Esquina). Conjuring an intersection in the city's Santa Tereza district (fig. 9.1), the group's moniker came from a 1970 song title that was used again for a landmark 1972 album.[1] Their music entered a crowded national stage of Música Popular Brasileira (MPB) that was alive with talent. By the early 1970s, the Clube included these core collaborators and others, listed here in alphabetical order: Lô Borges (Salomão Borges, voice, songwriter, guitar; b. 1952, Belo Horizonte); Beto Guedes (voice, guitar, multi-instrumentalist, songwriter; b. 1951, Montes Claros, MG), Toninho Horta (guitar, songwriter; b. 1948, Belo Horizonte); Tavinho Moura (voice, songwriter, guitar, viola; b. 1947, Juiz de Fora, MG); Novelli (Djair de Barros e Silva, bass, songwriter; b. 1945, Recife, Pernambuco); Nivaldo Ornelas (saxophone, composer; b. 1942, Belo Horizonte); Robertinho Silva (drums; b. 1943, Rio de Janeiro); and Wagner Tiso (keyboards, arranging; b. 1945, Três Pontas, MG). Lyrics to many Clube songs were penned by Márcio Borges (Lô's brother, b. 1946, Belo Horizonte); Fernando Brant (1946–2015, b. Caldas, MG); and Ronaldo Bastos (b. 1948, Niterói, Rio de Janeiro).

Their music was fused with folk, rock, jazz, classical, pop, and Brazilian styles brought by each member into the creative mix and flourished in multiple aesthetic and stylistic trajectories, some of which defy easy categorization. The collective's name appeared in sequel titles twice again: the 1972 song "Clube da Esquina No. 2," and the 1978 double album *Clube da Esquina 2*. Today, Clube members celebrate a nearly sixty-year legacy in popular Brazilian music. This chapter focuses on select Clube songs that develop musical and textual themes of Minas Gerais as a cultural territory, and arguably as a state of mind. The era of the military dictatorship (1964–1985) and Milton's discovery of Afro-Mineiro traditions are also discussed. As Fábio Zanon of Rádio Cultura FM stated:

> Clube da Esquina's music is recognizably Brazilian, but not with fundamentals of choro or samba. They use electric instruments as influenced by rock, but they do not sound like rock. The music is strong with asymmetric rhythms, but it is not dance music. Their harmony is dissonant, but not like bossa nova. I have a hunch: this music was baptized in baroque churches and has the introspection and solemnity of sacred Mineiro music, but the priests were the Mocambiqueans and Kayapos of the African mines.[2]

Depictions of both urban and rural Minas are hewn into select repertoire, conveying meanings through eclectic musical styles and the poetic, programmatic intentions of lyricists. In some of the songs, Minas Gerais emerges as the world writ large, with complex social landscapes and compelling narratives that foster not only regional identities but also universal themes recognized by national and international audiences. In addition to an examination of the regionalist subset of the collective's vast and varied catalog, brief biographical sketches are provided below to illustrate the group's roots in various parts of the state's interior. Importantly, the military dictatorship maps chronologically to the collective's formation and rise, and is reflected in regionalist themes that interweave with those of protest and resistance. As antidotes to modern alienation and the poisonous violence of the military government's authoritarianism, these songs offer a reenvisioning of citizenship and constructions of authenticity intertwined with regionalist tableaux in which Brazilians and foreigners alike were invited to recognize their own narratives.

Bruno Viveiros Martins's book *Som imaginário* (Imaginary sound) carries the subtitle "The reinvention of the city in songs of the Corner Club." In it, the author extolls the collective's poetic use of cityscapes as settings for communal narratives, as the streets on which friendships are created and tested, where the rites of citizenship occur, and where the political will of the people finds voice. Although some songs veil their urban locales, creating existential backdrops of action or alienation, others such as the Borges brothers' "Ruas da cidade" (City streets) and Lô Borges and Fernando Brant's "Paisagem da Janela" carry the specific imprint of Belo Horizonte. The cover of one edition of Martins's book features an atmospheric rendering of the iconic Santa Tereza viaduct, crossing the Arrudas River and linking downtown to the neighborhood of the same name briefly discussed above in the introduction. The district is home to the street "corner" that engendered the collective's name.

Belo Horizonte–based musician, composer, and producer Chico Amaral states that the Clube "wasn't a movement, but rather a moment—in which the musical experiences of those young people came together."[3] This chapter holds that some of those moments and experiences emerged from a range of identities tied to place. Warmly recalling years later the mid-1960s gatherings of Milton, Wagner Tiso, Tavinho Moura, and others at his home in Belo Horizonte's Nova Suíça district, saxophonist and composer Nivaldo Ornelas stated that back then, "the original group of musicians did not have a name; we were only 'the Mineiros.'"[4] Yet as Corner Club scholar Holly Holmes has noted, Brazilians tended to associate the Clube's regional characteristics with rural, pastoral, and rustic notions of Minas Gerais, rather than with the sprawling grit of provincial Belo Horizonte, where the collective was conceived and grew. She writes of the rural/urban dichotomy of the Clube da Esquina:

[Members'] rural childhood experiences led to coming-of-age and adulthood in an urban environment, and a stage of transition—perhaps lifelong—of reconciling urban and rural lifeways, habits, and values.... For fans in the 1970s, the rusticity portrayed in the music of the Clube da Esquina helped to reconcile urban and rural imaginaries at a time when the process of urbanization and industrialization was still unfolding and rural lifeways were undergoing powerful transformations.[5]

This urban/rural spectrum charted in the Clube catalog was both musical and textual. Rock, jazz, and progressive electric experimentalism portrayed the edgy parameters of urban life, as in the aggressive rock stylings of 1970's "Para Lennon e McCartney," mentioned in the introduction and further discussed below. The atmospheric landscapes and acoustic quietude of guitar-driven balladry often represented the calming reverberation of pastoral life, as in the two songs "Morro Velho" and "Três Pontas." Masterfully rendered texts by poet-lyricists reduced the complex pathos of both city and country life into clear, affective mantras, some speaking programmatically of utopias correlating Mineiro experience with hope, others of dystopias, the latter masking political protest that would otherwise attract the military government's censors. The interior Mineiro world was that of isolated small towns marked by the distances between, from the coast, and from the Belo Horizonte metropolitan area, which grew quickly throughout the twentieth century. Expressions of rurality include inspirational images of the natural world, simple ways of life, cultural traditions of quotidian routines, and observations on isolation, journeys, and escape. This work often poetically embraced a common thread held by both *mineiridade* and *música caipira*: a romantic, symbolic reverence for the natural environment. Here, the mountains and valleys, distant horizons, vast landscapes, and fazendas; the night sky and the mysteries of the *sertão*, all might serve as backdrops to coming-of-age narratives and tales characterizing ways of life. While sharing such textual themes, the Clube's rural sound grew from eclectic folk music, processions of popular Catholicism, and the iconicity of the acoustic guitar and soft timbral palettes integral to atmospheric production values of both geographical expanse and intimate storytelling. As Brazilianist literary scholar Charles Perrone stated, Milton was "bred in the mountainous interior state of Minas Gerais, whose musical heritage is quite different from the samba traditions of Rio de Janeiro or Salvador."[6] In addition to buttressing themes of hope, dreams, and Brazilian authenticity, a wonderment of place in many Clube recordings is conjoined in members' songwriting to notions of the Mineiro past, the historical depths partially illustrated by both the darkness of the Minas baroque and the brilliance of its golden splendor.

Mineiro identity emerged through Milton's and others' musical references to the *toada*, a word applied to traditional songs of processionals such as the Folia de Reis and an often generic term used for simple folk melodies. Jairo

Severiano states of Milton's earliest phase that his compositions were already "making supreme use of regional music of Minas Gerais . . . [and] motives inspired from the simple tradition of *toadas* and modinhas, transformed by the composer into sophisticated musical results."[7] As Milton later clarified: "[T]he *toada* is different according to the region. That of Dorival Caymmi is maritime. Mine has a connection with the region of Três Pontas. . . . I was greatly influenced by having grown up in Minas."[8] The Clube was thus imbued from the start with seeds of the rural interior. In prefacing his discussion of Milton's song "Morro Velho," discussed below, Perrone notes that the song "is an example of the so-called oxcart sound with sophisticated elaborations. . . . As far as Milton's narrative text is concerned, there are notable reflections of imbedded patterns of folk life and social relations."[9] Milton invoked this imagery when he later characterized the core of his music as being like the *toada*, "a kind of oxcart, something that unrolls and develops, a ballad," a point Perrone emphasizes by adding simply that "the deepest roots of Milton's music are in the folk songs of the interior of Minas Gerais."[10] By the mid-1960s, the musician had developed a highly individualistic trajectory and compositional techniques through hard work and studious interpretations of his Mineiro surroundings.

Beginning in the 1970s, Tavinho Moura's influential contributions to the Clube in this respect came in the form of concrete research into regional folkloric genres, primarily the Folia de Reis. Moura's "Calix bento" (Blessed chalice), an adaptation of a Folia de Reis *toada* from northern Minas, and "Lua girou" (The Moon turned), a "folkloric song from the Beira-Rio region of Bahia adapted and arranged by Milton Nascimento," both grace Milton's 1976 LP *Geraes*.[11] "Peixinhos do mar" (Little fish of the sea), an adaptation of a *marujada toada* arranged by Moura, appears on his 1980 LP *Tavinho Moura* and on the more widely heard version from his collaboration the same year with Milton on the latter's popular LP *Sentinela*. *Marujadas*, discussed in chapter 6, are maritime-themed reenactments of Reconquista battles between Iberian Christians and Moors. These are just a few examples of a larger component of the Clube catalog that's grounded in the folk music world. Both Moura and Beto Guedes significantly augmented the notion of regional and folk authenticity in the sound world of Clube recordings through their use of the viola. Yet musical and textual themes, both urban and rural, also weave portraits of provincialism, social alienation, and the variously cleaved identities of Belo Horizonte's gleaming modernism.

This discursive play around Mineiro identity, regionalist declarations, and their relationships with the rest of the world is at the heart of a song from the 1970 EMI-Odeon LP *Milton*, the rock-powered "Para Lennon e McCartney" by Milton, Lô, and Márcio Borges: "I am from South America, I know you won't know / Now I am a 'cowboy,' I am made of gold, I am you / I am of the world, I am Minas Gerais." The musical accompaniment has no stylistic connection to Minas's pastoral interior. Rather, with its aggressive rock and brash, confident tone, the song addresses more than simple notions of identities of place by mentioning Minas Gerais in an homage to the Beatles' primary writing partnership. The authors' regionalist trope is heightened by the historical *barroco mineiro* reference to gold, the geopolitical and cultural layer of South America, and the global, universal citizen tag of "the world." The electrifying tune is joined on the LP by the song "Clube da Esquina." If "Para Lennon e McCartney" is the outward-bound rocket of a regional anthem, "Clube da Esquina" illustrates the most intimate, inward poetics of an urban nocturne laced with local resonance. Its epicenter is nothing less than the collective's urban nucleus, the Clube's original corner at the intersection of Rua Divinópolis and Rua Paraisópolis, down the street from the Borges residence in Santa Tereza. As Milton mellifluously calls out to those listening: "Come to the corner / You do not know the future I am holding in my hands." The earliest Nascimento–Lô Borges collaboration, "Clube da Esquina" is a reflective ode to dreamy contemplation of life's meanings. Conjuring the city's past, the song references the village with roots in the colonial era that was razed in the early 1890s for the construction of Belo Horizonte: "And in the Curral D'el-Rey / windows open to the blackness of the lunar world / But I don't feel that I'm lost / At night's end my voice slips away." Brazilian listeners recognize this as Belo Horizonte, as dressed up as the reference is with historical color. The portrayal of a local sensibility is met with a near-equal sense of restlessness. Charles Perrone notes how "[t]he wistful 'Club da Esquina' established the name of the Minas Gerais music collective he [Milton] led; the lyric colors the intimacy and cohesion of the local group with the impulse to surpass limited horizons."[12] The song is a Mineiro calling card that still sounds today.

Milton and his friends bathed much of their 1970s output in various associations with this ultralocal Clube tag, a concept that grew to symbolize togetherness for all of Brazil. The regionalism found in the collective's output is often embedded in a universally attractive musical sophistication. The polystylism that accompanies the Clube's programmatic tour through Minas Gerais comes in many flavors. The rock of "Para Lennon e McCartney" and the introspective pop balladry of "Clube da Esquina" echo the modernizing effect bossa nova brought to two songs that earlier had helped launch Milton's career, and that depicted small-town life in autobiographical tones while spreading the gospel of Sul de Minas to the nation. The stories behind the origins of "Morro Velho" (composed by Milton) and "Três Pontas," with Ronaldo Bastos's lyrics about the small town where Milton and Clube cohort Wagner Tiso were raised, cast a spotlight on Milton's early life and upbringing.

Milton, "Morro Velho," and "Três Pontas": Trains and Bossa Nova in the Symbolic Environments of Two 1960s Songs about Sul de Minas

Adopted in Rio de Janeiro by a white couple after his birth mother died of tuberculosis, Milton was raised in the agricultural southern cone of Minas Gerais known as Sul de Minas. Once a student of Heitor Villa-Lobos, his adoptive mother Lília played piano regularly in the home, endearing Milton's young ear to that beloved Brazilian composer's thoughtful fusions of classical music and Debussian innovations with choro and other Brazilian styles. Following the family's move to his adoptive father Josino's Sul de Minas hometown of Três Pontas, a five-year-old Milton began playing harmonica, singing, and closely watching the Folia de Reis, Congado, the Semana Santa, and other public processionals of popular Catholicism. He initiated a life-long friendship with Wagner Tiso, whose mother was also a pianist and music teacher and whose uncle Mário was a violinist, accordion teacher, and conductor of the town's Fanfarra municipal band.[13] Milton and Wagner helped form a Platters-inspired vocal group, Luar de Prata (Silver Moon), and a dance band called W's Boys. Through recordings, radio, television, and the live performances of touring musicians, Milton's youthful immersion in Mineiro music was profoundly augmented by global forces, through which the young artist honed techniques of improvised vocalizations and a developed taste for more complex jazz harmonies, which further resonated with bossa nova influences.

Milton moved to Belo Horizonte in 1963, at the age of twenty. His career breakout songs, including "Morro Velho," were performed live on

TV Globo from Rio de Janeiro's Maracanãzinho Auditorium during the Second International Song Festival in 1967. His other festival songs were "Maria, minha fé" and "Travessia" (lyrics by Fernando Brant). "Morro Velho" is loosely based on the singer's recollections of visiting Fazenda da Cachoeira (Waterfall Farm), owned by Wagner Tiso's aunt and near Alfenas, a small town in the heart of coffee country thirty miles west of Três Pontas. Before moving to Belo Horizonte, Milton and Wagner briefly lived in Alfenas, where Wagner's father had been transferred for his job at Banco da Lavoura.[14] The story Milton invented for "Morro Velho" proved years later to be a premoni- tion that grew from his real-life acquaintance with Niceto Aniceto, a black farmhand living at Fazenda da Cachoeira. Niceto's son is portrayed in the song as having grown up on the farm with the white fazenda owner's son, childhood friends of the best kind.[15] Following the narrative's tranquil, pas- toral scenes of youths fishing in clear stream waters, and of playing songs on the viola, the painful coming-of-age story of divided racial and class lines sees the white son go away to college, returning years later to run the farm as a doctor with a beautiful new wife. His black childhood friend is now only another worker.

In the song's introductory lyrics, Milton pays tribute to the bucolic notions of rural Minas and its iconic instrument of choice, the viola: "In the interior of my land, the farm is a friend that gives up its land / The strong com- mitment is made, it seems that it is all yours / Just to sit on the hill and see everything green, beautiful growing / Proud comrade, a viola instead of a field hoe." Francisco Carlos Teixeira da Silva has commented on the "Morro Velho" theme, suggesting what he terms a "utopia of social reform" in which the landscape's idealized beauty and serenity mask social conflicts of class and race. Adding to his analysis of the song, he continues: "In 'Morro Velho,' social injustice forms an equation of equal terms with racism. It was not enough to denounce the latifundia, it was also necessary to show the most intimate structures of the social difference."[16] Returning to broader aspects of Clube ruralism, Holly Holmes points to the salvaging of country living in some of these nostalgic themes and how they "re-signify interior lifeways from representations of 'backwardness' or 'provinciality' to representations of spiritual connectedness to nature or fraternity around collective labor."[17]

Coffee farms surrounding towns similar to Alfenas throughout the Sul de Minas region, like the "Morro Velho" locale of Fazenda da Cachoeira, were the economic engines behind the early twentieth-century growth of the area's small urban populations. Then, there were a few towns of no more than ten to twenty thousand inhabitants, yet with public plazas, cinemas, and access to interior railroad transport; these towns sprouted in the generations preceding Milton's and Wagner's coming of age. When Severiano describes their W's Boys experience as "three years of crisscrossing the Gerais, animating dances," he meant driving all night from Três Pontas and Alfenas to these other small Sul de Minas towns.[18]

Nascimento's first solo record, *Travessia* (Codil, 1967), included his festival songs and the three primary Clube lyricists: Ronaldo Bastos, Fernando Brant, and Márcio Borges.[19] The album features another early MPB window into small-town life in the Mineiro interior, "Três Pontas," which also reflects Milton's coming-of-age experiences in southern Minas Gerais. Bastos, too, had childhood memories of fazenda life on his family's country home in rural Rio de Janeiro State, near the site of the *Clube da Esquina* LP cover photo taken by his friend Cafi years later. Bastos's playfully condescending portrayal of seemingly naïve Três Pontas residents, running to the station to meet an arriving train full of news and ideas from the outside world, comes with a backdrop of an isolated interior. The innocence in which the lyricist bathes rural folks was all about satisfying city-dweller perspectives: "And the town puts on its finest / to see the train . . . / Everyone comes running to see once again / People who left, planning to return some day . . . / They bring hope to those who want to find themselves in this land." Yet in the face of criticism he received from old friends still living there, Milton points to the train theme, and his recollections of having waited at the town's station, as both legitimately autobiographical and comforting.[20] These landscapes and rural memories have remained part of Milton's and Wagner's identities as seen in influential Clube songs, which convey a sometimes idealized sense of regionalist purpose, valorizing open spaces, small towns, and the special relationships conjured with the natural environment.

"Três Pontas," at once a narrative of rural Mineiro simplicity and its juxtaposition with the industrialized, transportive power of the railroad, is drenched in bossa nova stylings that sonically mark the train's modernity: the incessant "chugging" emerging from the acoustic bass and low-register piano, the guitar's driving repetitiveness, and the *pandeiro*'s ostinato. Back in the mix, dark choral voices appear and fade like steam. A jazzy flute solo hovers freely above, while during short, contrasting sections a classically styled cello line accompanies quiet reflection. These country visions of a bygone interior were wrapped in the hip, modern arrangements and bossa nova stylings of Eumir Deodato (b. 1943), and Milton's first album showcases his, and by later extension the Clube's, early foundational connection to bossa nova. But the remaining tracks of *Travessia* feature charts penned by Luiz Eça, whose Tamba 4 (previously the Tamba Trio) form Milton's session ensemble.[21] With modern sounds and styles gracing Sul de Minas regionalism, a combination of country charm and urban gleam, we begin to understand Severiano's read of Milton's "surprising use of regional music from Minas Gerais, treated with the exquisite harmonic resources of bossa nova, jazz, and the Beatles, three major influences on his work."[22]

Milton Comes to Belo Horizonte

Milton began studying accounting while a typist for Centrais Elétricas de Furnas as he searched for gigs. This regular grind brought him into contact with many of his future Clube friends, including Marilton Borges, with whom he formed the Grupo Evolussamba quartet with Wagner and Ferrari.[23] Milton appeared on his first recording on the band Holliday's 1964 release *Barulho de trem* around the same time the Maletta Building's Berimbau Club was launched, a small jazz venue featuring the Tempo Trio with Nivaldo Ornelas, drummer Paulinho Braga, and bassist Paulo Horta, the older brother of Clube member Toninho Horta. The Berimbau Club became a hot spot for the city's best musicians, including another trio composed of Paulinho Braga, Wagner on piano, and Milton on bass; it was here that Pacífico Mascarenhas first witnessed the talents of Milton and Wagner, later inviting them to join and record with his group. Now, in an invigorating urban environment, the twenty-one-year-old Nascimento was soon hanging out downtown at his new friend Marilton Borges's home in the Levy Building (fig. 9.2), where Grupo Evolussamba occasionally rehearsed. There, Milton met all of the Borges family, the parents (father Salomão was a respected journalist) and ten siblings, most importantly younger brothers Márcio, Lô, and Telo.[24] These connections formed the initial creative axis of the Clube.

Milton has commented on plying his musical trades at Musicians' Point in downtown Belo Horizonte during his earliest years there, a routine shared by the generation before him as described in chapter 8 above:

Musicians' Point was very cool because it was a place on the street where all the musicians went, near a bar. We would exchange ideas, talk, and go to the house of one. We would hang out at one another's houses, the mother of another. We created friendships, really . . . [with musicians such as] Hélvius Vilela, Ildeu Soares, Pascoal Meireles, Celinho [Balona], Figo Seco, the singer Helena Ribeiro, and guitarist Nazário Cordeiro. There was an exceptional, fantastic person, [a drummer named] Bosco. . . . I was very sad there at first [in Belo Horizonte]. He would take me to his house, and I'd stay there with his family, a wonderful thing. It's something I had in Belo Horizonte that I didn't have anywhere else.[25]

Pacífico Mascarenhas and bandleader Célio Balona both hired Milton and Wagner for gigs and recordings. During this time, Nivaldo Ornelas, then a twenty-one-year-old clarinetist, first heard recordings of saxophone great John Coltrane as well as Stan Getz's 1962 LP *Jazz Samba* featuring a Grammy-winning, million-record-selling version of the bossa nova classic "Desafinado." Ornelas's formal training in concert band and classical music combined with his love for regional popular Catholic festivities such as the Congado and Folia de Reis and the sound world of liturgical church repertoire.[26] Within these interstices of burgeoning cultural spheres, Ornelas took inspiration, bringing his newly acquired saxophone along as he joined the Conjunto Célio Balona. The timely switch to saxophone was Ornelas's contribution to the season of change sweeping through Belo Horizonte and the rest of Brazil. Ornelas helped run the Berimbau Club, which opened on April 1, 1964, the night of a military coup that ushered in a twenty-four-year dictatorship.

Regional Legacies in the 1970s LPs *Clube da Esquina, Minas, Geraes,* and *Clube da Esquina 2*

If Milton's early work of the 1960s brought Sul de Minas into view, later albums and songs of the 1970s set forth broader stylistic and literary palettes with which the collective portrayed regional identities. The 1972 LP *Clube da Esquina* further propelled the now-patented Corner Club label as a tag of regional identity in another song, the wordless, timeless "Clube da Esquina

No. 2" (Milton Nascimento, Lô Borges, Márcio Borges). The album cover's photo of two young boys resting on the side of a dirt road in the countryside promotes some of its songs' symbolic rurality and soothed the reality of the country's political turmoil, Brazil's industrialization, and explosive urbanization. Brazilian audiences knew that the music was coming to them from a certain place. The *Clube da Esquina* album's gatefold reveals a photo collage interspersed with rural images, a small map of Sul de Minas featuring Três Pontas, and a snapshot of the Rua Divinópolis street sign. Without directly mentioning the words "Minas Gerais," the music, lyrics, and graphics created a concept album about identities of place, both rural and urban, and about friendship.

Of the albums released by members of the collective during the 1970s, the two most convincingly regionalist follow-ups to the 1972 album are the programmatically titled Nascimento albums *Minas* (1975) and *Geraes* (1976). The title of the first was due to a friend's passing observation that "Minas" matched the first letters of his full name: *MI*-lton *NAS*-cimento. The *Minas* and *Geraes* titles, the latter using an archaic spelling, thus grew from the artist's personalized sense of regional identity. During this period, the collective fully blossomed with the inclusion of Tavinho Moura, Nivaldo Ornelas, and Novelli. Toninho Horta's considerable contributions on nylon-string and electric guitar, composition, and arranging also colored many of these recordings with a rich, chordal style full of harmonic intricacies that helped characterize a regional flair. Novelli's wordless hymn "Minas" begins Milton's powerful album of the same name, recorded in October 1975, a soaring, programmatic tribute to the region sonically emerging from the "Paula and Bebeto" theme heard later in the album, energetically intoned by an a cappella children's choir. Milton's solo voice carries the main melody with his arpeggiating guitar accompaniment, and it slowly grows stronger, his sustained tones contrasting and dovetailing with the fade-out of the restless kids' rhythmic repetition. The song continues as a lonely strand of notes assumes the spotlight, a particularly Mineiro isolation soon joined contrapuntally with Beto Guedes's high-register vocalese. A thick strain of men's choir comprising Horta, Tiso, Ornelas, Guedes, and the songwriter couples with a slight return of the children's driving theme spread out across a polyphonic tapestry, creating a near-baroque texture of what "Minas" might mean to an audience looking for authenticity and peace in Brazil in the mid-1970s. The many voices shaped by calming, hymn-like chord changes fade to the tireless children who introduced the song, the whole easily interpreted as a portrayal of the church-like atmosphere marking the region's religiosity without religion. Not a word is spoken in this reflective little piece of Minas, here a place of contemplation and reassurance.

Another song from *Minas* exhorting contemplation of regional identity is Milton's and Brant's "Ponta de Areia" (Sand Point), a poignant lament of isolation and the forlornness of the state's interior, landlocked inhabitants. The beautiful melody buoys the song's nostalgia, its musical expressivity conveying the loss of a vital railway connection to the Atlantic Ocean. Trains emerge as powerful symbols of a bygone era, but also of communal connection in a state where distances compound separation and loneliness, as railroad references do in both "Três Pontas" and "Morro Velho." In "Ponta de Areia," the *maria fumaça* (steam locomotive) stops sounding its whistle for the people and places that it passes by on its journeys between the coast and the interior stations of the Mineiro hinterland. "Sand Point, final stop / of the Bahia–Minas [rail line], a natural road / that linked Minas to the port, to the sea." The rails, "torn up and taken away," were sacrificed by the military government's 1960s modernization project, which channeled massive support to automobile manufacturing and infrastructure. Ornelas's soprano saxophone, both wistful and thorny, pronounces a short introduction that promptly fuses with the innocence of a children's choir sounding the declamatory melodic theme, followed by a lone rail station bell and a clearing, ghostly pause. From these layers emerges Milton's clear falsetto restating the melodic theme, at once both mournful and celebratory; and, like "Três Pontas" eight years earlier, a choir seems to create clouds of locomotive steam. The image of a train was adopted as a Clube da Esquina logo in the 1970s, a regional icon chosen by Milton for use on the *Geraes* album cover. "Ponta de Areia" languidly sings of the distances between loved ones, traditions of prosperous rail travel linked also to aspirations and opportunity. As the song's narrative is a solid poetic vision, its tight musical projection is a vehicle for Milton's marvelous vocal skills, propelled by the rhythm section of Novelli (bass), Wagner (keyboards), and Paulinho Braga (drums). Ornelas returns with a lilting solo over the churning progression. Later, a harsh cut to the melody's reiteration in the children's voices brings a quick fade, bidding farewell.

Minas sold hundreds of thousands of copies in Brazil and still ranks as one of Nascimento's best-selling LPs.[27] "Gran circo" (Great circus) by Milton and Márcio Borges, and Nelson Ângelo's "Simples" (Simply), also from the

Minas album, are discussed below as songs of political protest that carry powerful regional metaphors. From the seminal collective that had recorded the breakthrough *Clube da Esquina* album in 1972, a stately version of Som Imaginário (Imaginary Sound), a band formed in part to support Milton in 1970, was responsible for the core sound of Milton's subsequent recordings; the band reunited Nivaldo Ornelas and Toninho Horta with Wagner Tiso and Paulinho Braga. Nascimento filled the hole left by Som Imaginário bassist Luiz Alves by wisely collaborating with the multitalented and underrated Novelli.[28] Beto Guedes blends his high-register voice with that of Nascimento's on several tracks while lending his rock and regional chops on electric guitar and viola.

Nelson Ângelo's "Fazenda" opens side 1 of the 1976 Nascimento LP *Geraes*. The song is a nostalgic meditation on the family weekend country house, the *situ*, visited by cousins, uncles, and aunts and typically miles outside the city yet close enough for frequent visits. "Fazenda" celebrates the beauty of nature and its delicacies, laced with family experiences through the generations. It is an ode to the Mineiro sense of place. There are no apologies here for the happiness brought by extended family, the core of Mineiro society. Life is good: "Drinking water, backyard spring, a thirst to live everything and to forget was so normal that time stopped / We had the *sabiá* [singing thrush], the orange grove, we had the *manga-rosa* / and during the farewell, uncles on the veranda a Jeep on the road, and our heart left there."

Writing both words and music, Ângelo extols the vitality of this way of life and underlines its values, seen in children breathing the wind "until night fell," and the old folks who "spoke about things about this life." In the last line, Milton cajoles the listener into joining the dream: "I was a child then, today it is you, and tomorrow us." The musical arrangement speaks directly to this nostalgia, with its surging affects underpinning Milton's incredible voice. Ângelo also plays viola and conducts his own orchestration of strings, trumpet, English horn, bassoon, and an exceptional arrangement for six flutes. Beto Guedes excels in the high part of the backing chorus, which is mixed in the recording to expose his line, a falsetto that is an echo, a memory, calling forth as witness to the Mineiro traditions being described. The varied, subtle intricacies of Ângelo's convincing work masks a rock ballad, complete with driving rhythms and soaring instrumentation. The curious coda of strings and a restless percussion solo brings the song to a close on a point of arrival a half-step from the tonic. The gently unsettling modulation leaves a question mark as to the relationships we might have with these sweet memories. Three more songs from the *Geraes* album strongly link to regionalist perspectives: "Minas Gerais," "O cio da terra," and "Carro de boi."

MPB welcomed Mineiro themes into the national discourse on Brazilian identity, their intimacy and regional sensibilities of personal social space anchored to literary and musical notions of rebellion, history, and tradition. As Perrone comments on Milton and the rest of the Clube collective:

> These local or regional currents merge with others to speak to and identify with the Brazilian nation, Latin America, and the world at large. . . . The projection from Minas Gerais toward the outside world is present in two recurrent motifs of travel, the highway and the train, which express both a sense of personal adventure and a search for collective fulfillment.[29]

Profiles of Key Clube Participants as Windows into Mineiro Identity

Although Milton is often seen as the collective's predominant leader, the backgrounds of other members and their locally and regionally shaped experiences lend equally in illustrating the collective's deep Mineiro roots. Family profiles, early musical directions, diverse geographic origins from within the state, and the complex array of local, regional, national, and international musical influences taking shape in the collective help define its relationship to our studies of music and Minas Gerais.

Two rectangular, blue street signs with white lettering grace the exterior wall of a small apartment building sitting on the southeast corner of the intersection of Rua Divinópolis and Rua Paraisópolis, the street names taken from the names of small towns from diverse regions of Minas Gerais. They meet here in Belo Horizonte's tree-lined Santa Tereza district, the latter running uphill past Fernando's Mercearia e Padaria (Market and Bakery), its sign reading, "a tradition since 1973." This is *the* corner of the "Corner Club." A gleaming Museu Clube da Esquina plaque commemorates the spot (fig. 9.1), the mother of all the dozen or so such plaques proudly marking physical locations throughout Belo Horizonte that played important roles in the collective's local development.

Figure 9.1. "The Corner" at the Santa Tereza district intersection of Rua Divinópolis and Rua Paraisópolis, Belo Horizonte—the epicenter of the Clube da Esquina (Corner Club) collective's popular music revolution led by Milton Nascimento, the Borges brothers Lô and Márcio, and friends. (Photo by Jonathon Grasse.)

Figure 9.2. A Corner Club Museum plaque graces the entrance to downtown Belo Horizonte's Levy Building, commemorating the original meeting place of Milton, the Borges family, and others who later helped form the Corner Club. (Photo by Jonathon Grasse.)

Looking downhill, a view through the neighborhood trees and buildings affords at a five-mile distance the wide, iconic mountainside of the Serra do Curral that embraces Belo Horizonte's southeastern edge. The insistent, optimistic cries of the ubiquitous bird known colloquially, and onomatopoeically, as the *bem-te-vi* (good to see you) compete for attention with the emphatic chatter of the men hanging out at Fernando's Market, and with the background din of motorbikes, cars, and their squeaky brakes negotiating both hill and intersection. The Borges family moved back to this quiet, suburban *bairro* from the Levy Building downtown (with its own Museu Clube da Esquina plaque), where they had stayed temporarily during renovations of their Santa Tereza home. The whole family played music. Over the course of the late 1960s, Milton Nascimento had made his name in Belo Horizonte as well as Minas, Rio de Janeiro and the rest of Brazil, and the world via his television appearances, Brazilian and US recordings, and tours. He now returned to his friends, the Borges family, at this corner looking for a renewed sense of place and collaborative zeal. As Milton told the story following the release of the 1972 LP *Clube da Esquina*:

"I'm doing some stuff on the guitar and want to turn it into music and I can't work it out. Can you help me?" This conversation happened in a small bar in Santa Tereza . . . with a guy who at that very moment left behind the image I'd had of him: an eleven-year-old boy who had a little vocal quartet that sang Beatles songs. It was Lô.[30]

Lô, then seventeen and finishing high school, had developed a musical friendship with Beto Guedes. The two already had penned the hit "Feira moderna" and would go on to form the rock music axis of the Clube, representing the globalism that infused the local music scene. The youthful Lô Borges, who gained fame with the *Clube da Esquina* LP at age twenty, aimed his creative sites beyond the local and gave no concern to nationalist critics citing his dedication to the Beatles and rock as evidence of excessive foreign influence. Lô became iconic of Belo Horizonte's emerging rock music scene, a popular music star embodying the eclecticism of "Rock Mineiro" while avoiding obvious regionalist stylizations in his music. Rather, the three primary Corner Club lyricists—Lô's brother Márcio, Fernando Brant, and Ronaldo Bastos— among other collaborators, each penned profoundly regional themes to his rock- and pop-tinged music. Eschewing folk and regional music traditions for a popular rock trajectory that has lasted to the present, Lô Borges was the emergent 1970s-era rock star personified. In this sense, and for our purposes, his importance lies in this groundbreaking role: as the city's youthful rock lord, and proof of Belo Horizonte's arrival on the national rock music scene.

Beto Guedes

Beto Guedes developed into perhaps the most quixotic Clube artist while representing his family's musical legacy. Born Alberto de Castro Guedes in 1951, the singer, songwriter, and multi-instrumentalist originally from the northern Minas city of Montes Claros claimed the electric guitar as his primary instrument along with his fragile-sounding, high-register voice. Having formed a musical friendship with Lô, Beto appears as an unknown outside an immediate circle of friends on all but four of the 1972 *Clube da Esquina* LP's twenty-one tracks, his first recording.[31] Before embarking on his subsequent solo career, he contributed vocals and multi-instrumental performances on Milton's *Minas*, adding the song "Caso voce queira saber" as a bonus track to that album's 1994 Abbey Road remastering. Guedes's trio of late 1970s albums struck a chord with rock audiences: *A página do relâmpago eléctrico* (1977), *Amor de Índio* (1978), and *Sol de primavera* (1979) are classic pop and art-rock LPs, each featuring on their label an orange *pequi* fruit logo, a Mineiro twist in homage to the Beatles' Apple Records label design. It is such subtle attributes that help forge the Mineiro brand. Even considering his viola and *bandolim* playing, Beto's songwriting and stylistic influence on the Clube, like Lô's, had less to do with regional identity than with his unique brand of prog-rock and modern pop-rock, which helped to define the Rock Mineiro sound. Like Lô's national career beginning in the 1970s, Beto's became symbolic of rock's success in Belo Horizonte rather than of regionalism, or of Mineiro themes per se.

In embracing rock at an early age, Guedes grew a new branch in the family's musical tree while continuing the musicality of his father, Godofredo Guedes (1908–1983), also a composer and talented multi-instrumentalist within amateur *seresta*, choro, and samba traditions. Born in Riacho de Santana, Bahia, to composer and *sanfonista* Cazuza Guedes, Godofredo moved from Bahia to Montes Claros in 1935. There, as a pharmacist in the primary urban center of northern Minas, he made a name organizing and composing for weekend dances (bailes) and *serestas*, playing clarinet, saxophone, and violin. At some point during this time, Godofredo traveled the seven hundred kilometers of country roads from Montes Claros to Rio de Janeiro to record his music and to search out, unsuccessfully, opportunities for a music career. He moved his family to Belo Horizonte in 1960, likely inspiring his scenically titled choro "Belo Horizonte." A full-blown orchestral arrangement of Godofredo's "Noite sem luar" (Moonless night) ends Beto's 1981 LP *Cantos da lua vaga* (Tales of the wandering moon), a hit-filled, sentimental pop album tinged with eccentric phrasing and featuring his overdubbed multi-instrumentalism. Beto frequently included his father's catchy, sentimental songs on his records, creating a tangible nostalgia for Godofredo's catalog.[32] In 2004, Beto's son Gabriel Guedes, representing the Mineiro family's fourth generation of musical talent, recorded a CD of his grandfather's compositions, *Choros de Godofredo*, with Milton's participation.[33] In August 2008, centenary celebrations for Godofredo brought remembrances in Montes Claros and in Belo Horizonte's premier concert venue, the Grand Theater of the Palácio das Artes.

Wagner Tiso

Wagner's friendship with Milton forms the backbone of the Corner Club collective.[34] His father's family lineage includes eastern European roots, with the surname Tiso deriving from the Tisa River, which from its origins in Ukraine flows through Slovakia, Hungary, Serbia, and into the Danube north of Belgrade. With a small group of extended family, Wagner's grandfather arrived in Três Pontas. Wagner's father was born in Nepomuceno, Minas Gerais. His mother was born in Três Pontas, the daughter of Italian immigrants, and was a long-standing piano teacher in her hometown. Nearly everyone in the extended family played a musical instrument, versed in a variety of styles and familiar with classical repertoire. One of his mother's passions was Chopin. From his childhood, Wagner counts as important musical influences, in addition to his musical family, local religious processions and festivals along with the latest sounds in cinema and radio. His older brother Gileno was an early role model: he played trumpet and moved to Belo Horizonte in the late 1950s, where he studied with a professor of music.

Toninho Horta

Belo Horizonte's busy 1960s music scene nurtured the guitarist, songwriter, and arranger Toninho Horta (b. 1948), who quickly established an indelible position in the nascent Corner Club collective. In 1965, a seventeen-year-old Toninho serendipitously sat in for a missing guitarist: bossa nova godfather Vinícius de Moraes, in town from Rio de Janeiro for a big concert, auditioned Horta and hired him on the spot for his Belo Horizonte appearance, cementing the young musician as a budding Brazilian music legend.[35] The Horta family had long been establishing their own place in Minas musical lore. Toninho's maternal grandfather, João Horta, formed musical ensembles throughout the state as he traveled with the Central do Brasil railroad, involved with the construction of tracks connecting the otherwise isolated, small hinterland towns. With wife and children in tow while he was composing, forming bands, and conducting ensembles along the way, João Horta found time to nurture family musical practice by teaching piano to his wife Lucília, a native of Sabará, and daughter Geralda, Toninho's mother (b. 1909).[36] At an evening weekend dance in the Rio São Francisco town of Pirapora, in the state's northwest,

Geralda Horta met Prudente de Mello, an engineering student of Native Brazilian heritage enrolled in Ouro Preto's Escola de Minas (Mining School) and the son of a *fazendeiro* from the north of Minas. After briefly settling on his family's large fazenda near Montes Claros, Beto Guedes's hometown, the Hortas moved to Belo Horizonte's Floresta district, where Toninho was born in 1948. His older brother Paulo played an important role in the rise of postwar jazz in Belo Horizonte by mastering jazz bass, frequenting Musicians' Point, and founding the city's influential Jazz Fan Club.[37] With this strongly musical family, an adolescent Toninho studied guitar with seasoned guitarist Chiquito Braga. One night, Paulo brought Milton home for one of the family's *horas dançantes* (informal house parties), and Milton and Toninho hit it off, playing their compositions for each other and forming a bond of musical discovery and development.

Horta lent his songwriting, arranging, guitar-playing, and orchestrational gifts to many important Clube recordings, including performances on bass and piano.[38] His style brought a jazz flair and sensibility to those recordings that they would otherwise not have had. In terms of regional identity, the guitarist has always proclaimed a proud connection to Belo Horizonte. His most touching song came early in his career, a collaboration with Fernando Brant, "Manuel audaz" (Bold Manuel), recorded many years later on the 1980 *Toninho Horta* LP (EMI-Odeon). The story revolves around Brant's real-life trusted Jeep, pet-named Manuel, which would take him and his friends on excursions throughout the Belo Horizonte environs and its surrounding countryside. The track is a stirring ode to friendships and love of place. Horta and Brant's jazz-laced bossa nova "Aqui Oh!" reflects textually on displacement and wanderlust while extolling the region: "In Minas Gerais happiness is kept in trunks, cathedrals / On the veranda I find my love . . . Blessed is the fruit of this Minas Gerais." In his interpretation, Perrone sees in the song "the poetic theme of the journey as a Mineiro trait"[39] and points to the long-established outflow, since the post–gold boom economic decline, of young Mineiros from struggling rural enclaves and small towns seeking improved socioeconomic opportunities in Belo Horizonte, the coastal cities, São Paulo, and overseas. Unlike Toninho Horta, who temporarily relocated to New York in support of his international jazz guitar career, many who left Minas Gerais never returned. This is the bittersweet lyrical essence of "Aqui Oh!"; similar themes of travel and life journeys characterize much of this regional popular music.

Tavinho Moura

Born Otávio Augusto Pinto de Moura (1947, Juiz de Fora, MG), Tavinho's early memories recall his grandmother's stories about the coffee fazendas surrounding his hometown.[40] His grandfather Francisco Otávio Moura made ten-string violas, some fashioned out of repurposed mandolins. Both of his parents played guitar, with Dorival Caymmi's songs in Mrs. Moura's primary repertoire; the family radio was regularly tuned to *samba-canções* by Noel Rosa and Francisco Alves among others (Tavinho still collects old samba records). Following his father's tragic, untimely death, the eight-year-old Tavinho moved with his family to Belo Horizonte in 1954, where he soon met Toninho Horta in their Floresta neighborhood. Later in grade school, he befriended future Clube members Nelson Ângelo and Márcio Borges. One of Moura's teenage bandmates was a neighbor whose father had been the mayor of Porteirinha, a small town close to the border with Bahia in the state's extreme north. He joined the family on a trip to the isolated town, where he discovered as an adolescent his passion for the traditional Mineiro folk music of the *sertão*:

> I was sleeping and woke up in a room with a group playing handmade instru-
> ments: a viola, fiddle, and tambourine they had made themselves. The *caixas*
> were of deer leather . . . and the guys were singing a dialect I did not under-
> stand. Then I heard: "The sun comes through the door, the moon through
> the window, Oh my God, the moon through the window." I became very
> interested in that narrative, and I was just beginning to read [Mineiro author
> João Guimarães] Rosa. I thought this was a really fantastic universe. Then
> began a very natural passion.[41]

During an interview in Belo Horizonte's Savassi district, Moura shared with me his perspectives on the personification of the viola's dual role in Mineiro identity: first, as a voice of the backwoods, whereby the viola's timbres have come to represent the *sertão*; second, as a legitimate solo instrument of the concert stage in the sophisticated mix of the *música viola* world. Tavinho's research into regional folkloric material, mainly viola *toadas* and songs from the Folia de Reis, imbued his solo albums and other Clube collaborations with a unique regional aura. "Do not be afraid my boy / Of the night in the backlands," sings Milton in his 1984 song partnered with Tavinho, "Noites do sertão" (Backland nights). Through the use of folkloric themes, adapted tunes, and instrumentation including the viola, Tavinho's work finds elaborately conceived musical and textual tributes to Mineiro cultural landscapes.

The Belo Horizonte collective's strongest connection to this rural world of music, Moura's early creative phase was defined by a series of five albums released between 1978 and 1984. But it was in 1967, when he and Márcio Borges joined forces for the song "Como vai minha aldeia" (How are you, my little village), that Moura's early career was launched, the song later becoming the basis for his admirable 1978 debut album of the same name. The *Como vai minha aldeia* LP features a viola on almost every track, lending an unmistakable regional spark to this imaginative, classic Clube record.[42] Tavinho was part of a vanguard, beginning in the 1970s, in resuscitating the instrument, exploring its traditional repertoire and appropriating its regional profile for folk-inspired concert music compositions. He counts viola virtuoso Renato Andrade as a primary *mestre*, particularly mentioning that artist's seminal *A fantástica* LP, and his primary viola was crafted by Virgílio Lima.[43] Later in his career, his compositions continued to fuse new, challenging music with the *música caipira* traditions he had studied in the Mineiro *sertão*. His frequent *parceiro* (creative partner) and fellow Clube alumnus Fernando Brant, who died in 2015, stated that Moura's music and stories are "explosions of Minas-ness, Brazilian-ness, and humanity." Brant stated romantically:

> Tavinho Moura is of the forest, of the river, of the critters, and of the flora and fauna. He knows of the waters and of the fish of the [Rio] São Francisco. He is a master of speaking the way of the people living on the riverbank, at the river's edges, in that world far from cities. He knows the people of those places, the vegetation, the animals, the dangers and the joys, the pain and the beliefs, the legends and myths, the food and those ways of love and of life.[44]

Tavinho Moura (RCA Victor) was recorded at RCA studios in São Paulo in 1980, with some songs arranged and conducted by Nivaldo Ornelas, who also added soprano sax. The personnel included original members of the Belo Horizonte–based band 14 Bis and the experimental music ensemble Uakti.[45] In addition to "As meninas no trem de Sabará" (The girls on the train from Sabará) and "Cabaré mineiro," two more *Tavinho Moura* LP songs deal directly with regionalist themes: "Corte palavra" (by Moura and Márcio Borges) references the Corner Club with the line "Cut word / dancing on the street car / at the corner club / before the hunger."[46] And in one of Moura's many collaborations with Fernando Brant, "Nossa Senhora do Ó" brings to listeners images of the Rio das Velhas, vital to the environs of central Minas Gerais, and the gold and cathedrals of the Minas baroque: "My old master passed this way / bringing their Chinese / From the Rio das Velhas they saw Minas Gerais, immortal gold, death in the cathedrals / Here they planted the white church."[47]

The LPs *Cabaret mineiro* (1981), *Engenho trapizonga* (1982), and *Noites do sertão* (1984) round out the artist's early phase, in which Tavinho's compositional styles were not limited to any single genre or regionalist theme. In his twenties, he scored the music for Schubert Magalhães's 1972 film *O homen do corpo fechado*, an accomplishment that led to a career in film composition. His work in regional cinema is notable, particularly the scores to two films by Carlos Alberto Prates Correia: *Cabaret mineiro* (Minas cabaret, 1980) and *Noites do sertão* (Nights of the backlands, 1983). Setting text by legendary Mineiro poet Carlos Drummond de Andrade (1902–1987), Moura's "Cabaré mineiro" is an ode to the bohemian life of nightclubs and brothels of mid-twentieth-century Belo Horizonte: "Spanish dancer from Montes Claros / Dance, and dance again in the room of mixed-races / 100 brown eyes are undressing your corpulent body / a mosquito bite, a bullet mark in the right thigh."[48] Another song extolling the virtues of Belo Horizonte's labyrinthian nightlife was Moura and Murilo Antunes's "Montanhez danças," portraying the nightclub of the same name: "Dancing in the cabarets of Don Juan land, face-to-face tangos with you / I will go dancing, I know you in my bar, dreaming in the cabarets / you wanted to kiss me, kisses, face-to-face with you / I will go dancing, in naked movements, your body in medium light."[49]

Moura's subsequent creative phase as a member of the Clube da Esquina included a return to original compositions for viola, and a musical yearning for the Mineiro interior. His 1992 masterpiece album *Caboclo d'água*, subtitled *Instrumental de viola*, embraces the backland's myths and legends. This album's "Minas Texas" playfully compares Minas Gerais to the US state of Texas, stressing the expansive notion of rugged country and the two regions' shared sense of independence. The challenging originality of his 2001 release *Cruzada* includes a set of four viola/guitar duets with guitarist Beto Lopes, and "São Gonçalo do Rio Preto," dedicated to the small, isolated Mineiro town in the high region of the Jequitinhonha River Valley southeast of Diamantina. Moura's 2015 CD *Beira da linha*, like *Caboclo d'água* twenty-three years earlier, is also subtitled *Instrumental de viola*. Of its fourteen tracks, eleven are for solo viola. The title song is dedicated to fellow Mineiro, virtuoso *violeiro*, and scholar Ivan Vilela. Clube member Murilo Antunes connected Tavinho Moura to the interior's mystical, perhaps mythical past: "A composer faithful to performance technique, Tavinho honors partygoers, dancers, and Brazil's children with rhythmic cells of a viola universe that blends into the imaginary of a *sertão* that no longer exists."[50]

Political Resistance: "Beco do Mota," "Gran Circo," "Simples," and "Ruas da Cidade"

Clube da Esquina scholar Bruno Viveiros Martins could easily write of 1960s Belo Horizonte as having been quiet and provincial despite the city's population explosion and industrial activities. Between 1950 and 1970, the metropolitan area's population grew from 412,000 to nearly 1.5 million, with annual growth rates during those years of over 6.5 percent.[51] The cultural before-and-after effects of the 1960s speaks to the milieu in which the Clube came together and the local impact Milton and friends had on the city, and through their songs upon the region's image on Brazil's national stage:

> Belo Horizonte during the 1960s was still a sleepy town experiencing progress and its first steps of gigantic growth. The city was welcoming modern sounds from afar and the tender music learned from grandparents in the small towns, who lent their children to this urban growth. The great metropolis was the daughter of modernity's rational design, granddaughter of its master, conservative colonialism.[52]

The Clube's confrontation with the regime had its ironically ugly seeds planted on April 1, 1964: the night of the coup, and the opening of the Berimbau Club in Belo Horizonte's Maletta Building, where Milton, Wagner, Nivaldo, and others had briefly gigged in their pre-Clube days. Through a series of decrees, most infamously 1968's Institutional Act no. 5 (AI5), Brazilians saw their civil liberties carved up and replaced by draconian laws stripping citizens of their right to gather, form political parties, and organize opposition. The military regime further tightened their grip on society moving into the 1970s. Censorship became normalized, affecting all broadcast and print media and forcing songwriters to submit lyrics to federal censors. Telling are themes of warning and alarm that are found in the protest music of societies censored and bullied by agents of dictatorships and their secret police. Protest songs articulated too plainly resulted in brutal reprisals. Caetano Veloso and Gilberto Gil were exiled to the United Kingdom for their perceived subversions, while Chico Buarque and Geraldo Vandré both famously self-exiled to escape government harassment. All four singer-songwriters, among others who were censored, jailed, or simply forced underground with shattered careers, had engaged in 1960s protest. During this time, it was guns versus guitars; the poetics of resistance would have to wear veils of allegory and metaphor, and opposition voices in popular music would soon be masked by the wordless vocalese of censored songs. The textless voices, verbalizations, and shouting that characterize Milton's 1973 LP *Milagre dos peixes* (Miracle of the fish) were exactly that: censors forbade the recording's original lyrics. These were the so-called leaden years (*anos de chumbo*), the harshest period of the right-wing military government. The following year, *Milagre dos peixes ao vivo*, a double LP recorded live, developed from a series of concerts in Brazil's southeast; the sellout concerts demonstrated the resilience of Brazilian audiences and their clamor for freedom. Leonardo José Magalhães Gomes remarks on the political context enveloping the collective's formative years:

> The time during which the group began its musical activities was very difficult. We cannot forget that the dawn of the adult lives of a large majority of these [Clube] artists was also the first years of the Brazilian military dictatorship, when the dreams of a more just society were destroyed by the ferocious repressive force of an illegitimate power that feared terrorist bombs while the songs of poets fought against them with equal conviction. Various recourses were used for this: prisons, torture, and the censor, all of which impeded the most basic expression of an entire generation's discontent. Many were the songs that were prohibited, and that waited decades to be heard by the general public.[53]

The story does not end with censorship. In Belo Horizonte of the late 1960s, there were other forms and institutions of resistance: the Centro Popular de Cultura (CPC), a chapter of the União dos Estudantes (UNE), student activities at the Colégio Estadual Central, and the country's primary left-wing organization, Ação Popular (AP). Following the 1972 *Clube da Esquina* album release, a politically active Márcio Borges collaborated with UFMG student leader José Carlos Machado, who was later arrested and executed while in custody, a political prisoner of the brutal DOI/CODI police in São Paulo, one of more than five hundred Brazilian citizens known to have been executed by their dictatorial government.[54] The DOPS-MG headquarters in downtown Belo Horizonte had multiple subterranean levels accommodating politically related incarceration and torture sessions.[55] Another politically active Clube member, Murilo Antunes (b. 1950, Pedra Azul, MG), braved the dangers of the DOPS-MG by hiding student leader Etelvino Nunes in his parent's home for an entire month before Nunes escaped to Chile. With friends and acquaintances tortured, exiled, and murdered, the collective was deeply affected by the authoritarian government. As Martins writes, Clube songs became a defense of democratic urban landscapes, and the movement assumed a larger sociopolitical role as an artistic vehicle for social change and a return to democracy "During its artistic trajectory, the Clube da Esquina demonstrated that while facing the danger of lost liberty, one must dream of a possible future. In order to defy the authoritarianism restricting democracy, such as the depoliticalization of Brazilian cities, it was necessary to reconquer public space."[56]

Songs composed in commemoration and outrage transcend mere protest, amounting rather to quasi-ceremonial liturgies, such as Brant and Nascimento's religiously powerful song from 1969, "Sentinela." While not direct expressions of regional identity, songs of great spiritual import can be interpreted within the solemn Catholicism that imbued the culture of Minas Gerais. Perrone says of the song: "A nondoctrinaire, yet fundamentally Christian, ethic of solidarity and love is expressed and tied to cognitive responses to the death of the comrade." Martins characterizes the song—a heartbreaking lamentation over the death of a "brother" who, in real life, could have been any of those known by members of the collective to have been brutalized, murdered, or exiled by the dictatorship—as a funeral song from a collective voice: "Death, a candle, I am the sentinel / of the body of my brother, who has departed / Now I reflect upon what has happened, memory will not die."[57]

Appearing on the 1969 LP *Milton Nascimento*, the song "Beco do Mota" (Mota's Alley, lyrics by Brant) became a radio hit, with its catchy melody and clear pop music aesthetics, but it harbored a socially conscious twist bathed in regional significance. In Diamantina during the 1960s, Mota's Alley, near the old city's main cathedral, emerged as a hip, counterculture haven, an alternative street scene inhabited by politically conscious students, hippies, and marginalized residents trading goods, playing music, selling and experimenting with drugs, and soliciting prostitution. The locale's history as a red-light district stretched back to the eighteenth century. With pressure from local Catholic archbishop Don Sigaud and the far-right movement Tradição, Família e Propriedade (Tradition, Family, and Property), municipal leaders and the authoritarian government cleared out the area, closing down the enclave.[58] "Beco do Mota" ends with a warning: Diamantina is the alley, all of Minas Gerais is the alley, and Brazil itself is the alley. The last line, "Long live my country!," calls on listeners to open their eyes to the worsening political situation. The song arguably transformed the cherished hangout, with its colonial-era backdrop of baroque splendor, into a stand-in for liberty, and it threw a rare spotlight on the military regime's cultural war. "Beco do Mota," though a pop-tinged radio hit, telescoped into the national soul's wrestling match with itself.

Appearing on the *Minas* LP, "Gran circo" (Great circus) by Milton and Márcio Borges, and Nelson Ângelo's "Simples" (Simply), both invoke images of the interior and of the natural world, although in stark, metaphoric shards recast as protest themes aimed at the regime. The traveling circus of the former is a euphemism for the arbitrary chaos and catastrophe of authoritarianism, a traveling tent tour's ghastly array of horrors where a starving clown and an insane ballerina perform under threat of real injury and death. "Gran circo" draws from the tradition of traveling circuses described earlier in this book, but with a pointed stick: the tradition is flipped to portray the shame of a government perpetrating social violence. The bread and circuses entertaining this audience are accompanied by an unnerving collage of Milton's music, a near-Ivesian palette of contrasts underlining danger, complete with guest vocalist Fafá de Belém's soaring, cheap opera vocalese and Wagner Tiso's eerie orchestrations. Milton's final line, "A dream awaits the human circus, the heartbroken human circus," leaves the listener to the strange sonic juxtapositioning of the outro sequence: an absolutely faint, distant-sounding solo piano thoroughly out of character with the rest of the song. Was it all a dream?

After "Gran circo" gets under the skin, with its implication of a faltering civilization run amok, "Simples" inverts visual symbols of the interior's natural splendors with much the same dystopian outcome. Again, Nivaldo Ornelas's just-so virtuosity on soprano saxophone ushers in a queasy atmosphere transforming the beauty of the sun, the rivers, and the gold nuggets of Minas lore into references of corrosive corruption: "The spring waters [become] our sadness, the sun on the horizon, a wound," and the "mine's gold becomes poison." What has become of the beloved landscape of Minas, and Brazil's pastoral vision, is brought clearer with the closing line, a cry for rejuvenation in the face of state violence: "The blood on the ground becomes a toy, and that child sitting there." The words and music are both the admirable work of Nelson Ângelo, including the orchestrations he conducted for the recording session.

Although their involvement in Milton's 1978 sequel *Clube da Esquina 2* is minimal, Lô and Márcio Borges contribute the curiously sardonic "Ruas da cidade" (City streets). The song's deliberately outside-the-box chord progression, reminiscent of Lô's first solo LP *Lô Borges*, provides ironic accompaniment to the faux-civic boosterism at the heart of the text's ostensible celebration. The appropriation by city planners of regional Indian tribe names for the naming of streets crisscrossing downtown Belo Horizonte is here brought to task as part of colonialism's three hundred years of paving over indigenous societies. Now collapsed in anonymity underneath the rise of modern Minas, the collective memories of the peoples behind those names transcend the city planners' empty homage to their spirit. In "Ruas da cidade," Belo Horizonte's streets are depicted as well-trodden cemeteries, their uneasily solemn naming utterly failing to honor the rich ethnic, linguistic, and cultural histories of the indigenous peoples who once called the region home. As Márcio's lyrics state, they are "all in the ground" ("todos no chão"), reminding listeners of the Guiacurus, Caetés, Goitacazes, Tupinambás, Aimorés, Guajajaras, Tamoios, Tapuias, Timbiras, and Tupis.

The Guiacurus were forced westward from Minas during colonial times, into modern Goiás and Mato Grosso do Sul, adopting horses along the way to augment their resistance to the invading Portuguese. But such details are not the goal of "Ruas da cidade," and they would have weighed down what is certainly not a soapbox ballad of commemoration. Rather, the song's odd, playful mordancy and ironic deadpan turns the irredeemable celebration of these peoples, through the flaccid boosterism of city planners, into a questioning of those very intentions. The song jabs at the notion that street names do justice to injustice. Meanwhile, the pedestrian-sounding song takes us on a walk-through of those streets: where streetcars, cattle, and a tractor pass, where an airplane flies over "streets and kings / the city planted in the heart so many names of those who died."[59] The harmonica's melodic line, wandering in haphazardly halfway through the track, is suspiciously restless. Its out-of-place musical characteristic adds a disorienting element to this panorama of Belo Horizonte streets. Yet the attractively simple vocal lines and harmony, to which the errant harmonica is either antagonistic or oblivious, are pure pop, accompanying our sometimes ghostly visit to downtown Belo Horizonte, a walk through time and in full view of the ineffective monumentalizing of fallen civilizations. The fake banner of unification is rejected in favor of the simple conviction that too many indigenous people perished anonymously and without proper ceremony. While not dishonoring their memory, the streets of the city fail to commemorate their civilizations. The purposefully twisted echo that is "Ruas das cidades" speaks to genocide's abyss.

Clube da Esquina 2 is often referred to as an ode to Latin America; as Jairo Severiano states, it "marks the beginning of Milton's Latinization, or approximating Latin American themes."[60] Culminating the first decade of Milton's international stardom, the recording finds him collaborating with the Uruguayan folk ensemble Grupo Tacuabé, performing a song by Chilean folk singer Violeta Parra, and singing Chico Buarque and Pablo Milanes's Spanish-language "Canción por la unidad de Latino América" (Song for Latin American unity). Yet the album's very title suggests a simultaneous digging into the local and regional. *Clube da Esquina 2* stubbornly spotlights the Santa Tereza corner, the city of Belo Horizonte, and Minas Gerais, highlighting their inclusion in that rich South American landscape. While its Brazilian listeners were invited to glance beyond their borders, not to the United States or Great Britain but to their Spanish-speaking neighbors, they are also gaining entry once again to the Mineiro world.

More Regionalist Themes in the Work of Milton Nascimento, and His Return to Afro-Mineiro Heritage

Milton's song "Coisas de Minas" (Things of Minas) appeared on his formidable 1993 LP *Angelus*, which, in addition to stalwart Brazilian comrades, featured illustrious, international guest artists including singer-songwriters Peter Gabriel, James Taylor, and Jon Anderson and the jazz talents of Wayne

Shorter, Ron Carter, Jack DeJohnette, Herbie Hancock, and Pat Metheny. To the rustic timbres of Wilson Lopes's ten-string viola, "Coisas de Minas" playfully insinuates provincial stereotypes of guarded social insularity, secrecy, and unsolved mystery: "If I told what no one knows / About the people there / They would say it's a lie / It would end my career and what is left of me." The crooner from Três Pontas ends the track with: "The sun is going down, the silence lets you hear / Could it be an angel's sign, this breeze that transfigures my names?" The angel-brokered messages and environmental symbols form an idealized rural kingdom of natural wonders speaking directly to individual identity, where sunsets and magical winds envelope the self-(re)discovery of oneness with one's self.

To briefly introduce here the subject of Milton's rediscovery of certain Afro-Mineiro music, we must examine his 1982 project, *Missa dos Quilombos* (Mass for the *Quilombos*), through the Mineiro prism. Resonating with Minas Gerais's unique church tradition—its historically heightened role of Catholic lay brotherhoods, and its deep Catholic roots in general—Milton's LPs *Sentinela* (1980) and *Missa dos Quilombos* also mark the artist's collaboration with the so-called liberation theology vanguard of the Brazilian church. However, the broad intensions of these works are not directly aimed at Afro-Mineiro tradition. The 1952 founding of the Conferência Nacional dos Bispos do Brasil (CNBB; the National Conference of Brazilian Bishops) proved to be a basis for progressive social action within the church, or what became known by its loose belief system, liberation theology. One of the CNBB's founders, Archbishop Dom Hélder da Câmara (archbishop of Olinda and Recife from 1964 to 1985) arose as leader of the church in the northeast. By the early 1960s, an invigorated, politically active Catholic Left was formed, primarily around the creation of the group Ação Popular (Popular Action). Although certainly also the home of right-wing supporters of the military and vociferously anticommunist Catholic leaders, the CNBB gradually arose in opposition to the repressive crimes of the military's security apparatus and in defense of the marginalized masses and victims of torture. Following the 1964 military coup, it was not long before government security forces turned their abuses toward Brazilian clergy involved in resistance.

Both *Sentinela* and *Missa dos Quilombos* were recorded on the Ariola label, which Nascimento had chosen in order to more fully voice his socially conscious messages and political activism. In 1979, Milton read a book by Bishop Dom Pedro Casaldáliga (1928–2020, b. Spain; ordained in 1952) and traveled to the city of Goiânia to see the bishop's liberation theology–based liturgical work *Missa da terra sem males*, dedicated to Native Brazilian Indians. Subject to intense harassment and an assassination attempt by the military government, Dom Pedro nevertheless helped form a new path of progressive activism in the Brazilian Catholic Church by supporting the landless, socioeconomically marginalized populations he served. Dom Hélder was also in attendance at the Goiânia performance and suggested to Dom Pedro and Milton that they compose a Mass dedicated to the suffering of blacks, perhaps with the theme of *quilombos*. While on tour in support of the *Sentinela* album, Milton composed most of the *Missa* during 1981. Dom Pedro and poet Pedro Tierra set the Mass in eleven parts contrasting recitative, chant, song, dance, and musical numbers. In addition to those eleven parts, four songs were ultimately added: the opening "Trancados na noite" (lyrics by Pedro Tierra); "Ony saruê" (an Afro-Brazilian chant of Yoruban origin); the folkloric "Peixinhos do mar" by Tavinho Moura; and "Raça" (by Milton and Fernando Brant).

Following the premiere performance of *Missa dos Quilombos* at Recife's Praça do Carmo, the distinctive recording was completed in only two days in the French Lazarite monastery of the Santuário do Caraça, a picturesque complex situated within the confines of Parque Nacional do Caraça less than fifty kilometers southeast of Belo Horizonte.[61] The monastery was quickly transformed into a recording venue, with acoustic treatments and a tight work space for more than thirty musical and technical participants. Everyone had to meet the strict monastic codes of rising at six in the morning and observing silence throughout parts of the day and evening. Overseeing a logistically complicated recording inside this particular ritualistic site spoke to Milton's vision of the work's sacredness and authenticity. Two years earlier, Milton had arranged for Benedictine monks to sing in a remake of his powerful lamentation "Sentinela," recorded in Ipanema's Colégio Notre Dame Cathedral in Rio de Janeiro. Dom Pedro emphasized a universal message in his liner notes to the *Missa dos Quilombos* recording: "In the music of the black Mineiro, Milton and his singers and players offer to our only Lord the work, the struggles, the martyrdom of the black people from across time and from all places."[62]

The work's importance also sheds light on a crossroads of sorts: the path leading to, and the context of, the church's progressive Left during the military dictatorship, and how some aspects of racial politics of the Mineiro past flavors the *Missa*'s reception through a regional prism. Though projected onto the national stage, the work indirectly revisits the wedding of African-derived peoples and culture with the isolated, *irmandade*-based Catholicism characterizing the Afro-Mineiro past. The texts harken not a reemphasis of Black Catholicism, a label some have used for Afro-Mineiro practices of popular Catholicism, but rather an affirmation of an apology for the suffering caused by slavery and racism and a valorization of African cultural expressions. As Luíz Maciel tellingly states, the "involvement with this work allowed Milton to make a revealing trip to his African roots."[63] In an interview with *Jornal do Brasil*'s Tárik de Souza, Milton stated: "I did the eleven parts of the Mass as if rediscovering internal sensations. It touched my African side a lot. I didn't even know much about *maracatu*, samba, or Candomblé chants that were emerging." It is really to this end that the *Missa dos Quilombos* project plays such an important part in discussions of Milton's connections to the Afro-Mineiro music he would later discover.

The 1997 album *Nascimento* kicks off with a pulsating Afro-Mineiro beat in the song "Louva-a-deus" (Praying mantis), with lyrics by Fernando Brant. For his work on the album, Milton singles out Belo Horizonte–based drummer, percussionist, and producer Lincoln Cheib with a "very special thanks," crediting the go-to local musician with "research and adaptation of rhythms from Minas Gerais." The drummer brings it on this opening track, playing "pandereta" and "folia box." The former is a frame drum, not unlike a *pandeiro* but without metal jingle disks, and the latter is a *caixa* from the Folia de Reis processions of popular Catholicism (*caixa* is mistranslated as "box" in the liner notes). Milton exalts in song to the Virgin Mary: "Our Lady, I will give you my heart / Make a shrine out of me," as fierce pounding drums propel the listener to the core timbres and rhythms of a folk religion groove. Another song on the *Nascimento* album, "Os tambores de Minas" (Minas drums), gets right to the heart of the matter with Márcio Borges's lyrics: "There was one, there were two, there were three thousand drums, and the voices from beyond / Old hill, *senzala*, crowded shacks." The back narrative driving this song is the since more broadly recognized Açude community, specifically the small settlement with slavery-era roots in the Serra do Cipó region northwest of Belo Horizonte discussed in chapter 6. Here, the Minas drums are the legendary *tambu* drums pictured in that chapter, and as the song continues, they beat for the return of those who have passed, the ancestors. They once also lived in this village, and before that, in the nineteenth-century *senzalas* of the

Fazenda do Cipó just down the road, the former slave quarters still standing, next to the landowner's house, the *casa grande*. These drums will be played, Márcio writes, until the players' hands bleed; they will never go silent.[64]

"Os tambores de Minas" soon expanded into a collaborative concert project that came to fruition the following year, showcasing drumming and chant from the fragile *candombe* legacy discussed in chapter 6. Milton's take was that the epic scope of this particular vein of cultural gold could not be limited to one song. *Os tambores de Minas: Ao vivo* (1998) is the title of both a CD and a DVD based on concert presentations of Milton's freshly redirected focus on the black music of Minas Gerais. His connection with this treasured Afro-Mineiro musical legacy was aided by Belo Horizonte singer Marina Machado. In 1996, Machado initiated her own project assisting the Açude community by recording songs from their *candombe* tradition and arranging to have some of the recordings included in the CD *Cartografia musical brasileira: MG* (Musical cartography of Brazil).[65] Following up with this deep regional culture with new song ideas, Belo Horizonte writing team Flavio Henriques and Chico Amaral composed "Casa aberta" (Open house), a song later featured on Milton's 2002 CD *Pietá* that introduces members of the Açude community, matriarchs of the small settlement with roots in slavery-era Serra do Cipó: "The *tambu* drums sound in tune, within the open house / The night of the party, Geralda, Helena, and Flor dance / At the river's edge, Ramiro heard Dona Mercês play the drum."

Taking the ensemble name Candombe da Serra do Cipó, the musicians, singers, and dancers of the Açude community were invited by Milton in 2005 to participate in recordings and local, national, and international performances of a renewed Tambores de Minas project, now incorporating songs from the *Pietá* album:

Singer Milton Nascimento performed at the Arts Palace Theater in Belo Horizonte, featuring dance and music of the people of Açude. Milton joined Candombe [da Serra do Cipó] with the voice of young Mineira singer Marina Machado, who also performed on his recording *Pietá* and with whom he shared the stage in concerts in Brazil and several European countries. Besides having recorded Açude *candombe* songs on two albums, Marina also produced Candombe da Serra do Cipó's CD demo, with the voices of the people of Açude.[66]

The release of André Braga and Cardes Amâncio's award-winning 2004 film *Candombe do Açude: Arte, cultura e fé* marked a heightened awareness in Belo Horizonte of this core of tradition now being proclaimed in Milton's Clube da Esquina trajectory. The documentary spread the word of these musicians just northwest of the Mineiro capital, as the notes to the film's DVD release shared:

> Açude time is ancestral time, enshrined in the deepest Afro-Brazilian tradition. The space, too, is that same space. History accompanies each utterance, each gesture, each sign that is marked on the face of the people's struggle. Each beat of the *tambu* drum evokes the royal, warrior-like roots of the most genuine Brazilianness, brought on slave ships.

Conclusion

Let us recall from the introduction the three types of musical space that form layers of a deep regionalism among identities of place and music: the physical places of a cultural territory's geography; the historical-temporal spaces of past events and development informing communities; and the figurative spatiality of individual consciousness. Notions of regional identity and music flow from cultural territories, the past, and the interior lives of Mineiros as they perform, listen, dance, discuss, and write.

Interpreted as a set of behaviors, music represents a range of opportunities for personal experience of historical knowledge whereby elements of the past are somehow made present, and in which a dual embodiment can occur among participants who may stand as a trace of social memory or bring about within themselves mental images of historical otherness. Music helps illuminate the reality of the past. Participants in this sense include musicians, dancers, audience members, listeners, instrument makers, writers, and readers, among others, engaging in historical reckoning through music. Their calling forth of the past can be seen as acts of identity formation, of active embodiment and emplotment, accompanied by social and historical others invoked in part to reinforce their social and historical sameness or their empathetic understanding. One might say that we navigate the past's temporal distance through reenactments of our own mental design and sensibilities, informed by knowledge, memories, and feelings of meaningfulness conflating with our own identities.

Artifacts of the music and histories of Minas Gerais come in many forms, through varied experiences, and represent social divergences and confrontation as well as regional cohesiveness: the banda playing waltzes in the *coreto* of Belo Horizonte's Praça da Liberdade; a Congado praise song rising above Ouro Preto's cobblestone streets; a viola's ringing sonority slowly decaying amid the vast silence of the *mineiro sertão*; the melodies of a *música colonial* choral masterwork resonating in a small church interior gleaming with gold mined by those who sang vissungo; the calling forth of ancestral spirits through drumming and the dancing that erupts around a bonfire; the strumming of an electric guitar from a Clube da Esquina recording escaping a bedroom window into the narrow street of a small Sul de Minas town; an indigenous Brazilian's lonely chant lamenting the ongoing destruction of his world. Music is history in Minas Gerais.

This book touches on only slices of those experiences. Music is also sound, the "Hearing" of which brings about deeper understandings of others, and how we ourselves fit into the world. The Mineiro state of mind, its figurative spatiality of individual consciousness, is animated by a cultural territory's geography and the myths and legends of its historical-temporal spaces. The array of music examined here has made it difficult to reach any clear conclusion about Mineiro regional identity and music. As stated in the introduction, I selected particular musical topics to serve as inroads into historically rich strata of varied regional identities, conjured through descriptions and narratives of musical expression, and voices from pasts both near and distant. We can forget any notion of uniform attitudes about this matter, and rather consider the great variety of ways Mineiros express and sense their feelings of belonging through music.

Hearing Brazil ends with Milton Nascimento's "rediscovery" of Afro-Mineiro music, a closure meant to bring the reader full circle: from the international star of the Corner Club collective "back" to the drumming, dancing, and singing of black communities and their pasts that help define the region. How do each of these musical subjects appear in the arena of regional identity? Some of the chapters weave together themes and categorical relationships that help point to possible nodes of self-identification through music, or at least underscore broad historical solidarity. Calundú, vissungo, batuque, and Congado, for instance, constitute a strong foundation in understanding an incredibly diverse Afro-Mineiro cultural world. Although calundú violently disappeared under the weight of cultural genocide, batuque flourished among Mineiros of all colors, social backgrounds, and socio-economic standings. And as vissungo has virtually disappeared in practice, reduced to a nearly hidden legacy, Congado has grown in participation and appreciation, including by non-blacks. These studies reveal both serious racial division *and* unity, and conclusive language about this complex reality is elusive. Fallout from the human catastrophes of indigenous depopulation, colonization, and slavery, with its brutal segregation and dehumanization, still haunts Brazil, and it does so as sensitivity to that history, I feel, increases. Sacred *música colonial* relied on a heritage of racially mixed practitioners and is today a beloved, recovered part of the lives of many Mineiros, as the colonial past still contributes to the Mineiro experience. The living memory of architecture, of the dominance of the church, harken to the eighteenth-century origins of what any visitor sees here in the *cidades históricas*, with quaint neighborhoods and quiet cobblestone streets. The voices and instruments of the *barroco mineiro* transform these locales, in their contemporary realities, as they steadfastly maintain Golden Age music traditions, the breadth of which was rediscovered in earnest a mere eighty years ago. Only a large-scale musicological project could have reintroduced some of this regionally definitive music back into towns and cities, and indeed patience, sweat, and tears in archives both dusty and state-of-the-art have resulted in performance editions of the region's polished gold, its *música colonial* classics.

Discussion of Minas Gerais as a vast cultural territory has necessitated an examination of the viola, an instrument whose iconic presence today elicits the "Rural Dreams and Urban Realities" of chapter 7's subtitle. Indeed, the viola is found in Congado and Clube da Esquina, the concert hall and the marketplace *roda*, as it occupies a wide range of social niches: from its folkloric role in the settling of the region by coastal Brazilians and the Portuguese during an epic gold rush, to its place in locations both impoverished, such as the isolated hamlets of the *sertão*, and elite, such as the comfortably chic urban salons of the illustriously wealthy. Perhaps the very feeling of forgottenness paradoxically reminds Brazilians of this arc of history. That definitive rural/urban dichotomy, still developing, overlaps with chapter 8 on Belo Horizonte, where narratives of *violeiros*, luthiers, and collectors of an instrument regarded as a cultural treasure are enveloped by other musical landscapes, their modes of understanding place, and their sprawling, changing realities. Those contrasts sit waiting for Mineiros every day, where musical legacies navigate change, the kaleidoscopic whirlwind of contemporary life, technological progress, and social development. And this itself is not new. As we have seen, beginning in the 1960s, members of the Corner Club collective made use of a great many musical styles and references in their expressions of home, in their songs about Belo Horizonte and Minas Gerais, and in their perspectives on Brazil and the world. To Milton Nascimento and his many local collaborators, a sense of universalism grew unabashedly from Mineiro roots.

During my thirty-one years of Minas Gerais experiences, these histories as I have interpreted and researched them, and the musical forms and their sound worlds, their communities, instruments, and festivals, have guided me toward deeper understandings of Minas as a cultural territory that contrasts with the rest of Brazil in obvious and subtle ways. From my outsider's point of view, the region's joys and complexities, its tragedies, contradictions, and diverse depth of beauty, frequently resonate with a music all their own.

Appendix 1

The Música do Brasil Colonial series is published jointly by the Inconfidência Museum of Ouro Preto and the University of São Paulo Press.

Volume 1 (Régis Duprat, ed., 1994)

1. *Antífona* (*Regina caeli laetare*), José Joaquim Emerico Lobo de Mesquita (b. Serro, 1746?–1805)
2. *Responsório de Santo Antônio* (*Si quaeris miracula*), José Joaquim Emerico Lobo de Mesquita
3. *Gradual para Domingo da Ressurreição*, José Joaquim Emerico Lobo de Mesquita
4. *Ladainha em Ré*, Marcos Coelho Neto (b. Ouro Preto, 1740–1806)

Volume 2 (Régis Duprat, ed., 1999)

1. *Ladainha em Fá*, José Joaquim Emerico Lobo de Mesquita
2. *Gradual Christus factus est, para 5ª feira Santa*, José Joaquim Emerico Lobo de Mesquita
3. *Spiritus Domini*, Francisco Gomes da Rocha (b. Ouro Preto, 1746?–1808)
4. *Antífona Salve Regina*, Marcos Coelho Neto (the son, d. 1823)

5. *Antífona Crucem Tuam*, attributed to Marcos Coelho Neto
6. *Stabat Mater*, João de Deus de Castro Lobo (b. Ouro Preto, 1794–1832)
7. *Moteto O Vere Christe*, José Joaquim da Paixão (flourished early nine-teenth century)

Most of the works from volumes 1 and 2 were recorded by the Brasilessentia Voice and Orchestra Group, directed by Vitor Gabriel, and released on the CD *Música do Brasil colonial: Compositores mineiros* (Paulus, 1997).

Volume 3 (Régis Duprat, ed., 2004)

1. *Antífona Hosanna filio David, para Domingo de Ramos*, Antônio Martiniano da Silva Benfica (b. Aiuruoca, MG, 184?–1905)
2. *Inventório Admirabile* and *Hino Jesu Rex, para o Nome de Jesus*, Alberto Fernandes de Azevedo (active in Serro and Diamantina, end of eighteenth to early nineteenth centuries)
3. *Gradual Haec dies, para Domingo da Ressurreição*, Francisco Gomes da Rocha
4. *Marcha in G*, Francisco Gomes da Rocha
5. *Adoração da Cruz para Sexta-feira Santa*, anonymous
6. *Antífona O Beata Anna, para festas de Santa Ana*, anonymous
7. *Antífona Domine tu mihi* and *Hino Vexilla regis para Semana Santa*, anonymous
8. *Antífona Regina caeli, para festas de Nossa Senhora*, anonymous
9. *Lição VII, De Epistola beati Pauli . . . festinemus, para Ofício de Sexta-feira Santa ad matutinum*, anonymous
10. *Ofertório Beata es, para Missa de Nossa Senhora*, anonymous
11. *Ofertório Sacerdotes Domini, para Missa de Corpus Christi*, anonymous

Volume 4 (Mary Angela Biason, ed., 2015)

1. *Quando na Verde Campina* (modinha), anonymous
2. *Cupido Tu És Travesso* (lundu), anonymous
3. *Romântico* (lundu), anonymous
4. *Oh! Que Tormentos Eu Sofro* (modinha), anonymous

5. *Triste Lembrança* (modinha), Lucindo Pereira dos Passos (b. Minas Gerais, 1820–1891)

6. *A Saudade me Devora* (modinha), Manoel Severo Pires de Figueiredo Netto (b. Diamantina, 1825–1893)

7. *Entre os Tormentos* (modinha), Manoel Severo Pires de Figueiredo Netto

8. *Fui ao Templo de Cupido* (modinha), Manoel Severo Pires de Figueiredo Netto

9. *Se o Trácio, Cantor Sublime* (modinha), Manoel Severo Pires de Figueiredo Netto

10. *Viva Saudade* (modinha), Manoel Severo Pires de Figueiredo Netto

11. *Sobre um Rochedo* (modinha), anonymous

12. *Esta Minha Jovem Lilia* (modinha), anonymous

13. *Eu tenho o Peito Magoado* (modinha), Lucindo Pereira dos Passos

14. *Cativadora* (modinha), anonymous

15. *Tu És o Lírio* (modinha), anonymous

16. *A Mulata* (lundu), Xisto Bahia

17. *Hino da Independência do Brasil*, Dom Pedro I

18. *Contradança*, anonymous

19. *Valsa*, anonymous

20. *Ó Mulher se Tu me Adoras* (modinha), Vicente Ferreira do Espirito Santo (b. Ouro Preto, 1847–1911)

21. *Violeta* (polka), Justino da Conceição (b. Ouro Preto, 1875–1951)

22. *Amizade* (waltz), Justino da Conceição

23. *Uma Intriga* (waltz), anonymous

24. *Os Senhores Estudantes* (waltz), Manoel José Gomes (1792–1868, father of composer Antônio Carlos Gomes)

25. *Variações para Flauta e Cordas*, José Felipe Corrêa Lisboa (b. Mariana, 1770–1841)

26. *O Canto do Sabiá* (contradance), José Felipe Corrêa Lisboa

Appendix 2

Luso-African Roots of Congado Mineiro Heritage

Black Catholicism and the Brotherhood of the Rosary

Early thirteenth-century Catholic legend tells of an apparition of the Virgin Mary witnessed by Saint Dominic whereby the sacred rosary was subsequently adopted as a ritualized method and object of devotion, as a popular substitution for elaborate Liturgy. Nossa Senhora do Rosário (Our Lady of the Rosary) is the name attributed to this Marian apparition, and promotion of rosary bead devotion led to the establishment as early as 1475 of a confraternity dedicated to her devotional worship. The image of the Virgin Mary accompanied Portuguese forces in the Reconquista against the Moors and was used by European Christianity in militarized Crusades (1190s–1270s). Our Lady of the Rosary grew increasingly symbolic of Portugal's imperial designs, beginning with fifteenth-century maritime exploration and colonial expansion in Africa, Southeast Asia, India, the Far East, and the Americas.[1] The Virgin Mary was ceremoniously crowned mother queen of Catholicism's celestial court during the Council of Trent (1545–1563), forming the basis of the Festa do Reinado de Nossa Senhora do Rosário (Feast of the Reign of Our Lady of the Rosary), celebrated annually thereafter on the first Sunday of October in the church calendar. The 1571 victory of Christian states over the Ottoman navy at the Battle of Lepanto was attributed to her by the church.

Open to all without regard to race or social class, the brotherhood of Our Lady of the Rosary had already attracted those of low social standing. In Portugal, the brotherhood developed new associations with blacks and slaves. In a 1494 royal letter, King Dom João II of Portugal, "speaking highly of the spiritual works of the black brothers . . . forbade that the fraternity be taken away from their control, as was threatened."[2] By 1496, Lisbon's brotherhood had split along racial lines, with blacks forming their own group and retaining limited self-governing powers.[3]

In various African cultures, beads have long been held as sacred objects with magical and medicinal power, as highly valued adornments, and as symbols of wealth, often used as currency. The earliest Portuguese trade in West and Central Africa, beginning in the middle of the fifteenth century, incorporated European-made glass beads as trade and purchase currency based on Africa's broad use and varied cultural recognition of beads, shells, and amulets. Catholic rosary beads, and the iconic images of a crowned mother of the spiritual persona of the child Christ, may have resonated with manifestations of Ifá for some enslaved West Africans. Ifá represents the sacred liturgy, the word of Oludumare (supreme *orixá*) encompassing knowledge and wisdom, a system of divination, guidance, and principles of living, and a stand-in name for some *orixás*. Beaded bracelets (*ide*) adorned the wrists of *babalawo*, West African priests of a brotherhood dedicated to the Ifá spirit world, where beaded necklaces were worn as medicinal objects.[4] Laura de Mello e Souza suggests that Congolese Angolan slaves associated Catholic rosary beads with sacred Central African *minkisi* objects of Bakongo cosmology, influential within the general Bantu galaxy of beliefs and practices.[5] Likewise, recognition of the Yoruban *orixá* Yemanjá, the goddess of the sea, may have also crossed over into the symbolism of the white Virgin Mary rising from the waters, as the African deity in Brazil came to be identified by some believers in syncretic sects with the virgin mother.[6] In Congolese Bakongo cosmology, waters separate worlds of the living and the dead, suggesting the translation of the Virgin Mary into a heavenly figure at the gateway of the afterlife and the world of ancestral spirits. Although her whiteness may also have signified a spirit from the land of the dead, "Holy mother" translated to Kikongo as *ngudi a nkisi*, close to "a source of magic."[7] Today, Afro-Mineiro *congadeiros* descend from the brotherhood institution and wear the rosary as a ritualistic part of the Reinado. Their rosaries are often fashioned out of seeds of the *lágrimas de Nossa Senhora* plant (Our

Lady's tears). Also in contemporary Minas Gerais, Our Lady of the Rosary is enveloped in maritime and oceanic scenarios as part of a key origin myth of Congado, depicting her rising from the sea to be rescued by the sounds of black musicians and dancers.

English explorer and diplomat Richard Burton, writing of the Afro-Brazilian material culture he encountered in mid-nineteenth-century Rio de Janeiro and Minas Gerais, noted some blacks' high regard for the rosary, marking a similarity to the *popo* beads of West Africa used as currency and worn as finery.[8] In Brazil's culturally hybrid, pan-African world, where some Africans were already touched by missionary Catholicism and religious conversion, new beliefs developed around ritual objects and other facets of religious practice such as dance, costuming, song, and the music of communal devotional processions. Many enslaved Central Africans had been widely exposed to, or had converted to, Catholicism in their African homeland. Vital were the important roles of African-derived music, dance, language, and costume as festive pastimes associated with the brotherhood of Our Lady of the Rosary, including the election of a king. In the Congo, music played a significant, sacred role in ritualized ceremonies involving the king. Interpreting an account of Pedro II Nkanga a Mvika's 1622 coronation as king of Congo, Georges Balandier notes iron bells and the decorated *ngoma* drum's ritualized use, restricted to monarchic events:

[This place that was] even more sacred, bore the great drum known as both *simbu* and *busto*, which represented the royalty in its coercive and violent aspect. This drum embodied absolute power. It rested on a piece of ornate cloth, protected from the earth as the king himself had to be. It was [trimmed] with silken and gold embroidery to which teeth had been fastened. Near the drum, during the coronation, three men each held [iron bells]. . . . They strike them together, producing a sound similar to the one the blacksmith makes when he brings the hammer down on the anvil. They call this *zimie* (*zima*, to strike); it is the oldest royal symbol, and only the king and the duke of Batta may use it.[9]

In 1491, King Nzinga Nkuwu of the Congo converted to Christianity, renaming himself Dom João I. Churches dedicated to Our Lady of the Rosary were constructed in the Congo, and by the early seventeenth century, the Congolese royal family became prominent members of such a house of worship in São Salvador.[10] The Portuguese royal court, quick to use the conversion of the Congolese king as political cache and a boastful point of pride with the pope, sought to further Lisbon's already considerable favor with Rome in terms of commercial status, privilege, and monopolies. In recognizing the king of Congo, and by attempting to organize an actual Congolese embassy delegation to visit the pope, the Portuguese indirectly elevated the status of Congolese slaves, language, and culture within growing slave communities in Lisbon and other cities, and within the greater Luso-African world dominated by market slavers. The crowning ceremony, and the appointment of ambassadors, dramatized the factual historical diplomacy that occurred between Christian and non-Christian powers. Regardless of how, or what, Africans thought of these concepts, images, and practices of the brotherhood of the rosary and Catholicism in general, some blacks in Lisbon publicly manifested a new "Black Catholic" tradition before Europeans first traveled to the Americas.[11]

The 1575 founding of the trade fort in Luanda by the first Portuguese colonial governor of the region, Paulo Dias de Novais, was marked by a formal state reception by a Mbundu delegation of dignitaries. Here, the account of musical accompaniment to diplomatic events surrounding Novais's first visit illustrates the association of ambassadorial pomp and its place in Congado celebrations:

> The ambassador and his company were then brought in. Revered and personable . . . surrounded by a terrible noise made by earth's instruments (*cabaça* with pebbles, elephant tusk trumpet, one *ingoma* drum, sort of *alcantara* (bridge?), a bell, together with two rattles, a viola, and a snare-like buzzer), the *mogunge* (Mbundu ambassador), seeing the governor (Novais) from a distance, began to make great *sequirilas* (beats), clapping hands and playing instruments.[12]

In Lisbon's São Domingos de Lisboa Church, an altar for Our Lady of the Rosary dating to 1505 was central to the first documented coronation of an *irmandade's* black king.[13] In 1563, "the *corregador* of Colares—about 25 kilometers northwest of Lisbon, broke up a *festa dos negros* where the blacks had elected a king."[14] The Crown likely allowed, if not encouraged, black participation in official ceremonies as a means to display Portuguese colonial domination of foreign lands: the exoticism of the spectacle in the eyes of white Europe was proof of successful commercial, diplomatic, and evangelical relations abroad.[15] Lisbon's "proto-Congado" event celebrated simultaneously the high status allotted to the Kingdom of Congo within Portuguese colonial culture, though substituting a priest for the traditional Congolese religious presence of the Mani Vunda spiritual leader. Blacks began to organize their own public election spectacles, theatrical, dramatic dances, and processionals with music, dance, and praise songs. Elections of an "African king" became an important Luso-Brazilian musical celebration linked to the psychological organization and structures of everyday lives.[16] The brotherhoods had developed into important social institutions that also generated contexts for Congado. As A. C. de C. M. Saunders states:

> The blacks [in Lisbon] accordingly came to form a community of their own, speaking a distinct language (a hybrid form of Portuguese) and retaining African cultural traditions: even when they celebrated Christian festivals they did so with African songs and dances. After manumission, the freed blacks' poverty, occupations and experience of legal discrimination tended to approximate them to slaves, and the freed blacks of the religious confraternity of the Rosary came to provide leadership for the black community as a whole. The brothers not only promoted the interests of freedmen but also strove to facilitate the manumission of slaves.[17]

The first documented inclusion of an "ambassadors" plot (*embaixadores*) in a Reinado occurred not in Lisbon but in Recife, Brazil, in 1642.[18] This ritual was strongly echoed in eighteenth- and nineteenth-century Minas Gerais but arguably transformed into a liberating context by virtue of the region's banishment of the church's first-order hierarchy and comparatively autonomous Afro-Mineiro communities. The Congolese king, his ambassadors, and the heightened drama of diplomatic missions and military conquests of pagan nations were defining elements of Portuguese power, and they remain highly symbolic metaphors in contemporary Congado Mineiro. Alfredo Rabaçal outlines four leading Congado motifs found throughout Brazil: Christians defeating the Moors; the Charlemagne tales; battles between the king of Congo and Queen Ginga (Nzinga Mbandi, the queen of Angola who successfully resisted Portuguese troops); and both warring and peaceful dispatches of embassies to foreign countries.[19] Seventeenth-century Angolan wars of resistance headed by Queen Ginga against the Portuguese prompted the widespread inclusion of her legend in Congado narrative plots in Brazil. Kalle Kananoja notes the importance of brotherhoods of the Rosary in seventeenth-century Angola, with a presence in Luanda (founded soon after Queen Ginga's demise, in 1628) and Massangano.[20]

In the seventeenth-century, Atlantic creole Christianity expanded in Angola, bringing about a broad cultural base of so-called Black Catholicism at the dawn of the first gold discoveries in Minas Gerais. Kananoja comments:

> According to [António de Oliveira de] Cadornega, the [seventeenth-century] church of Luanda's black rosary brotherhood was well ornamented, with a frontal, pulpit, and vestry. Besides the image of the Virgin, the images of Saint Benedict of Nursia and Saint Dominic had been placed on the altars. A special place had been reserved for Saint Benedict the Moor. Because of his origin—his parents were black slaves from Africa living in Sicily—Saint Benedict received a dedicated following among Central Africans. . . . There was also a black rosary brotherhood in the village, which congregated three times a week to pray the rosary. By the late seventeenth century, churches dedicated to Our Lady of the Rosary had also been established in Cambambe and Presídio das Pedras. In 1693 [the year gold was discovered in Minas Gerais], a governor's report described that Luanda's rosary brotherhood was served by a chaplain paid by them, who officiated their feasts and masses on Saturdays, Sundays, and Saints' Days.[21]

Wracked by civil wars following Portuguese intrusion, the Kingdom of Congo suffered mightily from colonial trade and slavery, with the grandeur of its legacy and political autonomy compromised and forced into decline. The Antonian Movement of 1684–1706 was a radicalized black African effort led by Dona Beatriz Kimpa Vita (1684–1706) to rewrite a Christian hagiography incorporating black Africans as founders of the Catholic Church.[22] Dona Beatriz's struggle was equally one for political reunification, with a goal to restore the court of the King of Congo. The movement failed: Dona Beatriz was burned at the stake as a heretic in 1706, and a large number of her followers were enslaved and shipped to the New World between 1707 and 1715. In Brazil, the primary destination of these enslaved Congolese of Catholic orientation was Minas Gerais in the first decades following the gold discoveries.

By the 1730s, enslaved Central Africans swelled the ranks of rosary brotherhoods in Minas Gerais. The trail of forced labor to the gold mines also came through Bahia, from where blacks probably brought the Reinado to Minas. The earliest documented date for an election in Bahia is 1729.[23] John Thornton notes the influence of Catholicism among enslaved Congolese in Brazil:

> The Kongolese brought their language and their culture with them, but most notably and particularly, their Catholic faith. In the 1720s, when they began arriving in large numbers, quite a few may have had contact with the Antonian movement, if not its specifics. It is no wonder that they might have chosen to express their consternation at their enslavement in this strange land in religious terms.[24]

Marina de Mello e Souza found strong cultural and historical ties between Congolese culture and the Brazilian Reinado tradition:

> The coronations of the King of Congo connects the Christianization of the King of Congo at the end of the 15th century to the symbolic space that the Congo occupied in Central West Africa, both for Africans and for Portuguese, to the particular characteristics of the transatlantic slave trade and its descendants in Portuguese America, to the type of Catholicism practiced here [Brazil], and to the relations among the communities and slave-owning society. Having in the [Reinado] festival the moment of maximum visibility, those elections of kings expressed values and world views through the ritual ambient and the symbols utilized.[25]

Mello e Souza continues, noting nineteenth-century descriptions:

> The coronation of the King of Congo in Brazil, mainly as recorded in the 19th century, annually recollected the foundation myth of some black Catholic communities, in which the ancestral Africa was invoked in its Christianized version represented by the King of Congo. . . . Generally stemming from the lay brotherhoods, the communities that performed the *festa* assumed European forms of organization to manifest their own cultural values, permeated by African elements.[26]

As Elizabeth Kiddy suggests regarding colonial-era Mineiro society and the tight web formed by African religion, cosmology, and a broad range of sociocultural sensibilities and practices, the more interesting questions [concerning Congado] reside not in examining the syncretism between African "religions" and Christianity but rather in how the organization of society, the power structure that included the living as well as unseen forces, spirits, and ancestors, was reoriented as it came into contact with Christianity as expressed both in the lay brotherhood organizations and in colonial Mineiro society.[27]

Importantly, Afro-Mineiros also kept many of their non-Christian beliefs, modes of worship, and African cultural memories, with music a primary vehicle for most religious experiences, leading Núbia Pereira de Magalhães Gomes and Edimilson de Almeida Pereira to state that in Minas Gerais, "*irmandade*-based Catholicism produced for blacks a resistance that mythically engaged defenses, while only in outer appearances did African memory seem to disappear."[28] As Kananoja states:

> The [confraternity] celebrations in Minas Gerais also exhibited syncretistic tendencies early on, as ecclesiastical visitors to Cachoeira do Campo heard from several witnesses in August 1738. Although not directly citing brotherhoods as hotbeds of syncretism, the denunciations reveal the extent to which blacks interacted with some segments of the secular clergy in creating new norms of religious practice.[29]

Civil and church authorities in colonial Minas, and subsequently the empire's policies toward the nineteenth-century province, had inherited "Africanized" festivities of the Congado, allowing them to flourish. Notions of monarchic values, and the iconic power of the "king" in the Congado legacy, were only bolstered by the presence of the Portuguese court in Rio de Janeiro, which, during its relocation to Brazil, founded the United Kingdom of Portugal, Brazil, and the Algarves in 1815, dissolving it in 1822 upon the court's return to Lisbon.

Kiddy contrasts Minas Gerais, with its tradition of brotherhood-based rosary festivals and kings of Congo, with other Brazilian regions in terms of the Afro-Mineiro response to the conservative backlash of the Old Republic, and to the Vatican's rejection of Black Catholicism's profane activities:

> The Afro-Mineiro population took a different route, and in some ways a middle route, by continuing with its rosary festivals, which had long been

based on a Euro-Brazilian structure—the brotherhoods—with content that was a distinct mix of African and European traditions. The festivals, which had already become part of local custom, became one of the main expressions of Afro-Brazilian culture in the state. Changes in the church, however, were beginning to lay the groundwork for significant alterations in the brotherhood structure, especially in regard to the associations' relationship with the church, that would become manifest after 1930.[30]

The rise of the Old Republic threw church-state relations on their head with the disestablishment doctrine, the separation of church and state leading to a "secularization" and modernization of the Brazilian state, and subsequently the so-called Romanization of the Brazilian church. The church, while once relying on this partnership with the state, was forced to follow the Vatican's ultramontane, Romanizing movement, which favored greater absolute supremacy of papal order over national or diocesan authority throughout the Roman Catholic Church. In Minas at the dawn of the twentieth century, black brotherhoods were soon seen by conservative Catholics as "perniciously independent and rife with questionable practices," in which local conditions had resulted in vernacular permutations resignifying doctrine and orthodoxy.[31] At that time, the Catholic Church in Minas was stronger than ever, headed by Dom Silvério Gomes Pimenta (1840–1922), the mixed-race archbishop of Mariana and agent of Vatican decrees. Rome created three archbishoprics and nine new bishoprics in Minas between 1906 and 1924.

In 1935, national church leader Cardinal Sebastião Leme da Silveira Cintra founded Catholic Action, a newly invigorated nationwide movement embraced by Getúlio Vargas, president of the republic from 1930 to 1937 and then dictator from 1937 to 1945. In 1944, Belo Horizonte archbishop Dom Antônio dos Santos Cabral helped pen the archdiocese's first synod constitution, which called for combating and eliminating perceived festival abuses such as the dances of the Reinados. In the face of legal threats and oppressive police actions, Congado groups in Minas ended their processions for much of the 1940s. Today, the tradition flourishes in Minas Gerais, following a steady growth in acceptance since the late 1950s.

Notes

Chapter 1: Introduction

1. Jonathon Grasse, "Deep Regionalism and Music in Minas Gerais, Brazil," in *Musical Spaces: Place, Performance, and Power*, ed. James Williams and Samuel Horlor (Singapore: Jenny Stanford, 2021).

2. Robert Tombs, *The English and Their History* (New York: Vintage Books, 2014), 3.

3. Iris Marion Young, *Justice and the Politics of Difference* (Princeton, NJ: Princeton University Press, 1990).

4. Auguste de Saint-Hilaire, cited in Lady Isabel Burton, *The Romance of Isabel Lady Burton: The Story of Her Life* (New York: Dodd, Mead and Company, 1904), 271.

5. Eduardo das Neves (1874–1919) was one of Brazil's most beloved troubadour performers, championing a variety of popular music and performing in serenading groups (*serestas*) and traveling circuses.

6. Marcos A. Marcondes, ed., *Enciclopédia da música brasileira: Popular, erudita e folclórica*, 2nd ed. (São Paulo: Art Editora/Publifolha, 1998), 130. The singer known as Cadete (b. Manuel Evéncio da Costa Moreira, 1874–1960) was one of the first Brazilians to record on metal cylinders, in the late 1890s, and frequently joined Eduardo das Neves and composer Heitor Villa-Lobos in one of Rio de Janeiro's most memorable turn-of-the-century serenading groups.

7. "Tuas terras que são altaneiras / O seu céu é do puro anil / És bonita oh terra mineira / Esperança do nosso Brasil."

8. Márcio Borges, "O Clube da Esquina," in *Do Samba-canção à Tropicália*, ed. Paulo Sérgio Duarte and Santuza Cambraia Naves (Rio de Janeiro: Relume Dumará, 2003), 173.

9. "Eu sou da América do Sul ... Sou de ouro, eu sou vocês, sou do mundo, sou Minas Gerais."

10. Libério Neves, *Santa Tereza* (Belo Horizonte: Conceito, 2010), 49.

11. Cited in Michel Nicolau Netto, *Música brasileira e identidade nacional na mundialização* (São Paulo: Annablume, 2009), 12.

12. Netto, *Música brasileira*, 92–93.

13. Stanley E. Blake, *The Vigorous Core of Our Nationality: Race and Regional Identity in Northeastern Brazil* (Pittsburgh: University of Pittsburgh Press, 2011), 225–26.

14. Rosângela Pereira de Tugny and Ruben Caixeta de Queiroz, eds., *Músicas, africanas e indígenas no Brasil* (Belo Horizonte: Editora UFMG, 2006).

15. In 1999, UNESCO declared some of the larger remaining fragments of the Mata Atlântica as World Heritage Sites, none of which are in Minas Gerais. These include the Atlantic Forest Southeast Reserves in Paraná, São Paulo, and Rio de Janeiro States, and the Discovery Coast of Bahia and Espírito Santo.

16. The estimated total population of Minas Gerais following the gold-rush period grew as follows: 1776, 341,769; 1786, 393,788; 1808, 433,049; and 1821, 580,786. Hal Langfur, *The Forbidden Lands: Colonial Identity, Frontier Violence, and the Persistence of Brazil's Eastern Indians, 1750–1830* (Stanford, CA: Stanford University Press, 2006), 131.

17. C. R. Boxer, *The Golden Age of Brazil, 1695–1750* (Berkeley: University of California Press, 1962), 69.

18. Warren Dean, cited in Mário Lara, *Família, história e poder no Campo das Vertantes* (self-published, 2012), 84.

19. Laura de Mello e Souza, *Norma e conflito: Aspectos da história de Minas no século XVIII* (Belo Horizonte: Editora UFMG, 2006), 155.

20. Rafael de Bivar Marquese, "A dinâmica da escravidão no Brasil: Resistência escrava, tráfico negreiro e alforrias, séculos XVII a XIX," *Novos Estudos CEBRAP*, no. 74 (March 2006): 116.

21. Caio César Boschi, *Os leigos e o poder* (São Paulo: Editora Ática, 1986), 156. Note that "New Christian" was a legal category facilitating anti-Semitic and anti-Muslim purges, applied to those Muslim Moors, and Bene Israel and Sephardic Jews, who converted to Catholicism after the Spanish and Portuguese "Reconquest" of Iberia.

22. A. J. R. Russell-Wood, *The Black Man in Slavery and Freedom in Colonial Brazil* (Basingstoke, Hants., England: Palgrave Macmillan, 1982), 31.

23. Kenneth Maxwell, *Conflicts and Conspiracies: Brazil and Portugal, 1750–1808* (New York: Routledge, 2004), 91–92.

24. The indicated years listed below are followed by the estimated total population of Minas Gerais, the percentage of black slaves, and the percentage of all persons of color (cited in Langfur, *The Forbidden Lands*, 131): 1776: 341,769 total, 139,348 enslaved blacks (40.8%), 265,969 total persons of color (77.8%); 1786: 393,788, 166,840 (42.4%), 322,788 (81.9%); 1808: 433,049, 133,035 (30.7%), 326,365 (75.4%); and 1821: 580,786, 153,801 (26.5%), 418,986 (72.1%).

25. Alcide d'Orbigny, *Viagem pitoresca através do Brasil* (Belo Horizonte: Editora Itatiaia, 1976), 146.

26. Maxwell, *Conflicts and Conspiracies*, 63 and passim.

27. Maxwell, *Conflicts and Conspiracies*, 84.

28. Zanoni Neves, *Navegantes da integração: Os remeiros do Rio São Francisco*, 2nd ed. (Belo Horizonte: Editora UFMG, 2011), 25–26.

29. John D. Wirth, *Minas Gerais in the Brazilian Federation, 1889–1937* (Stanford, CA: Stanford University Press, 1977), 68–73.

30. Wirth, *Minas Gerais in the Brazilian Federation*, 65.

31. Caio César Boschi, "Convicções e coerências de um cultor de Clio," in *Diogo de Vasconcelos: O ofício do historiador*, ed. Adriana Romeiro and Marco Antonio Silveira (Belo Horizonte: Autêntica, 2014), 12.

32. Marco Antonio Silveira, "Diogo Vasconcelos e os demônios," in *Diogo de Vasconcelos: O ofício do historiador*, ed. Adriana Romeiro and Marco Antonio Silveira (Belo Horizonte: Autêntica, 2014), 143–44.

33. João Camilo de Oliveira Torres, *O homem e a montanha: Introdução ao estudo das influências da situação geográfica para a formação do espírito Mineiro* (1943; Belo Horizonte: Autêntica, 2011), 150.

34. Torres, *O homem e a montanha*, 149.

35. Torres, *O homem e a montanha*, 131.

36. Twentieth-century authors associated with *mineiridade* include Sylvio Vasconcelos, Alceu Lima, Antonio Cândido, and Fernando Dias.

37. Michael Mitchell, "Miguel Reale and the Impact of Conservative Modernization on Brazilian Race Relations," in *Racial Politics in Contemporary Brazil*, ed. Michael Hanchard (Durham, NC: Duke University Press, 1999), 117.

38. Andrea Schiavio, "Music in (En)Action: Sense-Making and Neurophenomenology of Musical Experience," PhD thesis, University of Sheffield, 2014, 9–10.

39. Alex Lawrey, "Putting the Psycho in Psychogeography: Tom Vague's Musical Mapping of Notting Hill," in *Sites of Popular Music Heritage: Memories, Histories, Places*, ed. Sara Cohen, Robert Knifton, Marion Leonard, and Les Roberts (New York: Routledge, 2015), 209.

40. Alessandra Ciucci, "'The Text Must Remain the Same': History, Collective Memory, and Sung Poetry in Morocco," *Ethnomusicology* 56, no. 3 (Fall 2012): 480.

41. Nancy Guy, "Flowing Down Taiwan's Tamsui River: Towards an Ecomusicology of the Environmental Imagination," *Ethnomusicology* 53, no. 2 (Spring–Summer 2009): 219.

42. Thomas Solomon, "Dueling Landscapes: Singing Places and Identities in Highland Bolivia," *Ethnomusicology* 44, no. 2 (Spring–Summer 2000): 275.

43. David M. Kaplan, *Ricoeur's Critical Theory* (Albany: State University of New York Press, 2003), 52–53.

44. Anna Schultz, "Hindu Nationalism, Music, and Embodiment in Marathi *Rāshṭrīya Kīrtan*," *Ethnomusicology* 46, no. 2 (Spring–Summer 2002), 307–22.

45. Schultz, "Hindu Nationalism, Music, and Embodiment."

46. Schultz, "Hindu Nationalism, Music, and Embodiment," 317.

47. Fiona Magowan and Louise Wrazen, eds., *Performing Gender, Place, and Emotion in Music: Global Perspectives* (Rochester, NY: University of Rochester Press, 2013), 6.

48. Lillie S. Gordon, review of *Performing Gender, Place, and Emotion in Music: Global Perspectives*, edited by Fiona Magowan and Louise Wrazen, *Ethnomusicology* 59, no. 3 (Fall 2015): 486.

49. Chris Gibson and Peter Dunbar-Hall, "Nitmiluk: Place and Empowerment in Australian Aboriginal Popular Music," *Ethnomusicology* 44, no. 1 (Winter 2000): 48.

50. Musical embodiment offers an opportunity to become part of who we are by fulfilling the expectations of others. A common usage of the term *embody* implies an individual's fulfillment of a heightened role, to meet the expectations for a full-fledged member of a social

group or even to represent/symbolize a region by metaphorically embodying its characteristics. Participants may be empowered to achieve some realized degree of idealization of values. For the social individual, this leads to a strengthened sense of belonging and identity. Through the embodiment of collective ideals, music behaviors are a means to perform identity.

51. Paul Ricoeur, *Memory, History, Forgetting*, trans. Kathleen Blamey and David Pellauer (Chicago: University of Chicago Press, 2004), 121.

52. Timothy Rice, "Time, Place, and Metaphor in Musical Experience and Ethnography," *Ethnomusicology* 47, no. 2 (Spring–Summer 2003): 161. Rice presents location, time, and musical metaphors as axes in his three-dimensional model of subject-centered musical ethnography.

53. Ricoeur, *Memory, History, Forgetting*, 227–28.

54. Neil Brenner and Stuart Elden, "Henri Lefebvre on State, Space, Territory," *International Political Sociology* 3, no. 4 (December 2009): 355.

55. Edward Soja, "Borders Unbound: Globalization, Regionalism, and the Postmetropolitan Transition," in *B/ordering Space*, ed. Henk Van Houtum, Olivier Kramsch, and Wolfgang Zierhofer (London: Ashgate Publishing, 2005), 33.

56. Elisa Larkin Nascimento, *The Sorcery of Color: Identity, Race, and Gender in Brazil* (Philadelphia: Temple University Press, 2007), 18.

57. Edwin E. Telles, *Race in Another America: The Significance of Skin Color in Brazil* (Princeton, NJ: Princeton University Press, 2004), 8, 12.

Chapter 2: *Calundú*: "Winds of Divination"

1. Donald Ramos, "A influência africana e a cultura popular em Minas Gerais: Um comentário sobre a interpretação da escravidão," in *Brasil: Colonização e escravidão*, ed. Maria Beatriz Nizza da Silva (Rio de Janeiro: Editora Nova Fronteira, 2000), 145.

2. Daniela Buono Calainho, *Metrópole das Mandingas* (Toronto: Garamond, 2008), 90.

3. James H. Sweet, *Recreating Africa: Culture, Kinship, and Religion in the African-Portuguese World, 1441–1770* (Chapel Hill: University of North Carolina Press, 2003), 7, 115, 151.

4. Kalle Kananoja, *Central African Identities and Religiosity in Colonial Minas Gerais* (Turku, Finland: Åbo Akademi University, 2012), 17–22.

5. José Jorge de Carvalho, "Black Music of All Colors: The Construction of Black Ethnicity in Ritual and Popular Genres of Afro-Brazilian Music," in *Music and Black Ethnicity: The Caribbean and South America*, ed. Gerard H. Béhague (New Brunswick, NJ: Transaction Publishers, 1994), 188.

6. Steven Eric Byrd, "Calunga, an Afro-Brazilian Speech of the Triângulo Mineiro: Its Grammar and History," PhD diss., University of Texas, 2005. Regarding the cultural and religious power of secretive, African-derived languages in Brazil more generally, see also Carlos Vogt and Peter Fry, *Cafundó: A África no Brasil* (São Paulo: Companhia das Letras, 1996).

7. Sweet, *Recreating Africa*, 140.

8. Sweet, *Recreating Africa*, 144.

9. Kananoja, *Central African Identities and Religiosity*, 202.

10. Sweet, *Recreating Africa*, 154.

11. Ilka Boaventura Leite, *Antropologia da viagem: Escravos e libertos em Minas Gerais no século XIX* (Belo Horizonte: Editora UFMG, 1996). Leite catalogues and details observations on Mineiro slaves and freed persons published by European visitors during the nineteenth century.

12. The *padroado real*, or royal patronage of the church, was an agreement confirmed by Pope Leo X in 1514 authorizing Portuguese royal court control over the church throughout the empire, including but not limited to the sites of new churches and the appointments of bishops and priests.

13. Anita Novinsky, *Inquisição: Prisioneiros do Brasil, séculos XVI–XIX* (Rio de Janeiro: Expressão e Cultura, 2002), 23–24.

14. Rogério Budasz, *A música no tempo de Gregório de Mattos* (Curitiba, Brazil: Editora do Departamento de Artes da Universidade Federal do Paraná, 2004), 12.

15. Laura de Mello e Souza, *The Devil and the Land of the Holy Cross: Witchcraft, Slavery, and Popular Religion in Colonial Brazil*, trans. Diane Grosklaus Whitty (Austin: University of Texas Press, 2003), 184–86.

16. Aldair Carlos Rodrigues, "A Inquisição na Comarca do Rio das Mortes: Os agentes," in *Travessias inquisitoriais das Minas Gerais aos cárceres do Santo Ofício: Diálogos e trânsitos religiosos no império luso-brasileiro (sécs. XVI–XVIII)*, ed. Júnia Ferreira Furtado and Maria Leônia Chaves de Resende (Belo Horizonte: Fino Traço, 2013), 108–11.

17. Auguste de Saint-Hilaire, *Viagem às nascentes do Rio São Francisco* (Belo Horizonte: Editora Itatiaia, 2004), 64.

18. Júnia Ferreira Furtado, "Barbeiros, cirurgiões e médicos na Minas colonial," *Revista do Arquivo Público Mineiro*, no. 41 (2005): 99.

19. D. Ramos, "A influência africana e a cultura popular," 142.

20. Roger Sansi-Roca, "The Fetish in the Lusophone Atlantic," in *Cultures of the Lusophone Black Atlantic*, ed. Nancy Priscilla Naro, Roger Sansi-Roca, and David H. Treece (New York: Palgrave Macmillan, 2007), 24.

21. Sansi-Roca, "The Fetish in the Lusophone Atlantic," 24–25.

22. Maria Leônia Chaves de Resende, "Minas Gerais sub examine: Inventário das denúncias nos Cadernos do Promotor da Inquisição de Lisboa (século XVIII)," in *Travessias inquisitoriais das Minas Gerais aos cárceres do Santo Ofício: Diálogos e trânsitos religiosos no império luso-brasileiro (sécs. XVI–XVIII)*, ed. Júnia Ferreira Furtado and Maria Leônia Chaves de Resende (Belo Horizonte: Fino Traço, 2013), 437, 415–75.

23. Furtado, "Barbeiros, cirurgiões e médicos na Minas colonial," 97.

24. Kananoja, *Central African Identities and Religiosity*, 232–37. Kananoja cites the Tribunal do Santo Oficial/Inquisição de Lisboa from the Instituto dos Arquivos Nacionais, Lisbon.

25. Kananoja, *Central African Identities and Religiosity*, 189, 197–98.

26. Sweet, *Recreating Africa*, 151. The Kingdom of Ndongo, located in what is today Angola, was first recorded in the sixteenth century.

27. D. Ramos, "A influência africana e a cultura popular," 144–45. Ramos cites Inquisition of Lisbon, no. 4853, July 5, 1798, Arquivo Nacional da Torre do Tombo, Lisbon.

28. D. Ramos, "A influência africana e a cultura popular," 148.

29. Donald Ramos, trans., "Inquisition Process: Luzia Pinta, Angolan Freedwoman," Inquisition of Lisbon, no. 252, Arquivo Nacional da Torre do Tombo, Lisbon, http://academic .csuohio.edu/as227/Lectures/Brazil/pinta_translation.htm. The "tabaque" is erroneously identified as a "small tambourine."

30. Laird W. Bergad, *Slavery and the Demographic and Economic History of Minas Gerais, Brazil, 1720–1888* (Cambridge: Cambridge University Press, 1999), 151.

31. Bergad, *Slavery and the Demographic and Economic History of Minas Gerais*, 230–31.

32. Kananoja, *Central African Identities and Religiosity*, 237. Kananoja cites the Tribunal do Santo Ofícial/Inquisição de Lisboa from the Instituto dos Arquivos Nacionais, Lisbon.

33. Stanley J. Stein, *Vassouras, a Brazilian Coffee County, 1850–1900: The Roles of Planter and Slave in a Plantation Society* (Princeton, NJ: Princeton University Press, 1985), 189, 205.

34. Facts about the life of Rosa Coura are cited from Luiz Mott, *Rosa Egipcíaca: Uma Santa Africana no Brasil* (Rio de Janeiro: Editora Bertrand Brasil, 1993).

35. Mott, *Rosa Egipcíaca*, 10.

36. John M. Janzen, *Ngoma: Discourses of Healing in Central and Southern Africa* (Berkeley: University of California Press, 1992).

37. Glaura Lucas, *Os sons do Rosário: O congado mineiro dos Arturos e Jatobá* (Belo Horizonte: Editora UFMG, 2002), 87.

38. Núbia Pereira de Magalhães Gomes and Edimilson de Almeida Pereira, *Os Arturos: Negras raízes Mineiros*, 2nd ed. (Belo Horizonte: Mazza Edições, 2000), 287.

39. Kananoja, *Central African Identities and Religiosity*, 219.

40. Sweet, *Recreating Africa*, 157.

41. Furtado, "Barbeiros, cirurgiões e médicos na Minas colonial," 99.

42. D. Ramos, "A influência africana e a cultura popular," 147.

43. Sansi-Roca, "The Fetish in the Lusophone Atlantic," 8.

44. Luiz Mott, "Santo Antônio, o Divino Capitão-do-Mato," in *Liberdade por um fio: História dos quilombos no Brasil*, ed. João José Reis and Flávio dos Santos Gomes (São Paulo: Companhia das Letras, 1996), 131. Mott cites the Inquisition of Lisbon, no. 134, Arquivo Nacional da Torre do Tombo, Lisbon.

45. Furtado, "Barbeiros, cirurgiões e médicos na Minas colonial."

46. Katia M. de Queirós Mattoso, *To Be a Slave in Brazil: 1550–1888*, trans. Arthur Goldhammer (New Brunswick, NJ: Rutgers University Press, 1987), 19; and Boxer, *The Golden Age of Brazil*, 45–46.

47. Elizabeth W. Kiddy, *Blacks of the Rosary: Memory and History in Minas Gerais, Brazil* (University Park: Pennsylvania State University Press, 2005), 45.

48. Robert F. Thompson, *Flash of the Spirit: African and Afro-American Art and Philosophy* (New York: Vintage Books, 1983), 56, 149; and Mary C. Karasch, *Slave Life in Rio de Janeiro, 1808–1850* (Princeton, NJ: Princeton University Press, 1987), 17.

49. Kiddy, *Blacks of the Rosary*, 50. Katia M. de Queirós Mattoso states that "Angolans" included enslaved Ovimbundu people from the Caconda trading post two hundred miles inland from Luanda (*To Be a Slave in Brazil*, 17). The coast of Angola was so quickly depleted of slave sources that for centuries the vast hinterland of southern Central Africa was victimized by slave raiding.

50. Laura de Mello e Souza, *O diabo e a terra de Santa Cruz: Feitiçaria e religiosidade popular no Brasil colonial* (São Paulo: Companhia das Letras, 1986), 37.

51. Kananoja, *Central African Identities and Religiosity*, 234. See also Marina de Mello e Souza, *Reis negros no Brasil escravista: História da festa de coroação de Rei Congo* (Belo Horizonte: Editora UFMG, 2002), 65; and Sweet, *Recreating Africa*, 144.

52. Roger Bastide, *The African Religions of Brazil: Toward a Sociology of the Interpenetration of Civilizations*, trans. Helen Sebba (Baltimore: Johns Hopkins University Press, 1978), 202.

53. L. Mello e Souza, *The Devil and the Land of the Holy Cross*, 171–72.

54. M. Resende, "Minas Gerais sub examine," 415–75.

55. M. Resende, "Minas Gerais sub examine," 415–75.

56. Calainho, *Metrópole das Mandingas*, 82.

57. Mott, *Rosa Egipcíaca*, 112.

58. L. Mello e Souza, *The Devil and the Land of the Holy Cross*, 255.

59. Sebastião José de Carvalho e Melo, First Marquis of Pombal, was the de facto head of the Portuguese state during the latter half of the eighteenth century. "Pombaline reforms" refer to his Enlightenment-era influences on the country's empire.

60. Carvalho, "Black Music of All Colors," 192.

61. Gomes and Pereira, *Os Arturos: Negras raízes Mineiras*, 139.

62. Renato da Silveira, "Calundu," March 29, 2011, https://dancasfolcloricas.blogspot.com /2011/03/calundu.html#more.

63. Carvalho, "Black Music of All Colors," 191.

64. Associação Filmes de Quintal, http://www.mapeandoaxe.org.br/terreiros/belohorizonte.

65. Gomes and Pereira, *Os Arturos: Negras raízes Mineiras*, 245.

66. Carlos Sandroni, *Feitiço decente: Transformações do samba no Rio de Janeiro (1917–1933)* (Rio de Janeiro: Jorge Zahar, 2001), 39. Sandroni states that Brazilian musicologist José Mozart de Araújo found no such references to lundu in the *manuelinas*, and no promulgations against African-derived dances in subsequent Portuguese royal ordinances. Rather than calundú, most scholars point to other origins of lundu and lundu song. Rogério Budasz cites José Ramos Tinhorão and Peter Fryer when correlating the word *gandu* with *landum*, an alternative term for the salon lundu song: the *gandu* form appears in the earliest known manuscripts of eighteenth-century viola repertoire in Portugal. Rogério Budasz, "Ecos do quilombo, sons da corte: Notas sobre o repertório português para viola (guitarra de cinco ordens)," in *A música no Brasil colonial*, ed. Rui Vieira Nery (Lisbon: Fundação Calouste Gulbenkian / Serviço de Música, 2001), 374.

67. Sweet, *Recreating Africa*, 46. Sweet cites from the *Cadernos do promotor* (Prosecutor's notebook of the Lisbon Inquisition), Arquivo Nacional da Torre do Tombo, Lisbon.

68. José Fernando Saroba Monteiro, "Lundu: Origem da música popular brasileira," Musica Brasilis, n.d., https://musicabrasilis.org.br/temas/lundu-origem-da-musica-popular-brasileira.

69. Marc A. Hertzman, *Making Samba: A New History of Race and Music in Brazil* (Durham, NC: Duke University Press, 2013), 20–21.

70. Sandroni, *Feitiço decente*, 39. Writers have suggested that the count was defending Afro-Brazilian dance from the Inquisition, an absurd claim considering that he was an

aristocratic Portuguese colonial administrator and a member of Queen Maria's court. In
Brazil for six years, he acted as governor of Pernambuco (1768–1769) and Bahia (1769–1774)
before returning to Lisbon and eventually becoming president of the Portuguese Senate
from 1786 to 1791.

71. Sandroni, *Feitiço decente*, 40.

72. Marcia Taborda, *Violão e identidade nacional* (Rio de Janeiro: Civilização Brasileira,
2011), 46–52. In lundu song, Barbosa had created a lyrical, popular urban musical form
embraced by salon society. He did so while attending Rio de Janeiro's prestigious Jesuit
College, where he rose in social rank; he left Brazil permanently in the mid-1760s, introducing these Brazilian popular song forms to the Portuguese court.

Chapter 3: *Vissungo's* "Songs of the Earth"

1. Aires da Mata Machado Filho, *O negro e o garimpo em Minas Gerais* (Rio de Janeiro:
Livraria José Olympio Editora, 1943), 7.

2. Francisco Eduardo de Andrade, "Viver a gandaia: Povo negro nos morros das Minas,"
in *Escravidão, mestiçagem e histórias comparadas*, ed. Eduardo França Paiva and Isnara
Pereira Ivo (São Paulo: Annablume, 2008), 175.

3. Machado Filho, *O negro e o garimpo em Minas Gerais*, cited in Alda Maria Palhares
Campolina, Cláudia Alves Melo, and Mariza Guerra de Andrade, *Escravidão em Minas
Gerais* (Belo Horizonte: Arquivo Público Mineiro, 1988), 68.

4. Andrade, "Viver a gandaia," 175. "Oenda auê, a a! Ucumbí oenda, auê, a / Oenda auê a a!
Ucumbi oenda, auê / no calunga Ucumbí oenda, ondoro onjo Ucumbí oenda ondoro onjo /
Iô vou oenda, pu curima auê / Iô vou oenda pu curima auê."

5. Such as this example of a miner complaining of being under a spell and thus unable
to work: "Uganda ô assomá qui popia qui dendengá uanga aué, uanga ô, assomá." Cited in
Bastide, *The African Religions of Brazil*, 202.

6. Cited from the English-language abstract of Marc-Antoine Camp, "Sung Penance:
Practice and Valorization of Afro-Brazilian Vissungo in the Region of Diamantina, Minas
Gerais," PhD thesis, University of Zürich, 2006.

7. Auguste de Saint-Hilaire, *Viagem pelo Distrito dos Diamantes e litoral do Brasil* (Belo
Horizonte: Editora Itatiaia, 2004), 17.

8. George Reid Andrews, *Afro-Latin America, 1800–2000* (New York: Oxford University
Press, 2004), 24.

9. Bastide, *The African Religions of Brazil*, 202.

10. Bastide, *The African Religions of Brazil*, 202.

11. José Jorge de Carvalho, "Um panorama da música afro-brasileira," in *Vissungo: Cantos
afro-descendentes em Minas Gerais*, ed. Neide Freitas Sampião (Belo Horizonte: Edições Viva
Voz, 2009), 24

12. Carvalho, "Um panorama da música afro-brasileira," 72.

13. Andréa Albuquerque Adour da Camara, "Vissungo: O cantar banto nas Américas,"
PhD thesis, Universidade Federal de Minas Gerais, 2013; and Lúcia Valéria do Nascimento,

"Vissungos: Uma prática social em extinção," master's thesis, Universidade Federal de Minas Gerais, 2006, 36.

14. Yeda Pessoa de Castro, *A língua Mina-Jeje no Brasil: Um falar africano em Ouro Preto do século 18* (Belo Horizonte: Coleção Mineiriana, 2002), 59.

15. Machado Filho, *O negro e o garimpo em Minas Gerais*, 121. He also cites in his coverage of African-derived dialects in the Serro Frio a few Brazilian scholars who had previously researched Afro-Brazilian linguistics, namely Artur Ramos, Jacques Raimundo, and Nina Rodrigues.

16. Rodrigo Castro Rezende, "As Nossas Áfricas: População escrava e identidades africanas nas Minas Setecentistas," master's thesis, Universidade Federal de Minas Gerais, 2006, 158–59.

17. Mônica Meyer, *Ser-tão natureza: A natureza de Guimarães Rosa* (Belo Horizonte: Editora UFMG, 2008), 160. See also Byrd, "Calunga, an Afro-Brazilian Speech"; and Vogt and Fry, *Cafundó: A África no Brasil*.

18. The historical argument for higher rates of manumission in Minas Gerais was most recently, and most strongly, argued by Andréa Lisly Gonçalves in *As margens da liberdade: Estudo sobre a prática de alforrias em Minas colonial e provincial* (Belo Horizonte: Fino Traço, 2011). See also Bergad, *Slavery and the Demographic and Economic History of Minas Gerais*, 125; Kathleen J. Higgins, *"Licentious Liberty" in a Brazilian Gold-Mining Region: Slavery, Gender, and Social Control in Eighteenth-Century Sabará, Minas Gerais* (University Park: Pennsylvania State University Press, 1999), 48; Marquese, "A dinâmica da escravidão no Brasil"; and Russell-Wood, *The Black Man in Slavery and Freedom*.

19. Marquese, "A dinâmica da escravidão no Brasil."

20. Emilia Viotti da Costa, *The Brazilian Empire: Myths and Histories*, rev. ed. (Chapel Hill: University of North Carolina Press, 2000), 186.

21. Georg Heinrich von Langsdorff, *Os diários de Langsdorff*, vol. 1: *Rio de Janeiro e Minas Gerais, 8 de maio de 1824 a 17 de fevereiro de 1825*, ed. Danuzio Gil Bernardino da Silva et al. (São Paulo: Fiocruz, 1997), 238.

22. George Gardner, *Travels in the Interior of Brazil, Principally through the Northern Provinces, and the Gold and Diamond Districts, during the Years 1836–1841* (London: Reeve Brothers, 1846). Cited in Robert M. Levine and John J. Crocitti, eds., *The Brazil Reader: History, Culture, Politics* (Durham, NC: Duke University Press, 1999), 53.

23. Saint-Hilaire, *Viagem pelo Distrito dos Diamantes*, 20.

24. Higgins, *"Licentious Liberty" in a Brazilian Gold-Mining Region*, 218.

25. Russell-Wood, *The Black Man in Slavery and Freedom*, 33.

26. Neide Freitas Sampião, ed., *Vissungo: Cantos afro-descendentes em Minas Gerais* (Belo Horizonte: Edições Viva Voz, 2009), 7.

27. It is worth noting that on the Endangered Music Project CD release *L. H. Corrêa de Azevedo: Music of Ceará and Minas Gerais* (Rykodisc, 1997), track no. 25, categorized as a vissungo titled "When Drying the Water (Mine Worker's Song)," is actually a child lollipop seller singing a *pregõe*, or vendor's song. This vendor's song, on the original, archived reel-to-reel recording, is adjacent to vissungo recordings and is mislabeled in the catalog entry, a fact that I confirmed during research at the American Folklife Center, Library of Congress,

in 2011. For this CD, I was employed by Endangered Music Project producer and former Grateful Dead drummer Mickey Hart to ascertain the playback quality of the original Brazilian acetate discs held at the Oneyda Alvarenga audio archive in São Paulo.

28. Cited in Z. Neves, *Navegantes da integração*, 64.

29. Edna Maria Resende, "Flagrantes do quotidiano: Um olhar sobre o universo cultural dos homens livres pobres em São João del-Rei (1840–1860)," in *Escravidão, mestiçagem e histórias comparadas*, ed. Eduardo França Paiva and Isnara Pereira Ivo (São Paulo: Annablume, 2008).

30. Ernst Hasenclever, *Ernst Hasenclever e sua viagem às províncias do Rio de Janeiro e Minas Gerais*, ed. Débora Bendocchi Alves (Belo Horizonte: Fundação João Pinheiro, 2015), 155. This German merchant visited the Gongo Soco mine when it was the largest, most productive gold mine in Brazil.

31. Julio Pinto Vallejos, "Slave Control and Slave Resistance in Colonial Minas Gerais, 1700–1750," *Journal of Latin American Studies* 17, no. 1 (May 1985), 7–8.

32. Fábio Henrique Viana, *A paisagem sonora de Vila Rica e a música barroca das Minas Gerais (1711–1822)* (Belo Horizonte: Editora C/Arte, 2012), 42–43.

33. Edison Carneiro, "O negro em Minas Gerais," in *Segundo seminário de estudos mineiros* (Belo Horizonte: Universidade de Minas Gerais, 1956), 7.

34. Mott, *Rosa Egipcíaca*, 154

35. Cited in Kiddy, *Blacks of the Rosary*, 99.

36. Cláudia Maria das Graças Chaves, *Perfeitos negociantes: Mercadores das Minas setecentistas* (São Paulo: Annablume, 1999), 57. See Viana, *A paisagem sonora de Vila Rica*, 43–44, regarding *negras de tabuleiro* in colonial Minas Gerais.

37. D. Ramos, "A influência africana e a cultura popular," 142.

38. Cited in Gonçalves, *As margens da liberdade*, 157.

39. Machado Filho, *O negro e o garimpo em Minas Gerais*, 142.

40. Elizabeth Farfán-Santos, *Black Bodies, Black Rights: The Politics of Quilombolismo in Contemporary Brazil* (Austin: University of Texas Press, 2016), 43.

41. Carlos Magno Guimarães, "Mineração, quilombos e Palmares," in *Liberdade por um fio: História dos quilombos no Brasil*, ed. João José Reis and Flávio dos Santos Gomes (São Paulo: Companhia das Letras, 1996), 14.

42. José Flávio Morais Castro, *Geoprocessamento de mapas de Minas Gerais nos séculos XVIII–XIX* (Belo Horizonte: Editora Pontifícia Universidade Católica de Minas Gerais, 2017), 135.

43. Cited in Cláudia Damasceno Fonseca, *Arraiais e vilas d'el rei: Espaço e poder nas Minas setecentistas* (Belo Horizonte: Editora UFMG, 2011), 302.

44. Tarcísio José Martins, *Quilombo do Campo Grande: A história de Minas que se devolve ao povo*, 3rd ed. (São Paulo: MG Quilombo, 2018), 455.

45. Regarding African-derived languages of Afro-Mineiro tradition still in use in the region of the Ambrósio quilombo, see Byrd, "Calunga, an Afro-Brazilian Speech."

46. See Tarcísio José Martins, *Quilombo do Campo Grande: Ladrões da história* (Belo Horizonte: Editora Santa Clara, 2011); and T. Martins, *Quilombo do Campo Grande*.

47. João Dornas dos Santos Filho, cited in Torres, *O homem e a montanha*, 165–66.

48. Lara, *Família, história e poder no Campo das Vertantes*, 195–202.

49. Tom Farias, *Carolina: Uma biografia* (Rio de Janeiro: Malê, 2018), 23–43. Miraculously, Carolina learned how to read and write during brief childhood studies at an unusually open-minded public school in Sacramento. She went on to become a literary legend, producing autobiographical narratives drawn from her early Minas diaries and her life as a single mother in the São Paulo favelas, where she relocated as a young woman.

50. T. Martins, *Quilombo do Campo Grande*, 463.

51. Vallejos, "Slave Control and Slave Resistance," 14.

52. Mott, "Santo Antônio, o Divino Capitão-do-Mato," 131. Mott cites the Inquisition of Lisbon, no. 1551, Arquivo Nacional da Torre do Tombo. Ricardo Ferreira Ribeiro, *Florestas anãs do sertão*, vol. 1 (Belo Horizonte: Autêntica, 2005), 321.

53. Bergad, *Slavery and the Demographic and Economic History of Minas Gerais*, 216.

54. Cited in Peter Fryer, *Rhythms of Resistance: African Musical Heritage in Brazil* (Hanover, NH: University Press of New England, 2000), 52.

55. Burton, *The Romance of Isabel Lady Burton*, 338.

56. Luis Heitor Corrêa de Azevedo, letter to Harold Spivacke, American Folklife Center, Library of Congress, Washington, DC.

57. Morton Marks, liner notes, *L. H. Corrêa de Azevedo: Music of Ceará and Minas Gerais*, Endangered Music Project (Rykodisc RCD 10404, 1997).

58. Vasco Mariz, *Três musicólogos brasileiros* (Rio de Janeiro: Civilização Brasileira, 1983), 134.

59. The Imperial Conservatory in Rio de Janeiro was founded in 1848. It was renamed the National Institute of Music (1890–1937), and then the National School of Music (1937–1965).

60. Marks, liner notes, *L. H. Corrêa de Azevedo*.

61. Paolo Dias and Edimilson de Almeida Pereira, liner notes, *Congado mineiro*, Documentos Sonoros Brasileiros series, vol. 1 (Associação Cultural Cachuera! / Coleção Itaú Cultural, 1997). The recordings for the CD were made in Minas Gerais and São Paulo during 1992–1997.

62. Maria Elisabete Gontijo dos Santos, Pablo Matos Camargo, João Batista de Almeida Costa, and José Augusto Laranjeiras Samião, *Comunidades quilombolas de Minas Gerais no século XXI* (Belo Horizonte: Centro de Documentação Eloy Ferreira da Silva / Autêntica, 2008), 67–68.

63. The Orquestra Afro-Brasileira's first LP, *Obaluayê* (Todamérica, 1957), mixes arrangements of traditional Afro-Brazilian genres with jazz, predating Moacir Santos's 1965 LP on the Forma label, *Coisas*, a widely renowned recording known for similar aesthetics and stylistic references. The ensemble's second LP, *Orquestra Afro-Brasileira* (CBS, 1968) was reissued on heavy vinyl by Polysom in 2014.

64. "Abigail Moura," Museu Afro Brasil, n.d., http://www.museuafrobrasil.org.br/noticias /2014/12/30/abigail-moura.

65. Felipe Castro, Janaína Marquesini, Luana Costa, and Raquel Munhoz, *Quelé, a voz da cor: Biografia de Clementina de Jesus*, 2nd ed. (Rio de Janeiro: Civilização Brasileira, 2017), 16. I have gotten some information about the *Os cantos dos escravos* LP, its producers, and its recording from this source. In the 1960s, Falcão helped form Recife's Popular Culture

Movement (Movimento de Cultura Popular, or MCP) with influential educator Paulo Freire (author of the 1968 book *Pedagogia do oprimido* [*Pedagogy of the Oppressed*]) and regionalist intellectual Ariano Suassuna, who had spearheaded the northeastern *armorial* arts movement.

66. Castro et al., *Quelé, a voz da cor*, 27–29.

67. Castro et al., *Quelé, a voz da cor*, 27.

68. Alexandre Lobão, *Quilombos e quilombolos: Passado e presente de lutas* (Belo Horizonte: Mazza Edições, 2014), 64.

69. Farfán-Santos, *Black Bodies, Black Rights*, 73.

Chapter 4: Sacred and Fine Art Music of the Colonial and Imperial Periods

1. Coral BDMG is sponsored by the Cultural Institute of the Minas Gerais Development Bank (Instituto Cultural Banco de Desenvolvimento de Minas Gerais).

2. Arnon Sávio Reis de Oliveira, interview with the author, Belo Horizonte, August 2013.

3. Rogério Budasz, "Zealous Clerics, Mischievous Musicians, and Pragmatic Politicians: Music and Race Relations in Colonial Brazil," *Diagonal* 6 (2010): 2, 10.

4. Maxwell, *Conflicts and Conspiracies*, 94–95.

5. Budasz, "Zealous Clerics," 12.

6. Active primarily in Vila Rica, the sculptor Antônio Francisco Lisboa (c. 1730–1814) became known as Aleijadinho (Little Cripple) due to a debilitating disease that forced him to strap hammer and chisel to his wrists. This mixed-race son of a Portuguese immigrant carpenter and his slave mistress became the most famous artist of the Minas baroque. Some controversy surrounds his legacy due to the lack of documentation.

7. Marília Scalzo and Celso Nucci, *Uma história de amor à música: São João del-Rei, Prados, Tiradentes* (São Paulo: BEÏ Editora, 2012), 15.

8. Francisco Curt Lange, cited in Viana, *A paisagem sonora de Vila Rica*, 66.

9. Eighteenth-century sacred and baroque music was also composed in other parts of Brazil, including the oldest source, found in the Municipal Historical Archive of Moji da Cruzes, São Paulo. Other primary sites include Recife, Salvador, and Rio de Janeiro. It is important to keep in mind the ban on printing presses in colonial Brazil: all original work, and their copies, are hand-drawn manuscripts.

10. After arriving in South America in 1923, Lange promoted the Americanismo Musical movement. Settling in Uruguay, he conducted research and worked in education, publishing musicological scholarship on New Music compositions. He cofounded the Instituto Interamericano de Musicologia (1938), the continuation of the Instituto de Estudios Superiores, and the Editorial Cooperativa Interamericana de Compositores (1941), among other South American organizations.

11. Francisco Curt Lange, "Archivo de música religiosa de la Capitania Geral das Minas Gerais (Brasil) (siglo XVIII)," Universidad Nacional de Cuyo, Escuela Superior de Música, Departamento de Musicología, Mendoza, Argentina, 1951.

12. José Ramos Tinhorão, *As festas no Brasil colonial* (São Paulo: Editora 34, 2000), 153. Tinhorão cites Béhague as erroneously stating: "Eighteenth-century Minas composers created a repertoire . . . within a sui generis style resulting from the sociocultural conditions of the artists of the time."

13. Budasz, "Zealous Clerics," 8: "There is no doubt Francisco Curt Lange knew Freyre's work when he first came up with the concept of *mulatismo musical* in a series of articles published in the 1940s. The German-Uruguayan musicologist brought to the international awareness a corpus of sacred music composed by mulattoes since the 1780s, an immense repertory unknown even to most Brazilians, which was still played in some small towns hidden in the mountains of Minas Gerais."

14. A team of musicologists including Mary Angela Biason, Paulo Castagna, Carlos Alberto Baltazar, and Maria Conceição Rezende, among others, undertook the long process of editing the performance editions and analyzing the holdings. They helped form the museum's Programa de Organização e Valorização do Acervo de Manuscritos Musicais (Program of Organization and Evaluation of the Musical Manuscripts Collection).

15. See the Mariana Museum Music Project website at http://www.mmmariana.com.br /restauracao_difusao/index2.htm. In 2002, a third such volume was published by UFMG and the Museu da Inconfidência, with the help of museum director Rui Mourão, the federal Ministry of Culture, and the Vitae Foundation, raising the number of cataloged themes to 628. The University of São Paulo Press published its first performance editions of Mineiro *música colonial* in 1994, a collection featuring an introduction by Duprat, three compositions by José Joaquim Emerico Lobo de Mesquita, and one by Marcos Coelho Neto.

16. Silva Benfica was an acquaintance of Emperor Dom Pedro II, for whom he composed the work *Te Deum Laudamus* and from whom he received the imperial Order of the Rose. Silva Benfica directed the band in his hometown of Aiuruoca, Minas Gerais.

17. Arnon Sávio Reis de Oliveira, interview with the author, Belo Horizonte, August 2013.

18. Inês Guimarães, "A Obra 'Dominica in Palmis' (1782) de Lobo de Mesquita," in *A música no Brasil colonial*, ed. Rui Vieira Nery (Lisbon: Fundação Calouste Gulbenkian / Serviço de Música, 2001), 216.

19. Sergio Macedo Pires, "Sources, Style, and Context for the *Te Deum* of José Joaquim Emerico Lobo de Mesquita (1746?–1805): A Critical Edition," PhD diss., Boston University, 2007, 21–31.

20. Maria Volpe notes that, previous to the appearance of the Brotherhood of Saint Cecilia in 1815, "[t]here is no evidence that the brotherhoods operated as a [musicians] union. . . . Nothing in their statutes concerns the regulation or protection of professional categories." Maria Alice Volpe, "Irmandades e ritual em Minas Gerais durante o período colonial: O triunfo eucarístico de 1733," *Revista Música* 8, nos. 1–2 (May–November 1997), 29.

21. Rubens Ricciardi, "Manuel Dias de Oliveira: Esboço biográfico e a partitura de 'Eu Vos Adoro,'" in *A música no Brasil colonial*, ed. Rui Vieira Nery (Lisbon: Fundação Calouste Gulbenkian / Serviço de Música, 2001), 236. Though little is known about them or their work, other Vila Rica composers of that generation included Inácio Parreiras Neves (dates unknown), Jerónimo de Souza Queiroz (d. 1828), and Antônio dos Santos Cunha (dates unknown).

22. The Vila Rica Opera House was the brainchild of wealthy business leader João de Sousa Lisboa, a very wealthy Portuguese official contracted by the Portuguese Crown to collect both the duties on certain goods entering Minas Gerais (*entradas*), and the 10 percent colonial tithe known as the *dízimos*. Lisboa counted on the help of the twenty-six-year-old Minas Gerais captaincy governor, José Luís Abranches, in promoting and financing the opera house.

23. Rosana Marreco Brescia, *A Casa da Ópera de Vila Rica (1770–1822)* (São Paulo: Paco Editorial, 2012), 78.

24. In 1996, under the direction of Carlos Alberto Pinto Fonseca, UFMG's choir, the Ars Nova Coral, released the recording *Mestres da música colonial mineira*, vol. 1 (Masters of the colonial music of Minas, vol. 1) featuring works by Lobo de Mesquita, Manoel Dias de Oliveira, and Marcos Coelho Neto (VPE 0027). The following year, the Brasilessentia Grupo Vocal e Orquestra, under the baton of Vitor Gabriel, released the recording *Música do Brasil colonial: Compositores mineiros* (Music of colonial Brazil: Mineiro composers), with works by Lobo de Mesquita, Marcos Coelho Neto, Francisco Gomes da Rocha, José Joaquim da Paixão, João de Deus de Castro Lobo, and anonymous composers (Museu da Inconfidência, 11562-2).

25. Mary Angela Biason, ed., *Música do Brasil colonial (IV)* (São Paulo: Editora da Universidade de São Paulo, 2015), 16, 21–22. From the series Museu da Inconfidência.

26. Ouro Preto's Museu da Inconfidência also archives scores of nineteenth-century secular, popular music such as polkas, waltzes, modinhas, and lundus.

27. In 1993, the Centro Pró-Música de Juiz de Fora recorded Padre João de Deus de Castro Lobo's *Te Deum* for chorus and chamber orchestra (conducted by Nélson Nilo Hack), and his Mass in D Major for orchestra and chorus (conducted by Sérgio Dias), as part of the Federal University of Juiz de Fora's Fourth International Festival of Colonial Brazilian Music and Early Music (GT-002).

28. Some of the composers of this original repertoire include those discussed in relation to the Diamantina and Ouro Preto circles. Among many others local to the Campo das Vertentes are Antônio dos Santos Cunha, Presciliano José da Silva, Martiniano Ribeiro Bastos, Joaquim de Paula Souza Bonsucesso, João Feliciano de Souza, and Francisco Martiniano Paula Miranda. Scalzo and Nucci, *Uma história de amor à música*, 17.

29. Scalzo and Nucci, *Uma história de amor à música*, 14. Much of the information that I provide on the music of São João del-Rei, Prados, and Tiradentes is from this source.

30. Suzel Ana Reily, "Remembering the Baroque Era: Historical Consciousness, Local Identity and the Holy Week Celebrations in a Former Mining Town in Brazil," *Ethnomusicology Forum* 15, no. 1 (June 2006): 39–62.

31. Marcelo Ramos, liner notes, *Padre José Maria Xavier, Ofício de Trevas*, vol. 2 (Palácio das Artes, n.d.).

32. Olga G. Cacciatore, *Dicionário biográfico de música erudita brasileira* (Rio de Janeiro: Editora Forense Universitária, 2005), 480–81.

33. Maria José Turri Nicoliello, liner notes, *Francisco Raposo* (CMCG, 2010).

34. See Appendix 2. In 1900, approximately forty-one thousand missionizing Catholics were dispersed throughout the world, including approximately eight thousand European

priests and twenty-seven thousand sisters and lay workers. Carlton J. H. Hayes, *A Generation of Materialism: 1871–1900* (New York: Harper and Row, 1963), 150.

35. Cited in Scalzo and Nucci, *Uma história de amor à música*, 26.

36. Reily, "Remembering the Baroque Era," 57.

37. Paulo Castagna and Jaelson Trindade, "Chapelmasters and Musical Practice in Brazilian Cities in the Eighteenth Century," in *Music and Urban Society in Colonial Latin America*, ed. Geoffrey Baker and Tess Knighton (Cambridge: Cambridge University Press, 2011), 138.

38. Cited in Viana, *A paisagem sonora de Vila Rica*, 70.

39. Ricciardi, "Manuel Dias de Oliveira," 238.

40. Paulo Castagna, "O 'estilo antigo' no Brasil, nos séculos XVIII e XIX," in *A música no Brasil colonial*, ed. Rui Vieira Nery (Lisbon: Fundação Calouste Gulbenkian / Serviço de Música, 2001), 199.

41. Bastide, *The African Religions of Brazil*, 115. Bastide cites Raymundo Octavio da Trinidade, *São Francisco de Assis de Ouro Prêto: Crônica narrada pelos documentos da ordem* (Rio de Janeiro: Diretoria do Patrimônio Histórico e Artístico Nacional, 1951).

42. The most regionally important genre not discussed in this book, the Folia de Reis are ensembles that perform Christmastime reenactments of the visitation of Wise Men to Bethlehem. Also known as companies of kings (*companhias de reis*), these musical groups are usually composed of low-income rural laborers. Suzel Ana Reily's *Voices of the Magi: Enchanted Journeys in Southeast Brazil* (Chicago: University of Chicago Press, 2002) remains the most valuable English-language study.

43. Robert Walsh, *Notícias do Brasil* (Belo Horizonte: Editora Itatiaia, 1985), 60.

44. Hermann Burmeister, *Viagem ao Brasil através das províncias do Rio de Janeiro and Minas Gerais* (Belo Horizonte: Editora Itatiaia, 1980), 275.

45. Saint-Hilaire, *Viagem pelo Distrito dos Diamantes*, 65.

46. Tinhorão, *As festas no Brasil colonial*, 138–39.

47. Camila Fernanda Guimarães Santiago, *A Vila em rica festas: Celebrações promovidas pela Câmara de Vila Rica (1711–1744)* (Belo Horizonte: Editora C/Arte / Fundação Mineira de Educação e Cultura, Faculdade de Ciências Empresariais, 2003), 17.

48. Lisa Voigt, *Spectacular Wealth: The Festivals of Colonial South American Mining Towns* (Austin: University of Texas Press, 2016), 142.

49. Kiddy, *Blacks of the Rosary*, 88.

50. Maria Conceição Rezende, *A música na história de Minas Colonial* (Belo Horizonte: Editora Itatiaia, 1989), 221.

51. Suzel Ana Reily, "The 'Musical Human' and Colonial Encounters in Minas Gerais, Brazil," *South African Music Studies* 29 (2009): 71.

52. Francisco Curt Lange, "A música barroca," in *Minas Gerais: Terra e povo*, ed. Guilhermino Cesar (Rio de Janeiro: Editora Globo, 1969), 242.

53. Lange, "A música barroca," 242.

54. Tamara Elena Livingston-Isenhour and Thomas George Caracas Garcia, *Choro: A Social History of a Brazilian Popular Music* (Bloomington: Indiana University Press, 2005), 61.

55. As the Minas School of liturgical music flourished, the Portuguese Inquisition was crushing what remained of calundú religious and healing practices, harassing participants of secular batuque as it spread throughout Brazilian society.

56. M. Rezende, *A música na história de Minas Colonial*, 667. As noted by John Wirth (*Minas Gerais in the Brazilian Federation*, 83), some of these associations were akin to civic organizations such as social clubs and dramatic groups, which in all numbered close to six hundred throughout Minas Gerais by the 1920 census.

57. Manuela Areias Costa, "'Vivas à República': Representações da banda 'União XV de Novembro' em Mariana, MG (1901–1930)," PhD diss., Universidade Federal Fluminense, 2012, 55.

58. Castagna and Trindade, "Chapelmasters and Musical Practice," 22.

59. M. Rezende, *A música na história de Minas Colonial*, 545.

60. José Ramos Tinhorão, *Os sons que vem da rua* (São Paulo: Editora 34, 2005), 109.

61. Clotildes Avellar Teixeira, *Marchinhas e retretas: História das corporações musicais civis de Belo Horizonte* (Belo Horizonte: Autêntica, 2007), 34.

62. Maurício Monteiro, *A Construção do gosto: Música e sociedade na corte do Rio de Janeiro, 1808–1821* (São Paulo: Ateliê Editorial, 2008), 219.

63. Tinhorão, *Os sons que vem da rua*, 110.

64. Cited in Wirth, *Minas Gerais in the Brazilian Federation*, 82.

65. James C. Fletcher and Daniel P. Kidder, *Brazil and the Brazilians: Portrayed in Historical and Descriptive Sketches* (1857; London: Kegan Paul, 2005), 441–42.

66. Livingston-Isenhour and Garcia, *Choro: A Social History*, 62.

67. These and other composers created musical accompaniment for the *maxixe*, a sort of Brazilianized polka that became a national genre despite its then scandalous choreography, and which developed into an international "exotic" dance craze. Casa Edison's turn-of-the-century catalog of recordings, and Brazilian publishers, used the term "tango" to distance the genre from its "lascivious" reputation. Andréa Mendonça Lage da Cruz and Joana Domingues Vargas note the arrival of these popular dance musics to the salon-based culture of Ouro Preto's soiree-like *partida* social gatherings, where they were performed by bandas. Andréa Mendonça Lage da Cruz and Joana Domingues Vargas, "A vida musical nos salões de Belo Horizonte (1897–1907)," *Análise & Conjuntura* 4, no. 1 (January–April 1989): 120–35.

68. Erminia Silva, "As múltipas linguagens na teatrilidade circense: Benjamin Oliveira e o circo-teatro no Brasil no final do século XIX e início do XX," PhD thesis, Universidade Estadual de Campinas, 2003, 42–43.

69. José Ramos Tinhorão, *A música popular no romance brasileiro*, vol. 2: *Século XX (primeira parte)* (São Paulo: Editora 34, 2000), 327.

70. Regina Horta Duarte, *Noites circenses: Espetáculos de circo e teatro em Minas Gerais no século XIX* (Campinas, Brazil: Editora da Unicamp, 1995), 199.

71. Duarte, *Noites circenses*, 200–201. Duarte cites Joaquim da Costa, *Conceição do mato dentro: Fonte da saudade* (Belo Horizonte: Editora Itatiaia, 1975).

72. Castagna and Trindade, "Chapelmasters and Musical Practice," 16.

73. Influential Brazilian musicologist Mário de Andrade (1893–1945) published his seminal work *Modinhas imperiais* in 1930, including extensive scores and annotations of salon-based repertoire.

74. As a harmonic accompaniment instrument for lyrical salon repertoire, the viola lost its place to the harpsichord, piano, and *violão* (guitar). During the nineteenth century, the viola gradually became associated with the lower socioeconomic classes, while the piano was found in more prosperous homes. Ivan Vilela, *Cantando a própria história: Música caipira e enraizamento* (São Paulo: Editora da Universidade de São Paulo, 2013), 45. See also Renato Moreira Varoni de Castro, "O violão substitui a viola de arame na cidade de Rio de Janeiro no século XIX," paper presented at the XV Congresso da Associação Nacional de Pesquisa e Pós-Graduação em Música, Rio de Janeiro, 2005; and Ivan Vilela, "Os caminhos da viola no Rio de Janeiro do século XIX," master's thesis, University Federal de Rio de Janeiro, 2007.

75. Reily, "Remembering the Baroque Era," 24.

Chapter 5: *Batuque*

1. Burmeister, *Viagem ao Brasil*, 279.

2. Viana, *A paisagem sonora de Vila Rica*, 50–51. In this excerpt, Viana quotes the following sources, respectively: Ecclesiastical Archives of the Archbishop of Mariana, *Devassas*, 1763-1764, f. 10v, cited in Luciano Figueiredo, *O avesso da memória: Cotidiano e trabalho da mulher em Minas Gerais no século XVIII* (Rio de Janeiro: Livraria José Olympio Editora / Brasília: Editora Universidade de Brasília, 1993), 175; Figueiredo, *O avesso da memória*, 171; and José Vieira Couto, *Memória sobre a Capitania das Minas Gerais: Seu território, clima e produções metálicas* (Belo Horizonte: Fundação João Pinheiro, 1994), 76.

3. Marcia Amantino, "Caxambu, cateretê e feitiçaria entre os escravos do Rio de Janeiro e Minas Gerais no século XIX," in *Escravidão, mestiçagem e histórias comparadas*, ed. Eduardo França Paiva and Isnara Pereira Ivo (São Paulo: Annablume, 2008).

4. A later echo of Lisbon's poorly documented Luso-African dance culture of the late 1400s, the Spanish *mangana* and its music of "a sad sound" from the thriving black community of fifteenth-century Castile has been described as a popular dance known well past the fifteenth century. According to A. C. de C. M. Saunders, "there must have been other dances, probably similar to the *undul, guineo, ye-ye*, and *zarembeque*, all of which, together with the *mangana*, were danced by Blacks in Castile during the sixteenth century." A. C. de C. M. Saunders, *A Social History of Black Slaves and Freedmen in Portugal, 1441–1555* (Cambridge: Cambridge University Press, 1982), 105–6.

5. Edison Carneiro, *Religiões Negras: Negros Bantos* (Rio de Janeiro: Civilização Brasileira, 1937).

6. Helena Morley, *The Diary of "Helena Morley,"* trans. Elizabeth Bishop (New York: Farrar, Straus and Giroux, 1995), 176–77. Morley's diary was originally published in Portuguese as *Minha vida de menina* in 1942.

7. David Eltis, "The Nineteenth-Century Transatlantic Slave Trade: An Annual Time Series of Imports into the Americas Broken Down by Region," *Hispanic American Historical Review* 67, no. 1 (February 1987): 109–38. A clear pattern of four-year alternations between higher and lower slave importation numbers occurs in shipments to "South of Bahia":

1826–1830, 176,000; 1831–1835, 57,000; 1836–1840, 202,000; 1841–1845, 90,000; and 1846–1850, 208,000.

8. See Manolo Florentino, *Em costas negras* (São Paulo: Companhia das Letras, 1997), 38.

9. Gerhard Kubik, *Angolan Traits in Black Music, Games and Dances of Brazil* (Lisbon: Junta de Investigações Científicas do Ultramar, Centro de Estudos de Antropologia Cultural, 1979), 18.

10. José Ramos Tinhorão, *Os sons dos negros do Brasil* (São Paulo: Art Editora, 1988), 72.

11. Richard Burton, *Viagem de canoa de Sabará ao Oceano Atlântico* (Belo Horizonte: Itatiaia, 1977), 63–64.

12. Sandroni, *Feitiço decente*, 85.

13. Renato Ortiz, *Cultura brasileira and identidade nacional* (São Paulo: Editora Brasiliense, 1985), 43–44.

14. Andréa Silva Dominguesi, "Cultura e identidade: Festa da igreja para os padres, e a festa de Nossa Senhora do Rosário para as pessoas do cativeiro," paper presented at the XXVI Simpósio Nacional de História, São Paulo, July 2011, 5.

15. Langsdorff, *Os diários de Langsdorff*, 198.

16. Johann Baptist von Spix and Carl Friedrich Philipp von Martius, *Viagem pelo Brasil, 1817–1820*, vol. 1, 2nd ed. (São Paulo: Edições Melhoramentos, 1981), 191.

17. Gomes and Pereira, *Os Arturos: Negras raízes Mineiras*, 449–50.

18. M. Rezende, *A música na história de Minas Colonial*.

19. Quoted in Fryer, *Rhythms of Resistance*, 167, 221.

20. Kubik, *Angolan Traits in Black Music*, 120.

21. See Fryer, *Rhythms of Resistance*, 161–69, for African instruments in Brazil, including those fallen from use.

22. Auguste de Saint-Hilaire, *Viagem pelas Províncias de Rio de Janeiro e Minas Gerais*, vol. 1 (São Paulo: Companhia Editora Nacional, 1938), 119.

23. Fryer, *Rhythms of Resistance*, 101.

24. Saint-Hilaire, *Viagem pelas Províncias de Rio de Janeiro e Minas Gerais*, 143–44

25. G. W. Freireyss, *Viagem ao interior do Brasil* (Belo Horizonte: Editora Itatiaia, 1982), 40.

26. Freireyss, *Viagem ao interior do Brasil*, 44.

27. Freireyss, *Viagem ao interior do Brasil*, 114.

28. Alexander Caldcleugh, *Viagens na América do sul: Extrato da obra contendo relato sobre o Brasil*, trans. Júlio Jeha (Belo Horizonte: Coleção Mineiriana, 2000), 133.

29. Francis de la Porte Castelnau, *Expedição às regiões centrais da América do Sul*, vol. 1 (São Paulo: Companhia Editora Nacional, 1949), 106.

30. Walsh, *Notícias do Brasil*, 91–92.

31. Saint-Hilaire, *Viagem pelas Províncias de Rio de Janeiro e Minas Gerais*, 69–70.

32. Torres, *O homem e a montanha*, 142–44.

33. D'Orbigny, *Viagem pitoresca através do Brasil*, 147.

34. Judy Bieber, "When Liberalism Goes Local: Nativism and Partisan Identity in the *Sertão Mineiro*, Brazil, 1831–1850," *Luso-Brazilian Review* 37, no. 2 (Winter 2000): 76.

35. Bieber, "When Liberalism Goes Local," 78.

36. Carlos Rodrigues Brandão, *A Clara cor da noite escura: Escritos e imagens de mulheres e homens negros de Goiás e Minas Gerais* (Goiânia, Brazil: Editora da Universidade Católica de Goiás / Uberlândia, Brazil: Universidade Federal de Uberlândia, 2009), 78.

37. Spix and Martius, *Viagem pelo Brasil*, vol. 1, 191.

38. Louis Agassiz and Mrs. Louis Agassiz [Elizabeth Cabot Cary Agassiz], *Journey in Brazil* (1868; Boston: Houghton Mifflin, 1964), 76, 103–4. Agassiz also wrote about the deforestation of the Mineiro Mata Atlântica. He noted during his coffee fazenda stay that, after less than thirty years, "the shrubs and the soil [of the coffee plantation] are alike exhausted, and, according to the custom of the country, the fazendeiro cuts down a new forest and begins a new plantation, completely abandoning his old one. . . . [E]xtensive as are the forests, they will not last forever," 113.

39. Agassiz and Agassiz, *Journey in Brazil*, 114–15.

40. Duarte, *Noites circenses*, 94–95.

41. Burmeister, *Viagem ao Brasil*, 275.

42. Stein, *Vassouras, a Brazilian Coffee County*, 204–7. See also Amantino, "Caxambú, cateretê e feiticaría," 257–76. According to Peter Fryer (*Rhythms of Resistance*, 141), drumming is briefly described in a 1717 Minas document relating how the "slaves sang melancholy songs in the Bantu dialect . . . [and] invoked the protection of the orixás by means of dances like the caxambú accompanied by a chocalho [rattle] and foot stomping." (The term "Bantu" was later coined in the 1860s to designate a group of African languages.)

43. Stein, *Vassouras, a Brazilian Coffee County*, 207.

44. Fazenda São Jose's *caxambú* recordings are featured on the compilation compact disc *Batuques do Sudeste*, Documentos Sonoros Brasileiros series, vol. 2 (Associação Cultural Cachuera!, 2000). Also featured is a *caxambú* track recorded in Santo Antônio de Pádua, a Rio de Janeiro hamlet five miles from the border with Minas Gerais.

45. Leda Maria Martins, *Afrografias da memória* (Belo Horizonte: Mazza Edições, 1997), 83.

46. Núbia Pereira de Magalhães Gomes and Edimilson de Almeida Pereira, *Mundo encaixado: Significação da cultura popular* (Belo Horizonte: Mazza Edições, 1992), 350.

47. Glaura Lucas, interview with the author, Belo Horizonte, August 16, 2013.

48. Kananoja, *Central African Identities and Religiosity*, 189, 223.

49. Cited in Viana, *A paisagem sonora de Vila Rica*, 50.

50. M. Rezende, *A música na história de Minas Colonial*, 221.

51. Kananoja, *Central African Identities and Religiosity*. Kananoja cites the *Devassas eclesiásticas*, book 1734, f. 96v, from the Ecclesiastical Archives of the Archbishop of Mariana.

52. Kananoja, *Central African Identities and Religiosity*, 224–25.

53. Campolina et al., *Escravidão em Minas Gerais*, 73.

54. Bastide, *The African Religions of Brazil*, 55.

55. Carlos Décio Mostaro, João Medeiros Filho, and Roberto Faria de Medeiros, *História recente da música popular brasileira em Juiz de Fora* (Juiz de Fora, Brazil: self-published, 1977), 253–55. The ensemble came under the direction of Eugênio da Silva in 1971, with folklorist Marisa Tavares d'Agosto becoming president.

56. Abigail Moura, liner notes, *Orquestra Afro-Brasileira* (Polysom 33160-1, 1968). The album was reissued in a remastered, heavy-vinyl limited edition by Polysom in 2014.

57. Arina Gomes Foscarini, "As manifestações culturais populares como atrativos turísti-cos: Estudo de caso do batuque em Lapinha da Serra/MG," Instituto de Geociências, Universidade Federal de Minas Gerais, Belo Horizonte, 2009.

58. Santos et al., *Comunidades quilombolas de Minas Gerais*, 237–90. The nongovernmen-tal agency Federação das Comunidades Quilombolas de Minas Gerais (N'golo) currently acts in conjunction with local, state, and federal government agencies in advocating for the legal rights of residents in marginalized African-descendant communities. The Centro de Documentação Eloy Ferreira da Silva (CEDEFES), a nonprofit NGO based in Belo Horizonte advocating for social justice on behalf of rural workers, indigenous Brazilians, and other marginalized social groups, has joined in these efforts. Founded in 1985 and named after a rural activist from Minas's São Francisco River Valley who was assassinated in 1984, CEDEFES has researched and published numerous studies pertaining to *comunidades quilombolas*.

59. Maria Irenilda Pereira, "Músico cria projeto para preservar tradições em comunidade quilombola," Centro de Documentação Eloy Ferreira da Silva, May 14, 2018, http://www.cedefes .org.br/musico-cria-projeto-para-preservar-tradicoes-em-comunidade-quilombola/.

Chapter 6: Congado in Minas Gerais

1. The festival is known throughout Minas Gerais by several related names: Festa do Rosário, Festa do Reinado de Nossa Senhora do Rosário, Festa de Nossa Senhora do Rosário, and Reinado do Rosário, for example. See Gomes and Pereira, *Os Arturos: Negras raízes Mineiras*, 539–46; and the interview with João Lopes by Glaura Lucas, "As falas da ingoma," in *Músicas, africanas e indígenas no Brasil*, ed. Rosângela Pereira de Tugny and Ruben Caixeta de Queiroz (Belo Horizonte: Editora UFMG, 2006), 101.

2. Vânia Noronha, "Reinado de Nossa Senhora do Rosário: A constituição de uma reli-giosidade mítica afrodescendente no Brasil," *Horizonte* 9, no. 21 (April–June 2011): 268.

3. Along Brazil's coast during the colonial era, election ceremonies of the Reinado some-times featured the *cucumbi* (also *quicumbi*), a dance of Angolan heritage known as *paracu-mbé*, or simply *cumbé*.

4. Lucas, *Os sons do Rosário*, 43. Cited from a *moçambique guarda* song: "Ê nego veio de muito longe / Veio de Angola, do Congo / Para as minas de Minas Gerais."

5. L. Martins, *Afrografias da memória*, 164.

6. "Lyric poetry" and "guiding principles" are my translations of *cantopoemas* and *pre-ceito*, respectively, as used by Núbia Pereira de Magalhães Gomes and Edimilson de Almeida Pereira in *Ouro Preto da Palavra: Narrativas de preceito do Congado em Minas Gerais* (Belo Horizonte: Editora PUC Minas, 2003), 14.

7. Larissa Oliveira e Gabarra, "Mihangas e bastões: Culturas materiais através do Atlântico," in *Objeto da escravidão: Abordagens sobre a cultura material da escravidão e seu legado*, ed. Camilla Agostini (Rio de Janeiro: 7Letras, 2013), 253.

8. Y. Castro, *A língua Mina-Jeje no Brasil*, 25–26. "O povo de Congo é povo Valente / Seu Rei de Congo já chegou /Ele veio de Aruanda, com toda a sua Banda."

9. Lucas, *Os sons do Rosário*, 43. Cited from a *moçambique* song: "É nego veio de muito longe / Veio de Angola, do Congo / Para as minas de Minas Gerais."

10. A compact disc featuring Congado in Minas Gerais is *Congado mineiro*, volume 1 of the series Documentos Sonoros Brasileiros (Associação Cultural Cachuera! / Coleção Itaú Cultural, 1997). Select tracks were recorded between 1992 and 1998 in the following locations: Milho Verde, Fidalgo, Ribeirão das Neves, Contagem, Serro, Jatobá, Sete Lagoas, Oliveira, and Pedro Leopoldo. Other CDs with Congado include *Festa do Rosário: Serro, MG, 1724–2000* (Secretaria de Estado de Cultura e Turismo de Minas Gerais CRI 169), recordings made in Serro in July 2000; *Os Negros do Rosário* (Lapa Discos LAPA 005, 1998), recordings made in Oliveira in 1986–1987; and *Festa de Nossa Senhora do Rosário: Conceição do Mato Dentro, MG* (Secretaria de Estado de Cultura e Turismo de Minas Gerais CXR 04), recordings made in Conceição do Mato Dentro, January 1, 1999.

11. "All of the groups proudly present among their lines of participants a good number of children. . . . It is a pleasure seeing them dance and sing, with all of the force of their innocence, revealing the dancers of tomorrow." These comments on the *festa* in São Gonçalo do Sapucaí in Sul de Minas appeared in an August 1954 article, "Danças populares da melhor tradição em São Gonçalo do Sapucaí," in the newspaper *Tribuna de Minas*. Cited in Alfredo João Rabaçal, *As congadas no Brasil* (São Paulo: Secretaria da Cultura, Ciência e Tecnologia / Conselho Estadual de Cultura, 1976), 180–81.

12. Oliveira e Gabarra, "Mihangas e bastões," 245–46.

13. Nei Lopes, *Bantos, malês e identidade negra* (Rio de Janeiro: Editora Forense Universitária, 1988), 229; cited in L. Martins, *Afrografias da memória*, 155.

14. L. Martins, *Afrografias da memória*, 155.

15. Hermano Vianna and Beto Villares, liner notes, *Música do Brasil* (Abril Entretenimento, n.d.).

16. Filipe Generoso Brandão Murta Gaeta, "O Panorama atual da marujada de Conceição do Mato Dentro/MG: Uma análise da interferência de agentes externos sobre sua cultura musical tradicional," master's thesis, Universidade Federal de Minas Gerais, Escola de Música, 2013, 18.

17. Regarding the *catopê*, see Gabriela Korossy, "Deus não sobe meia ladeira," in *Da senzala à capela: From Senzala to Chapel*, ed. Laycer Tomaz (Brasília: Editora Universidade Brasília, 2000), 42. Regarding the *vilão*, see Maria Amalia Corrêa Giffoni, *Reinado do Rosário de Itapecerica* (São Paulo: Palas Athena do Brasil, 1989), 68: "The *Vilão* constitutes a living memory, exposed to the public gaze, of what was and remains the conscience of those people who are gradually fleeing the stigma placed upon them and finally conquering the spaces previously denied to them." Rogério Budasz places the *vilão* dance (also *viollano*) of southern Brazil within the group of dances used in the all-night fandango tradition. Rogério Budasz, liner notes, *Iberian and African-Brazilian Music of the 17th Century* (Naxos, 2006).

18. L. Martins, *Afrografias da memória*, 159. "Ó viva Maria no céu / com o Rosário na mão / contemplando o mistério."

19. Also used for an Afro-Uruguayan dance, the term "candombe" may be derived from the Kimbundu dance *kanome* and reinforced by the same, adapted Kikongo word used in South America's Southern Cone for any black cultural custom. The Río de la Plata region of

Uruguay and Argentina witnessed a nineteenth-century dance known as *candombe*, eventually influencing the tango and milonga traditions. Nineteenth-century Rio de Janeiro was home to a dance and ritual known as *candombe*, which spread throughout parts of Brazil as an African-derived circle dance. Candombe became associated with the rural southeastern pan-Bantu complex of music culture, cited as a quasi-religious slave dance of the interior and within the galaxy of the *bailes de congos* (dances of the Congado). There is no clear understanding of how the term became incorporated into the Reinado tradition, or if candombe dance influenced the most sacred components of Congado in Minas Gerais.

20. Jonathon Grasse, "Calundu's Winds of Divination: Music and Black Religiosity in Eighteenth and Nineteenth-Century Minas Gerais, Brazil," *Yale Journal of Music and Religion* 3, no. 2 (2017): 43–63.

21. Paulo Dias, liner notes, *Batuques do Sudeste*, Documentos Sonoros Brasileiros series, vol. 2 (Associação Cultural Cachuera!, 2000). This collection of field recordings features candombe performances from five contemporary Mineiro communities located in, or in proximity to, the Belo Horizonte metropolitan region: Contagem, Jatobá, Mato do Tição, Matozinhos, and Justinópolis.

22. Glaura Lucas, interview with the author, August 16, 2013. See also Edimilson de Almeida Pereira, *Os tambores estão frios: Herança cultural e sincretismo religioso de candombe* (Belo Horizonte: Mazza Edições, 2005).

23. Gomes and Pereira, *Mundo encaixado*, 351.

24. Santos et al., *Comunidades quilombolas de Minas Gerais*, 69.

25. José Jorge de Carvalho, "Afro-Brazilian Music and Rituals, part 1: From Traditional Genres to the Beginnings of Samba," Duke/University of North Carolina Program in Latin American Studies, Working Paper Series, Durham, North Carolina, 2000, 14–15.

26. Santos et al., *Comunidades quilombolas de Minas Gerais*, 63–74. Santos and her coauthors account for more than 430 such marginalized communities in Minas Gerais.

27. Afonso Capelas Jr., "As donas da história," *Revista Raiz*, 2nd ed., 2005, http://revista-raiz.uol.com.br/portal/index.php?Itemid=96&id=82&option=com_content&task=view.

28. Capelas, "As donas da história."

29. André Braga and Cardes Amâncio, dirs., *Candombe do Açude: Arte, cultura e fé* (Avesso Filmes, 2004); and Sérgio Bairon and José da Silva Ribeiro, dirs., *Tá caindo fulô . . . Tambús de candombe de comunidade do Açude* (2012).

30. Lucas, *Os sons do Rosário*, 89. See also P. Dias, liner notes, *Batuques do Sudeste*; and Gomes and Pereira, *Os Arturos: Negras raízes Mineiras*.

31. Lucas, *Os sons do Rosário*, 285–86.

32. Glaura Lucas notes certain secretive candombe musical features "echoing" in the *moçambique guarda* of the Os Arturos Congado procession. Lucas, *Os sons do Rosário*, 224; and Glaura Lucas, interview with the author, Belo Horizonte, August 16, 2013.

33. L. Martins, *Afrografias da memória*, 167. "Se a morte não me matar, tamborim / Se a terra não me comer, tamborim / Ai, ai, ai, tamborim / Para o ano eu voltarei, tamborim."

34. Budasz, *A música no tempo de Gregório de Mattos*, 10–12. In this description, the musical bow associated with Brazilian capoeira, the *berimbau*, is joined by a fanciful array of strings, aerophones, and percussion. The guitar could have been a ten-string viola, which

retains a regional role in *guardas* throughout Minas Gerais. The board-shaped guitar description suggests a nonincurved waist body type, such as the flat, oval-shaped *moresca* guitar, or an African plucked lute. *Arranhol* may refer to a scraped instrument (*arranhar*, "to scratch"), while the *cocoa* violin may refer to any number of West African fiddles with various resonator types (or perhaps a bowed lute or harp with a round resonator). The meaning of *gral* appears to be unknown, and the term *cumbe* likely relates to the Angolan *cumbé* dance, also known as *paracumbé*. Budasz cites *Folhetos de ambas lisboas, in provas e suplementos a história annual chronologica, e política do mundo, e principalmente da Europa*, booklet 3, August 1730. See also José Ramos Tinhorão, *Os negros em Portugal: Sécs. XV a XIX* (Lisbon: Commisão Nacional para as Comemorações dos Descobrimentos Portugueses, 1999), 169.

35. Lucas, *Os sons do Rosário*, 144–45. Patrícia Brandão Couto notes the term *caixa de guerra* (war drum) in *Festa do Rosário: Iconografia e poética de um rito* (Rio de Janeiro: Editora da Universidade Federal Fluminense, 2003), 251.

36. Lucas, *Os sons do Rosário*, 87.

37. Gomes and Pereira, *Os Arturos: Negras raízes Mineiras*, 287.

38. Lucas, *Os sons do Rosário*, 166. Glaura Lucas has provided the only thorough musicological analysis of Congado drumming patterns, revealing basic cells and variations in two separate Congado communities in the Belo Horizonte municipality.

39. Lucas, *Os sons do Rosário*, 95.

40. L. Martins, *Afrografias da memória*, 173. "Canta e dança, crioulo / Que a força vem de Zambi."

41. P. Couto, *Festa do Rosário*, 132.

42. P. Couto, *Festa do Rosário*, 131.

43. Salwa El-Shawan Castelo-Branco, liner notes, *Musical Traditions of Portugal* (Smithsonian Folkways, 1994); and Tiago de Oliveira Pinto, "As bandas-de-pífanos no Brasil: Aspectos de organologia, repertorio e função," in *Portugal e o mundo: O encontro de culturas na música*, ed. Salwa El-Shawan Castelo-Branco (Lisbon: Dom Quixote, 1997), 566. Pinto notes that the *gaita de foles* is played in the northeastern Portuguese district of Trás-os-Montes.

44. Daniel Lima Magalhães, *Canudos, gaitas e pífanos: As flautas do norte de Minas* (Belo Horizonte: self-published, 2010).

45. Magalhães, *Canudos, gaitas e pífanos*, 18.

46. Johann Baptist von Spix and Carl Friedrich Philipp von Martius, *Viagem pelo Brasil, 1817–1820*, vol. 2, 2nd ed. (São Paulo: Edições Melhoramentos, 1976), 70.

47. Magalhães, *Canudos, gaitas e pífanos*, 8, 30–31.

48. John Luccock, *Notas sobre de Rio de Janeiro e partes meridionais do Brasil* (São Paulo: Livraria Martins, 1942), 352.

49. Castelnau, *Expedição às regiões centrais da América do Sul*, 171–72.

50. Burmeister, *Viagem ao Brasil*, 264.

51. Lady Burton, *The Romance of Isabel Lady Burton*, 331.

52. Sweet, *Recreating Africa*, 7, 109, 112.

53. Kananoja, *Central African Identities and Religiosity*.

54. Sweet, *Recreating Africa*, 104.

55. Gomes and Pereira, *Os Arturos: Negras raízes Mineiras*, 139.

56. L. Mello e Souza, *The Devil and the Land of the Holy Cross*, 50.

57. Kiddy, *Blacks of the Rosary*, 148–49.

58. Boschi, *Os leigos e o poder*, 79–80. The first manifestation of the Crown's political moves against the church's activities in Minas came in a 1709 *carta régia* issued following the end of the War of the Emboabas. Throughout the remainder of the first half of the eighteenth century, a series of *cartas, ordens*, and *avisos régios* issued by the Crown to Mineiro captaincy governors, and to Rio de Janeiro and Bahia bishops, detailed the exclusion of clerics and religious orders from Minas Gerais.

59. Renato da Silva Dias, "Na Africa eu nasci, no Brasil eu me criei," in *Escravidão, mestiçagem e histórias comparadas*, ed. Eduardo França Paiva and Isnara Pereira Ivo (São Paulo: Annablume, 2008), 303, 307.

60. Lucas, *Os sons do Rosário*, 44–45.

61. Wladimir Alves de Souza, *Guia dos bens tombados Minas Gerais* (Rio de Janeiro: Expressão e Cultura, 1984), 53, 80, 179.

62. Kananoja, *Central African Identities and Religiosity*, 190.

63. Burmeister, *Viagem ao Brasil*, 216.

64. Richard Graham, "Free African Brazilians and the State in Slavery Times," in *Racial Politics in Contemporary Brazil*, ed. Michael Hanchard (Durham, NC: Duke University Press, 1999), 37.

65. Guilherme Guimarães Leonel, "Entre a cruz e os tambores: Estratégias de resistência e perspectivas de controle, coerção e tolerância às Festas do Reinado em Divinópolis/MG," in *História e memória do Centro-Oeste Mineiro*, ed. Batistina Maria de Souza Corgozinho, Leandro Pena Catão, and Mateus Henrique de Faria Pereira (Belo Horizonte: Crisálida, 2009), 122.

66. Suzel Ana Reily, "To Remember Captivity: The *Congados* of Southern Minas Gerais," *Latin American Music Review* 22, no. 1 (Spring–Summer 2001), 10.

67. Cited in Gomes and Pereira, *Os Arturos: Negras raízes Mineiras*, 14. See also Dominguesi, "Cultura e identidade." The latter work examines conflicts between priests and Congado communities in Sul de Minas.

68. Wagner Rodrigues da Cruz, "Congado: Memória de um povo," in *História e memória do Centro-Oeste Mineiro*, ed. Batistina Maria de Souza Corgozinho, Leandro Pena Catão, and Mateus Henrique de Faria Pereira (Belo Horizonte: Crisálida, 2009), 195. See also Rubens Alva de Silva, "Chico Rei Congo do Brasil," in *Memória afro-brasileira: Imaginário, cotidiano e poder*, ed. Vagner Gonçalves da Silva (São Paulo: Editora Selo Negro, 2007).

69. Tarcísio José Martins, "Chico Rei, nem história e nem lenda: É só uma Nota de Rodapé," Quilombo Minas Gerais, 2003, https://www.mgquilombo.com.br/artigos/pesquisas-escolares/chico-rei-nem-historia-e-nem-lenda-e-so-uma-nota-de-rodape/.

70. I completed fieldwork at Ouro Preto's the Faith that Sings and Dances festival in 2015, 2016, and 2018.

71. Elias Gibran and Pedro Kalil, eds., *De Camarões: Veredas de Maurício Tizumba*. (Belo Horizonte: Editora Nandyala, 2018).

Chapter 7: The Viola in Minas Gerais

1. Rodrigo Delage, liner notes, *Viola Caipira Instrumental* (self-released, n.d.).

2. Oneyda Alvarenga (1911–1984, b. Varginha, MG) published her prize-winning 1937 work *Cateretês do sul de Minas Gerais* (*Cateretês* in southern Minas Gerais) following studies with visiting French anthropologists Claude and Dina Levi-Strauss.

3. Vilela, *Cantando a própria história*, 37.

4. In Mato Grosso, these folk violas became known as *viola cocho*, and in 2004 they were designated by Brazil's Ministry of Culture as a national heritage musical instrument.

5. Cited in Elizabeth Travassos, "O destino dos artefatos musicais de origem Ibérica e a modernização no Rio de Janeiro (ou como a viola se tornou caipira)," in *Artifícios & artefactos: Entre o literário e o antropológico*, ed. Gilda Santos and Gilberto Velho (Rio de Janeiro: 7Letras, 2006), 128.

6. Rosa Nepomuceno, *Música caipira: Da roça ao rodeio* (São Paulo: Editora 34, 1999), 56.

7. Martha de Ulhôa Carvalho, "Musical Style, Migration, and Urbanization: Some Considerations on Brazilian *Música Sertaneja*," *Studies in Latin American Popular Culture* 12 (1993): 75–76.

8. Angela Vianna Botelho and Carla Anastasia, *D. Maria da Cruz e a Sedição de 1736* (Belo Horizonte: Autêntica, 2012), 9.

9. Paulo Freire, liner notes, *Violeiros do Brasil: Músicas e conversas com artistas da viola brasileira* (Projeto Memória Brasileira, 2008).

10. Chaves, *Perfeitos negociantes*, 57.

11. Saint-Hilaire, *Viagem pelo Distrito dos Diamantes*, 23.

12. Saint-Hilaire, *Viagem pelas Províncias de Rio de Janeiro e Minas Gerais*, 70–71.

13. Maxwell, *Conflicts and Conspiracies*, 87–88.

14. Wirth, *Minas Gerais in the Brazilian Federation*, 36.

15. Spix and Martius, *Viagem pelo Brasil*, vol. 1, 202.

16. Cited in Fryer, *Rhythms of Resistance*, 98.

17. Spix and Martius, *Viagem pelo Brasil*, vol. 1, 191.

18. Campolina et al., *Escravidão em Minas Gerais*, 24.

19. Cited in Francisco Curt Lange, *História da música na Capitania Geral das Minas Gerais*, vol. 8 (Belo Horizonte: Conselho Estadual de Cultura, 1982), 453.

20. Célio Hugo Alves Pereira, *Efemérides do arraial do tejuco a Diamantina* (Belo Horizonte: Edições CLA, 2007), 48.

21. Hasenclever, *Ernst Hasenclever e sua viagem*, 134, 141

22. Francisco Vidal Luna and Iraci del Nero da Costa, "A vida quotidiana em julgamento: Devassas em Minas Gerais," in *Minas colonial: Economia e sociedade*, by Francisco Vidal Luna and Iraci del Nero da Costa (São Paulo: Pioneira, 1982), 55–77.

23. Luzimar Paulo Pereira, "A viola do diabo: Nota sobre narrativas de pactos demoníacos no norte e noroeste Mineiro," in *Leituras sobre music popular: Reflexões sobre sonoridades e cultura*, ed. Emerson Gumbelli, Julio Diniz, and Santuza Cambraia Naves (Rio de Janeiro: 7Letras, 2008), 380. Master violeiro Roberto Corrêa is among others who have commented

on this aspect of *viola caipira* lore in Minas Gerais, in *A arte de pontear viola*, 2nd ed. (Brasília: Editora Viola Corrêa, 2002), 46–53.

24. Vilela, *Cantando a própria história*, 46.

25. Luzimar Paulo Pereira, *Os giros do sagrado: Um estudo etnográfico sobre as folias em Urucuia, MG* (Rio de Janeiro: 7Letras, 2010), 199–207. Volume 4 of the Documentos Sonoros Brasileiros series (Associação Cultural Cachuera!) is titled *Famaliá sons do Urucuia* and is dedicated to the musical arts of the town of Urucuia.

26. Travassos, "O destino dos artefatos musicais de origem Ibérica," 121–30.

27. Travassos, "O destino dos artefatos musicais de origem Ibérica," 121–30.

28. The "illiterate maestro" characterization is taken from Luiz Faria and Matheus Calil, liner notes, *Clube da Viola: Raízes*, vol. 2 (BMG Brasil, 2003).

29. Burton, *The Romance of Isabel Lady Burton*, 366.

30. Burton, *The Romance of Isabel Lady Burton*, 360.

31. Corrêa, *A arte de pontear viola*, 27.

32. Myriam Taubkin, liner notes, *Violeiros do Brasil: Músicas e conversas com artistas da viola brasileira* (Projeto Memória Brasileira, 2008).

33. Lyrics to this public domain song are printed in the liner notes to Rodrigo Delage's CD *Viola Caipira Instrumental*.

34. Elizabeth Travassos and Alexander Dent identify Pires's uncle, the linguist Amadeu Amaral (founder in 1921 of the Society for Paulista Studies), as an influence on his nephew's push toward citing "caipira" as a label for music. Amaral "produced the first detailed analysis of caboclo language of the Central-South." Alexander Sebastian Dent, *River of Tears: Country Music, Memory, and Modernity in Brazil* (Durham, NC: Duke University Press, 2009), 129.

35. Belo Horizonte's population by decade is as follows: 1890 (Curral D'el-Rey), 8,009; 1900, 13,472; 1920, 55,563; 1940, 211,377; 1950, 352,724; 1960, 693,328; 1970, 1,255,415; 1980, 1,789,855; and 1991, 2,048,851. Cited in Marshall C. Eakins, *Tropical Capitalism: The Industrialization of Belo Horizonte, Brazil* (New York: Palgrave, 2001), 37. The Brazilian Institute of Geography and Statistics lists Belo Horizonte's 2015 official population as 2,502,557.

36. Eakins, *Tropical Capitalism*, 172.

37. Elizabeth Akemi, *Revista Tempo*, May 2012, http://www.revistatempo.com.br/index.php/noticias/detalhes/cultura/946.

38. Also in 2013 in the Latin Grammys, Azevedo had another recording in the running for the roots category, "O Velho Chico: Sob olhar januarense" (The Old São Francisco River as seen by residents of Januária), referring to the river port in the extreme north of Minas.

39. Carlos Felipe, liner notes, Zé Coco do Riachão, *Vôo das garças* (Lapa, 1997).

40. Vilela, *Cantando a própria história*, 47.

41. Rosa Nepomuceno uses the term *novos-caipiras* to describe the virtuoso *violeiros* ascending in the late 1970s who championed concert instrumental music; Nepomuceno, *Música caipira*, 34.

42. Vilela, *Cantando a própria história*, 45; R. Castro, "O violão substitui a viola de arame na cidade"; and Vilela, "Os caminhos da viola no Rio de Janeiro."

43. Cited in José Ramos Tinhorão, *Domingos Caldas Barbosa: O poeta da viola, da modinha e do lundu (1740–1800)* (Lisbon: Caminho, 2004), 20. Marcia Taborda cites other scholars in her claim that these prominent men of letters played the five-course viola; Taborda, *Violão e identidade nacional*.

44. "Gisela Nogueira: Brazilian Baroque Guitar," Anima, n.d., http://www.animamusica .art.br/site/lang_en/pages/musicos/gisela.html. The Mineiro town of Capivari is today known as Consolacão, twenty kilometers from the São Paulo border.

45. Vilela, *Cantando a própria história*, 41.

46. The title's use of "armorial mineira" references the populist spirit of the 1970s Movimento Armorial artistic movement that developed in Brazil's Nordeste region (armorial means "book of heraldic arms"). Initially, under the leadership of Pernambucano writer Ariano Suassuna (1927–2014), the *armorial* aesthetic challenged the fine arts to infuse, reference, and absorb ideals from popular Nordeste culture, and it took hold among playwrights, novelists, composers, and visual artists.

47. Langsdorff, *Os diários de Langsdorff*, 249.

48. Nepomuceno, *Música caipira*, 73.

Chapter 8: Belo Horizonte Nocturne

1. Leonardo José Magalhães Gomes, *A música da cidade: Cartografia musical de Belo Horizonte* (Belo Horizonte: Editora Gomes, 2011), 44.

2. Bruno Viveiros Martins, *Som imaginário: A reinvenção da cidade nas canções do Clube da Esquina* (Belo Horizonte: Editora UFMG, 2009),14.

3. B. Martins, *Som imaginário*, 14.

4. Castelnau, *Expedição às regiões centrais da América do Sul*, 179–81.

5. Berenice Martins Guimarães, "Minas Gerais: A construção da nova ordem e a nova capital," *Análise & Conjuntura* 8, nos. 2–3 (May–December 1993), 25. To Guimarães, the "order" of Belo Horizonte's plan reveals more: "The Congress and the Cathedral are located on Avenida Afonso Pena, the principle axis of the city: the Congress in the center, at Praça da República, situated lower than the Palace, representing its submission to the executive branch, and the Cathedral at the edge of the urban zone, separated from Congress and the Palace, symbolizing the separation between church and state" (26).

6. Márcia Cruz, *Morro do Papagaio* (Belo Horizonte: Conceito, 2009), 18–22.

7. B. Guimarães, "Minas Gerais," 29.

8. Wirth, *Minas Gerais in the Brazilian Federation*, 94.

9. Cruz and Vargas, "A vida musical nos salões de Belo Horizonte," 129. *A rainha da festa* was researched by Francisco Curt Lange and incorporated into his library in Uruguay.

10. "Sociedade Musical Carlos Gomes, cem anos marcando o compass da nossa história," (Prefeitura Municipal, Secretaria de Cultura, Belo Horizonte, 1995, 28. Originally named Cidade de Minas (City of the Mines), Belo Horizonte (also initially *Bello* Horizonte) took its name from a very small, local settlement at the margins of Curral D'el-Rey.

11. Today, more than thirty thousand musicians statewide form more than eight hundred bands.

12. Teixeira, *Marchinhas e retretas*, 35.

13. "Sociedade Musical Carlos Gomes," 23.

14. The Portuguese painter, photographer, and engineer Francisco Soucasseaux (1856–1904) constructed the building and is credited with creating the first cinematography of the city. His colored postcard set depicting the city's important buildings and plazas sold widely. Francisco Soucasseaux, "Cartão postal em Belo Horizonte," http://www.cartaopostal.fot.br /conteudo.asp?p=p000018. A photograph of the Orquestra Soucasseaux identifies players as: Antônio Sardinha, violin; D. Silvestre Moreira, baritone horn; A. Naronha, flute; Francisco (Chico) Torres, violin; Francisco (Chichico) Vieitas, viola; Domingos Monteiro, cello; Paulo de Souza, double bass; João Pereira da Silva, baritone horn; Eugênio Velasco, clarinet/*requinta*; Nenem Trajano, trumpet; Rodrigo Miranda, clarinet; and Jeronimo Correia, ophicleide.

15. Maria Ferreira de Oliveira, "Sérgio Magnani: Sua influência no meio musical de Belo Horizonte," master's thesis, Universidade Federal de Minas Gerais, 2008, 10.

16. "Sociedade Musical Carlos Gomes," 31; and Cruz and Vargas, "A vida musical nos salões de Belo Horizonte," 127.

17. Gomes, *A música da cidade*, 60; and Teixeira, *Marchinhas e retretas*, 53.

18. Teixeira, *Marchinhas e retretas*, 55.

19. Camila Frésca, *Uma extraordinária revelação de arte: Flausino Vale e o violino brasileiro* (São Paulo: Annablume, 2010), 30.

20. Aideone Bertussi, *A banda do Alto da Cruz* (Ouro Preto, Brazil: Instituto de Artes e Cultura / Universidade Federal de Ouro Preto, 1985).

21. Cruz and Vargas, "A vida musical nos salões de Belo Horizonte," 123.

22. Gomes, *A música da cidade*, 61.

23. Cruz and Vargas, "A vida musical nos salões de Belo Horizonte," 129.

24. Cruz and Vargas, "A vida musical nos salões de Belo Horizonte," 129.

25. Cacciatore, *Dicionário biográfico*, 148.

26. Cruz and Vargas, "A vida musical nos salões de Belo Horizonte," 124.

27. Cruz and Vargas, "A vida musical nos salões de Belo Horizonte," 129.

28. Universidade Federal Campina Grande, http://www.dec.ufcg.edu.br/biografias/Mano JMac.htm.

29. Cacciatore, *Dicionário biográfico*, 87.

30. *Pattápio Silva, Mestres Brasileiros*, vol. 5, liner notes (V&M, Sonhos e Sons, 2004). Afonso Pena helped spearhead the founding of Belo Horizonte after becoming the first freely elected governor of Minas Gerais in 1892 (his name graces one of the city's most important avenues).

31. Cited in Paulinho Assunção, *Maletta* (Belo Horizonte: Conceito, 2010), 80.

32. Gomes, *A música da cidade*, 62.

33. Sérgio Freire, *Do conservatório à escola: 80 anos de criação musical em Belo Horizonte* (Belo Horizonte: Editora UFMG, 2006), 12. The rest of the quartet included E. Guardagnin, second violin; L. Cioglia, viola; and T. Matta, cello.

34. Jader de Oliveira, *No tempo mais que perfeito: Vida e sonhos de Belo Horizonte nos anos 50* (self-published, 2009), 44.

35. Oliveira, *No tempo mais que perfeito*, 132.

36. Oliveira, *No tempo mais que perfeito*, 132. The Comércio's orchestra appears in a dated photo in Freire, *Do conservatório à escola*, 2006.

37. "Sociedade Musical Carlos Gomes," 29. Other cinemas and their opening dates in Belo Horizonte include the Cinema Avenida, 1910; Parque Cinema, 1911; Cine Odeon, 1912; Cinema Lagoinha, 1913; and Cinema Floresta, 1915. The Banda Carlos Gomes's conductor, Henrique Passos, was hired in 1914 to form and direct the orchestra at the Cine Odeon. Camila Frésca (*Uma extraordinária revelação de arte*, 32) lists other theaters that had opened by 1910, including the Cine Central and Cine Ideal.

38. Marcondes, *Enciclopédia da música brasileira*, 74–75.

39. Celina Albano, *Cine Pathé* (Belo Horizonte: Conceito, 2008), 16.

40. Cacciatore, *Dicionário biográfico*, 33.

41. Frésca, *Uma extraordinária revelação de arte*, 33. The school received no state support. Others assisting in the school's creation were José Nicodomos, José Ramos de Lima, Ismael Franzen, and Alfred Furst. Courses were offered in piano, violin, cello, harmony, and solo and choral singing.

42. In 1949, the state-run UMG transformed into the Universidade Federal de Minas Gerais (UFMG), with all but the music conservatory later moving to the Cidade Universitária, a large campus located in Belo Horizonte's Pampulha district.

43. Bernardo Novais da Mata-Machado, *Do transitório ao permanente: Teatro Francisco Nunes, 1950–2000* (Belo Horizonte: Preifetura Belo Horizonte, 2002), 33.

44. Marcelo Bortoloti, *Guignard: Anjo mutilado* (São Paulo: Companhia das Letras, 2020), 307. Guignard's Escola de Belas Artes quickly merged with Department of Architecture of the Institute of Fine Arts of Belo Horizonte to form the Escola Guignard. In the late 1980s, the school became part of the State University of Minas Gerais (Universidade do Estado de Minas Gerais), and in 1994 the Escola Guignard moved to Mineiro architect Gustavo Penna's distinctive, newly designed building in the city's Mangabeiras district.

45. Information on these composers is from Cacciatore, *Dicionário biográfico*.

46. Cacciatore, *Dicionário biográfico*, 92.

47. Wirth, *Minas Gerais in the Brazilian Federation*, 84.

48. Jan Dewilde and Annelies Focquaert, "Bosmans, Arthur," Studiecentrum voor Vlaamse Muziek, n.d. https://www.svm.be/content/bosmans-arthur?display=biography&language=en.

49. Dewilde and Focquaert, "Bosmans, Arthur."

50. Oiliam José Lanna (b. 1953, Visconde do Rio Branco, MG) studied music in his hometown before graduating from UFMG under the tutelage of Bosmans. Following a graduate degree in music from the University of Montreal, he returned to Belo Horizonte, where he became a professor of composition, counterpoint, and orchestration at his alma mater.

51. M. Oliveira, "Sérgio Magnani," 30.

52. Frésca, *Uma extraordinária revelação de arte*, 40.

53. Frésca, *Uma extraordinária revelação de arte*, 40. In partnership with the SCA's creation were Carlos Vaz de Carvalho and music critic Celso Brant.

54. Vera Chacham, "A memória dos pequenos lugares e a construção da grande cidade," *Varia História*, no. 13 (June 1994): 132–46.

55. From Tavinho Moura's LP *Como vai minha aldeia* (RCA, 1978).

56. Márcio Rubens Prado, *Montanhez* (Belo Horizonte: Conceito, 2010), 22–23.

57. J. Oliveira, *No tempo mais que perfeito*, 105.

58. Prado, *Montanhez*, 30.

59. Prado, *Montanhez*, 29.

60. "Rômulo Paes," November 7, 2010, http://cifrantiga2.blogspot.com/2010/11/romulo-paes.html; and Penido Neto, liner notes, *Rômulo Paes e coisas mais* (Minas Trabalho Cantando / Paralelos, n.d.).

61. J. Oliveira, *No tempo mais que perfeito*, 61.

62. B. Martins, *Som imaginário*, 42.

63. J. Oliveira, *No tempo mais que perfeito*, 37. Sílvio Caldas and Cyro Monteiro were leading *sambistas* from Rio de Janeiro.

64. Wander Piroli, *Lagoinha* (Belo Horizonte: Conceito, 2003), 29.

65. All information on Mestre Conga is from Júlio Coelho Rosa's liner notes for *Mestre Conga: Decantando em sambas* (Navegador Musicas / Bananaouro, 2006).

66. Serviço Social do Comércio Palladium, http://circuitosesc.com.br/index.php/front-sesc/2-destaques-da-semana/cultura/107-noticias/noticias-sesc-palladium/2745-cine-sesc-palladium-exibe-documentario-sobre-mestre-conga.

67. Other key members included Oscar "Kalu" Baldvino, Alírio de Paula, José Alvino, José "Ze Preto" Ferreira, and others. Rosa, liner notes, *Mestre Conga*.

68. Serviço Social do Comércio Palladium.

69. Gomes, *A música da cidade*, 68. Rádio Experimental Mineira changed its name to Rádio Mineira in 1931.

70. J. Oliveira, *No tempo mais que perfeito*, 76.

71. J. Oliveira, *No tempo mais que perfeito*, 76.

72. Frésca, *Uma extraordinária revelação de arte*, 39.

73. J. Oliveira, *No tempo mais que perfeito*, 80.

74. Camila Frésca (*Uma extraordinária revelação de arte*, 37) states that beginning in 1930, Belo Horizonte witnessed a surge of new casinos but offers no details on names or locations.

75. Prado, *Montanhez*, 55–57.

76. Cited in Frésca, *Uma extraordinária revelação de arte*, 38. Delê was a photographer for the *Estado de Minas* newspaper in Belo Horizonte.

77. The information on Chiquito Braga is from Klenio Daniel, "Memória: Há dois meses morria Chiquito Braga, precursor da harmonia mineira de violão," *Violão Brasileiro*, February 22, 2018, https://www.violaobrasileiro.com/blog/memoria-ha-dois-meses-morria-chiquito-braga-precursor-da-harmonia-mineira-de-violao/208.

78. J. Oliveira, *No tempo mais que perfeito*, 44. Small groups included those directed by Pacífico Mascarenhas, Célio Balona, Paulo Modesto, Walter Gonçalves, and former members of Delê's large dance orchestra Gilberto Santana and pianist Túlio Silva.

79. The Maletta Building includes 319 apartments, 72 storefronts at street level, 74 stores in the mezzanine complex, and 642 offices and commercial spaces, including restaurants, bars,

and cafés. Museu da Pessoa, interview with Wagner Tiso, https://acervo.museudapessoa
.org/pt/conteudo/historia/entrevista-de-wagner-tiso-45809.

80. J. Oliveira, *No tempo mais que perfeito*, 80.

81. Maria Dolores, *Travessia: A vida de Milton Nascimento* (Rio de Janeiro: Editora
Record, 2006), 81.

82. J. Oliveira, *No tempo mais que perfeito*, 44.

83. B. Martins, *Som imaginário*, 41.

Chapter 9: Regionalist Themes in the Songs of the Corner Club

1. See *The Corner Club*, this author's book examining the 1972 LP *Clube da Esquina* (New
York: Bloomsbury, 2020).

2. Maria Tereza R. Arruda Campos, *Toninho Horta: Harmonia compartilhada* (São Paulo:
Imprensa Oficial do Estado de São Paulo, 2010), 64.

3. Cited in Andréa Estanislau, "Da música para a musica," in *Coração Americano: 35 anos
do álbum Clube da Esquina*, ed. Andréa Estanislau (Belo Horizonte: Prax, 2008), 62.

4. Museu Clube da Esquina, interview with Nivaldo Ornelas, 2010–2012. The website no
longer exists, and the URL cannot be cited.

5. Holly L. Holmes, "Milton Nascimento and the Clube da Esquina: Popular Music,
Politics, and Fraternity during Brazil's Military Dictatorship (1964–85)," PhD diss.,
University of Illinois, 2017, 98.

6. Charles A. Perrone, *Masters of Contemporary Brazilian Song: MPB, 1965–1985* (Austin:
University of Texas Press, 1989), 130.

7. Jairo Severiano, *Uma história da música popular brasileira* (São Paulo: Editora 34,
2008), 370.

8. Museu Clube da Esquina, interview with Milton Nascimento, 2010–2012. The website
no longer exists, and the URL cannot be cited.

9. Perrone, *Masters of Contemporary Brazilian Song*, 140.

10. Perrone, *Masters of Contemporary Brazilian Song*, 132

11. Liner notes, Milton Nascimento, *Geraes* (EMI, 1976).

12. Perrone, *Masters of Contemporary Brazilian Song*, 135.

13. Perrone, *Masters of Contemporary Brazilian Song*, 58.

14. Museu da Pessoa, interview with Milton Nascimento, http://www.museudapessoa.net
/MuseuVirtual/.

15. Milton Nascimento, liner notes, *Travessia* (Dubas Música, 2002). "This image came
to mind and I composed 'Morro Velho.' And curiously this story I created ended up coming
true," Milton states, referring to an eerily similar relationship actually coming to fruition at
Fazenda da Cachoeira years later.

16. Francisco Carlos Teixeira da Silva, "Da bossa nova à tropicália: As canções utópicas,"
in *Do samba-canção à tropicália*, ed. Paulo Sérgio Duarte and Santuza Cambraia Naves (Rio
de Janeiro: Relume Dumará, 2003), 141.

17. Holmes, "Milton Nascimento and the Clube da Esquina," 36.

18. Severiano, *Uma história da música popular brasileira*, 369.

19. It was Brant's arcane idea to title his first songwriting partnership with Nascimento by lifting "Travessia" for the title track, the very last word from Mineiro literary legend João Guimarães Rosa's epic *Grande Sertão: Veredas*, a classic Brazilian novel.

20. Nascimento, liner notes, *Travessia*.

21. Dolores, *Travessia*, 73. For the *Travessia* sessions at Codil's Rio de Janeiro studios on Avenida Rio Branco, Eça brought in Rubens Ohana on drums, bassist Dorio Ferreira, and Bebeto Castilho on flute.

22. Severiano, *Uma história da música popular brasileira*, 370.

23. Márcio Borges, *Os sonhos não envelhecem: Histórias do Clube da Esquina*, 6th ed. (São Paulo: Geração Editorial, 2010), 28.

24. Cited in Estanislau, "Da música para a musica," 76.

25. Museu Clube da Esquina, interview with Milton Nascimento.

26. Nivaldo Ornelas, personal communication, December 30, 2009.

27. Dolores, *Travessia*, 199.

28. An important addition from the Nordeste to the collective, Novelli (Djair de Barros e Silva) met Milton Nascimento at the 1967 International Song Festival, where he played bass with the group MPB4.

29. Perrone, *Masters of Contemporary Brazilian Song*, 133–34.

30. Estanislau, "Da música para a musica," 27.

31. Along with Toninho Horta, Novelli, and Dorival Caymmi, Guedes almost landed his first solo album deal in the immediate aftermath of the *Clube da Esquina* record, as part of 1973's *O disco do quatro*: the original idea was to have each release a solo album as an immediate follow-up to *Clube da Esquina*.

32. Guedes presented his father's song "Cantar" during his fiftieth birthday concert held on September 11, 2001, in Belo Horizonte's Teatro Francisco Nunes. The performance included special appearances by Milton Nascimento, Lô Borges, and Tavinho Moura and was released on an Epic label DVD as *Beto Guedes: 50 anos ao vivo*.

33. Eduardo Tristão Girão, "Centenario de Godofredo Guedes e comemorado em Montes Claros e BH," *Estado de Minas*, July 21, 2008.

34. Biographical information on Tiso from Museu da Pessoa, interview with Wagner Tiso.

35. Campos, *Toninho Horta*, 40–41

36. Campos, *Toninho Horta*, 15.

37. Sisters Letícia and Gilda Horta sang operettas with the Minas Gerais Symphony and organized what became a family tradition of the *hora dançante*. Another sister, Lena, became an accomplished flutist and talent agent. Campos, *Toninho Horta*, 15–22, 25.

38. In 1974, Horta chose to play with Som Imaginário and Nascimento on the *Milagre dos peixes* album, foregoing the singular opportunity to join the backup band for one of Brazil's most famous duets: Tom Jobim and Elis Regina. His first solo LP, *Terra dos pássaros* (Birdland), which had been recorded several years earlier in Los Angeles, was released in 1980, quickly followed that same year by his second LP, *Toninho Horta*.

39. Perrone, *Masters of Contemporary Brazilian Song*, 144.

40. Museu Clube da Esquina, interview with Tavinho Moura, 2010–2012. The website no longer exists, and the URL cannot be cited.

41. Museu Clube da Esquina, interview with Tavinho Moura.

42. Although Moura later played viola on many of his later recordings, the *violeiros* credited on his 1978 recordings are Zéduardo and Paulão.

43. During an interview I had with Lima, the luthier pointed to a photograph hanging on the wall of Tavinho Moura holding a remarkable-looking viola he had constructed in his shop, and he said, "People write asking me to make for them a viola exactly like that one I made for Tavinho." Virgílio Lima, interview with the author, Sabará, August 7, 2013.

44. Tavinho Moura, *Maria do matué: Uma estória do Rio São Francisco* (self-published, 2007).

45. 14 Bis members included Flávio Venturini (piano, accordion), Vermelho (keyboards), and Hely Rodrigues (drums). 14 Bis was the model number of Brazilian aviator Alberto Santos Dumont's first successfully flown airplane. Moura brought the Belo Horizonte–based avant-garde ensemble Uakti into the Clube circle after befriending Marco Antônio Guimarães and using that group for his score for the 1979 film *Cabaré Mineiro*. Guimarães studied with composer Walter Smetak in Bahia and formed Uakti in 1978 with members of Belo Horizonte's Orquestra Sinfônica, including Paulo Santos and Cláudio Luz.

46. "Corte palavra / balanço do bonde / no clube da esquina / de antes da fome."

47. "Por aqui passou meu velho mestre / levando os seus chinesas / Do rio das velhas viu. Minas Gerais, Ouro immortal, Morte nas catedrais / Por aqui plantou a igreja branca."

48. "A dançarinha espanhola de Montes Claros / dança e redança na sala mestiça / cem olhos morenos estão despindo seu corpo gordo / picado de mosquito / tem um sinal da bala / na coxa direita."

49. "Bailando nos cabarés de um país don juan, tangos cara a cara com você / eu vou bailando, eu conheci você no meu bar, sonhando nos cabarés / você quis me beijar, beijos cara a cara com você / eu vou bailando, em movimentos nús, seu corpo a média luz."

50. Murilo Antunes, liner notes, *Caboclo d'água* (Bemol, 1992).

51. "Belo Horizonte, Brazil Metro Area Population 1950–2021," Macrotrends, https://www.macrotrends.net/cities/20183/belo-horizonte/population.

52. Bruno Viveiros Martins, "Clube da Esquina: Viagens, sonhos e canções," bachelor's thesis, Universidade Federal de Minas Gerais, 2005, 14.

53. Gomes, *A música da cidade*, 82.

54. B. Martins, *Som imaginário*, 117. DOI/CODI was the Destacamento de Operações de Informações/Centros de Operações de Defensa Interna (Operation and Information Detachment/Centers for Internal Defense Operations).

55. B. Martins, *Som imaginário*, 117. A Getúlio Vargas–era agency known as the Delegacia de Ordem Pública (DOP; Department of Public Order, created 1931) became in 1956 the Departamento de Ordem Política e Social de Minas Gerais.

56. B. Martins, *Som imaginário*, 178.

57. "Morte, vela / Sentinela sou, / Do corpo desse meu irmão que já se vai / Revejo nessa hora tudo que ocorreu / Memória não morrerá."

58. B. Martins, *Som imaginário*, 63.

59. "Passa bonde, passa boiada / Passa trator, avião / Ruas e reis / A cidade plantou no curação / Tantos nomes de quem morreu."

60. Severiano, *Uma história da música popular brasileira*, 369.

61. *Missa dos Quilombos* was also performed at the invitation of the Spanish government on the occasion of the five hundredth anniversary of Christopher Columbus's first arrival in the Americas, at a concert held at the Santiago de Compostela Sanctuary in 1992. Another notable performance was for the three hundredth anniversary of the death of Zumbi of Palmares, held in 1995 at the Aparecida do Norte Church in São Paulo.

62. Dom Pedro Casaldáliga, liner notes, *Missa dos Quilombos*, by Milton Nascimento (Ariola, 1982).

63. Luíz Maciel, liner notes, *Missa dos Quilombos*, by Milton Nascimento (Abril Coleções, 2012).

64. "Os tambores de Minas" (Minas drums) by Milton Nascimento and Márcio Borges, from the CD *Nascimento* (1997). "Os tambores de Minas" was later released on the CD and DVD, Milton Nascimento, *Tambores de Minas: Ao vivo* (WEA, 1998).

65. *Cartografia musical brasileira: MG* (Rumos Itaú Cultural Música CMB81, 2001–2002) was part of a nationwide fieldwork project undertaken by Hermano Vianna and Benjamim Taubkin that produced a set of ten CDs.

66. Braga and Amâncio, *Candombe do Açude*.

Appendix 2: Luso-African Roots of Congado Mineiro Heritage

1. Juliana Beatriz de Almeida Souza, "Virgem imperial: Nossa Senhora e império marítimo português," *Luso-Brazilian Review* 45, no. 1 (2008): 35.

2. Saunders, *A Social History of Black Slaves and Freedmen*, 217.

3. Kiddy, *Blacks of the Rosary*, 30.

4. William Bascom, *Ifa Divination: Communication between Gods and Men in West Africa* (Bloomington: Indiana University Press, 1969), 84.

5. L. Mello e Souza, *The Devil and the Land of the Holy Cross*, 161.

6. Bastide, *The African Religions of Brazil*, 256; and Kiddy, *Blacks of the Rosary*, 60.

7. Kiddy, *Blacks of the Rosary*, 61.

8. Stein, *Vassouras, a Brazilian Coffee County*, 202.

9. Georges Balandier, *Daily Life in the Kingdom of the Kongo: From the Sixteenth to the Eighteenth Century* (London: George Allen and Unwin, 1968), 200–202.

10. Kiddy, *Blacks of the Rosary*, 32.

11. Nancy Priscilla Naro, "Colonial Aspirations: Connecting Three Points of the Portuguese Black Atlantic," in *Cultures of the Lusophone Black Atlantic*, ed. Nancy Priscilla Naro, Roger Sansi-Roca, and David H. Treece (New York: Palgrave Macmillan, 2007), 131–32.

12. Lopes, *Bantos, malês e identidade negra*, 151.

13. Tinhorão, *Os sons dos negros do Brasil*, 98.

14. Saunders, *A Social History of Black Slaves and Freedmen*, 106.

15. L. Mello e Souza, *The Devil and the Land of the Holy Cross*, 165.

16. Marcelo de Andrade Vilarino, "D'África ao Brasil: Elementos hi[e]stóricos coformadores e estruturantes do Congado belo-horizontino," in *Variações sobre o reinado: Um*

rosário de experiências em louvor a Maria, ed. Léa Freitas Perez, Marcos da Costa Martins, and Rafael Barros Gomes (Porto Alegre: Medianiz, 2014), 84.

17. Saunders, *A Social History of Black Slaves and Freedmen*, 2.

18. Tinhorão, *Os negros em Portugal*, 142.

19. Rabaçal, *As congadas no Brasil*, 210–11.

20. Kananoja, *Central African Identities and Religiosity*, 176.

21. Kananoja, *Central African Identities and Religiosity*, 176. António de Oliveira de Cadornega (1623–1690) was a Portuguese soldier and historian.

22. John K. Thornton, *The Kongolese Saint Anthony: Dona Beatriz Kimpa Vita and the Antonian Movement, 1684–1706* (Cambridge: Cambridge University Press, 1998).

23. Kiddy, *Blacks of the Rosary*, 105.

24. Thornton, *The Kongolese Saint Anthony*, 211.

25. M. Mello e Souza, *Reis negros no Brasil escravista*, 18.

26. M. Mello e Souza, *Reis negros no Brasil escravista*, 19.

27. Kiddy, *Blacks of the Rosary*, 40–41.

28. Gomes and Pereira, *Os Arturos: Negras raízes Mineiras*, 36.

29. Kananoja, *Central African Identities and Religiosity*, 188.

30. Kiddy, *Blacks of the Rosary*, 177–78.

31. Kiddy, *Blacks of the Rosary*, 179.

Works Cited

Books

Agassiz, Louis, and Mrs. Louis Agassiz [Elizabeth Cabot Cary Agassiz]. *Journey in Brazil.* Boston: Houghton Mifflin, 1964. First published, Boston: Ticknor and Fields, 1868.

Albano, Celina. *Cine Pathé.* Belo Horizonte: Conceito, 2008.

Amaral, Chico. *A música de Milton Nascimento.* Belo Horizonte: Editora Gomes, 2013.

Andrews, George Reid. *Afro-Latin America, 1800–2000.* New York: Oxford University Press, 2004.

Assunção, Paulinho. *Maletta.* Belo Horizonte: Conceito, 2010.

Balandier, Georges. *Daily Life in the Kingdom of the Kongo: From the Sixteenth to the Eighteenth Century.* London: George Allen and Unwin, 1968.

Bascom, William. *Ifa Divination: Communication between Gods and Men in West Africa.* Bloomington: Indiana University Press, 1969.

Bastide, Roger. *The African Religions of Brazil: Toward a Sociology of the Interpenetration of Civilizations.* Translated by Helen Sebba. Baltimore: Johns Hopkins University Press, 1978.

Bergad, Laird W. *Slavery and the Demographic and Economic History of Minas Gerais, Brazil, 1720–1888.* Cambridge: Cambridge University Press, 1999.

Bertussi, Aideone. *A Banda do Alto da Cruz.* Ouro Preto, Brazil: Instituto de Artes e Cultura / Universidade Federal de Ouro Preto, 1985.

Biason, Mary Angela, ed. *Música do Brasil colonial (IV).* São Paulo: Editora da Universidade de São Paulo, 2015.

Blake, Stanley E. *The Vigorous Core of Our Nationality: Race and Regional Identity in Northeastern Brazil.* Pittsburgh: University of Pittsburgh Press, 2011.

Borges, Márcio. *Os sonhos não envelhecem: Histórias do Clube da Esquina.* 6th ed. São Paulo: Geração Editorial, 2010.

Bortoloti, Marcelo. *Guignard: Anjo mutilado.* São Paulo: Companhia das Letras, 2020.

Boschi, Caio César. *Os leigos e o poder.* São Paulo: Editora Ática, 1986.

Botelho, Angela Vianna, and Carla Anastasia. *D. Maria da Cruz e a Sedição de 1736*. Belo Horizonte: Autêntica, 2012.

Boxer, C. R. *The Golden Age of Brazil, 1695–1750*. Berkeley: University of California Press, 1962.

Braga, Reginaldo Gil. *Batuque jêje-ijexá em Porto Alegre*. Porto Alegre: Fumproarte / Secretaria Municipal de Cultura, 1998.

Brandão, Carlos Rodrigues. *A Clara cor da noite escura: Escritos e imagens de mulheres e homens negros de Goiás e Minas Gerais*. Goiânia, Brazil: Editora da Universidade Católica de Goiás / Uberlândia, Brazil: Universidade Federal de Uberlândia, 2009.

Brescia, Rosana Marreco. *A Casa da Ópera de Vila Rica (1770–1822)*. São Paulo: Paco Editorial, 2012.

Budasz, Rogério. *A música no tempo de Gregório de Mattos*. Curitiba, Brazil: Editora do Departamento de Artes da Universidade Federal do Paraná, 2004.

Burmeister, Hermann. *Viagem ao Brasil através das províncias do Rio de Janeiro and Minas Gerais*. Belo Horizonte: Itatiaia, 1980.

Burton, Lady Isabel. *The Romance of Isabel Lady Burton: The Story of Her Life*. New York: Dodd, Mead and Company, 1904.

Burton, Richard. *Viagem de canoa de Sabará ao Oceano Atlântico*. Belo Horizonte: Itatiaia, 1977.

Cacciatore, Olga G. *Dicionário biográfico de música erudita brasileira*. Rio de Janeiro: Editora Forense Universitária, 2005.

Calainho, Daniela Buono. *Metrópole das Mandingas*. Toronto: Garamond, 2008.

Caldcleugh, Alexander. *Viagens na América do sul: Extrato da obra contendo relato sobre o Brasil*. Translated by Júlio Jeha. Belo Horizonte: Coleção Mineiriana, 2000.

Campolina, Alda Maria Palhares, Cláudia Alves Melo, and Mariza Guerra de Andrade. *Escravidão em Minas Gerais*. Belo Horizonte: Arquivo Público Mineiro, 1988.

Campos, Maria Tereza R. Arruda. *Toninho Horta: Harmonia compartilhada*. São Paulo: Imprensa Oficial do Estado de São Paulo, 2010.

Carneiro, Edison. *Religiões Negras: Negros Bantos*. Rio de Janeiro: Civilização Brasileira, 1937.

Castelnau, Francis de la Porte. *Expedição às regiões centrais da América do Sul*. Vol. 1. São Paulo: Companhia Editora Nacional, 1949.

Castro, Felipe, Janaína Marquesini, Luana Costa, Raquel Munhoz. *Quelé, a voz da cor: Biografia de Clementina de Jesus*. 2nd ed. Rio de Janeiro: Civilização Brasileira, 2017.

Castro, José Flávio Morais. *Geoprocessamento de mapas de Minas Gerais nos séculos XVIII–XIX*. Belo Horizonte: Editora Pontifícia Universidade Católica de Minas Gerais, 2017.

Castro, Yeda Pessoa de. *A língua Mina-Jeje no Brasil: Um falar africano em Ouro Preto do século 18*. Belo Horizonte: Coleção Mineiriana, 2002.

Chaves, Cláudia Maria das Graças. *Perfeitos negociantes: Mercadores das Minas setecentistas*. São Paulo: Annablume, 1999.

Claudio, Luíz. *Minas sempre-viva: Pesquisa histórica do folclore musical mineiro*. Rio de Janeiro: Léo Christiano Editorial, 1983.

Corrêa, Roberto. *A arte de pontear viola*. 2nd ed. Brasília: Editora Viola Corrêa, 2002.

Costa, Emilia Viotti da. *The Brazilian Empire: Myths and Histories*. Rev. ed. Chapel Hill: University of North Carolina Press, 2000.

Costa, Joaquim da. *Conceição do mato dentro: Fonte da saudade*. Belo Horizonte: Editora Itatiaia, 1975.

Couto, José Vieira. *Memória sobre a Capitania das Minas Gerais: Seu território, clima e produções metálicas*. Belo Horizonte: Fundação João Pinheiro, 1994.

Couto, Patrícia Brandão. *Festa do Rosário: Iconografia e poética de um rito*. Rio de Janeiro: Editora da Universidade Federal Fluminense, 2003.

Cruz, Márcia. *Morro do Papagaio*. Belo Horizonte: Conceito, 2009.

Dent, Alexander Sebastian. *River of Tears: Country Music, Memory, and Modernity in Brazil*. Durham, NC: Duke University Press, 2009.

Dolores, Maria. *Travessia: A vida de Milton Nascimento*. Rio de Janeiro: Editora Record, 2006.

D'Orbigny, Alcide. *Viagem pitoresca através do Brasil*. Belo Horizonte: Editora Itatiaia, 1976.

Duarte, Regina Horta. *Noites circenses: Espetáculos de circo e teatro em Minas Gerais no século XIX*. Campinas, Brazil: Editora da Unicamp, 1995.

Eakins, Marshall C. *Tropical Capitalism: The Industrialization of Belo Horizonte, Brazil*. New York: Palgrave, 2001.

Estanislau, Andréa. "Da música para a musica." In *Coração Americano: 35 anos do álbum Clube da Esquina*, edited by Andréa Estanislau. Belo Horizonte: Prax, 2008.

Farfán-Santos, Elizabeth. *Black Bodies, Black Rights: The Politics of Quilombolismo in Contemporary Brazil*. Austin: University of Texas Press, 2016.

Farias, Tom. *Carolina: Uma biografia*. Rio de Janeiro: Malê, 2018.

Figueiredo, Luciano. *O avesso da memória: Cotidiano e trabalho da mulher em Minas Gerais no século XVIII*. Rio de Janeiro: Livraria José Olympio Editora / Brasília: Editora Universidade de Brasília, 1993.

Fletcher, James C., and Daniel P. Kidder. *Brazil and the Brazilians: Portrayed in Historical and Descriptive Sketches*. London: Kegan Paul, 2005. First published, Philadelphia: Childs and Peterson, 1857.

Florentino, Manolo. *Em costas negras*. São Paulo: Companhia das Letras, 1997.

Fonseca, Cláudia Damasceno. *Arraiais e vilas d'el rei: Espaço e poder nas Minas setecentistas*. Belo Horizonte: Editora UFMG, 2011.

Freire, Sérgio. *Do conservatório à escola: 80 anos de criação musical em Belo Horizonte*. Belo Horizonte: Editora UFMG, 2006.

Freireyss, G. W. *Viagem ao interior do Brasil*. Belo Horizonte: Editora Itatiaia, 1982.

Frésca, Camila. *Uma extraordinária revelação de arte: Flausino Vale e o violino brasileiro*. São Paulo: Annablume, 2010.

Fryer, Peter. *Rhythms of Resistance: African Musical Heritage in Brazil*. Hanover, NH: University Press of New England, 2000.

Gardner, George. *Travels in the Interior of Brazil, Principally through the Northern Provinces, and the Gold and Diamond Districts, during the Years 1836–1841*. London: Reeve Brothers, 1846.

Gibran, Elias, and Pedro Kalil, eds. *De Camarões: Veredas de Maurício Tizumba*. Belo Horizonte: Editora Nandyala, 2018.

Giffoni, Maria Amalia Corrêa. *Reinado do Rosário de Itapecerica*. São Paulo: Palas Athena do Brasil, 1989.

Gomes, Leonardo José Magalhães. *A música da cidade: Cartografia musical de Belo Horizonte*. Belo Horizonte: Editora Gomes, 2011.

Gomes, Núbia Pereira de Magalhães, and Edimilson de Almeida Pereira. *Mundo encaixado: Significação da cultura popular*. Belo Horizonte: Mazza Edições, 1992.

Gomes, Núbia Pereira de Magalhães, and Edimilson de Almeida Pereira. *Os Arturos: Negras raízes Mineiros*. 2nd ed. Belo Horizonte: Mazza Edições, 2000.

Gomes, Núbia Pereira de Magalhães, and Edimilson de Almeida Pereira. *Ouro Preto da Palavra: Narrativas de preceito do Congado em Minas Gerais*. Belo Horizonte: Editora PUC Minas, 2003.

Gonçalves, Andréa Lisly. *As margens da liberdade: Estudo sobre a prática de alforrias em Minas colonial e provincial*. Belo Horizonte: Fino Traço, 2011.

Grasse, Jonathon. *The Corner Club*. New York: Bloomsbury, 2020.

Hasenclever, Ernst. *Ernst Hasenclever e sua viagem às províncias do Rio de Janeiro e Minas Gerais*. Edited by Débora Bendocchi Alves. Belo Horizonte: Fundação João Pinheiro, 2015.

Hayes, Carlton J. H. *A Generation of Materialism: 1871–1900*. New York: Harper and Row, 1963.

Hertzman, Marc A. *Making Samba: A New History of Race and Music in Brazil*. Durham, NC: Duke University Press, 2013.

Higgins, Kathleen J. *"Licentious Liberty" in a Brazilian Gold-Mining Region: Slavery, Gender, and Social Control in Eighteenth-Century Sabará, Minas Gerais*. University Park: Pennsylvania State University Press, 1999.

Janzen, John M. *Ngoma: Discourses of Healing in Central and Southern Africa*. Berkeley: University of California Press, 1992.

Kananoja, Kalle. *Central African Identities and Religiosity in Colonial Minas Gerais*. Turku, Finland: Åbo Akademi University, 2012.

Kaplan, David M. *Ricoeur's Critical Theory*. Albany: State University of New York Press, 2003.

Karasch, Mary C. *Slave Life in Rio de Janeiro, 1808–1850*. Princeton, NJ: Princeton University Press, 1987.

Kiddy, Elizabeth W. *Blacks of the Rosary: Memory and History in Minas Gerais, Brazil*. University Park: Pennsylvania State University Press, 2005.

Kubik, Gerhard. *Angolan Traits in Black Music, Games and Dances of Brazil*. Lisbon: Junta de Investigações Científicas do Ultramar, Centro de Estudos de Antropologia Cultural, 1979.

Lange, Francisco Curt. *História da música na Capitania Geral das Minas Gerais*. Vol. 8. Belo Horizonte: Conselho Estadual de Cultura, 1982.

Langfur, Hal. *The Forbidden Lands: Colonial Identity, Frontier Violence, and the Persistence of Brazil's Eastern Indians, 1750–1830*. Stanford, CA: Stanford University Press, 2006.

Langsdorff, Georg Heinrich von. *Os diários de Langsdorff*. Vol. 1: *Rio de Janeiro e Minas Gerais, 8 de maio de 1824 a 17 de fevereiro de 1825*. Edited by Danuzio Gil Bernardino da Silva, et al. São Paulo: Fiocruz, 1997.

Lara, Mário. *Família, história e poder no Campo das Vertentes*. Self-published, 2012.

Leite, Ilka Boaventura. *Antropologia da viagem: Escravos e libertos em Minas Gerais no século XIX*. Belo Horizonte: Editora UFMG, 1996.

Levine, Robert M., and John J. Crocitti, eds. *The Brazil Reader: History, Culture, Politics*. Durham, NC: Duke University Press, 1999.

Livingston-Isenhour, Tamara Elena, and Thomas George Caracas Garcia. *Choro: A Social History of a Brazilian Popular Music*. Bloomington: Indiana University Press, 2005.

Lobão, Alexandre. *Quilombos e quilombolos: Passado e presente de lutas*. Belo Horizonte: Mazza Edições, 2014.

Lopes, Nei. *Bantos, malês e identidade negra*. Rio de Janeiro: Editora Forense Universitária, 1988.

Lucas, Glaura. *Os sons do Rosário: O congado mineiro dos Arturos e Jatobá*. Belo Horizonte: Editora UFMG, 2002.

Luccock, John. *Notas sobre de Rio de Janeiro e partes meridionais do Brasil*. São Paulo: Livraria Martins, 1942.

Machado Filho, Aires da Mata. *O negro e o garimpo em Minas Gerais*. Rio de Janeiro: Livraria José Olympio Editora, 1943.

Magalhães, Daniel Lima. *Canudos, gaitas e pífanos: As flautas do norte de Minas*. Belo Horizonte: self-published, 2010.

Magowan, Fiona, and Louise Wrazen, eds. *Performing Gender, Place, and Emotion in Music: Global Perspectives*. Rochester, NY: University of Rochester Press, 2013.

Marcondes, Marcos A., ed. *Enciclopédia da música brasileira: Popular, erudite e folclórica*. 2nd ed. São Paulo: Art Editora/Publifolha, 1998.

Mariz, Vasco. *Três musicólogos brasileiros*. Rio de Janeiro: Civilização Brasileira, 1983.

Martins, Bruno Viveiros. *Som imaginário: A reinvenção da cidade nas canções do Clube da Esquina*. Belo Horizonte: Editora UFMG, 2009.

Martins, Leda Maria. *Afrografias da memória*. Belo Horizonte: Mazza Edições, 1997.

Martins, Tarcísio José. *Quilombo do Campo Grande: A história de Minas que se devolve ao povo*. 3rd ed. São Paulo: MG Quilombo, 2018.

Martins, Tarcísio José. *Quilombo do Campo Grande: Ladrões da história*. Belo Horizonte: Editora Santa Clara, 2011.

Mata-Machado, Bernardo Novais da. *Do transitório ao permanente: Teatro Francisco Nunes, 1950–2000*. Belo Horizonte: Preifetura Belo Horizonte, 2002.

Mattoso, Katia M. de Queirós. *To Be a Slave in Brazil: 1550–1888*. Translated by Arthur Goldhammer. New Brunswick, NJ: Rutgers University Press, 1987.

Maxwell, Kenneth. *Conflicts and Conspiracies: Brazil and Portugal, 1750–1808*. New York: Routledge, 2004.

Mello e Souza, Laura de. *The Devil and the Land of the Holy Cross: Witchcraft, Slavery, and Popular Religion in Colonial Brazil*. Translated by Diane Grosklaus Whitty. Austin: University of Texas Press, 2003.

Mello e Souza, Laura de. *O diabo e a terra de Santa Cruz: Feitiçaria e religiosidade popular no Brasil colonial*. São Paulo: Companhia das Letras, 1986.

Mello e Souza, Laura de. *Norma e conflito: Aspectos da história de Minas no século XVIII*. Belo Horizonte: Editora UFMG, 2006.

Mello e Souza, Marina de. *Reis negros no Brasil escravista: História da festa de coroação de Rei Congo*. Belo Horizonte: Editora UFMG, 2002.

Meyer, Mônica. *Ser-tão natureza: A natureza de Guimarães Rosa*. Belo Horizonte: Editora UFMG, 2008.

Monteiro, Maurício. *A Construção do gosto: Música e sociedade na corte do Rio de Janeiro, 1808–1821*. São Paulo: Ateliê Editorial, 2008.

Morley, Helena. *The Diary of "Helena Morley."* Translated by Elizabeth Bishop. New York: Farrar, Straus and Giroux, 1995.

Mostaro, Carlos Décio, João Medeiros Filho, and Roberto Faria de Medeiros. *História recente da música popular brasileira em Juiz de Fora*. Juiz de Fora, Brazil: self-published, 1977.

Mott, Luiz. *Rosa Egipcíaca: Uma Santa Africana no Brasil*. Rio de Janeiro: Editora Bertrand Brasil, 1993.

Moura, Tavinho. *Maria do matué: Uma estória do Rio São Francisco*. Self-published, 2007.

Nascimento, Elisa Larkin. *The Sorcery of Color: Identity, Race, and Gender in Brazil*. Philadelphia: Temple University Press, 2007.

Nepomuceno, Rosa. *Música caipira: Da roça ao rodeio*. São Paulo: Editora 34, 1999.

Netto, Michel Nicolau. *Música brasileira e identidade nacional na mundialização*. São Paulo: Annablume, 2009.

Neves, Libério. *Santa Tereza*. Belo Horizonte: Conceito, 2010.

Neves, Zanoni. *Navegantes da integração: Os remeiros do rio São Francisco*. 2nd ed. Belo Horizonte: Editora UFMG, 2011.

Novinsky, Anita. *Inquisição: Prisioneiros do Brasil, séculos XVI–XIX*. Rio de Janeiro: Expressão e Cultura, 2002.

Oliveira, Jader de. *No tempo mais que perfeito: Vida e sonhos de Belo Horizonte nos anos 50*. Self-published, 2009.

Ortiz, Renato. *Cultura brasileira e identidade nacional*. São Paulo: Editora Brasiliense, 1985.

Pereira, Célio Hugo Alves. *Efemérides do arraial do tejuco a Diamantina*. Belo Horizonte: Edições CLA, 2007.

Pereira, Edimilson de Almeida. *Os tambores estão frios: Herança cultural e sincretismo religioso de candombe*. Belo Horizonte: Mazza Edições, 2005.

Pereira, Luzimar Paulo. *Os giros do sagrado: Um estudo etnográfico sobre as folias em Urucuia, MG*. Rio de Janeiro: 7Letras, 2010.

Perrone, Charles A. *Masters of Contemporary Brazilian Song: MPB, 1965–1985*. Austin: University of Texas Press, 1989.

Piroli, Wander. *Lagoinha*. Belo Horizonte: Conceito, 2003.

Prado, Márcio Rubens. *Montanhez*. Belo Horizonte: Conceito, 2010.

Rabaçal, Alfredo João. *As congadas no Brasil*. São Paulo: Secretaria da Cultura, Ciência e Tecnologia / Conselho Estadual de Cultura, 1976.

Reily, Suzel Ana. *Voices of the Magi: Enchanted Journeys in Southeast Brazil*. Chicago: University of Chicago Press, 2002.

Rezende, Maria Conceição. *A música na história de Minas Colonial*. Belo Horizonte: Editora Itatiaia, 1989.

Ribeiro, Ricardo Ferreira. *Florestas anãs do sertão*. Vol. 1. Belo Horizonte: Autêntica, 2005.

Ricoeur, Paul. *Memory, History, Forgetting*. Translated by Kathleen Blamey and David Pellauer. Chicago: University of Chicago Press, 2004.

Rugendas, Johann Moritz. *Voyage pittoresque dans le Brésil*. Paris: Engelmann et Cie, 1835.

Russell-Wood, A. J. R. *The Black Man in Slavery and Freedom in Colonial Brazil*. Basingstoke, Hants., England: Palgrave Macmillan, 1982.

Saint-Hilaire, Auguste de. *Viagem às nascentes do Rio São Francisco*. Belo Horizonte: Editora Itatiaia, 2004.

Saint-Hilaire, Auguste de. *Viagem pelas Províncias de Rio de Janeiro e Minas Gerais*. Vol. 1. São Paulo: Companhia Editora Nacional, 1938.

Saint-Hilaire, Auguste de. *Viagem pelo Distrito dos Diamantes e litoral do Brasil*. Belo Horizonte: Editora Itatiaia, 2004.

Sampião, Neide Freitas, ed. *Vissungo: Cantos afro-descendentes em Minas Gerais*. Belo Horizonte: Edições Viva Voz, 2009.

Sandroni, Carlos. *Feitiço decente: Transformações do samba no Rio de Janeiro (1917–1933)*. Rio de Janeiro: Jorge Zahar, 2001.

Santiago, Camila Fernanda Guimaraes. *A Vila em rica festas: Celebrações promovidas pela Câmara de Vila Rica (1711–1744)*. Belo Horizonte: Editora C/Arte / Fundação Mineira de Educação e Cultura, Faculdade de Ciências Empresariais, 2003.

Santos, Maria Elisabete Gontijo dos, Pablo Matos Camargo, João Batista de Almeida Costa, and José Augusto Laranjeiras Samião. *Comunidades quilombolas de Minas Gerais no século XXI*. Belo Horizonte: Centro de Documentação Eloy Ferreira da Silva / Autêntica, 2008.

Saunders, A. C. de C. M. *A Social History of Black Slaves and Freedmen in Portugal, 1441–1555*. Cambridge: Cambridge University Press, 1982.

Scalzo, Marília, and Celso Nucci. *Uma história de amor à música: São João del-Rei, Prados, Tiradentes*. São Paulo: BEÏ Editora, 2012.

Severiano, Jairo. *Uma história da música popular brasileira*. São Paulo: Editora 34, 2008.

Souza, Wladimir Alves de. *Guia dos bens tombados Minas Gerais*. Rio de Janeiro: Expressão e Cultura, 1984.

Spix, Johann Baptist von, and Carl Friedrich Philipp von Martius. *Viagem pelo Brasil, 1817–1820*. Vol. 1. 2nd ed. São Paulo: Edições Melhoramentos, 1981.

Spix, Johann Baptist von, and Carl Friedrich Philipp von Martius. *Viagem pelo Brasil, 1817–1820*. Vol. 2. 2nd ed. São Paulo: Edições Melhoramentos, 1976.

Stein, Stanley J. *Vassouras, a Brazilian Coffee County, 1850–1900: The Roles of Planter and Slave in a Plantation Society*. Princeton, NJ: Princeton University Press, 1985.

Sweet, James H. *Recreating Africa: Culture, Kinship, and Religion in the African-Portuguese World, 1441–1770*. Chapel Hill: University of North Carolina Press, 2003.

Taborda, Marcia. *Violão e identidade nacional*. Rio de Janeiro: Civilização Brasileira, 2011.

Teixeira, Clotildes Avellar. *Marchinhas e retretas: História das corporações musicais civis de Belo Horizonte*. Belo Horizonte: Autêntica, 2007.

Telles, Edwin E. *Race in Another America: The Significance of Skin Color in Brazil*. Princeton, NJ: Princeton University Press, 2004.

Thompson, Robert F. *Flash of the Spirit: African and Afro-American Art and Philosophy*. New York: Vintage Books, 1983.

Thornton, John K. *The Kongolese Saint Anthony: Dona Beatriz Kimpa Vita and the Antonian Movement, 1684–1706*. Cambridge: Cambridge University Press, 1998.

Tinhorão, José Ramos. *A música popular no romance brasileiro*. Vol. 2: *Século XX* (*primeira parte*). São Paulo: Editora 34, 2000.

Tinhorão, José Ramos. *As festas no Brasil colonial*. São Paulo: Editora 34, 2000.

Tinhorão, José Ramos. *Domingos Caldas Barbosa: O poeta da viola, da modinha e do lundu (1740–1800)*. Lisbon: Caminho, 2004.

Tinhorão, José Ramos. *Os negros em Portugal: Sécs. XV a XIX*. Lisbon: Commisão Nacional para as Comemorações dos Descobrimentos Portugueses, 1999.

Tinhorão, José Ramos. *Os sons dos negros do Brasil*. São Paulo: Art Editora, 1988.

Tinhorão, José Ramos. *Os sons que vem da rua*. São Paulo: Editora 34, 2005.

Tinhorão, José Ramos. *Rei de Congo: A mentira histórica que virou folklore*. São Paulo: Editora 34, 2016.

Tombs, Robert. *The English and Their History*. New York: Vintage Books, 2014.

Torres, João Camilo de Oliveira. *O homem e a montanha: Introdução ao estudo das influências da situação geográfica para a formação do espírito Mineiro*. Belo Horizonte: Autêntica, 2011. First published, 1943.

Trinidade, Raymundo Octavio da. *São Francisco de Assis de Ouro Prêto: Crônica narrada pelos documentos da ordem*. Rio de Janeiro: Diretoria do Patrimônio Histórico e Artístico Nacional, 1951.

Tugny, Rosângela Pereira de, and Ruben Caixeta de Queiroz, eds. *Músicas, africanas e indígenas no Brasil*. Belo Horizonte: Editora UFMG, 2006.

Viana, Fábio Henrique. *A paisagem sonora de Vila Rica e a música barroca das Minas Gerais (1711–1822)*. Belo Horizonte: Editora C/Arte, 2012.

Vilela, Ivan. *Cantando a própria história: Música caipira e enraizamento*. São Paulo: Editora da Universidade de São Paulo, 2013.

Vogt, Carlos, and Peter Fry. *Cafundó: A África no Brasil*. São Paulo: Companhia das Letras, 1996.

Voigt, Lisa. *Spectacular Wealth: The Festivals of Colonial South American Mining Towns*. Austin: University of Texas Press, 2016.

Walsh, Robert. *Notícias do Brasil*. Belo Horizonte: Editora Itatiaia, 1985.

Wirth, John D. *Minas Gerais in the Brazilian Federation, 1889–1937*. Stanford, CA: Stanford University Press, 1977.

Chapters in Books and Anthologies, and Conference Papers

Amantino, Marcia. "Caxambú, cateretê e feiticaría entre os escravos do Rio de Janeiro e Minas Gerais no século XIX." In *Escravidão, mestiçagem e histórias comparadas*, edited by Eduardo França Paiva and Isnara Pereira Ivo. São Paulo: Annablume, 2008.

Andrade, Francisco Eduardo de. "Viver a gandaia: povo negro nos morros das Minas." In *Escravidão, mestiçagem e histórias comparadas*, edited by Eduardo França Paiva and Isnara Pereira Ivo. São Paulo: Annablume, 2008.

Avelar, Idelbar. "Defeated Rallies, Mournful Anthems, and the Origins of Brazilian Heavy Metal." In *Brazilian Popular Music and Citizenship*, edited by Idelbar Avelar and Christopher Dunn. Durham, NC: Duke University Press, 2011.

Borges, Márcio. "O Clube da Esquina." In *Do Samba-canção à Tropicália*, edited by Paulo Sérgio Duarte and Santuza Cambraia Naves. Rio de Janeiro: Relume Dumará, 2003.

Boschi, Caio César. "Convicções e coerências de um cultor de Clio." In *Diogo de Vasconcelos: O ofício do historiador*, edited by Adriana Romeiro and Marco Antonio Silveira. Belo Horizonte: Autêntica, 2014.

Budasz, Rogério. "Ecos do quilombo, sons da corte: Notas sobre o repertório português para viola (guitarra de cinco ordens)." In *A música no Brasil colonial*, edited by Rui Vieira Nery. Lisbon: Fundação Calouste Gulbenkian / Serviço de Música, 2001.

Carneiro, Edison. "O negro em Minas Gerais." In *Segundo seminário de estudos mineiros*. Belo Horizonte: Universidade de Minas Gerais, 1956.

Carvalho, José Jorge de. "Black Music of All Colors: The Construction of Black Ethnicity in Ritual and Popular Genres of Afro-Brazilian Music." In *Music and Black Ethnicity: The Caribbean and South America*, edited by Gerard H. Béhague. New Brunswick, NJ: Transaction Publishers, 1994.

Carvalho, José Jorge de. "Um panorama da música afro-brasileira." In *Vissungo: Cantos afro-descendentes em Minas Gerais*, edited by Neide Freitas Sampião. Belo Horizonte: Edições Viva Voz, 2009.

Castagna, Paulo. "O 'estilo antigo' no Brasil, nos séculos XVIII e XIX." In *A música no Brasil colonial*, edited by Rui Vieira Nery. Lisbon: Fundação Calouste Gulbenkian / Serviço de Música, 2001.

Castagna, Paulo, and Jaelson Trindade. "Chapelmasters and Musical Practice in Brazilian Cities in the Eighteenth Century." In *Music and Urban Society in Colonial Latin America*, edited by Geoffrey Baker and Tess Knighton. Cambridge: Cambridge University Press, 2011.

Castro, Renato Moreira Varoni de. "O violão substitui a viola de arame na cidade de Rio de Janeiro no século XIX." Paper presented at the XV Congresso da Associação Nacional de Pesquisa e Pós-Graduação em Música, Rio de Janeiro, 2005.

Cruz, Wagner Rodrigues da. "Congado: Memória de um povo." In *História e memória do Centro-Oeste Mineiro*, edited by Batistina Maria de Souza Corgozinho, Leandro Pena Catão, and Mateus Henrique de Faria Pereira. Belo Horizonte: Crisálida, 2009.

Dias, Renato da Silva. "Na Africa eu nasci, no Brasil eu me criei." In *Escravidão, mestiçagem e histórias comparadas*, edited by Eduardo França Paiva and Isnara Pereira Ivo. São Paulo: Annablume, 2008.

Dominguesi, Andréa Silva. "Cultura e identidade: Festa da igreja para os padres, e a festa de Nossa Senhora do Rosário para as pessoas do cativeiro." Paper presented at the XXVI Simpósio Nacional de História, São Paulo, July 2011.

Graham, Richard. "Free African Brazilians and the State in Slavery Times." In *Racial Politics in Contemporary Brazil*, edited by Michael Hanchard. Durham, NC: Duke University Press, 1999.

Grasse, Jonathon. "Deep Regionalism and Music in Minas Gerais, Brazil." In *Musical Spaces: Place, Performance, and Power*, edited by James Williams and Samuel Horlor. Singapore: Jenny Stanford, 2021.

Guimarães, Carlos Magno. "Mineração, quilombos e Palmares." In *Liberdade por um fio: História dos quilombos no Brasil*, edited by João José Reis and Flávio dos Santos Gomes. São Paulo: Companhia das Letras, 1996.

Guimarães, Inês. "A Obra 'Dominica in Palmis' (1782) de Lobo de Mesquita." In *A música no Brasil colonial*, edited by Rui Vieira Nery. Lisbon: Fundação Calouste Gulbenkian / Serviço de Música, 2001.

Korossy, Gabriela. "Deus não sobe meia ladeira." In *Da senzala à capela: From Senzala to Chapel*, edited by Laycer Tomaz. Brasília: Editora Universidade Brasília, 2000.

Lange, Francisco Curt. "A música barroca." In *Minas Gerais: Terra e povo*, edited by Guilhermino Cesar. Rio de Janeiro: Editora Globo, 1969.

Lawrey, Alex. "Putting the Psycho in Psychogeography: Tom Vague's Musical Mapping of Notting Hill." In *Sites of Popular Music Heritage: Memories, Histories, Places*, edited by Sara Cohen, Robert Knifton, Marion Leonard, and Les Roberts. New York: Routledge, 2015.

Leonel, Guilherme Guimarães. "Entre a cruz e os tambores: Estratégias de resistência e perspectivas de controle, coerção e tolerância às Festas do Reinado em Divinópolis/MG." In *História e memória do Centro-Oeste Mineiro*, edited by Batistina Maria de Souza Corgozinho, Leandro Pena Catão, and Mateus Henrique de Faria Pereira. Belo Horizonte: Crisálida, 2009.

Lucas, Glaura. "As falas da ingoma." In *Músicas, africanas e indígenas no Brasil*, edited by Rosângela Pereira de Tugny and Ruben Caixeta de Queiroz. Belo Horizonte: Editora UFMG, 2006.

Luna, Francisco Vidal, and Iraci del Nero da Costa. "A vida quotidiana em julgamento: Devassas em Minas Gerais." In *Minas colonial: Economia e sociedade*, by Francisco Vidal Luna and Iraci del Nero da Costa. São Paulo: Pioneira, 1982.

Mitchell, Michael. "Miguel Reale and the Impact of Conservative Modernization on Brazilian Race Relations." In *Racial Politics in Contemporary Brazil*, edited by Michael Hanchard. Durham, NC: Duke University Press, 1999.

Mott, Luiz. "Santo Antônio, o Divino Capitão-do-Mato." In *Liberdade por um fio: História dos quilombos no Brasil*, edited by João José Reis and Flávio dos Santos Gomes. São Paulo: Companhia das Letras, 1996.

Naro, Nancy Priscilla. "Colonial Aspirations: Connecting Three Points of the Portuguese Black Atlantic." In *Cultures of the Lusophone Black Atlantic*, edited by Nancy Priscilla Naro, Roger Sansi-Roca, and David H. Treece. New York: Palgrave Macmillan, 2007.

Oliveira e Gabarra, Larissa. "Mihangas e bastões: Culturas materiais através do Atlântico." In *Objeto da escravidão: Abordagens sobre a cultura material da escravidão e seu legado*, edited by Camilla Agostini. Rio de Janeiro: 7Letras, 2013.

Pereira, Luzimar Paulo. "A viola do diabo: Nota sobre narrativas de pactos demoníacos no norte e noroeste Mineiro." In *Leituras sobre music popular: Reflexões sobre sonoridades e cultura*, edited by Emerson Gumbelli, Julio Diniz, and Santuza Cambraia Naves. Rio de Janeiro: 7Letras, 2008.

Pinto, Tiago de Oliveira. "As bandas-de-pífanos no Brasil: Aspectos de organologia, repertorio e função." In *Portugal e o mundo: O encontro de culturas na música*, edited by Salwa El-Shawan Castelo-Branco. Lisbon: Dom Quixote, 1997.

Ramos, Donald. "A influência africana e a cultura popular em Minas Gerais: Um comentário sobre a interpretação da escravidão." In *Brasil: Colonização e escravidão*, edited by Maria Beatriz Nizza da Silva. Rio de Janeiro: Editora Nova Fronteira, 2000.

Resende, Edna Maria. "Flagrantes do quotidiano: Um olhar sobre o universo cultural dos homens livres pobres em São João del-Rei (1840–1860)." In *Escravidão, mestiçagem e histórias comparadas*, edited by Eduardo França Paiva and Isnara Pereira Ivo. São Paulo: Annablume, 2008.

Resende, Maria Leônia Chaves de. "Minas Gerais sub examine: Inventário das denúncias nos Cadernos do Promotor da Inquisição de Lisboa (século XVIII)." In *Travessias inquisitoriais das Minas Gerais aos cárceres do Santo Ofício: Diálogos e trânsitos religiosos no império luso-brasileiro (sécs. XVI–XVIII)*, edited by Júnia Ferreira Furtado and Maria Leônia Chaves de Resende. Belo Horizonte: Fino Traço, 2013.

Ricciardi, Rubens. "Manuel Dias de Oliveira: Esboço biográfico e a partitura de 'Eu Vos Adoro.'" in *A música no Brasil colonial*, edited by Rui Vieira Nery. Lisbon: Fundação Calouste Gulbenkian / Serviço de Música, 2001.

Rodrigues, Aldair Carlos. "A Inquisição na Comarca do Rio das Mortes: Os agentes." In *Travessias inquisitoriais das Minas Gerais aos cárceres do Santo Ofício: Diálogos e trânsitos religiosos no império luso-brasileiro (sécs. XVI–XVIII)*, edited by Júnia Ferreira Furtado and Maria Leônia Chaves de Resende. Belo Horizonte: Fino Traço, 2013.

Sansi-Roca, Roger. "The Fetish in the Lusophone Atlantic." In *Cultures of the Lusophone Black Atlantic*, edited by Nancy Priscilla Naro, Roger Sansi-Roca, and David H. Treece. New York: Palgrave Macmillan, 2007.

Silva, Francisco Carlos Teixeira da. "Da bossa nova à tropicália: As canções utópicas." In *Do samba-canção à tropicália*, edited by Paulo Sérgio Duarte and Santuza Cambraia Naves. Rio de Janeiro: Relume Dumará, 2003.

Silva, Rubens Alva de. "Chico Rei Congo do Brasil." In *Memória afro-brasileira: Imaginário, cotidiano e poder*, edited by Vagner Gonçalves da Silva. São Paulo: Editora Selo Negro, 2007.

Silveira, Marco Antonio. "Diogo Vasconcelos e os demônios." In *Diogo de Vasconcelos: O ofício do historiador*, edited by Adriana Romeiro and Marco Antonio Silveira. Belo Horizonte: Autêntica, 2014.

Soja, Edward. "Borders Unbound: Globalization, Regionalism, and the Postmetropolitan Transition." In *B/ordering Space*, edited by Henk Van Houtum, Olivier Kramsch, and Wolfgang Zierhofer. London: Ashgate Publishing, 2005.

Travassos, Elizabeth. "O destino dos artefatos musicais de origem Ibérica e a modernização no Rio de Janeiro (ou como a viola se tornou caipira)." In *Artifícios & artefactos: Entre o literário e o antropológico*, edited by Gilda Santos and Gilberto Velho. Rio de Janeiro: 7Letras, 2006.

Vilarino, Marcelo de Andrade. "D'África ao Brasil: Elementos hi[e]stóricos coformadores e estruturantes do Congado belo-horizontino." In *Variações sobre o reinado: Um rosário de experiências em louvor a Maria*, edited by Léa Freitas Perez, Marcos da Costa Martins, and Rafael Barros Gomes. Porto Alegre: Medianiz, 2014.

Young, Iris Marion. *Justice and the Politics of Difference*. Princeton, NJ: Princeton University Press, 1990.

Articles from Journals

Bieber, Judy. "When Liberalism Goes Local: Nativism and Partisan Identity in the *Sertão Mineiro*, Brazil, 1831–1850." *Luso-Brazilian Review* 37, no. 2 (Winter 2000): 75–93.

Brenner, Neil, and Stuart Elden. "Henri Lefebvre on State, Space, Territory." *International Political Sociology* 3, no. 4 (December 2009): 353–77.

Budasz, Rogério. "Zealous Clerics, Mischievous Musicians, and Pragmatic Politicians: Music and Race Relations in Colonial Brazil." *Diagonal* 6 (2010): 1–12.

Carvalho, Martha de Ulhôa. "Musical Style, Migration, and Urbanization: Some Considerations on Brazilian *Música Sertaneja*." *Studies in Latin American Popular Culture* 12 (1993): 75–94.

Chacham, Vera. "A memória dos pequenos lugares e a construção da grande cidade." *Varia História*, no. 13 (June 1994): 132–46.

Ciucci, Alessandra. "'The Text Must Remain the Same': History, Collective Memory, and Sung Poetry in Morocco." *Ethnomusicology* 56, no. 3 (Fall 2012): 476–504.

Cruz, Andréa Mendonça Lage da, and Joana Domingues Vargas. "A vida musical nos salões de Belo Horizonte (1897–1907)." *Análise & Conjuntura* 4, no. 1 (January–April, 1989): 120–35.

Eltis, David. "The Nineteenth-Century Transatlantic Slave Trade: An Annual Time Series of Imports into the Americas Broken Down by Region." *Hispanic American Historical Review* 67, no. 1 (February 1987): 109–38.

Furtado, Júnia Ferreira. "Barbeiros, cirurgiões e médicos na Minas colonial." *Revista do Arquivo Público Mineiro*, no. 41 (2005): 88–105.

Gibson, Chris, and Peter Dunbar-Hall. "Nitmiluk: Place and Empowerment in Australian Aboriginal Popular Music." *Ethnomusicology* 44, no. 1 (Winter 2000): 39–64.

Gordon, Lillie S. Review of *Performing Gender, Place, and Emotion in Music: Global Perspectives*, edited by Fiona Magowan and Louise Wrazen. *Ethnomusicology* 59, no. 3 (Fall 2015): 483–88.

Grasse, Jonathon. "Calundu's Winds of Divination: Music and Black Religiosity in Eighteenth and Nineteenth-Century Minas Gerais, Brazil." *Yale Journal of Music and Religion* 3, no. 2 (2017): 43–63.

Guimarães, Berenice Martins. "Minas Gerais: A construção da nova ordem e a nova capital." *Análise & Conjuntura* 8, nos. 2–3 (May–December 1993): 16–31.

Guy, Nancy. "Flowing Down Taiwan's Tamsui River: Towards an Ecomusicology of the Environmental Imagination." *Ethnomusicology* 53, no. 2 (Spring–Summer 2009): 218–48.

Marquese, Rafael de Bivar. "A dinâmica da escravidão no Brasil: Resistência escrava, tráfico negreiro e alforrias, séculos XVII a XIX." *Novos Estudos CEBRAP*, no. 74 (March 2006): 107–23.

Noronha, Vânia. "Reinado de Nossa Senhora do Rosário: A constituição de uma religiosidade mítica afrodescendente no Brasil." *Horizonte* 9, no. 21 (April–June, 2011): 268–83.

Reily, Suzel Ana. "The 'Musical Human' and Colonial Encounters in Minas Gerais, Brazil." *South African Music Studies* 29 (2009): 61–79.

Reily, Suzel Ana. "Remembering the Baroque Era: Historical Consciousness, Local Identity and the Holy Week Celebrations in a Former Mining Town in Brazil." *Ethnomusicology Forum* 15, no. 1 (June 2006): 39–62.

Reily, Suzel Ana. "To Remember Captivity: The *Congados* of Southern Minas Gerais." *Latin American Music Review* 22, no. 1 (Spring–Summer 2001): 4–30.

Rice, Timothy. "Time, Place, and Metaphor in Musical Experience and Ethnography." *Ethnomusicology* 47, no. 2 (Spring–Summer 2003): 151–79.

Schultz, Anna. "Hindu Nationalism, Music, and Embodiment in Marathi *Rāshṭrīya Kīrtan.*" *Ethnomusicology* 46, no. 2 (Spring–Summer 2002): 307–22.

Solomon, Thomas. "Dueling Landscapes: Singing Places and Identities in Highland Bolivia." *Ethnomusicology* 44, no. 2 (Spring–Summer 2000): 257–80.

Souza, Juliana Beatriz de Almeida. "Virgem imperial: Nossa Senhora e império marítimo português." *Luso-Brazilian Review* 45, no. 1 (2008): 30–52.

Vallejos, Julio Pinto. "Slave Control and Slave Resistance in Colonial Minas Gerais, 1700–1750." *Journal of Latin American Studies* 17, no. 1 (May 1985): 1–34.

Volpe, Maria Alice. "Irmandades e ritual em Minas Gerais durante o período colonial: O triunfo eucarístico de 1733." *Revista Música* 8, nos. 1–2 (May–November 1997): 6–55.

Monographs

Carvalho, José Jorge de. "Afro-Brazilian Music and Rituals, part 1: From Traditional Genres to the Beginnings of Samba." Duke/University of North Carolina Program in Latin American Studies, Working Paper Series, Durham, North Carolina, 2000.

Foscarini, Arina Gomes. "As manifestações culturais populares como atrativos turísticos: Estudo de caso do batuque em Lapinha da Serra/MG." Instituto de Geociências, Universidade Federal de Minas Gerais, Belo Horizonte, 2009.

Lange, Francisco Curt. "Archivo de música religiosa de la Capitania Geral das Minas Gerais (Brasil) (siglo XVIII)." Universidad Nacional de Cuyo, Escuela Superior de Música, Departamento de Musicología, Mendoza, Argentina, 1951.

"Sociedade Musical Carlos Gomes, cem anos marcando o compass da nossa história." Prefeitura Municipal, Secretaria de Cultura, Belo Horizonte, 1995.

Theses and Dissertations

Byrd, Steven Eric. "Calunga, an Afro-Brazilian Speech of the Triângulo Mineiro: Its Grammar and History." PhD diss., University of Texas, 2005.

Camara, Andréa Albuquerque Adour da. "Vissungo: O cantar banto nas Américas." PhD thesis, Universidade Federal de Minas Gerais, 2013.

Camp, Marc-Antoine. "Sung Penance: Practice and Valorization of Afro-Brazilian Vissungo in the Region of Diamantina, Minas Gerais." PhD thesis, University of Zürich, 2006.

Costa, Manuela Areias. "'Vivas à República': Representações da banda 'União XV de Novembro' em Mariana, MG (1901–1930)." PhD diss., Universidade Federal Fluminense, 2012.

Gaeta, Filipe Generoso Brandão Murta. "O Panorama atual da marujada de Conceição do Mato Dentro/MG: Uma análise da interferência de agentes externos sobre sua cultura musical tradicional." Master's thesis, Universidade Federal de Minas Gerais, Escola de Música, 2013.

Holmes, Holly L. "Milton Nascimento and the Clube da Esquina: Popular Music, Politics, and Fraternity during Brazil's Military Dictatorship (1964–85)." PhD diss., University of Illinois, 2017.

Martins, Bruno Viveiros. "Clube da Esquina: Viagens, sonhos e canções." Bachelor's thesis. Universidade Federal de Minas Gerais, 2005.

Nascimento, Lúcia Valéria do. "Vissungos: Uma prática social em extinção." Master's thesis, Universidade Federal de Minas Gerais, 2006.

Oliveira, Maria Ferreira de. "Sérgio Magnani: Sua influência no meio musical de Belo Horizonte." Master's thesis, Universidade Federal de Minas Gerais, 2008.

Pires, Sergio Macedo. "Sources, Style, and Context for the *Te Deum* of José Joaquim Emerico Lobo de Mesquita (1746?–1805): A Critical Edition." PhD diss., Boston University, 2007.

Rezende, Rodrigo Castro. "As Nossas Áfricas: População escrava e identidades africanas nas Minas Setecentistas." Master's thesis, Universidade Federal de Minas Gerais, 2006.

Schiavio, Andrea. "Music in (En)Action: Sense-Making and Neurophenomenology of Musical Experience." PhD thesis, University of Sheffield, 2014.

Silva, Erminia. "As múltipas linguagens na teatrilidade circense: Benjamin Oliveira e o circo-teatro no Brasil no final do século XIX e início do XX." PhD thesis, Universidade Estadual de Campinas, 2003.

Vilela, Ivan. "Os caminhos da viola no Rio de Janeiro do século XIX." Master's thesis, Universidade Federal do Rio de Janeiro, 2007.

Websites

Anima. "Gisela Nogueira: Brazilian Baroque Guitar." Anima, n.d. http://www.animamusica .art.br/site/lang_en/pages/musicos/gisela.html.

Associação Filmes de Quintal. http://www.mapeandoaxe.org.br/terreiros/belohorizonte.

Capelas, Afonso, Jr. "As donas da história." *Revista Raiz*, 2nd ed., 2005. http://revistaraiz.uol
.com.br/portal/index.php?Itemid=96&id=82&option=com_content&task=view.

Daniel, Klenio. "Memória: Há dois meses morria Chiquito Braga, precursor da harmonia
mineira de violão." Violão Brasileiro, February 22, 2018. https://www.violaobrasileiro.com
/blog/memoria-ha-dois-meses-morria-chiquito-braga-precursor-da-harmonia-mineira
-de-violao/208.

Dewilde, Jan, and Annelies Focquaert. "Bosmans, Arthur." Studiecentrum voor Vlaamse
Muziek, n.d. https://www.svm.be/content/bosmans-arthur?display=biography&langua
ge=en.

Mariana Museum Music Project. http://www.mmmariana.com.br/restauracao_difusao
/index2.htm.

Martins, Tarcísio José. "Chico Rei, nem história e nem lenda: É só uma Nota de Rodapé."
Quilombo Minas Gerais, 2003. https://www.mgquilombo.com.br/artigos/pesquisas
-escolares/chico-rei-nem-historia-e-nem-lenda-e-so-uma-nota-de-rodape/.

Minas Faz Ciência. http://revista.fapemig.br/materia.php?id=452.

Monteiro, José Fernando Saroba. "Lundu: Origem da música popular brasileira." Musica
Brasilis, n.d. https://musicabrasilis.org.br/temas/lundu-origem-da-musica-popular
-brasileira.

Museu Afro Brasil. "Abigail Moura." N.d. http://www.museuafrobrasil.org.br/noticias/2014
/12/30/abigail-moura.

Museu Clube da Esquina. Interviews with Tavinho Moura, Milton Nascimento, and
Nivaldo Ornelas, 2010–2012.

Museu da Pessoa. Interview with Milton Nascimento. http://www.museudapessoa.net
/MuseuVirtual/.

Museu da Pessoa. Interview with Wagner Tiso. https://acervo.museudapessoa.org/pt/con
teudo/historia/entrevista-de-wagner-tiso-45809.

Pereira, Maria Irenilda. "Músico cria projeto para preservar tradições em comunidade
quilombola." Centro de Documentação Eloy Ferreira da Silva, May 14, 2018. http://www
.cedefes.org.br/musico-cria-projeto-para-preservar-tradicoes-em-comunidade
-quilombola/.

Ramos, Donald, trans. "Inquisition Process: Luzia Pinta, Angolan Freedwoman." Inquisition
of Lisbon, no. 252, IArquivo Nacional da Torre do Tombo, Lisbon. http://academic
.csuohio.edu/as227/Lectures/Brazil/pinta_translation.htm.

"Rômulo Paes." November 7, 2010. http://cifrantiga2.blogspot.com/2010/11/romulo-paes
.html.

Serviço Social do Comércio Palladium. http://circuitosesc.com.br/index.php/front-sesc/2
-destaques-da-semana/cultura/107-noticias/noticias-sesc-palladium/2745-cine-sesc-
palladium-exibe-documentario-sobre-mestre-conga.

Silveira, Renato da. "Calundu." March 29, 2011. https://dancasfolcloricas.blogspot.com/2011
/03/calundú.html.

Soucasseaux, Francisco. "Cartão postal em Belo Horizonte." http://www.cartaopostal.fot.br
/conteudo.asp?p=p000018.

Universidade Federal Campina Grande. http://www.dec.ufcg.edu.br/biografias/ManoJMac
.htm.

CDs and CD Liner Notes

Antunes, Murilo. Liner notes. *Caboclo d'água*, by Tavinho Moura. Bemol, 1992.

Batuques do Sudeste. Documentos Sonoros Brasileiros series, vol. 2. Associação Cultural
Cachuera!, 2000.

Budasz, Rogério. Liner notes. *Iberian and African-Brazilian Music of the 17th Century.*
Naxos, 2006.

Casaldáliga, Dom Pedro. Liner notes. *Missa dos Quilombos*, by Milton Nascimento. Ariola,
1982.

Castelo-Branco, Salwa El-Shawan. Liner notes. *Musical Traditions of Portugal.* Smithsonian
Folkways, 1994.

Delage, Rodrigo. Liner notes. *Viola Caipira Instrumental.* Self-released, n.d.

Dias, Paulo. Liner notes. *Batuques do Sudeste.* Documentos Sonoros Brasileiros series, vol. 2.
Associação Cultural Cachuera!, 2000.

Dias, Paulo, and Edimilson de Almeida Pereira. Liner notes. *Congado mineiro.* Documentos
Sonoros Brasileiros series, vol. 1. Associação Cultural Cachuera! / Coleção Itaú Cultural,
1997.

Faria, Luiz, and Matheus Calil. Liner notes. *Clube da Viola: Raízes*, vol. 2. BMG Brasil, 2003.

Felipe, Carlos. Liner notes. Zé Coco do Riachão, *Vôo das garças.* Lapa, 1997.

Freire, Paulo. Liner notes. *Violeiros do Brasil: Músicas e conversas com artistas da viola brasileira.* Projeto Memória Brasileira, 2008.

Geraes, by Milton Nascimento. Liner notes. EMI, 1976.

Maciel, Luíz. Liner notes. *Missa dos Quilombos,* by Milton Nascimento. Abril Coleções, 2012.

Marks, Morton. Liner notes. *L. H. Corrêa de Azevedo: Music of Ceará and Minas Gerais.*
Endangered Music Project. Rykodisc RCD 10404, 1997.

Moura, Abigail. Liner notes. *Orquestra Afro-Brasileira.* Polysom 33160-1, 1968.

Nascimento, Milton. Liner notes. *Travessia.* Dubas Música, 2002.

Neto, Penido. Liner notes. *Rômulo Paes e coisas mais.* Minas Trabalho Cantando / Paralelos,
n.d.

Nicoliello, Maria José Turri. Liner notes. *Francisco Raposo.* CMCG, 2010.

Pattápio Silva, Mestres Brasileiros, vol. 5. Liner notes. V&M, Sonhos e Sons, 2004.

Ramos, Marcelo. Liner notes. *Padre José Maria Xavier, Ofício de Trevas,* vol. 2. Palácio das
Artes, n.d.

Rosa, Júlio Coelho. Liner notes. *Mestre Conga: Decantando em sambas.* Navegador Musicas
/ Bananaouro, 2006.

Taubkin, Myriam. Liner notes. *Violeiros do Brasil: Músicas e conversas com artistas da viola
brasileira.* Projeto Memória Brasileira, 2008.

Vianna, Hermano, and Beto Villares. Liner notes. *Música do Brasil.* Abril Entretenimento, n.d.

Films

Bairon, Sérgio, and José da Silva Ribeiro, dirs. Tá caindo fulô . . . Tambús de candombe de comunidade do Açude. 2012.

Braga, André, and Cardes Amâncio, dirs. Candombe do Açude: Arte, cultura e fé. Avesso Filmes, 2004.

Personal Interviews

Lima, Virgílio. Unpublished interview. Sabará, August 7, 2013.

Lucas, Glaura. Unpublished interview. Belo Horizonte, August 16, 2013.

Moura, Tavinho. Unpublished interview. Belo Horizonte, January 2016.

Oliveira, Arnon Sávio Reis de. Unpublished interview. Belo Horizonte, August 2013.

Newspaper Articles

Girão, Eduardo Tristão. "Centenário de Godofredo Guedes e comemorado em Montes Claros e BH." Estado de Minas, July 21, 2008.

Index

Page numbers in **bold** refer to illustrations.

About the Author

Ethnomusicologist, composer, and guitarist Jonathon Grasse has researched music in Minas Gerais, Brazil, for over twenty-five years and has published journal articles, chapters, and books on the subject. He is a professor of music at California State University, Dominguez Hills, where he has developed courses and material on Brazilian music.

CPSIA information can be obtained
at www.ICGtesting.com
Printed in the USA
BVHW081706220322
631905BV00002B/6